MOBILE THEATER

ARCHITECTURAL COUNTERCULTURE ON STAGE

Fernando Quesada

Foreword 4

Mobile Theater Design 6

The Disintegration of Theatrical Space 30

Introduction. Experiments in Situation 42

Chapter 1.
Temple – Machine – Caravan 56
The Triple Theatrical System 58
The Metropolitan Civic Temple 66
The Avant-Garde Machine 70
Taking Back the Streets 78

Chapter 2.
Environment 88
Tragedies in a Garage 93
Action, Space and Environment 97
Urban Scores 99
The Environmental Canon 103
Transactions on Space 108

Chapter 3.
Poor – Popular – Pop 118
The 13 Rows in Opole 122
The Canopied Container 127
Thespis' Wagon with a Combustion Engine 134
The Kinetic Decorated Shed 139

Cover Image: Logotype for the Mobile Theater © *Javier Navarro de Zuvillaga.*

Chapter 4.
The electric Decade 148
The Electric Drama of Dissolution 151
Cybernetic Circuses 158
The Repose of the Masses 164
Technodevices for Social Emergencies 168

Chapter 5.
The Pneumatic Community 182
Theaters of Air 185
Peaceful Atoms 189
The Dissolution of the Great Machine 198
The Counterculture Campaign 205

Chapter 6.
Sacred Geometries 212
Order, Technocracy and Industry 215
The Great Mystic Campout 220
Lines and Time Tunnels 227
Technowalden 235

Conclusions. ***Et in Arcadia Ego*** 242

This book seeks to tell the story of a very particular moment in history, using a metaphor we will call the Mobile Theater. This metaphor has been embodied in many different examples, but just one of them will serve as the main story line – although not the only one – in the narrative presented here. Our focus is the degree project developed by the Spanish architect Javier Navarro de Zuvillaga (Madrid, 1942) for his studies at the Architectural Association School of Architecture in London, which we have reproduced here in its entirety.

In addition to this project, Navarro de Zuvillaga published an article in 1976, also included in this book, which laid out the foundations for his research. Navarro's project and the themes from his article were the conceptual drivers behind this book, which aims not only to disseminate them, because of their importance and their exceptional quality in the context of Spanish architectural culture, but also to situate them in a broader context, both geographically and culturally, within a rich international framework.

Therefore, and despite what it might seem, this book is not a monograph about a design by an author – or it isn't only that. It is the story of a highly complex, and chronologically clear-cut, cultural network. Over the course of this narrative, Javier Navarro's Mobile Theater appears and disappears, only to reappear again, as a point of reference and a specter that haunts the investigation as a whole. Moreover, this discontinuous structure is also characterized by a series of themes, each providing a title for a chapter, which are independent from one another, but globally they offer a comprehensive portrait of the cultural climate in London in which Javier Navarro's project took shape. In that sense, we have aimed to produce, or reproduce, a certain critical cultural atmosphere, rather than a narrative that is closed off, conclusive or dogmatic.

The period during which this book's title project was developed is of great interest today, because it outlines cultural, economic and social conditions that are somewhat similar to our own. What should most interest us today about that chapter in history is not its premonitory character – which can only be evidenced in hindsight, by a nostalgic or even opportunistic outlook – but rather how the main characters in the story were able to navigate, almost blindly, the contradictions of their times. What honors almost all the architectural experiments that are reviewed in this book is not their anticipation of certain phenomena that are predominant, accepted and ubiquitous today: just the opposite, it is their enormous antagonism with respect to the dominant architectural culture of their time.

This book is an homage to that tenacious antagonism, not an instrumental document to validate the subsequent imitators of the Mobile Theater.

Although it is impossible to list everyone who contributed to this effort, there are some people who need to be mentioned by name. I would like to thank Javier Navarro de Zuvillaga for his continued help with this research, for his generosity, commitment, friendship and acuity. Thanks are also due to María Teresa Muñoz for her keen revisions of the manuscripts and our long conversations about the period it deals with. To Angela Kay Bunning for her excellent translation into English. To Ricardo Devesa, editor in chief at Actar, for his confidence in this project from the outset. To José Miguel de Prada Poole and Antonio Fernández Alba for our meetings and conversations about their work. To María and Diego Fullaondo for their warm generosity. To Antonio Cobo for his patient research and friendship. To Francesco Moschini, from the Accademia di San Luca, and Elena Tinacci, from the MAXXI in Rome, for their kindness regarding the reproduction of images. To Arnold Aronson for his valuable insight into Environmental Scenography in North America and for his pioneering work in the field. To Juan José Montijano for his contagious enthusiasm for popular variety theater. To Ken Turner and Tony Murchland for their warmth and sincerity in talking about their lives with a stranger. To Richard Schechner and Joanne Pattavina (Jerry Rojo's widow), for their generosity with my requests. To Toni Martin for his availability to answer my doubts and questions. To Peter Sciscioli, from Meredith Monk's Studio, for his kindness and great help. To Gerzy Gurawski for his complicity during a memorable phone conversation. To Antoni Verdaguer for his complicity. And to Raphael Chau, from Jeffery Shaw's Studio, for his disinterested contribution.

Finally, I would like to deeply thank the many people from the libraries and archives I have consulted for their help over such an extended period of time. This book has been produced thanks to the funding provided by two research projects from the National Research Plan of the Ministry of Education of Spain: Expanded Theatricalities HAR2015-63984-P, and The New Loss of the Centre. Critical Practices of the Live Arts and Architecture in the Anthropocene PID2019-105045GB-I00, but also thanks to the Schindler Prize, gained by my former student Elías Sancho de Agustin and myself, with Elías's Thesis Project at the School of Architecture of Universidad de Alcala. I deeply thank Elías Sancho, the School of Architecture, and the support of Julio Arce and Rosa Amat, who lead this initiative of the Schindler Group Elevators.

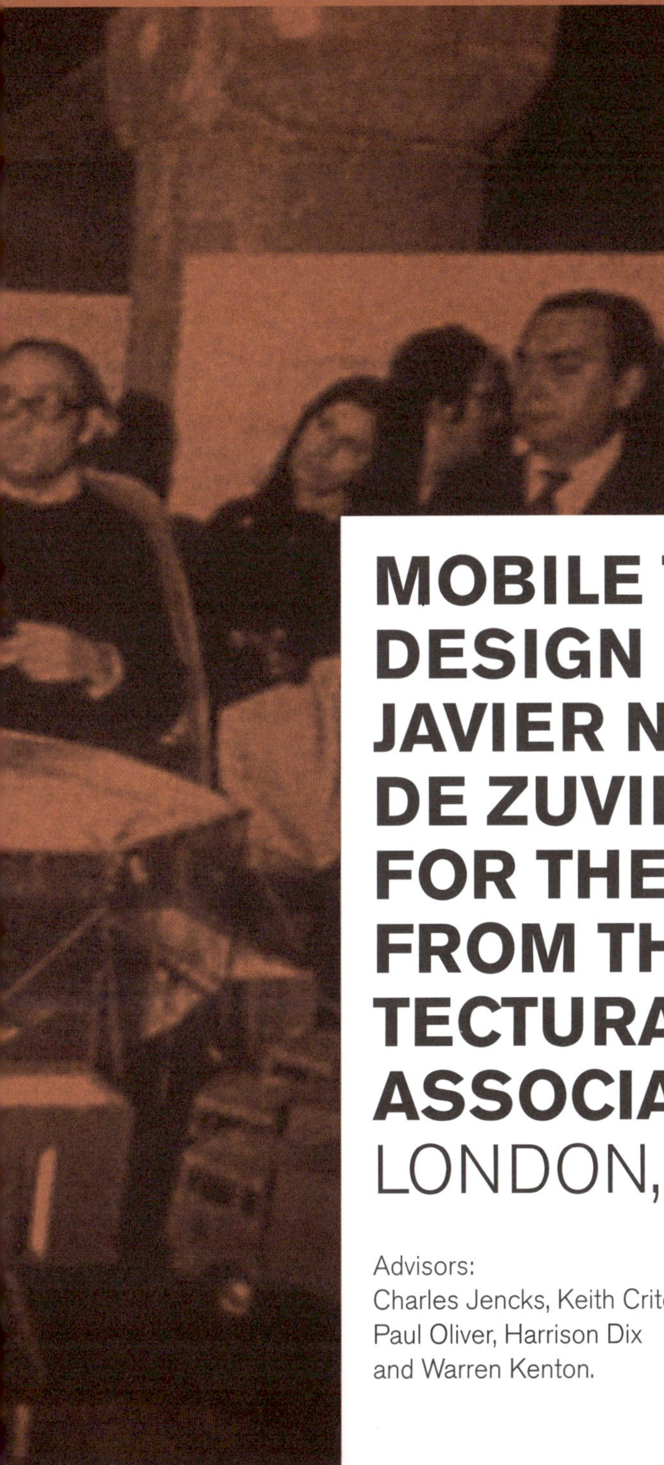

MOBILE THEATER DESIGN BY JAVIER NAVARRO DE ZUVILLAGA FOR THE DEGREE FROM THE ARCHITECTURAL ASSOCIATION, LONDON, JUNE 1971

Advisors:
Charles Jencks, Keith Critchlow, Paul Oliver, Harrison Dix and Warren Kenton.

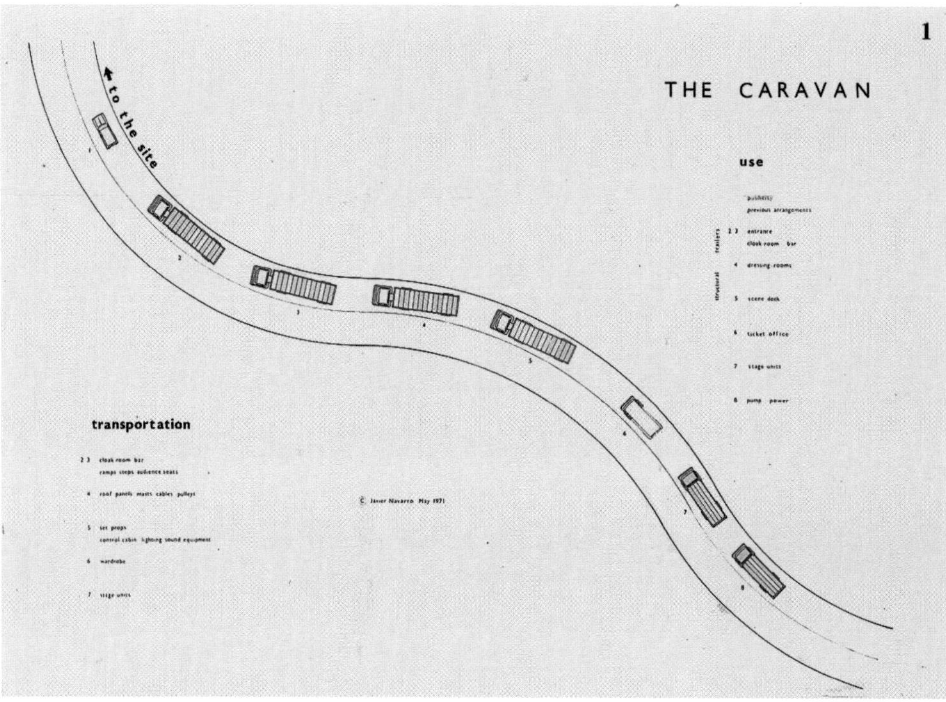
1
THE CARAVAN
to the site
use
previous arrangements
structural trailers
2 3 entrance
cloak-room bar
4 dressing-rooms
5 scene dock
6 ticket office
7 stage units
8 pump power
transportation
2 3 cloak-room bar
ramps steps audience seats
4 roof panels masts cables pulleys
5 set props
control cabin lighting sound equipment
6 wardrobe
7 stage units
C Javier Navarro May 1971

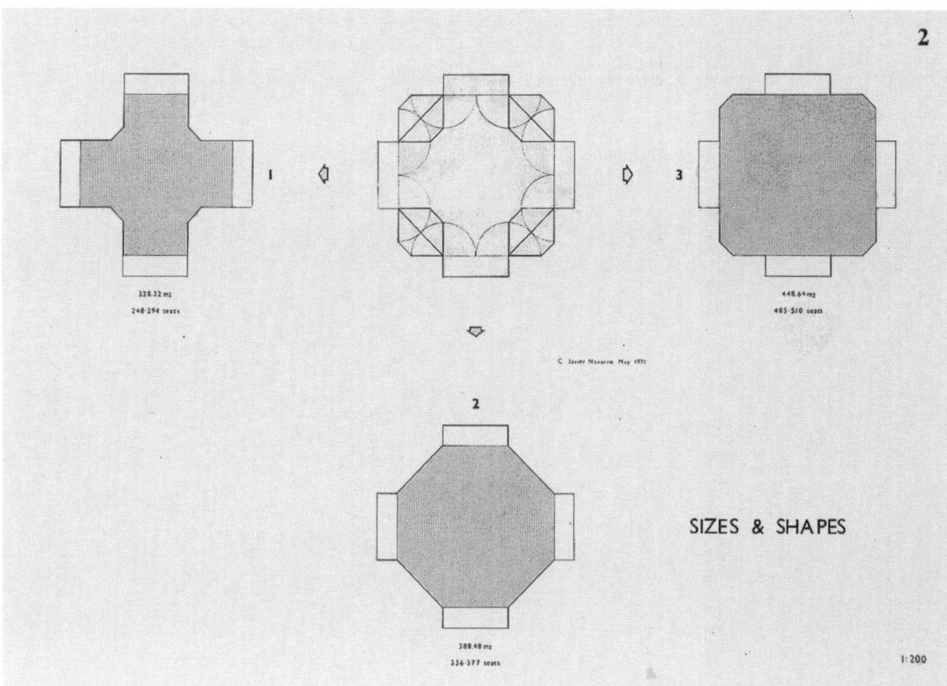
2
1
3
328.32 m2
248-294 seats
448.64 m2
485-510 seats
C Javier Navarro May 1971
2
SIZES & SHAPES
388.48 m2
336-377 seats
1:200

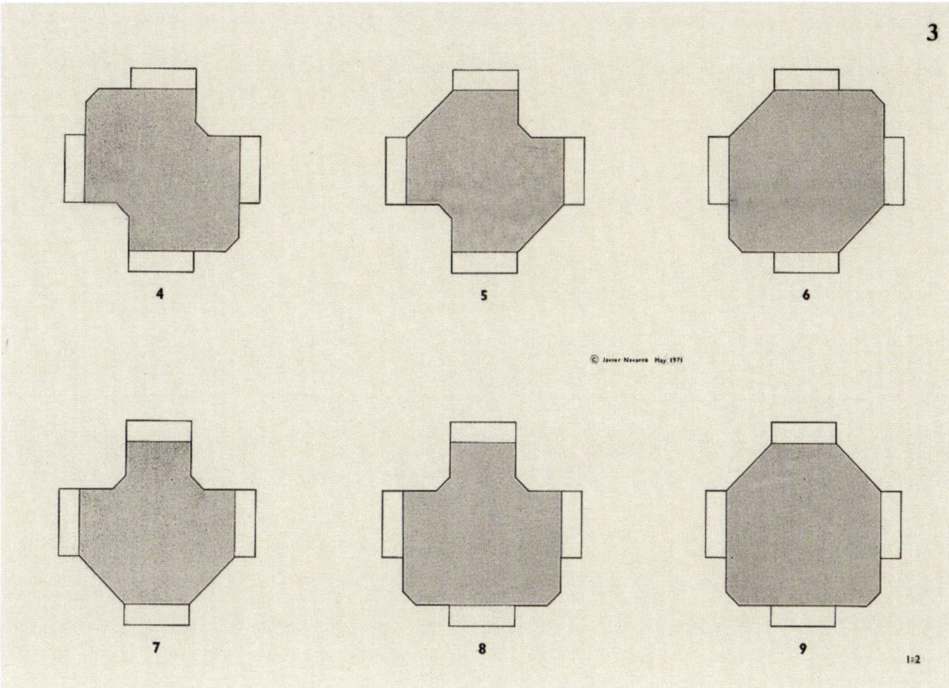
3
4
5
6
© Javier Navarro May 1971
7
8
9
1:2

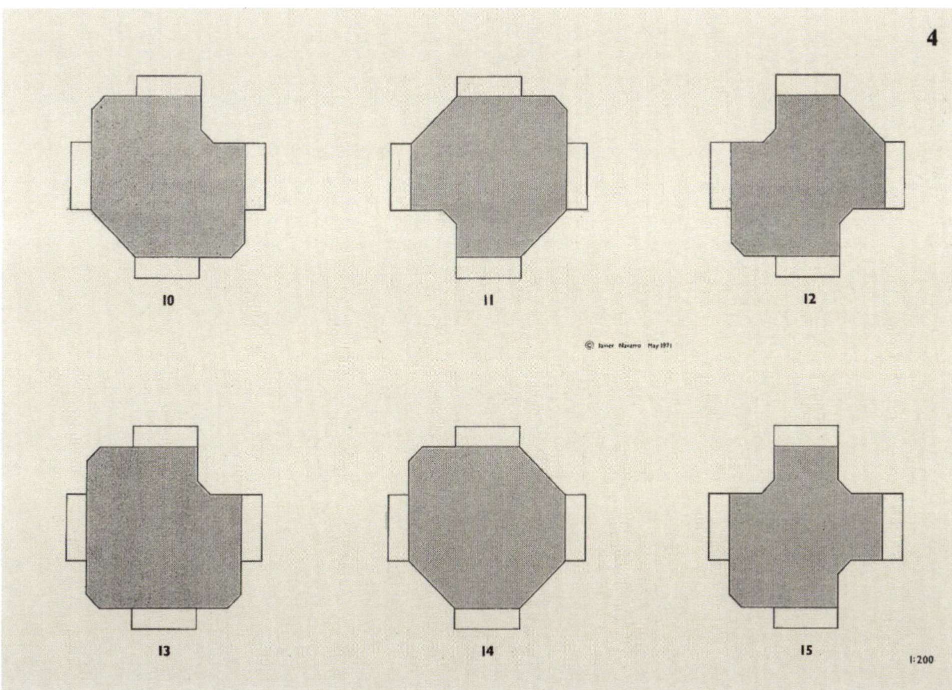
4
10
11
12
© Javier Navarro May 1971
13
14
15
1:200

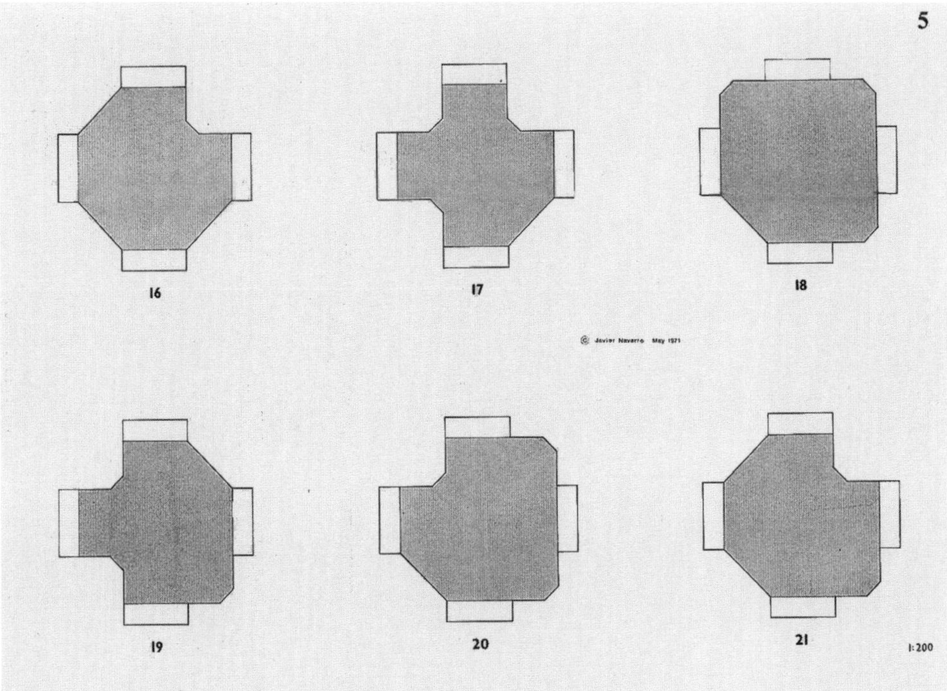
5
16
17
18
© Javier Navarro May 1971
19
20
21
1:200

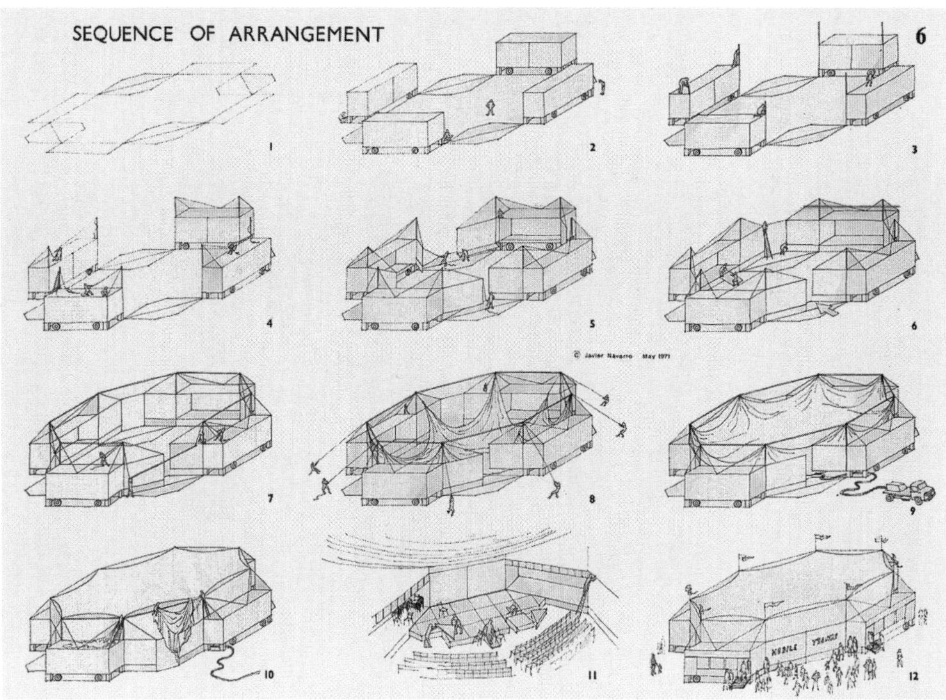
SEQUENCE OF ARRANGEMENT
6
1
2
3
4
5
6
© Javier Navarro May 1971
7
8
9
10
11
12

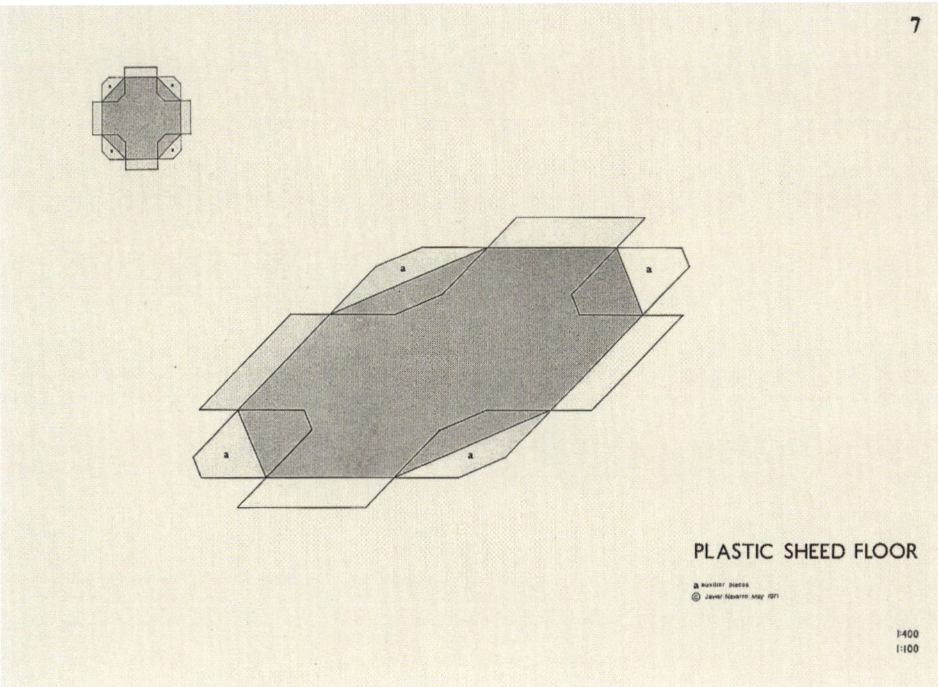
7
a
a
a
a
PLASTIC SHEED FLOOR
a auxiliar pieces
© Javier Navarro May 1971
1:400
1:100

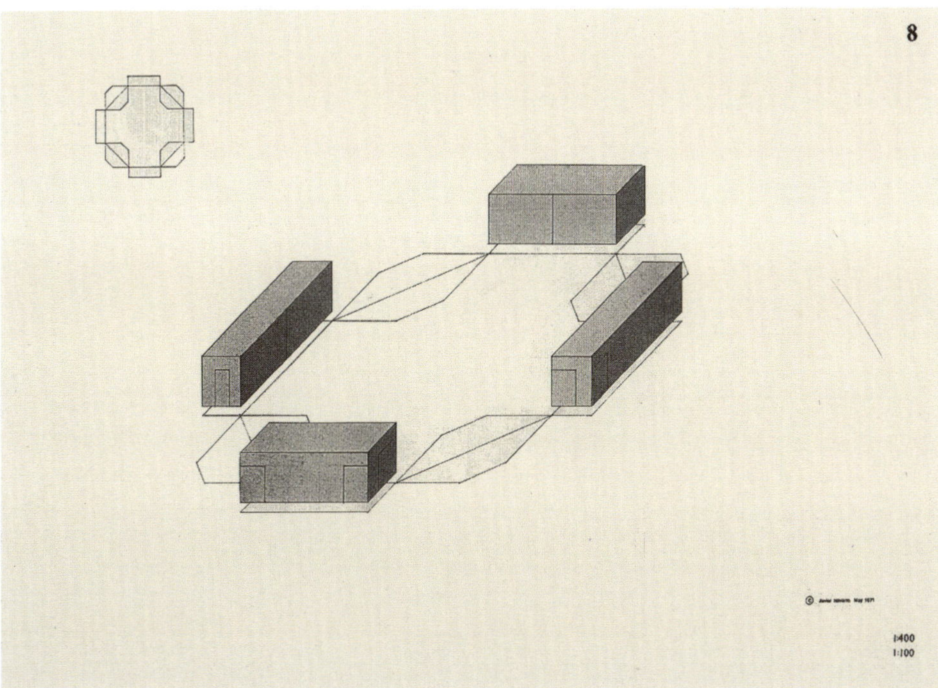
8
1:400
1:100

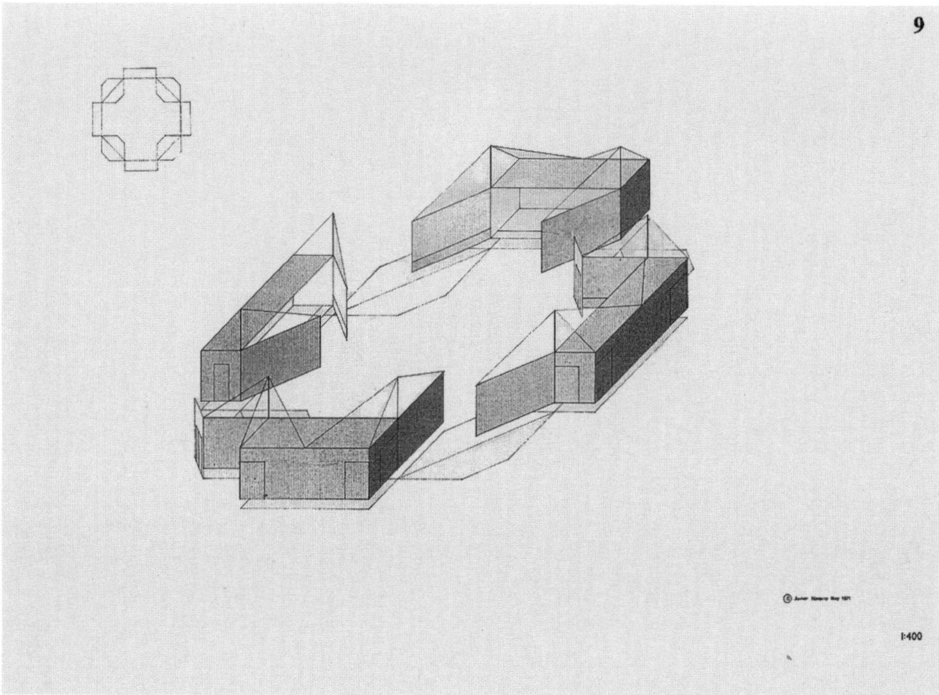
9
1:400

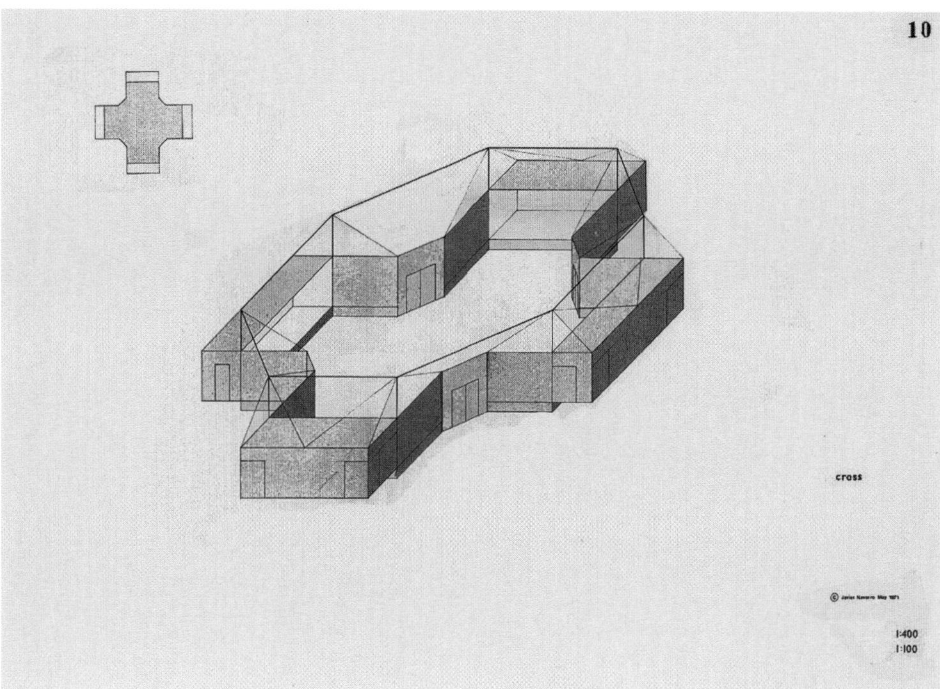
10
cross
1:400
1:100

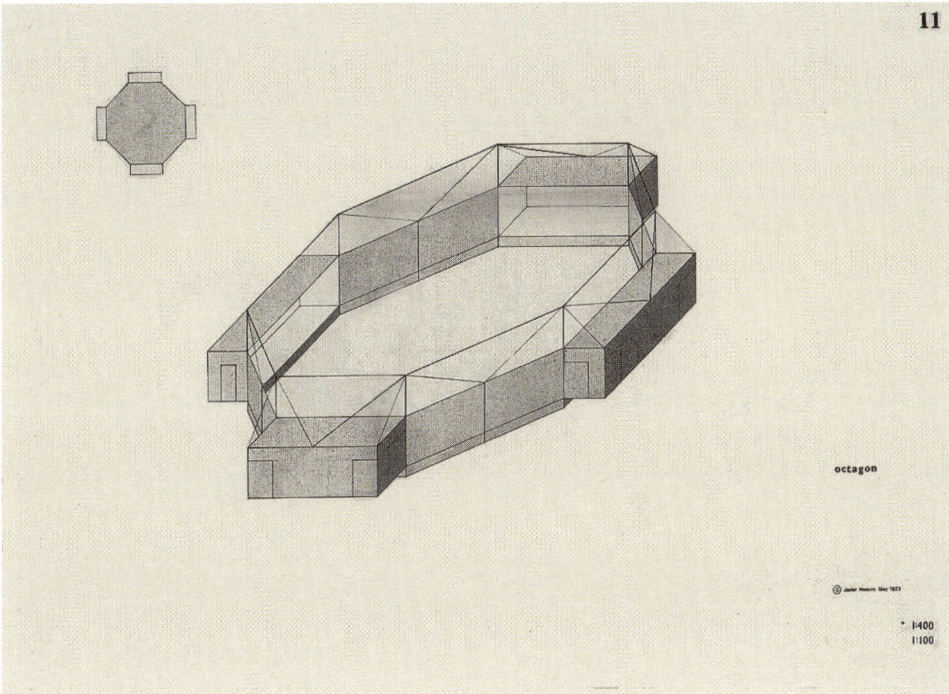
11
octagon
1:400
1:100

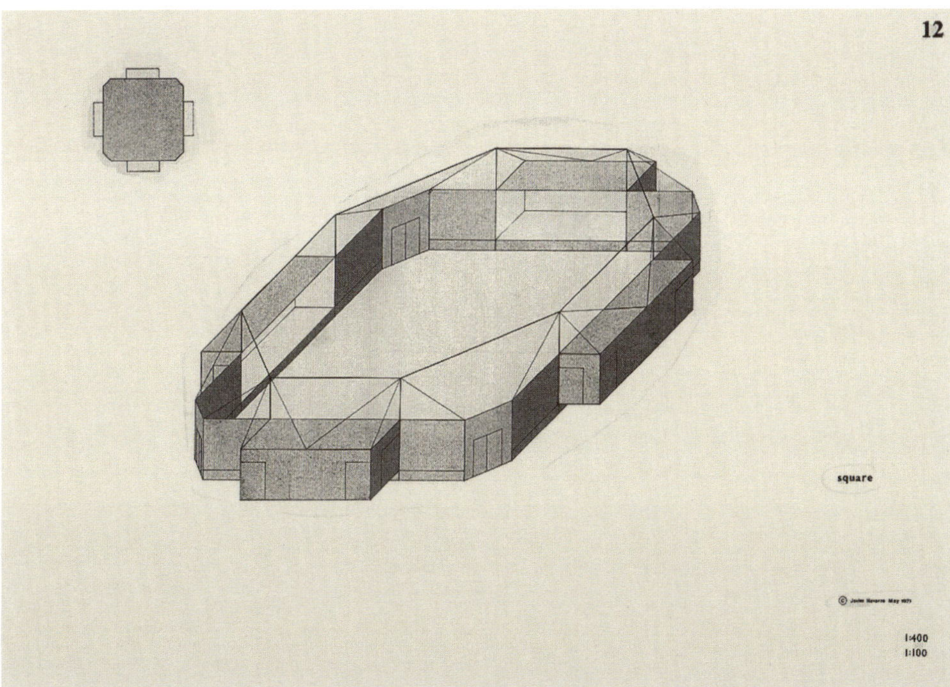
12
square
1:400
1:100

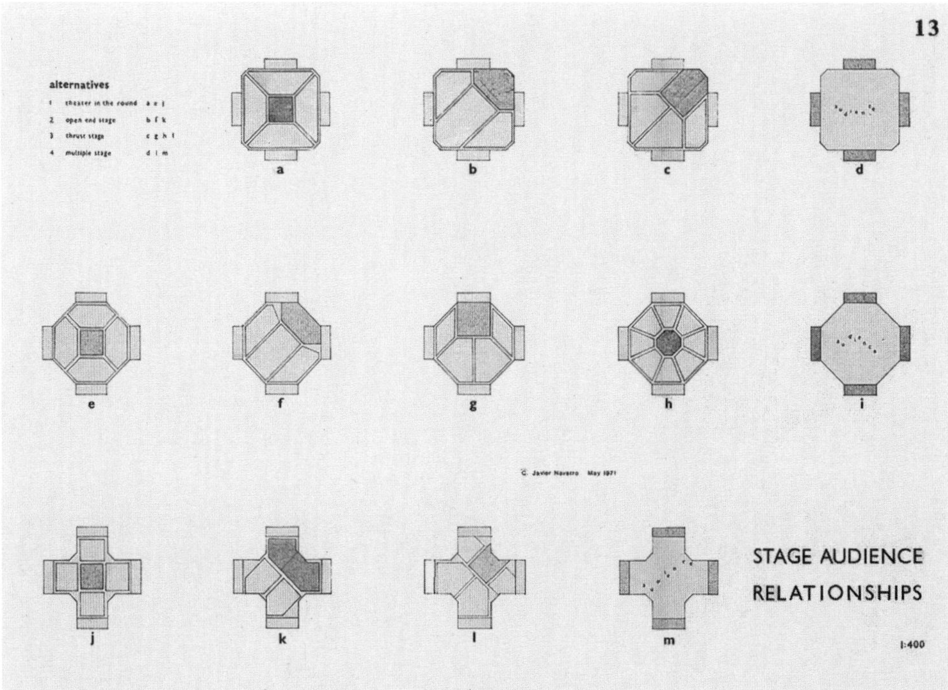
13
alternatives
1 theater in the round a e j
2 open end stage b f k
3 thrust stage c g h l
4 multiple stage d i m
a
b
c
d
e
f
g
h
i
© Javier Navarro May 1971
j
k
l
m
STAGE AUDIENCE
RELATIONSHIPS
1:400

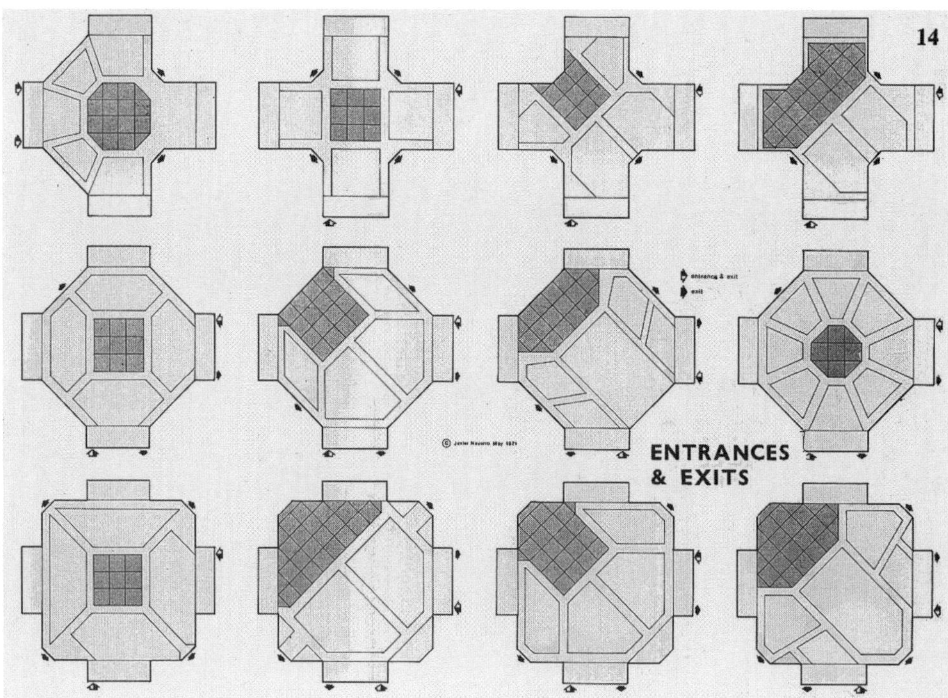
14
entrance & exit
exit
© Javier Navarro May 1971
ENTRANCES
& EXITS

ARRANGEMENTS OF THE TRAILERS 15

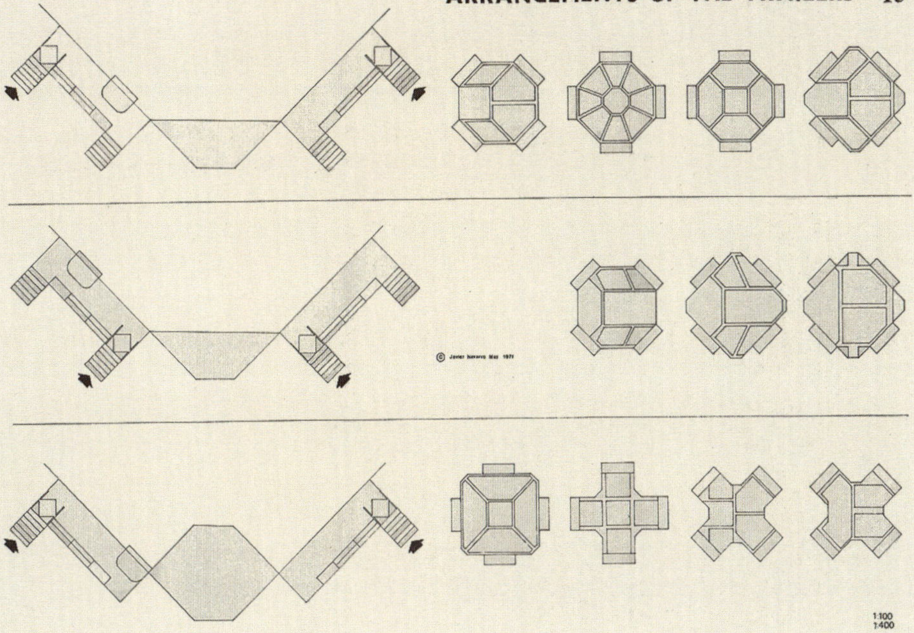

© Javier Navarro May 1971

1:100
1:400

16

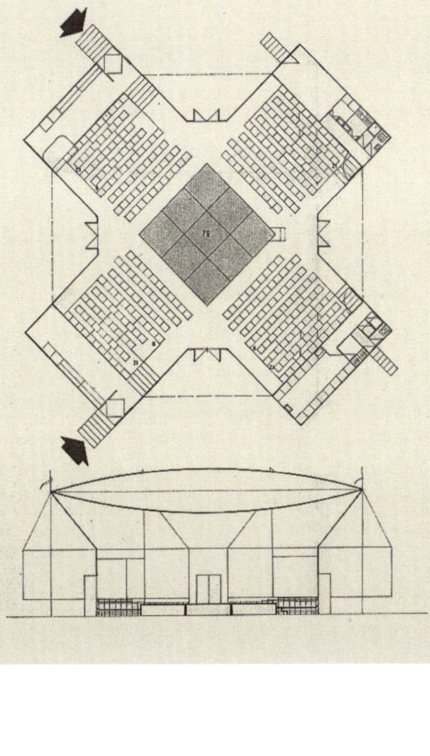

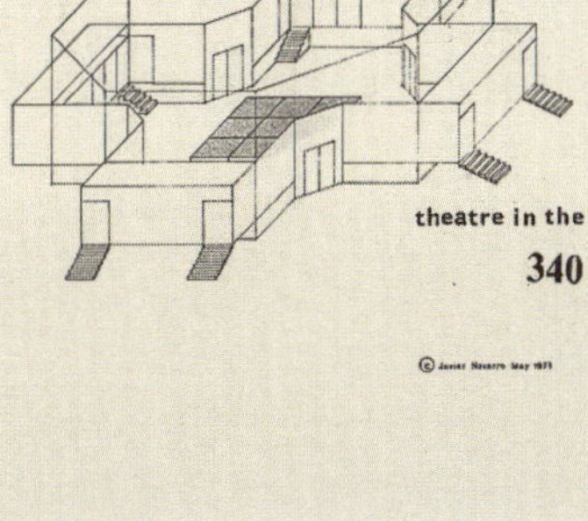

cross

theatre in the round

340 seats

© Javier Navarro May 1971

1:100

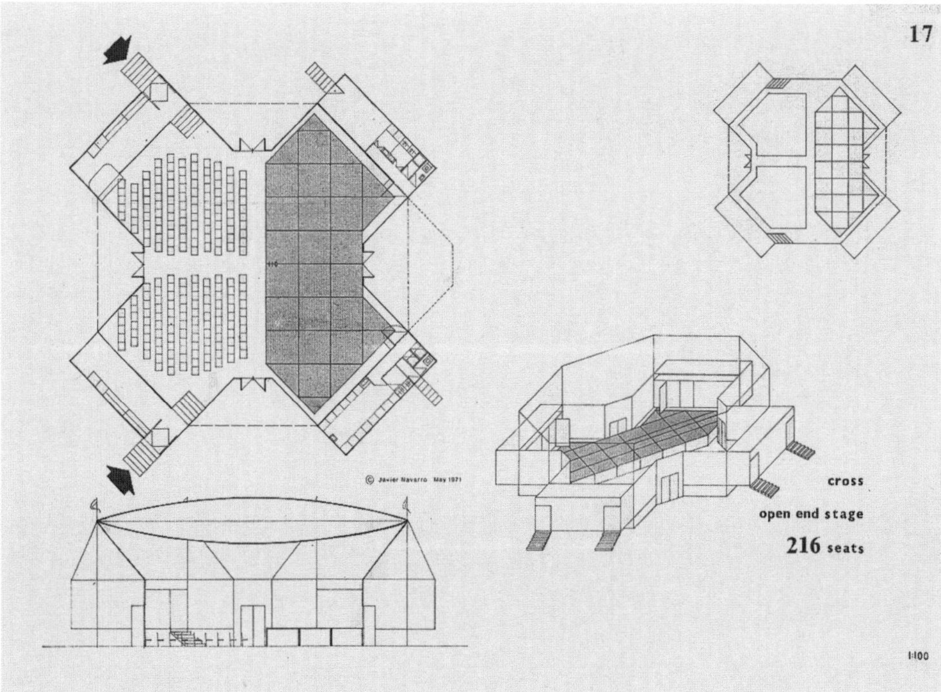
17
© Javier Navarro May 1971
cross
open end stage
216 seats
1:100

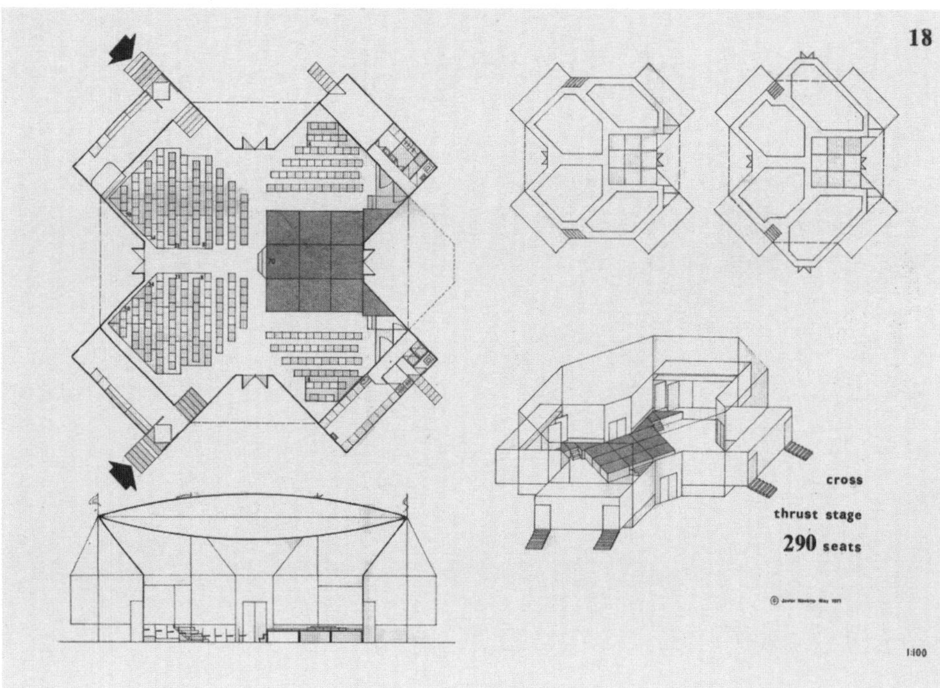
18
cross
thrust stage
290 seats
1:100

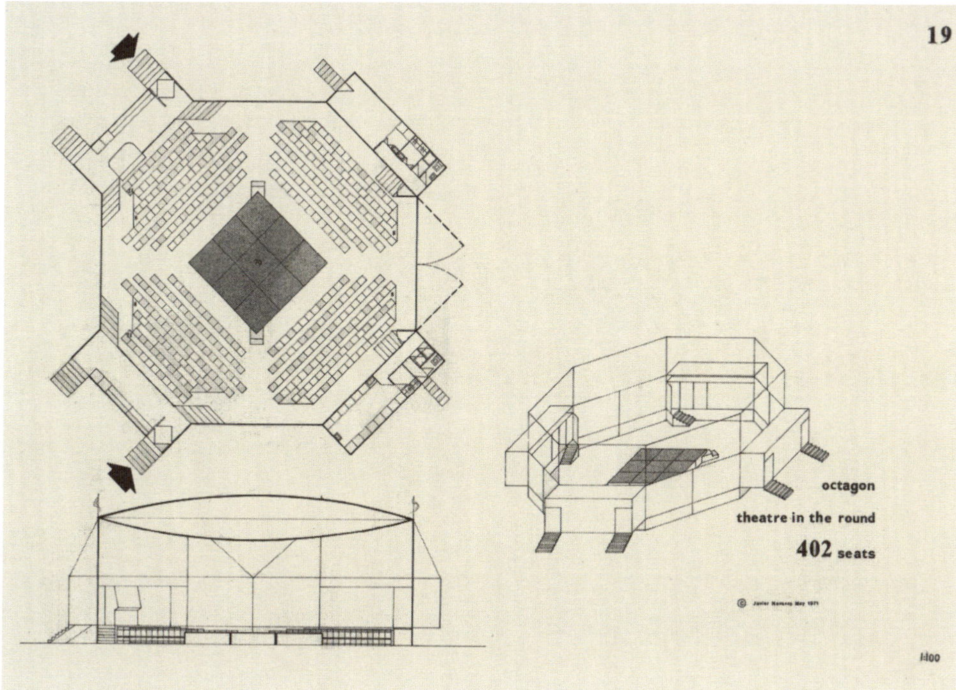
19
octagon
theatre in the round
402 seats
1:100

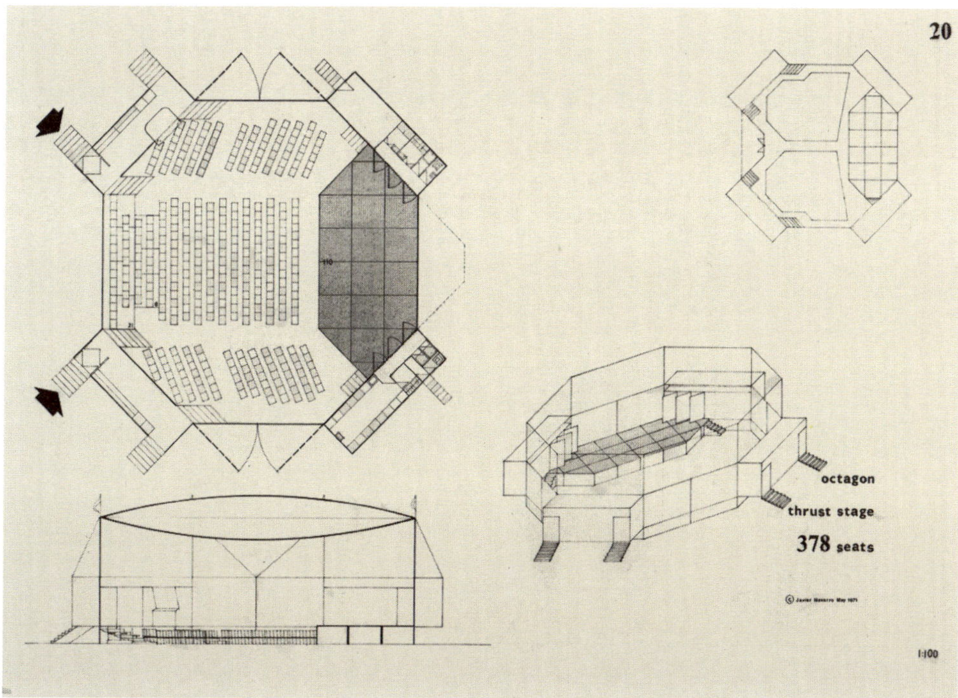
20
octagon
thrust stage
378 seats
1:100

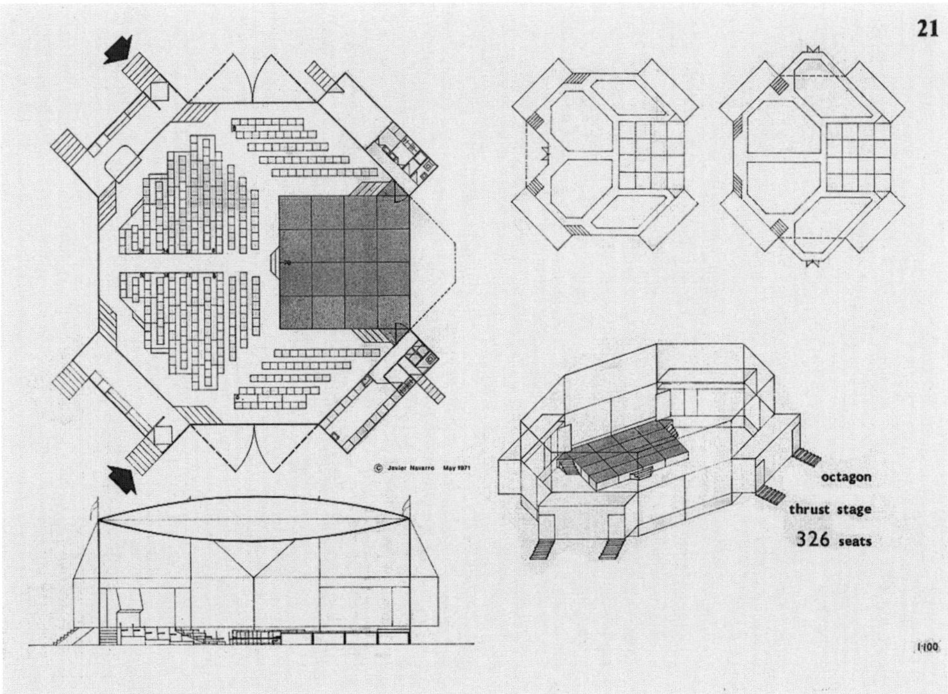
21
© Javier Navarro May 1971
octagon
thrust stage
326 seats
1:100

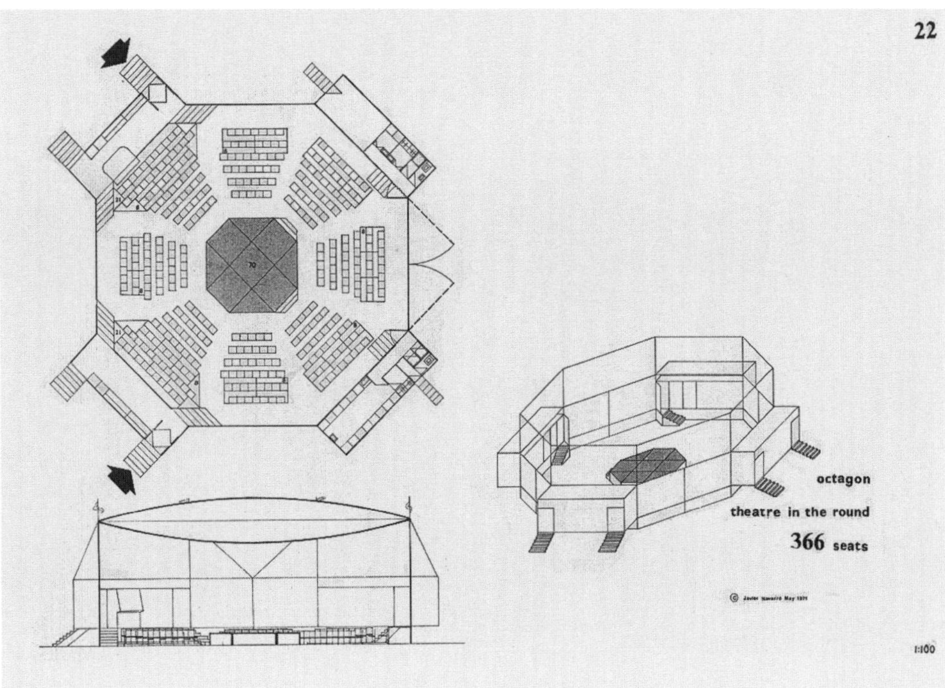
22
octagon
theatre in the round
366 seats
© Javier Navarro May 1971
1:100

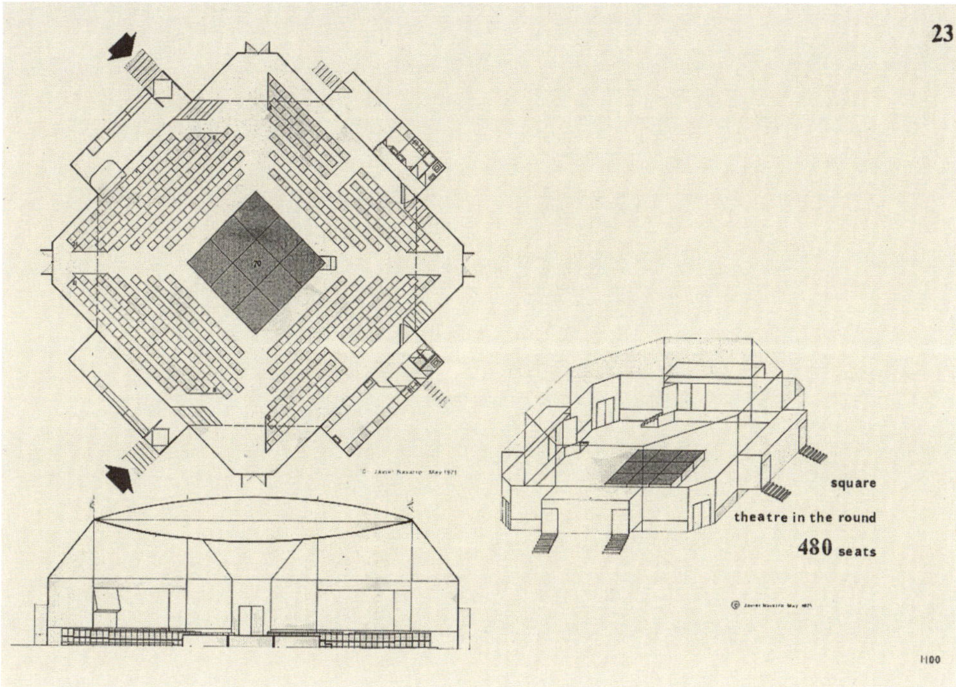
23
square
theatre in the round
480 seats
1:100

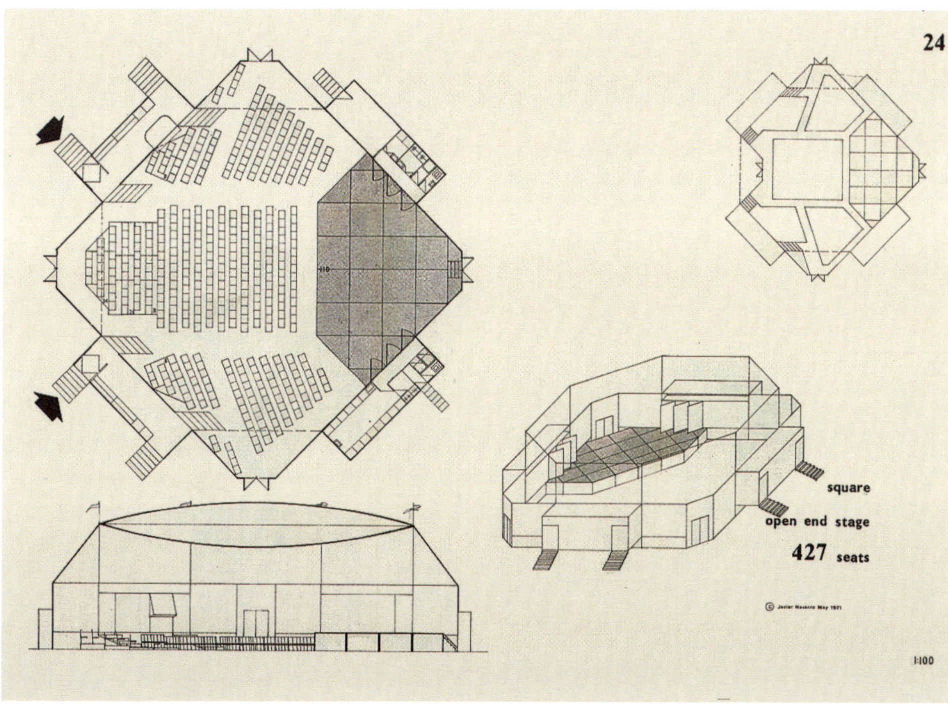
24
square
open end stage
427 seats
1:100

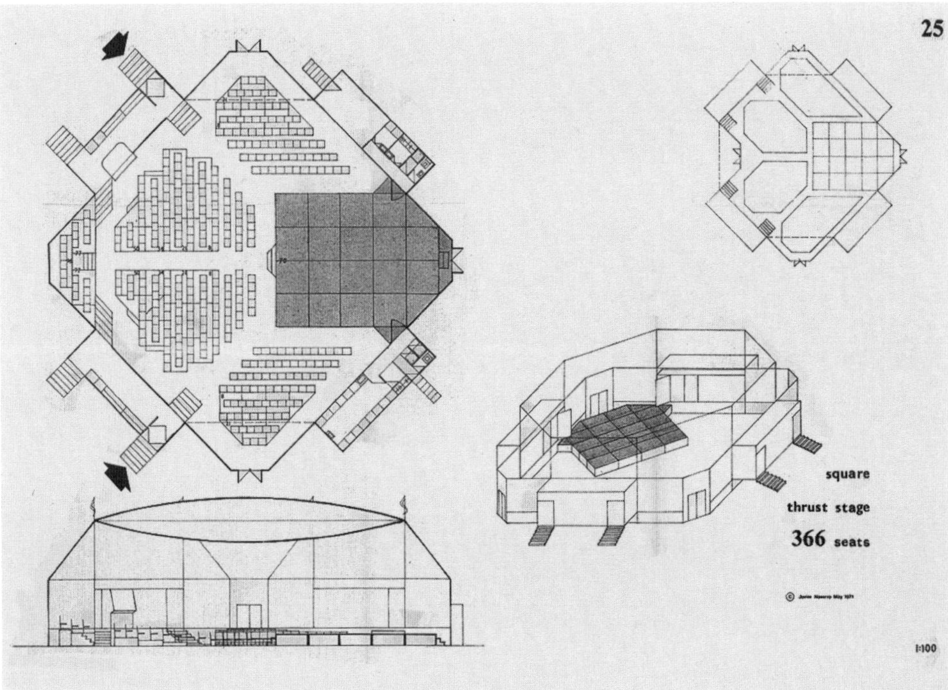
25
square
thrust stage
366 seats
1:100

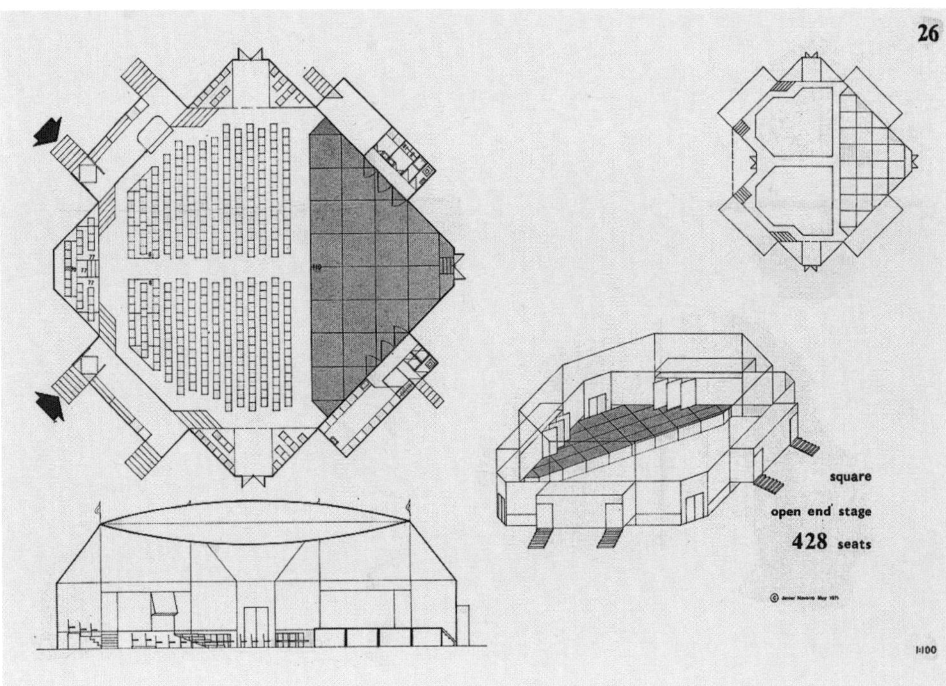
26
square
open end stage
428 seats
1:100

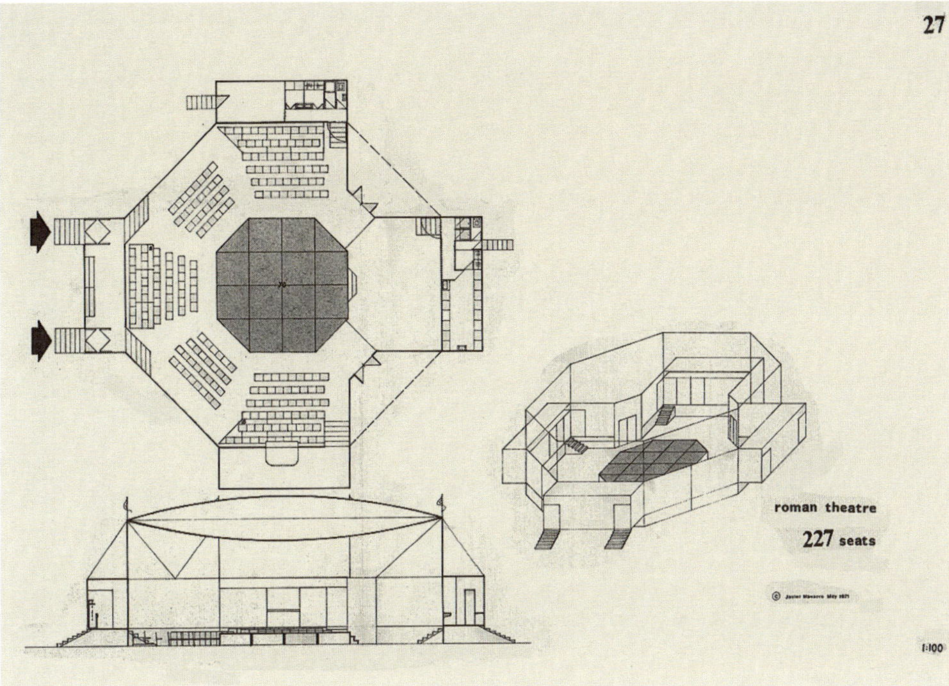
27
roman theatre
227 seats
1:100

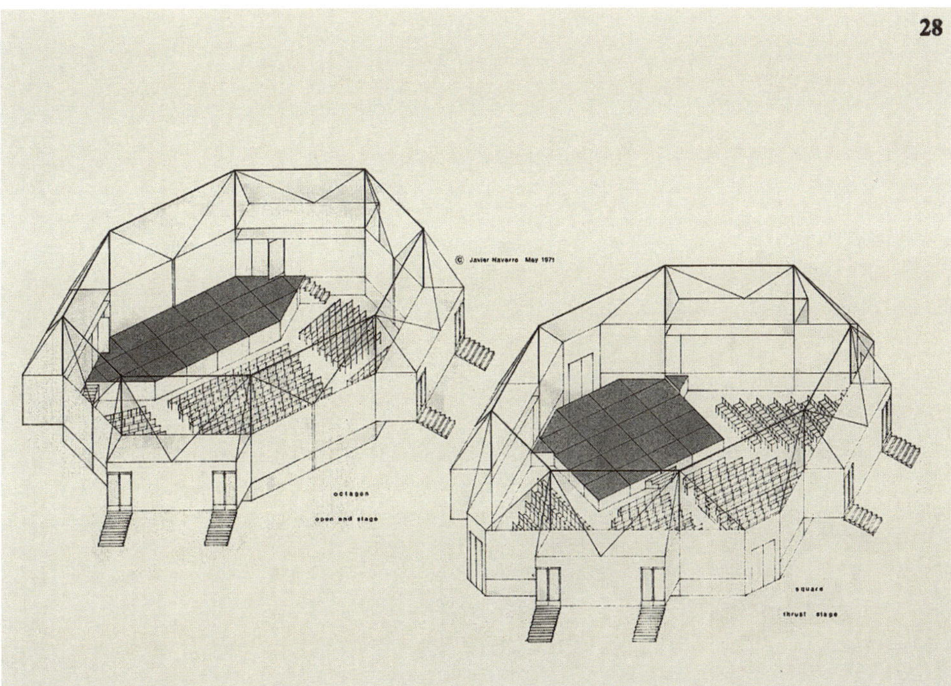
28
© Javier Navarro May 1971
octagon
open end stage
square
thrust stage

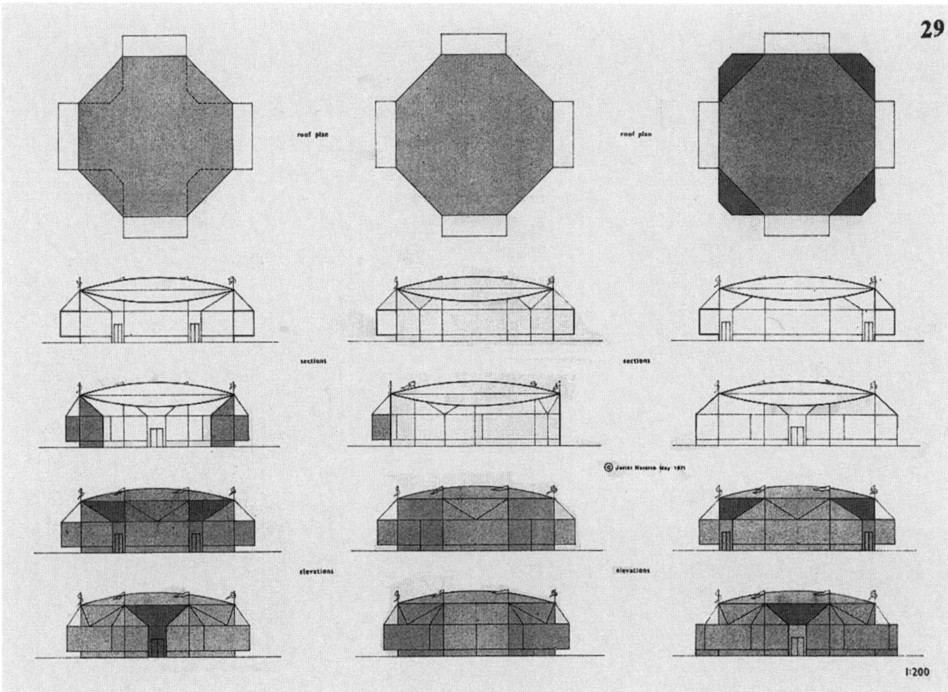
29
roof plan
roof plan
sections
sections
© Javier Navarro May 1971
elevations
elevations
1:200

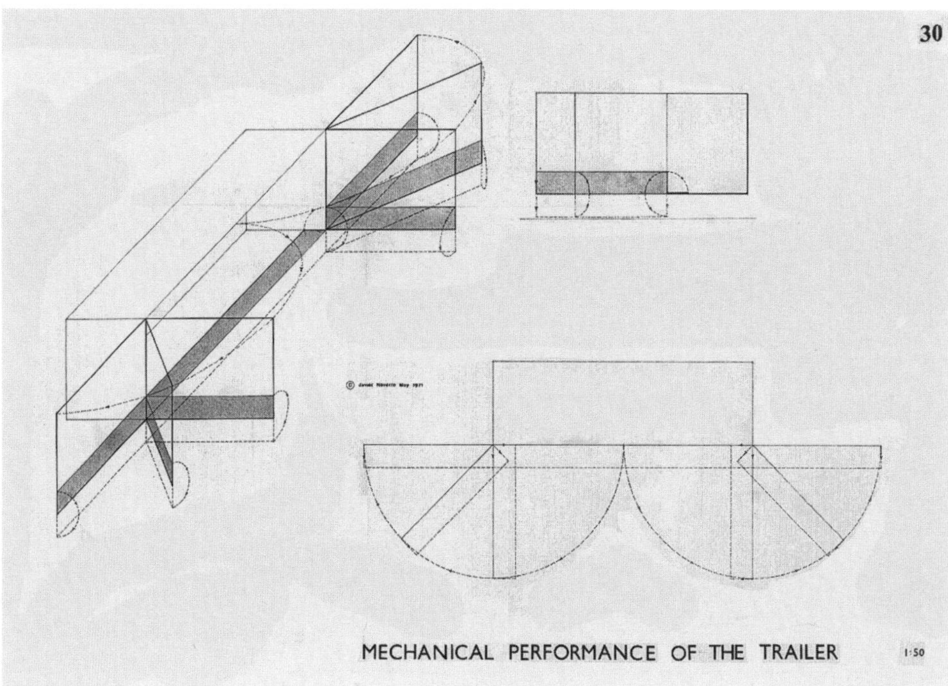
30
MECHANICAL PERFORMANCE OF THE TRAILER
1:50

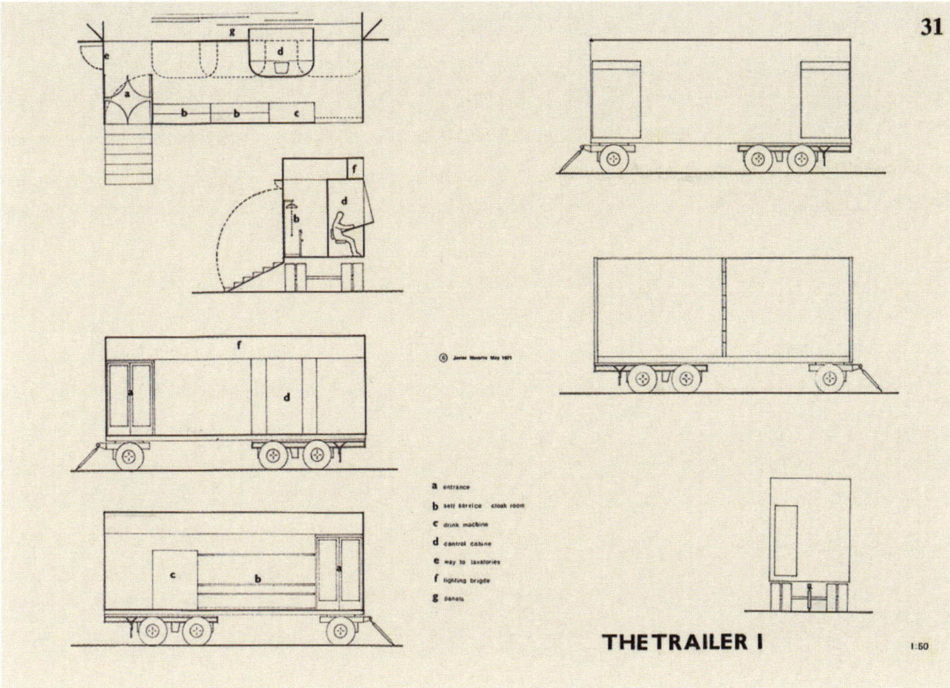
31
g
d
e
a
b
b
c
f
d
b
f
a
d
a entrance
b self service cloak room
c drink machine
d control cabine
e way to lavatories
f lighting bridge
g panels
c
b
a
THE TRAILER I
1:50

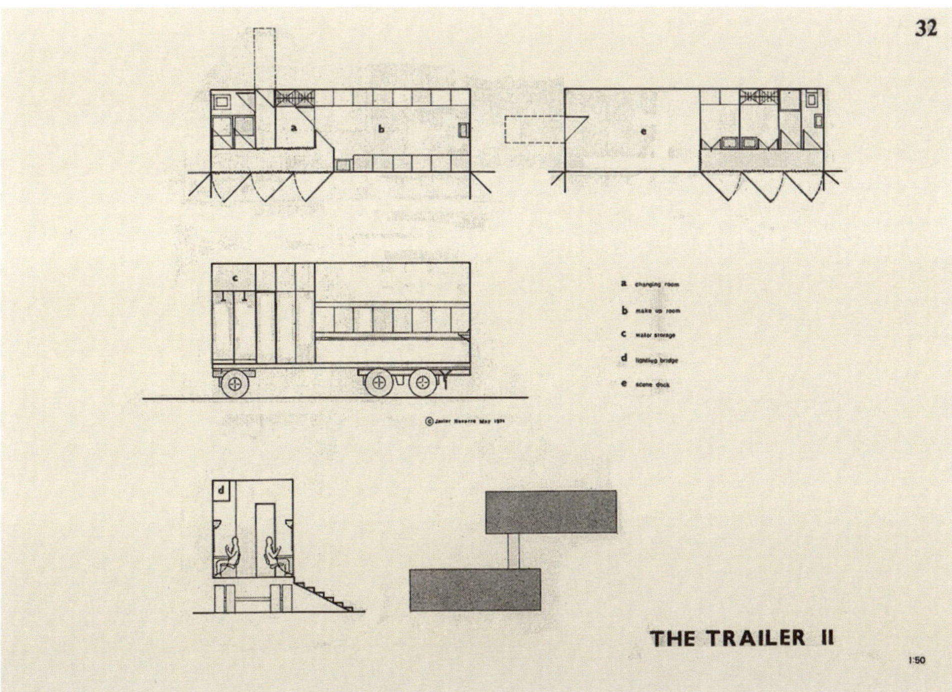
32
a
b
e
c
a changing room
b make up room
c water storage
d lighting bridge
e scene dock
d
THE TRAILER II
1:50

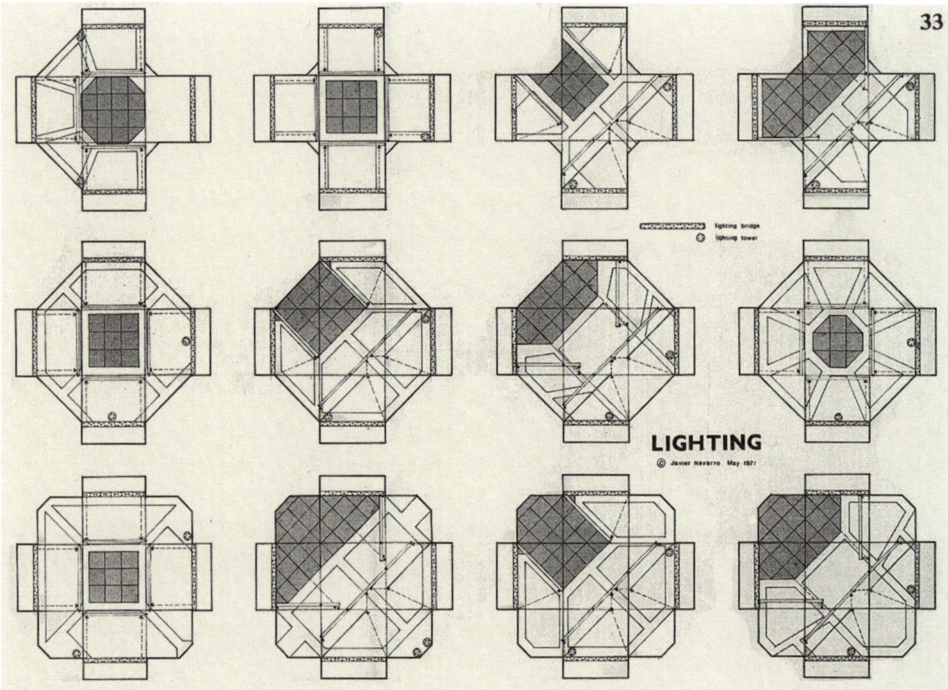
33
lighting bridge
lighting tower
LIGHTING
© Javier Navarro May 1971

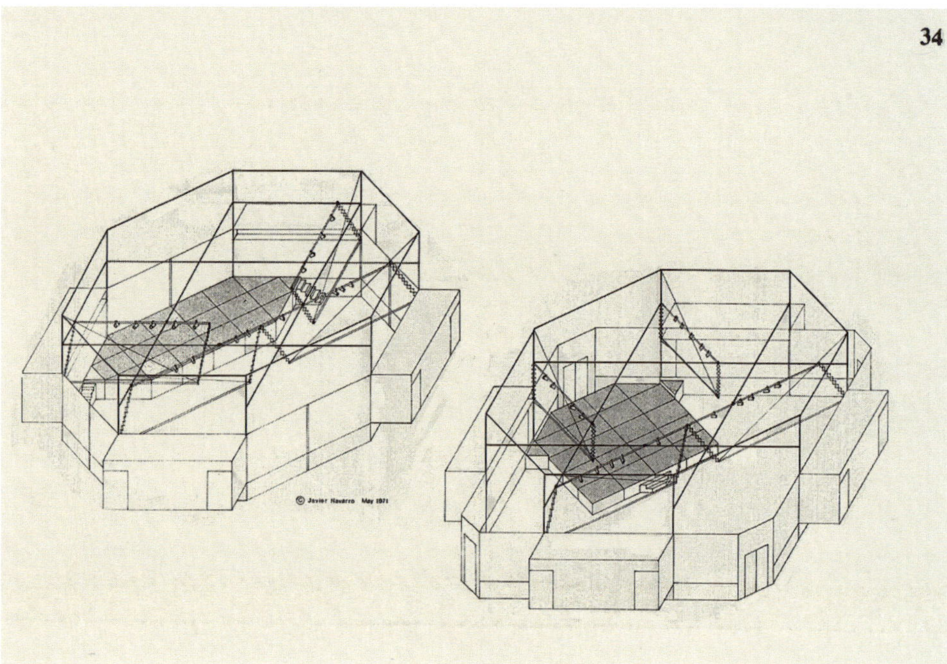
34
© Javier Navarro May 1971

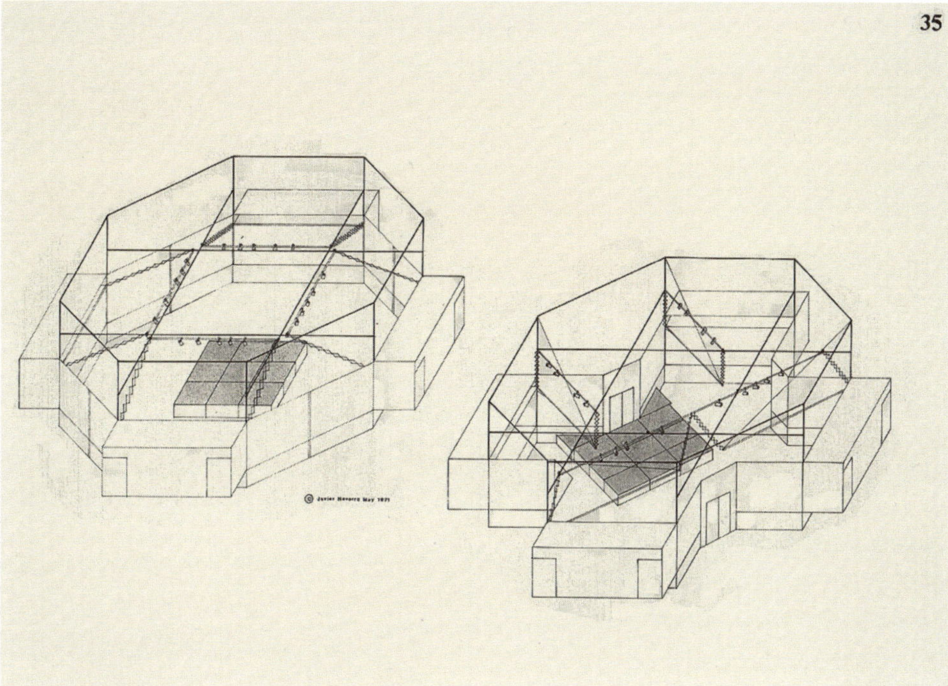

35

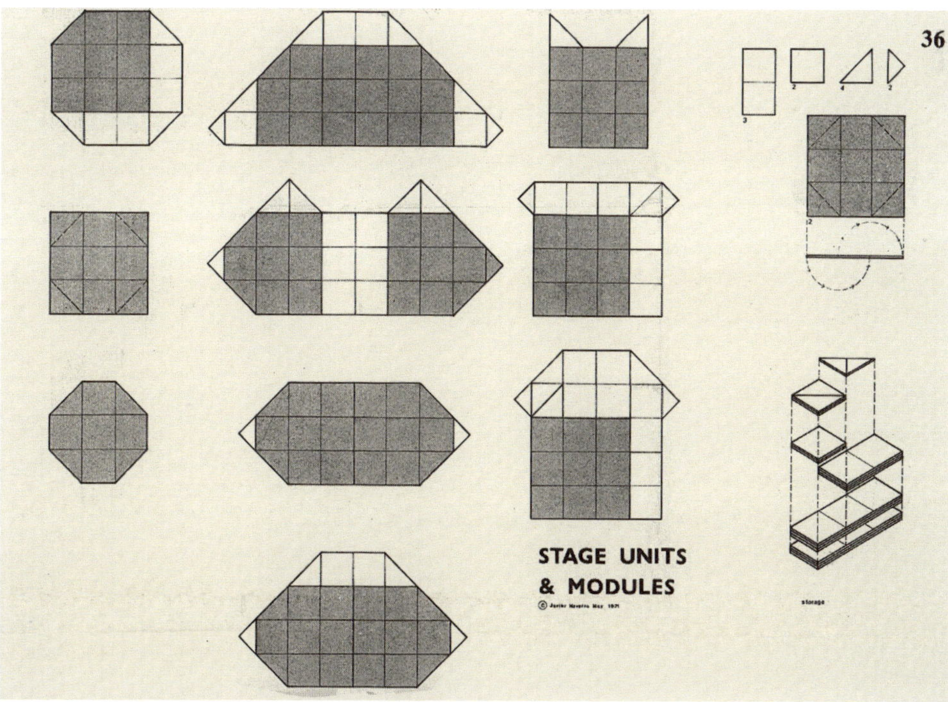

36

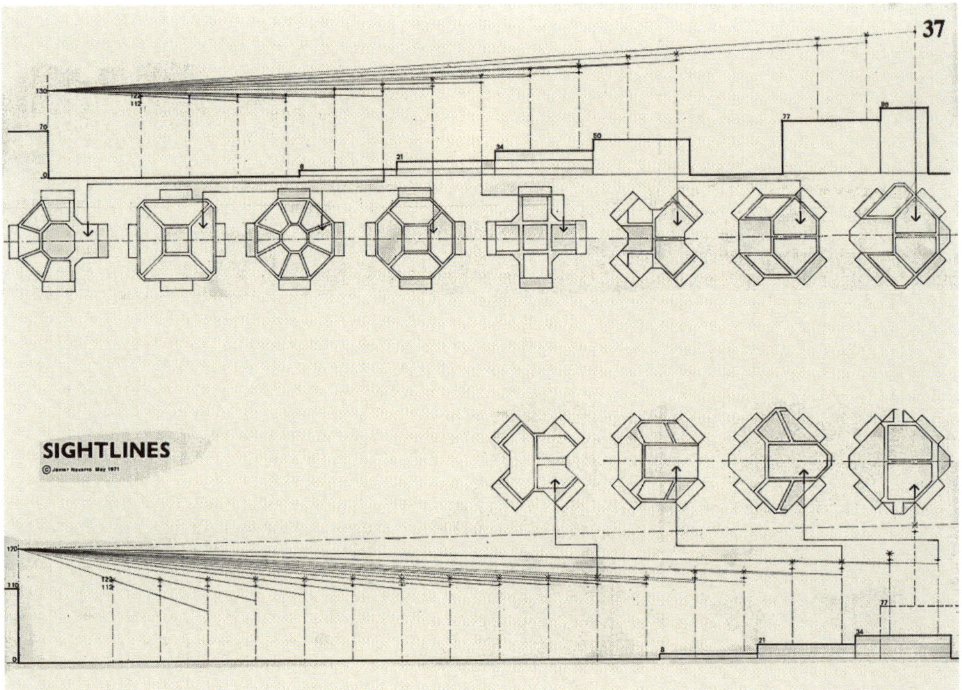
37
SIGHTLINES
© Javier Navarro May 1971

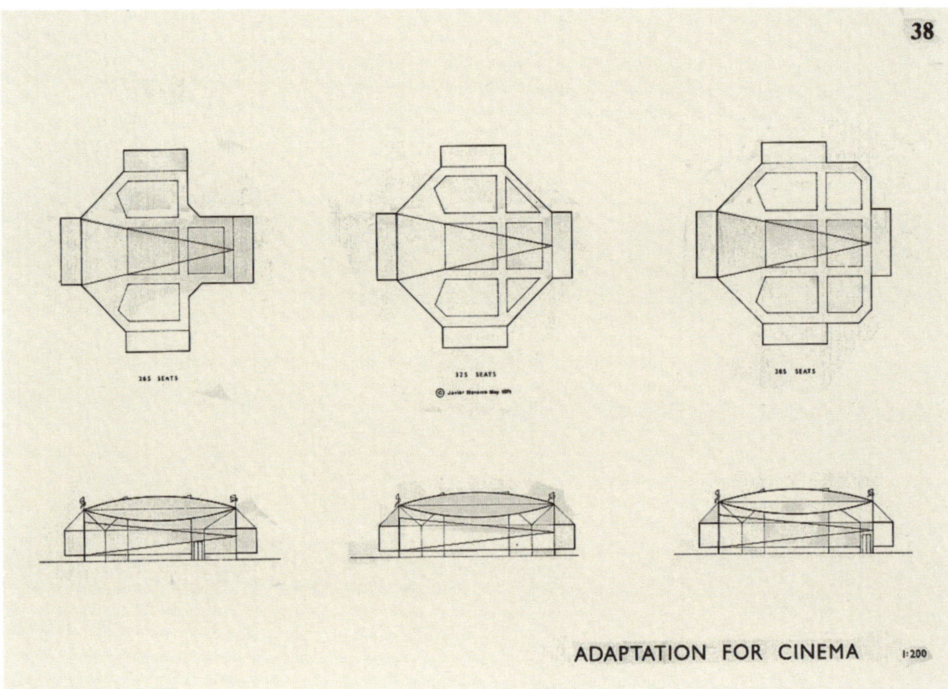
38
265 SEATS
325 SEATS
385 SEATS
© Javier Navarro May 1971
ADAPTATION FOR CINEMA
1:200

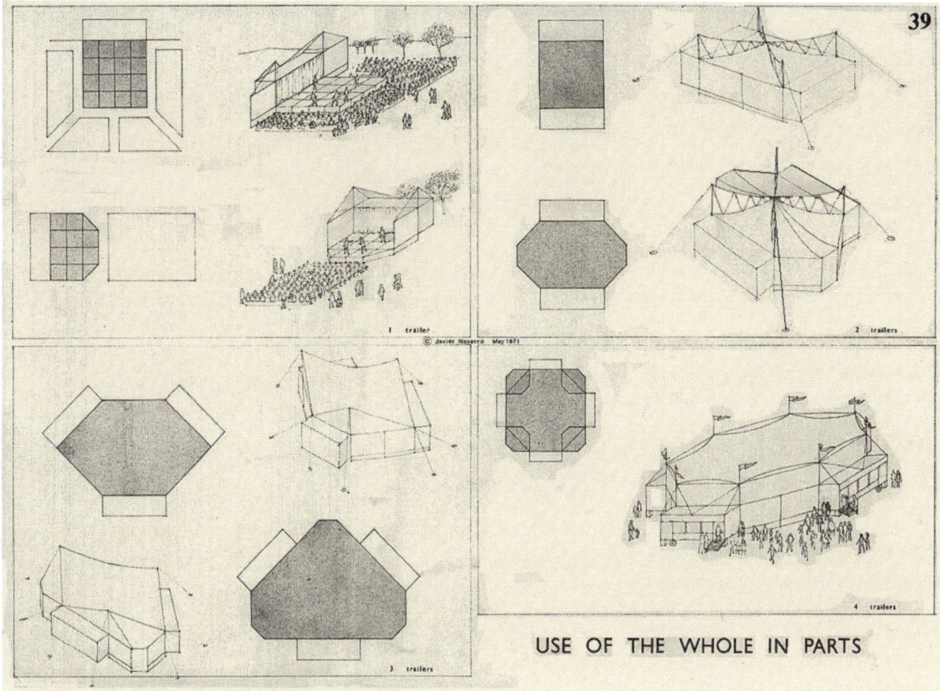
39
1 trailer
2 trailers
© Javier Navarro May 1971
3 trailers
4 trailers
USE OF THE WHOLE IN PARTS

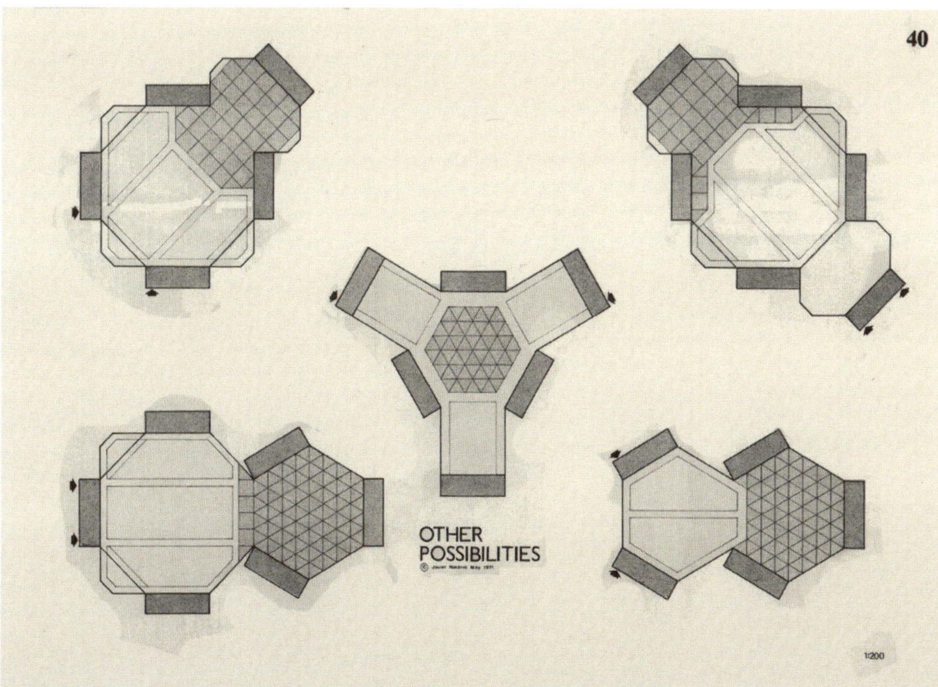
40
OTHER
POSSIBILITIES
1:200

Model of the setup sequence, 1974

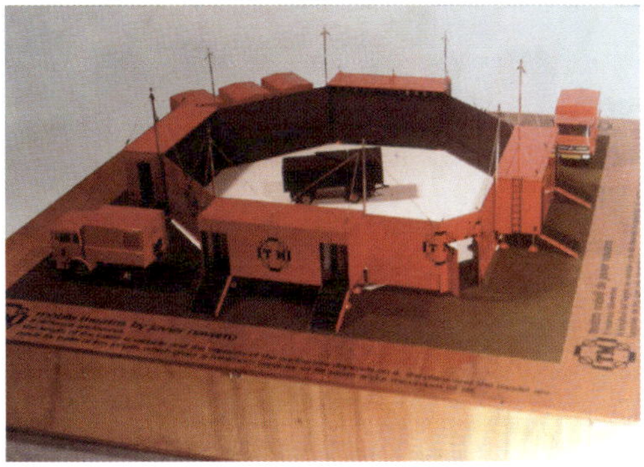

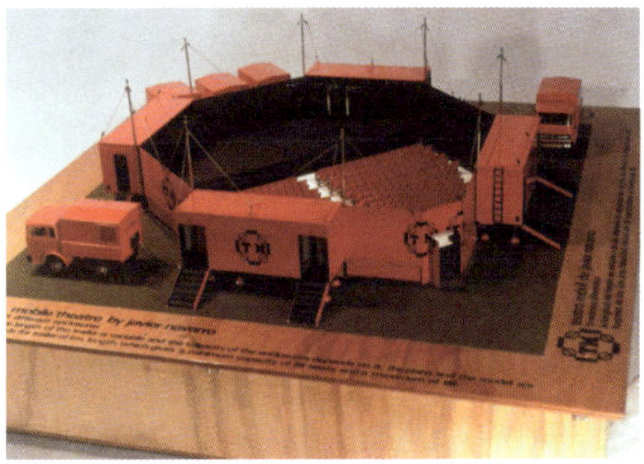

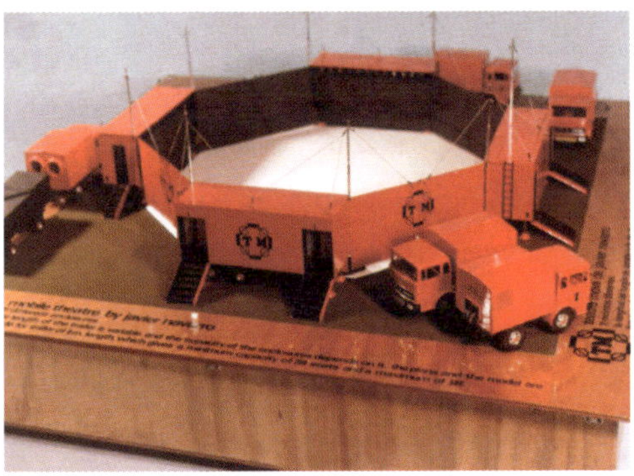

THE DISINTEGRATION OF THEATRICAL SPACE

JAVIER NAVARRO DE ZUVILLAGA

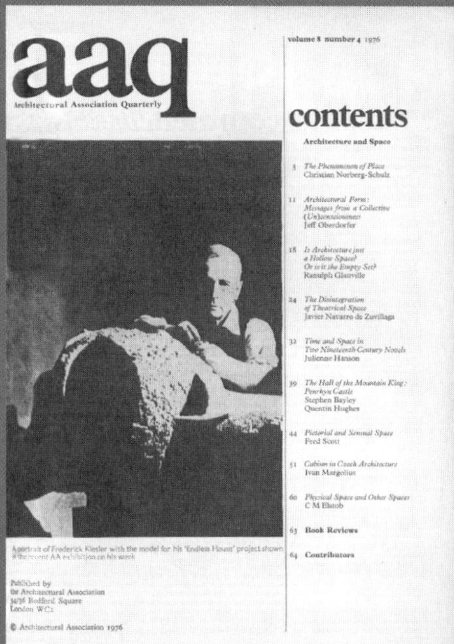

aaq
Architectural Association Quarterly

volume 8 number 4 1976

contents

Architecture and Space

3 *The Phenomenon of Place*
Christian Norberg-Schulz

11 *Architectural Form: Messages from a Collective (Un)consciousness*
Jeff Oberdorfer

18 *Is Architecture just a Hollow Space? Or is it the Empty Set?*
Ranulph Glanville

24 *The Disintegration of Theatrical Space*
Javier Navarro de Zuvillaga

32 *Time and Space in Two Nineteenth Century Novels*
Julienne Hanson

39 *The Hall of the Mountain King: Penrhyn Castle*
Stephen Bayley
Quentin Hughes

44 *Pictorial and Sensual Space*
Fred Scott

51 *Cubism in Czech Architecture*
Ivan Margolius

60 *Physical Space and Other Spaces*
C M Elstob

63 **Book Reviews**

64 **Contributors**

A portrait of Frederick Kiesler with the model for his 'Endless House' project shown at the recent AA exhibition on his work

Published by
the Architectural Association
34/36 Bedford Square
London WC1

© Architectural Association 1976

Transcription of the original text published in English in *Architectural Association Quarterly*, London, vol: 8, n 4, 1976. Pages 24-31.

The tradition of the poor, the theatre in its purest and quintessential form, is alive and well. This tradition proceeds from the very origins of theatre and has always shown itself with greatest intensity in those periods of history when the theatre has been attempting to seek out its own space, either because no theatres existed, as in the beginning, or during the Middle Ages, or because the theatre was restricted by conventional spaces, as happens nowadays.

It could be said the one thing which most strongly characterises current theatrical practice is that instead of creating theatre in an appropriate place or space, on occasion it looks for the appropriate space to perform particular types of theatre. This phenomenon, which could be easily mistaken for indifference towards theatrical space, is, in fact, not so. It is quite the opposite; it implies greater concern for theatrical space by considering that theatrical space could be anywhere— in an ancient or modern theatre, open air or enclosed, a sports arena, a square, a park, a factory. It is clear that in order to revitalize itself theatre needed to get out of theatres, although occasionally it returns to them with a new spatial approach.

Appia introduced this need at the beginning of this century. He said, "Let us abandon our theatres to their death throes and let us construct basic buildings, designed simply to cover the space in which we are working".[1]

Through this manner of understanding theatrical space, it can be classified, using G. Canella's definition, as Mobile Theatre.[2] But just as Temple Theatre and Theatre Machine portray themselves in characteristic buildings with very concrete examples, in Mobile Theatre we come up against a problem. Whereas the Temple Theatre and Theatre Machine were conceived in a search for a new integrated theatrical space, Mobile Theatre is a response to a tendency towards the disintegration on theatrical space.

But why should theatrical space be disintegrating? It should come as no surprise at all to us after the toil of Appia, Craig, Meyerhold, Piscator and Artaud, to name only the most significant. All their work during the first part of this century had to bear fruit and the way I see it, this fruit is Theatre Machine which was gestating for years and whose development was interrupted by two world wars, and Mobile Theatre, which in its manifold forms is the most direct response to the ephemeral character of the theatre.

I would put it this way. "What is a theatre? It is a place where theatre happens. But what is theatre considered as an activity? Theatre is a representation of activities, of all the activities imaginable, that is to say, the representation of anything. But each and every one of these activities requires a space for its performance and this space is the theatre. Thus, in the same way that the actor is a 'place of personalities,' the theatre is the 'place of places,' of all the places imaginable: it is a place fiction."[3]

This approach to theatrical space requires that the theatre building should not, in fact, be one building or if it is it should be multifaceted. It is not, as is commonly supposed by some people who cannot conceive of theatre outside "the theatre building," a matter of ending with theatre, but rather, on the contrary, of preventing theatre from dying inside theatres. Although there are precedents, it is really the matter of a new approach to theatrical space.

It is clear that wherever theatre is performed the boundaries of a theatrical space are required. But this is space whose architecture, like theatrical space itself, must be ephemeral. In this respect the worlds of Celan are particularly important: "In order to be theatre, theatre must flee from itself from the possibility of ending up inevitably as an institution."[4] And a theatre which flees from itself cannot take place in an institutionalized theatrical space.

This is obviously connected with "traveling theatre" from Thespis to the Middle Ages, from the sacramental acts up to today. But there is an aspect which clearly differentiates Mobile Theatre from its historic precedents; even though it also returns to its origins, although it too is searching for its own space and its own style it does so with a tendency towards ritualized action, it starts out from a replanning or restating of theatrical space based on a denial —although not total one— of the concept which preceded it as unitary and differentiated space.

Mobile Theatre is essentially experimental theatre, since, in every situation and in every place, it searches for theatrical space appropriate to the circumstances.

When Gropius, in his Total Theatre Project, attempted to bring about the disappearance of the hall by the use of projection all around its perimeter, his aim was for the disintegration of conventional theatrical space. The Infinidome of Blanding Sloan, who, in the thirties already conceived theatrical spectacle as the cosmic spectacle of the Planetarium, its precedent, the Fortuny dome, Suspended Theatre of New York —all these are approaches, by means of technological solutions, to the idea of "environment theatre" which is the most prolific and most characteristic expression of Mobile Theatre.

Apart from the whole of the secular tradition —what Peter Brooks calls "coarse theatre"[5]— preoccupations are manifested which predate the appearance of "environmental theatre." Perhaps it was Artaud who most precisely expressed the theme: "We have suppressed the hall and the stage which are then replaced by a single space without dividing walls, partitions or barriers of any description and that will be the actual theatre of the action? [...] the spectator, situated in the centre of the action will see himself surrounded and traversed by it. This involvement has its origins in the proper layout of the hall."[6]

This is a redefinition of theatrical space which for Artaud was involved in the spatial translation of his idea of addressing oneself directly to the public through their feeling and not their understanding of the spoken word. And it is this idea and its consequential spatial planning which inspired theatre for more than a decade; especially today's version of environmental theatre.

After working on their own account both Grotowski and the Living Theatre, after discovering Artaud, found themselves identified in great measure with the Theatre of Cruelty. Not very long ago Grotowski began a dissertation by saying, "We have entered the era of Antonin Artaud."

And perhaps Grotowski, leading the Theatre Laboratory, is one of those who did most to rediscover theatre by replanning theatrical space, "attempting to avoid eclecticism, opposing the idea that the theatre is a combination of disciplines."[7]

Confronting the essence of theatre directly, he has rediscovered the "theatre of the poor," finding that representation is an act of transgression (the incarnation of Dionysus by Thespis was a transgression) and consequently that theatre can exist without a separate acting area. Thus he challenged the notion of the theatre as the synthesis of unequal creative disciplines (what he calls "synthetic" or "rich" theatre) from which the Theatre Machine has been the inevitable architectural outcome, in its attempts to reconcile spatially all the possibilities of theatre: "However much theatre may extend and explore its mechanical resources, it will remain inferior to cinema and television. For this reason as much as anything, I propose poverty within the theatre."[8] This is a question of poverty of material means, not of means of expression, based on the direct actor-audience relationship. A shared living of the act of theatre in a common space: environmental theatre.

This "essential vitality" which Artaud was putting forward, was taken up not only by Grotowski but also by many other groups. The adherents of Living Theatre, in honour of his name, declared in 1969: "We used to think that theatre and life were two separate things but this was completely untrue." Ronnie Davis, founder of the San Francisco Mime Troup, said in 1970: "Acting does not exists for us, we do not act, we are." And Peter Schumann, director of the Bread and Puppet maintains, "We have no solution to the problem, what should theatre's function be? What is its form? It all depends on the place where we happen to be or the moment in which we are living."

These statements contained the spirit of Mobile Theatre whose spatial translation is sketched in by Jérôme Savary, director of the Grand Magic Circus: "Basically, the works of the Magic Circus cannot be peformed in theatres because we start from the point of view that there are far more places in which to perform theatre than the theatres themselves. The ideal place is a gymnasium, a garage or a public square, an open-air site where there is nothing and it is possible to place a few useful objects and put out some chairs."

Thus it remains clear that Mobile Theatre rejects as its theatrical space what we have hitherto known as theatre and seeks through its experiences for a new expression of theatrical space, an expression we might call "vital"; a space which lives during the performance and which should be a protagonist of the performance as much as the actors and the audience. It would not be inappropriate to try and clarify slightly the multifaceted panorama of what we call Mobile Theatre and we shall do this from the point of view of the theatrical space which it delineates or which it employs in each case.

This first group, which we can consider, is that theatre which is performed in a place previously chosen for the purpose as a setting for actors and audience, hardly requiring changes to its (pre-) existing configuration. It follows the great tradition of royal entrances, of festival processions and public parades, of the chariot of Thespis and of medieval troupes of strolling players.

It is possible to call this first group "Mobile Theatre of the found environment," or "street theatre" to which those groups just mentioned all correspond, each in their own way. It is characterised by a high degree of flexibility in the action-audience relationship, insofar as, since it is taking place in a public street or square, the spectator can choose whether or not to take any notice of the action. And this is one important characteristics: that the places chosen always offer the possibilities of finding an audience[9] which is an essential element in the political and guerrilla theatres of the sixties.

Its theatrical space is an urban space which may be transformed, according to circumstances, to a greater or lesser degree. Royal entrances with their triumphal arches, their false (although theatrically authentic) façades, which still survive, through often very diminished, in official visits of foreign presidents and in the big public displays which some governments still organise, correspond to a greater degree of transformation or theatricalization. The street performances of so many groups, from the medieval *farandula* to Bread and Puppet, who limit themselves to erecting a platform or making a procession, correspond to a lesser degree of transformation of the surroundings. And the fact of the matter is that, quite independent of the previous transformation of space, there always exists a spatial transgression which is unique to the theatrical performance.

Within this group it is possible to include some other less theatrical social and religious spectacles such as fairs and *verbenas* (the celebration to mark the eve of a saint's day), pagan and religious parades and processions (Holy Week in Spain is pretty theatrical) and the political and labour demonstrations of our century (dialectical materialism being the more or less official religion of our times, it can be said that these demonstrations are the religious processions of today).

Taking another criterion, that of prior election of the space to be used, we can consider the most simple, a street or square, right up to the most spectacular —particularly in terms of its dimensions. The storming of the Winter Palace, a commemorative spectacle of the third anniversary of the Russian Revolution, took place within an enormous integrated theatrical space: two giant platforms, linked by a huge bridge, the square, the palace and a cruiser anchored in the Neva: the participants numbered more than 6000, the audience more than 100000.

In Vermont Bread and Puppet, in the summer of 1974 offered a spectacle (Domestic Resurrection Fair and Circus) in a vast meadow surrounded by hills. The action took place in the meadow and was watched by spectators situated on the surrounding hills. An urban version "in negative" of the same thing was put on in Manhattan; in this the spectators were located on the terrace of a building, while the dancers —in this case it was a ballet—performed on the terraces of other buildings surrounding the spectators on all sides. Meredith Monk went even further with her production *Vessel*, using three different spaces; her own home, the Performing Garage (of which we will talk later) and a site intended for car parking.[10] And finally we must mention Spoleto, a theatre-city, the zenith of theatrical spaces integrated into the urban space, the scene of theatrical festivals.

The second group of Mobile Theatre which we shall consider is that of the "prepared environment." It unfolds within a closed space which is conveniently prepared for each production, but always based on the assumption that this space is common to actors and spectators (although the action occasionally marks out inevitable differences) — which they share jointly during the time of the performance. This idea of living together and the vital common experience within the same space is its clearest characteristic.

A reference to liturgical drama is inescapable. For a performance of the martyrdom of Saint Apollonia (a French performance given in the open air in 1460) an "environment" was created in relation to the grouping of the surrounding dwellings, where a common space was used by both actors and audience. The latter intervened indirectly in the action through the figure of the emperor. Other more primitive examples of liturgical drama held in church interiors, even though based on different assumptions, pointed the way towards the current concept of the spectator within this space and within the action. But let us analyse the current assumptions.

Grotowski says, of theatrical space: "We have renounced the stage-auditorium plan; for each production a new space is designed for actors and audience. Thus an infinite variation of the actor-audience relationship is possible [...] The essential thing is to find the appropriate actor-audience relationship for each type of performance and to give a body to this decision by material arrangements."[11]

It is, as Artaud wanted, a matter of surrounding and traversing the audience with the action, of making the spectator an actor, not just a person for whom the actors exists but part of the action; of involving the spectator in the action not by technical means as the Theatre Machine did, but by experiencing the common sharing of space and time.

Jerry N. Rojo, a pioneer of environmental theatre and designer of various well-known American productions, says that the designer of the theatrical environment "begins with the notion that the production develops from the starting point of a given space, that it occupies it in its totality, and that for actor and audience, time, space and materials exist just as they are;"[12] that is to say, not an appearance of reality but a vital realism which, as we shall see, makes way for performances positively removed from traditional realism.

We have to return to Appia to understand this new process of the "realistic approach to theatre." His desire to emphasize the spatial-temporal relationships of the actors with the stage —in which light is fundamental— is no more than the seed, which starting with stage space ended up invading all theatrical space.

Why should only the actor and not the public as well, feel a relationship with a dramatic space and time in a direct manner? This is one question which Appia, Meyerhold, Copeau, Artaud, Piscator and Brecht all seem to have asked themselves. The consequence of their answers to it would be environmental theatre. The Happening, the outcome of Surrealist and Dadaist experiments with which Artaud was so closely linked, is a clear precedent of this way of understanding theatrical space. The prophetic visions of the creations of the Theatre of Cruelty, seems to be confirmed by Rojo: "Each environment performance creates a sense of total involvement."[13]

Apart from other experiments (Eisenstein, Okhlopkov, Copeau and St Doeis), Brecht went along with this way of understanding theatrical space. "Make them dream in full light," Brecht said to the lighting technicians, referring to the audience.[14] Use blinding illumination from the stage and let the audience see the spotlights; these were Brecht's two proposals. On the other hand, the interpretative technique made the actors insert, from the realism of their own experiences, directions and comments addressed to the public about the performance itself.

The effects of all these shock tactics contribute to the audience's living the performance within realistic space-time coordinates. Brecht did not touch directly upon the problem of theatrical space insofar as he was modifying the spatial actor-audience relationship, as others have done, but he certainly did so indirectly through the lighting and the interpretative techniques. And his way of living theatrical space has had a great influence on the "prepared environment" theatre.

In this connection Rojo explains: "The traditional division of space into foyer, stage and theatrical areas, forum and auditorium should not be considered immutable for this class of theatre, but should be subjected to a reorganisation according to the idea for an individual production [...] in essence, the designer becomes a hybrid architect-designer who conceives a completely new theatre for every production."[15]

This is already fact. Peter Brook, another of the directors who has experimented mostly in this type of environment theatre, says clearly: "Year after year, the most vital theatrical experiments take place outside the halls built for just that purpose."[16] Which does not prevent theatres from being used as theatrical spaces, although with different criteria, as Living Theatre did with the Auditorium of the Academy of Music in Brooklyn in *Paradise Now*. Taking up Peter Brooks words again, it boils down to the fact that "the decorating principle is an integrating part of the theatrical space, not part of the play."[17]

Thus it becomes clear how in Mobile Theatre, the settings tends to be the architecture of theatrical space, architecture which in its own time tends to become a stage setting in the sense that it is not formalised with the same sense of permanence and definition with which the Temple Theatre and the Theatre Machine are, but is faithful to the fleeting character of the theatre, it serves as a "theatre" for the performance, only to disappear once it is over. It is, to put it another way, an architecture of representation or a representation of architecture.

Examples of this new conception of theatrical space are the productions of the Performing Group which Richard Schechner directs in the Performing Garage, with spaces designed by Rojo; Grotowski's Theatre Laboratory with designs by the architect J. Gurawski; Living Theatre; Bread and Puppet; the Grand Magic Circus; Chaikin's Open Theatre; Lee Breuer's Mabou Mimes; Foreman's Ontological Hysteric Theatre; Anne West's I; the Theatre of Vasilicó; J. Roose-Evans' Stage Two; and those of many other groups all over the world, which are responding to the idea of the theatre of mobility.

To complete this panorama of the conception and the use of theatrical space today, there remains a third group which, with no further words, is perfectly described by the term Mobile Theatre. To understand it better we have to make two prior observations. The first is that this kind of theatre also corresponds, to what we have called Theatre Machine. The second is that, one way or another, it is also an example of what is commonly known as travelling theatre, thus it is a mixture of "theatre of the found" and "theatre of the prepared environment": its aim is to install itself in any place; it also responds in various ways to previous designs with a greater degree of flexibility.

Its historical antecedents are the same as those of the two preceding groups, but this is the one which follows most directly the tradition of the strolling *farandula*.

Naturally the examples which we are going to quote correspond in general to the various criteria. But there is one which is common to all of them; the aim of taking theatre from one place to another.

Previously, when nobody conceived of performing out of theatres the idea was to take the theatre to those places which lacked one. This criterion, which remains valid in many locations and situations, has lost part of its strength with the expansion of the concept of theatrical space. Effectively, even though no theatre exists, performances can take place on any other site or in the street.

With the growth of cities and all that entails, a Mobile Theatre is conceivable which, rather than going from city to city, goes from one location to another within the same city. An interesting example of this possibility is offered by the proposal for the theatre of Udine by N. Dardi and M. Ricci. This is a modular organism, which can be modified on demand, consisting of a stock of demountable, portable, cubic modules that can be carried or transported to another part of the city. "The theatrical activity begin with the public dismantling of a part of the 'mother theatre', the transporting of the pieces through the streets and their re-erection in the place chosen on the basis of the elements necessary for the performance itself."[18]

The Mobile Theatre always offer the additional spectacle of the assembly of the structure. It starts with the very simple element: a lorry —previously it was a cart with mules—, which transports the essential parts to be set up as a scenario or as a stage-set in the open air, with curtains and spotlights. A typical example in Spain was García Lorca's *La Barraca* (The Hut). There are also simple structures, all demountable and thus transportable, which provide an enclosed space for the performance and whose composition and assembly procedures offer different solutions. These include the traditional *Envelats* (awnings or canopies) of Catalonia and the Levante. Domenech i Montaner describes them thus: "The envelat, a tent of monumental proportions, has as its object, the provision within a few hours of a large hall (salon) with no internal support, adequate for two or three thousand people assembled for a party".[19] It could well be a theatrical party. It consists of a canvas ingeniously draped from poles by means of cords.

Another example in Spain is the very popular theatre of Manolita Chen, intended for variety shows. This comprises a canvas held up by very light rods. The Spanish architect E. Pérez Piñero has designed some demountable geodesic domes which, when covered with canvas, offer an enclosed site for performances.

Hans Walter-Muller came up with an inflatable theatre, easily dismantled and transported, for the Maeght Foundation in Saint-Paul-de-Vence in France. The Bubble Theatre used an enclosure called Tensi-Dome formed from an elastic cloth stretched over two inclined arches. Perhaps the simplest example of the enclosed area is the convertible dome designed by a group of Dutch architects to house happenings in the streets of Amsterdam.

Another group always have the common characteristic of being self-transporting, that is to say that the transport elements (vans, containers) form part of the structure, whether enclosed or in the open air. The technology employed in these examples varies from the most elementary to the most sophisticated. A simple example is the Belgian Théâtre de Travers, a small space formed starting with one van. On the same lines but using a railway carriage and diferent solutions are the design of M. Matinen (1966) and of Murchland, Ridou and Farrel (1972) the latter based on the use of a bus.

In 1971 K. Karou presented a model of a mobile open air theatre using three lorries at the Prague Quadrennial. K. Kotami designed a travelling and adaptive theatre based on five lorries covered by a parabolic canvas. The Delacorte Theatre of New York is a mobile, open-air theatre which uses four lorries. My own Mobile Theatre (1971) is the only case I know of which forms an enclosure with the trailers themselves. Four of these trailers are in fixed positions yet 21 different enclosures can be obtained. Each of these is different in form and size and can be created within the same inflatable covering.

The Travelling Theatre by A. Stinco (1967) uses the lorries to anchor the pneumatic structure. The Travelling Theatre designed by J. Aubert (1968) and the Mobile auditorium of D. Patterson (1972) accommodate 5000 spectators each, one using 31 lorries, the other 46 containers.

As we have seen, this class of Mobile Theatre is extremely varied in its architectural solutions; so much so that it could include such examples as floating theatres; the Arena Teaterbåten which runs along the Swedish Coasts performing in the ports and the theatre-ship which the University of Minnesota launched in 1959 on the Mississippi.

We have categorised this third group of Mobile Theatre according to the technical solutions which each brings to the ideals of travelling theatre in accordance with the way that it corresponds most closely to the idea of the Theatre Machine. Not only because its technology constitutes a great machinery, but also because it corresponds to the character of adaptability. But the possibility of its total disappearance as theatrical space, given its demountable structure, is another response to the spirit of direct living together of time and space which revitalises current theatre. When, in addition, it offers us the possibility of changing its internal and external configuration —see my Mobile Theatre— then it corresponds even in greater measure to what we have called Mobile Theatre in more general terms. On the other hand, the ephemeral character of theatrical space which most of the different solutions to Mobile Theatre tend to display, is in line with the responses which architecture and design can offer in territories far removed from the theatre.

In the human environment, which is conditioned each day by man himself, the need emerges for it to possess certain flexibility which makes it capable of some degree of modification. This flexibility can be obtained in two ways, either by including it in the design of new environments —adaptability and mobility of the theatrical space— or by designing environments which can be superimposed on those already existing —environmental theatre— from the Suitaloon of M. Webb (1968) to P. Cook's Instant City (1969). As the latter suggests perhaps "the future of architecture lies in the explosion of architecture."[20]

It is also possible that the future of the theatre will be found in blowing the theatre apart. The explosion has already started. How, otherwise, can we explain the disintegration of theatrical space?

Notes

1. A. Appia, *L'oeuvre d'art vivant*, Geneva 1921.

2. G. Canella, *Ulisse* vol. II 1969. Speaking of modern theatre Canella considers three fundamental types: the Temple Theatre, the Theatre Machine and Mobile Theatre. He refers to the Classical examples and the Wagnerian prototype of Bayreuth and, as modern examples, the Lincoln Centre, New York, the Opera House in Sydney and the National Theatre in London as the first type. The Theatre Machine derives from the Constructivist models and the Total Theatre of Gropius. The Mobile Theatre tends towards the disintegration of theatrical space, by means of a freer relationship between public and performance.

3. Javier Navarro, *Mobility in the Theatre*, a paper presented in the course on Theatre Architecture at the Centro Internazionalle di Studi di Architettura Andrea Palladio, Vicenza 1975.

4. Celant, *Sipario*, n. 7, 1970, p.8.

5. P. Brook, *El espacio vacío*, Península, Barcelona 1973.

6. A. Artaud, *El teatro de la crueldad* (First Manifesto), from *El teatro y su doble*, Sudamericana, Buenos Aires 1971.

7. J. Grotowski, *Towards a Poor Theatre*, Methuen, London 1969.

8. J. Grotowski, Opus cit.

9. See Brooks McNamara, "Performance Space, The Environmental Tradition", *Architectural Association Quarterly*, vol. 7, n. 2, April-June 1975, London.

10. B. McNamara, opus. cit.

11. J. Grotowski, opus cit.

12. Jerry N. Rojo, "Environmental Design", in *Contemporary Stage Design USA*, ITI, New York 1974.

13. J. N. Rojo, opus cit.

14. B. Brecht, *Schriften zum Theater*, Frankfurt am Main, 1957.

15. B. Brecht, opus cit.

16. B. Brecht, opus cit.

17. P. Brook in *L'Architecture d'Ajourd d'hui*, n. 152, 1970.

18. M. Manieri-Elia, "Il Teatro Contemporaneo", course in Vicenza 1975.

19. Doménech i Montaner, *Historia General del Arte*, Barcelona 1886.

20. P. Cook, *Experimental Architecture*, Studio vista, London 1970, p. 152.

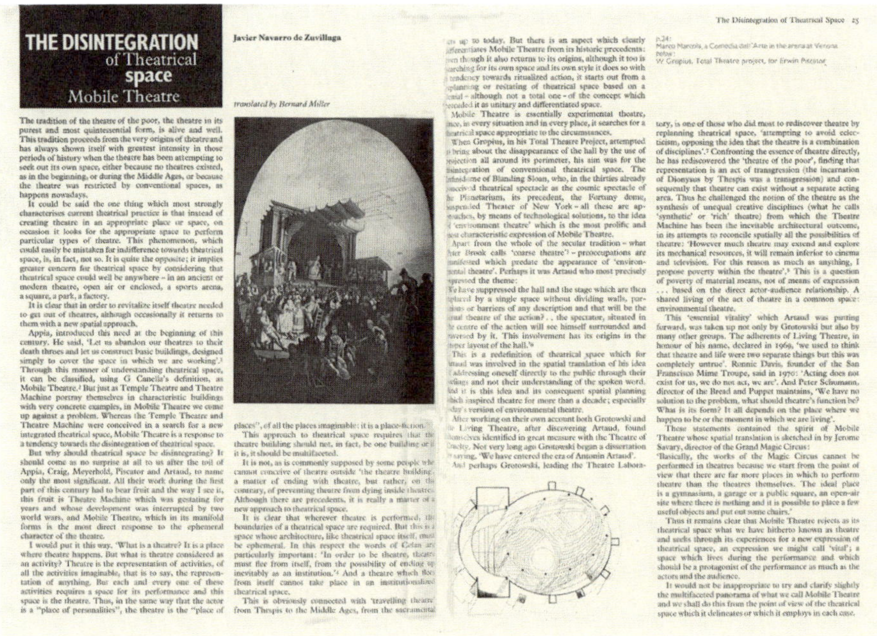

The Disintegration of Theatrical Space 25

THE DISINTEGRATION of Theatrical space
Mobile Theatre

Javier Navarro de Zuvillaga

translated by Bernard Miller

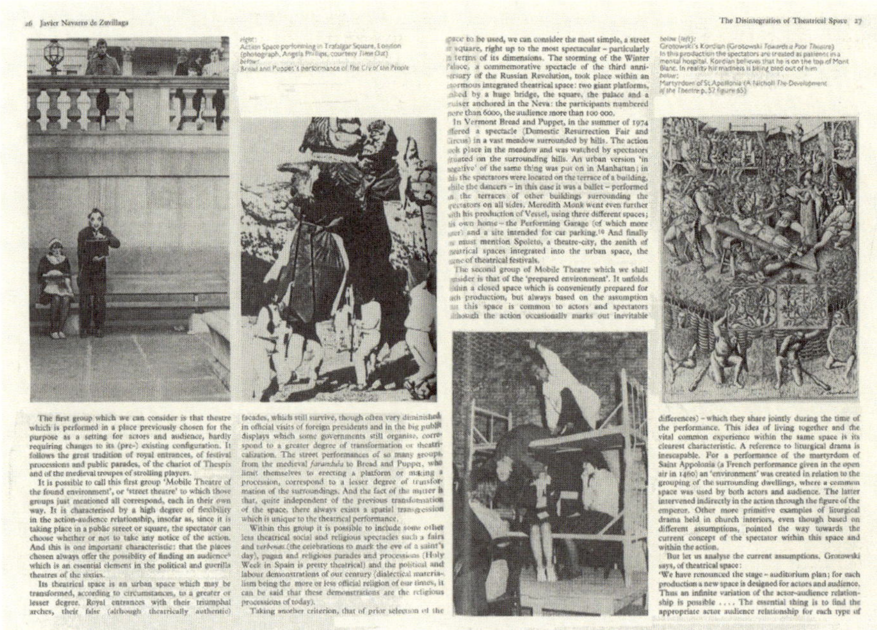

26 Javier Navarro de Zuvillaga

The Disintegration of Theatrical Space 27

performance and to give a body to this decision by material arrangements.'[11]

It is, as Artaud wanted, a matter of surrounding and traversing the audience with the action, of making the spectator an actor, not just a person for whom the actors exist but part of the space and of the action; of involving the spectator in the action not by technical means as the Theatre Machine did, but by experiencing the common sharing of space and time.

Jerry N Rojo, a pioneer of environmental theatre and designer of various well-known American productions, says that the designer of the theatrical environment 'begins with the notion that the production develops from the starting point of a given space, that it occupies it in its totality and that for actor and audience, time, space and materials exist just as they are;'[12] that is to say, not an appearance of reality but a vital realism which, as we shall see, makes way for performances positively removed from traditional realism.

We have to return to Appia to understand this new process of the 'realistic approach to theatre'. His desire to emphasize the spatial-temporal relationships of the actors with the stage – in which light was fundamental – is no more than the seed, which starting with the stage space ended up invading all theatrical space.

Why should only the actor and not the public as well, feel a relationship with dramatic space and time in a direct manner? This is one question which Appia, Meyerhold, Copeau, Artaud, Piscator and Brecht all seem to have asked themselves. The consequence of their answers to it would be environmental theatre. The Happening, the outcome of Surrealist and Dadaist experiments with which Artaud was so closely linked, is a clear precedent of this way of understanding theatrical space. The prophetic visions of the creator of the Theatre of Cruelty, seems to be confirmed by Rojo: 'Each environment performance creates a sense of total involvement.'[13] Apart from other experiments (Eisenstein, Okhlopkov, Copeau and St Doeis), Brecht went along with this way of understanding theatrical space. 'Make them dream in the light' Brecht said to the lighting technicians, referring to the audience.[14] Use blinding illumination from the stage and let the audience see the spotlights; these were Brecht's two proposals. On the other hand, the interpretative technique made the actors insert, from the realism of their own experiences, directions and comments addressed to the public about the performance itself. The effects of all these shock tactics contribute to the audience's living the performance within realistic space-time co-ordinates. Brecht did not touch directly upon the problem of theatrical space insofar as he was modifying the spatial actor-audience relationship, as others have done, but he certainly did so indirectly through the lighting and the interpretative techniques. And his way of living theatrical space has had a great influence on the 'prepared environment' theatre.

In this connection Rojo explains, 'The traditional division of space into foyer, stage and technical areas, forum and auditorium should not be considered immutable for this class of theatre, but should be subjected to a reorganisation according to the idea for an individual production . . . in essence, the designer becomes a hybrid architect-designer who conceives a completely new theatre for every production.[15]

This is already fact. Peter Brook, another of the directors who has experimented mostly in this type of environmental theatre, says clearly, 'Year after year, the most vital

below:
Living Theatre's *Paradise Now*
(photograph, Donald Cooper, courtesy *Time Out*)

A catalunian Envelat (*Arquitecturas Bis* number 5)

theatrical experiments take place outside the halls built for just that purpose.'[16] Which does not prevent theatres from being used as theatrical spaces, although with different criteria, as Living Theatre did with the Auditorium of the Academy of Music in Brooklyn in *Paradise Now*.

Taking up Peter Brook's words again, it boils down to the fact that 'the decorating principle is an integrating part of the theatrical space, not part of the play.'[17]

Thus it becomes clear how in Mobile Theatre, the setting tends to be the architecture of theatrical space, architecture which in its own time tends to become a stage setting in the sense that it is not formalised with the same sense of permanence and definition with which the Temple Theatre and Theatre Machine are, but is faithful to the fleeting character of the theatre, it serves as a 'theatre' for the performance, only to disappear once it is over. It is, to put it another way, an architecture of representation or a representation of architecture.

Examples of this new conception of theatrical space are the productions of:

- the Performing Group which Richard Schechner directs in the Performing Garage, with spaces designed by Rojo;
- Grotowski's Theatre Laboratory with designs by the architect J Gurawski;
- Living Theatre,
  Bread and Puppet,
- the Grand Magic Circus,
- Chaikin's Open Theatre,
- Lee Breuer's Mabou Mimes,
- Foreman's Ontological Hysteric Theatre,
- Anne West's I,
- the Theatre of Vasilico,
- J Roose-Evans' Stage Two

and those of many other groups all over the world, which are responding to the idea of the theatre of mobility.

To complete this panorama of the conception and the use of theatrical space today, there remains a third group which, with no further words, is perfectly described by the term Mobile Theatre. To understand it better we have to make two prior observations. The first is that this kind of theatre also corresponds, to what we have called Theatre Machine. The second is that, one way or another, it is also an example of what is commonly known as travelling theatre, thus it is a mixture of 'theatre of the found' and theatre of the prepared environment': its aim is to install itself in any place; it also responds in various ways to previous designs with a greater or lesser degree of flexibility.

Its historical antecedents are the same as those of the two preceding groups, but this is the one which follows most directly the tradition of the strolling *farandula*.

Naturally the examples which we are going to quote, correspond in general to the various criteria. But there is one which is common to all of them; the aim of taking theatre from one place to another.

Previously, when nobody conceived of performing out of theatres the idea was to take the theatre to those places which lacked one. This criterion, which remains valid in many locations and situations has lost part of its strength with the expansion of the concept of theatrical space. Effectively, even though no theatre exists, performances can take place on any other site or in the street.

With the growth of cities and all that that entails, a Mobile Theatre is conceivable which, rather than going from city to city, goes from one location to another within the same city. An interesting example of this possibility is offered by the proposals for the theatre of Udine by N Dardi and M Ricci. This is a modular organism which can be modified on demand, consisting of a stock of demountable, portable, cubic modules which can be carried or transported to another part of the city. 'The theatrical activity begins with the public dismantling of a part of the "mother theatre", the transporting of the pieces through the streets and their re-erection in the place chosen on the basis of the elements necessary for the performance itself.'[18]

The Mobile Theatre always offers the additional spectacle of the assembly of the structure. It starts with the very simplest element: a lorry – previously it was a cart with mules – which transports the essential parts to be set up as a scenario or as a stage-set in the open air, with curtains and spotlights. A typical example in Spain was Garcia Lorca's *La Barraca* (*The Hut*). There are also simple structures, all demountable and thus transportable, which provide an enclosed space for the performance and whose composition and assembly procedures offer different solutions. These include the traditional 'Envelats' (awnings or canopies) of Catalunia and the Levante. Domenech i Montaner describes them thus: 'The envelat, a tent of monumental proportions, has as its object, the provision within a few hours of a large hall (salon) with no internal support, adequate for two or three thousand people assembled for a party.'[19] It could well be a theatrical party. It consists of a canvas ingeniously draped from poles by means of cords.

Another example in Spain is the very popular theatre of Manolita Chen, intended for variety shows. This comprises a canvas held up by very light rods.

The Spanish architect E Perez Pinero has designed some demountable geodesic domes which, when covered with canvas, offer an enclosed site for performances.

Hans Walter-Muller came up with an inflatable theatre, easily dismantled and transported, for the Maeght Foundation in St Paul de Vance in France. The Bubble Theatre used an enclosure called the Tensi-Dome formed from an elastic cloth stretched over two inclined arches. Perhaps the simplest example of the enclosed area is the convertible dome designed by a group of Dutch architects to house happenings in the streets of Amsterdam.

Another group always have the common characteristic

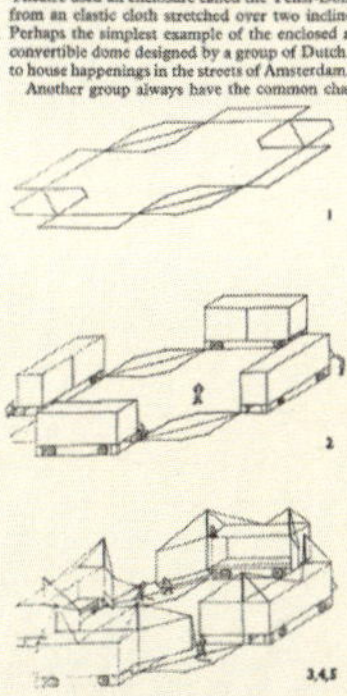

of being self-transporting, that is to say that the transport elements (vans, containers) form part of the structure, whether enclosed or in the open air. The technology employed in these examples varies from the most elementary to the most sophisticated. A simple example is the Belgian Theatre de Travers, a small space formed starting with one van. On the same lines but using a railway carriage and different solutions are the design of M Matinen (1966) and of Murchland, Ridout and Farrell (1972) the latter based on the use of a bus.

In 1971 K Kaoru presented a model of a Mobile open-air Theatre using three lorries at the Prague Quadriennial. K Kotami designed a Travelling and Adaptable Theatre based on five lorries covered by a parabolic canvas. The Delacorte Theatre of New York is a mobile, open-air theatre which uses four trailers. My own Mobile Theatre (1971) is the only case I know of which forms an enclosure with the trailers themselves. Four of these trailers are in fixed positions yet 21 different enclosures can be obtained. Each of these is different in form and size and can be created within the same inflatable covering.

below (left and right):
A mobile theatre project produced at the AA by the author. The reference numbers indicate the various stages in the process of erection of the mobile theatre
bottom:
A Stinco's Travelling Hall (Cook *Experimental Architecture* p

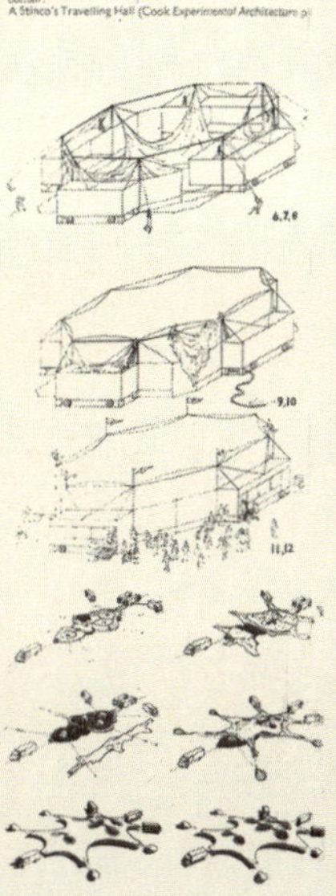

Cook's Instant City

The Travelling Hall by A Stinco (1967) uses the lorries to anchor the pneumatic structure.

The Travelling Theatre designed by J Aubert (1968) and the Mobile Auditorium of D Patterson (1972) accommodate 5000 spectators each, one using 31 lorries, the other 46 containers.

As we have seen, this class of Mobile Theatre is extremely varied in its architectural solutions; so much so that it could include such examples as floating theatres; the Arena Teaterbåten which runs along the Swedish coasts performing in the ports and the theatre-ship which the University of Minnesota launched in 1959 on the Mississippi.

We have categorised this third group of Mobile Theatre according to the technical solutions which each brings to the ideals of travelling theatre in accordance with the way that it corresponds most closely to the idea of the Theatre Machine. Not only because its technology constitutes a great machinery, but also because it corresponds to the character of adaptability. But the possibility of its total disappearance as theatrical space, given its demountable nature, is another response to the spirit of direct living together of time and space which revitalises current theatre. When, in addition, it offers us the possibility of changing its internal and external configuration – see my Mobile Theatre – then it corresponds in even greater measure to what we have called Mobile Theatre in more general terms. On the other hand, the ephemeral character of theatrical space which most of the different solutions to Mobile Theatre tend to display, is in line with the responses which architecture and design can offer in territories far removed from the theatre.

In the human environment, which is conditioned each day by man himself, the need emerges for it to possess certain flexibility which makes it capable of some degree of modification. This flexibility can be obtained in two ways; either by including it in the design of new environments – adaptability and mobility of the theatrical space – or by designing environments which can be superimposed on those already existing – environment theatre – from the Suitaloon of M Webb (1968) to P Cook's Instant City (1969). As the latter suggests perhaps 'the future of architecture lies in the explosion of architecture.'[20]

It is also possible that the future of the theatre will be found in blowing the theatre apart. The explosion has already started. How otherwise, can we explain the disintegration of theatrical space?

References

1
A Appia *L'Oeuvre d'Art Vivant* Geneva 1921.

2
G Canella *Ulisse* volume 11, 1919. Speaking of modern theatre Canella considers three fundamental types: the Temple Theatre, the Theatre Machine and Mobile Theatre. He refers to the Classical examples and the Wagnerian prototype of Bayreuth and, as modern examples, the Lincoln Centre, New York, the Opera House in Sidney and the National Theatre in London as the first type. The Theatre Machine derives from the Constructivist models and the total theatre of Gropius. The Mobile Theatre tends towards the disintegration of theatrical space, by means of a freer relationship between public and performance.

3
Javier Navarro *Mobility in the Theatre* a paper presented in the course on Theatre Architecture at the Centro Internazionale di Studi di Architettura Andrea Palladio, Vicenza 1975.

4
Celant *Sipario* number 7, 1970, p.8.

5
P Brook *El Espacio Vacio* Peninsula, Barcelona 1973.

6
A Artaud *El Teatro de la Crueldad (First Manifesto) from El Teatro y su Doble* Sudamericana, Buenos Aires 1971.

7
J Grotowski *Towards a Poor Theatre* Methuen, London 1969.

8
Op cit.

9
See Brooks McNamara 'Performance Space, The Environmental Tradition' *AAQ* volume 7 number 2, April-June 1975, Architectural Association London.

10
B McNamara, op cit.

11
J Grotowski, op cit.

12
Jerry N Rojo 'Environmental Design' *Contemporary Stage Design USA* ITI, New York 1974.

13
J N Rojo, op cit.

14
B Brecht *Schriften zum Theater* Frankfurt am Main, 1957.

15
Op cit.

16
Op cit.

17
P Brook *L'Architecture d'Aujourd'hui* number 152.

18
M Manieri-Ellia 'Il Teatro Contemporaneo', course in Vicenza 1975.

19
Doménech i Montaner *Historia General del Arte* Barcelona 1886.

20
P Cook *Experimental Architecture* Studio Vista, London 1970, p.152.

INTRODUCTION_ EXPERIMENTS IN SITUATION

The architect Javier Navarro de Zuvillaga (1942) earned his degree in architecture from the Superior Technical School of Architecture of Madrid. During the academic year 1970-1971, he travelled from Madrid to London on a scholarship from the British Council to complete his education at the Architectural Association School of Architecture. There, from September to July, he developed a project called the Mobile Theater, consisting of a stage mechanism made up of a series of carefully designed 8 x 2.5 meter trucks, which could be joined to form a space for performances or other collective uses, covered by an inflatable structure, with a total assembly time of six and a half hours for four operators. His design, exhibited and published internationally from 1971 to 1975, was never realized. In June of 1976, the project was rounded out with a brilliant and ambitious 15-page text called "The Disintegration of Theatrical Space", published in the journal *Architectural Association Quarterly*, and an architectural adaptation, developed in 1974, of the original theater design for use as emergency housing instead. This valuable material has remained partially unpublished and has not been subject to detailed study despite its originality, rigor and cultural value.

This book aims to present a detailed portrait of the project and to situate it culturally in its time and place, London in 1971, where, after the events of May '68, architectural counterculture took up arms on a series of very different fronts, from disciplinary retreat to guerilla positions, and under a broad range of ideologies. Navarro's architectural design renders an account of those events, since its development over time extends beyond its conception as an artifact: its unsuccessful construction process resulted in an inner history that ran from 1969 until 1976. During that period, the Mobile Theater was presented by its author or exhibited in London (The Architectural Association School of Architecture 1971, 1974 and Slade School of Art 1972), York (International Youth Arts Festival 1971), Salzburg (Seminar on American Studies 1972), New York (International Theatre Institute 1972), New Haven, Connecticut (Long Wharf Theater 1972), Dallas (Dallas Theatre Center 1973), Madrid (Club Pueblo 1973), Tarragona (II Setmana de Teatre 1973), Barcelona (Museu del Teatre, Palau Güell 1973), Salamanca (Aula Juan de la Enzina, Universiad de Salamanca 1974), Málaga (Escuela de Arte Dramático 1974), Geneva (Salon International des Inventions, Second Gold Medal 1974), Vicenza (Centro Internazionale di Studi di Architettura Andrea Palladio 1975) and the 13th São Paolo Art Biennial in 1975. It was published in part in the following journals: *Arquitectura*, Madrid, May 1972; *Architectural Design*, London, January 1973; *ABC de las Américas*, New York, February 1973; *Primer Acto*, Madrid, February 1973; *Jano*, Barcelona, March 1973; *Mobelart*, Barcelona, June 1973; *Arte y Cemento*, Bilbao, July 1973;

Yorick, Barcelona, June-July 1973 and *Architectural Association Quarterly*, London, vol. 8, no. 4, 1976.

In 1969, Javier Navarro founded the Teatro Independiente de Situación (TIS), after leading a university theater group for a number of years. That experience culminated with the staging of a play called *Experimento de situación* during the cycle Teatro Nacional de Cámara y Ensayo at the Teatro Marquina in Madrid on May 31, 1970, just months before his departure for London. The piece, as recounted in the advertisement published in the newspaper *ABC* on that day, was based on the first act of the play *Pictures from the Insects' Life* by the Čapek brothers, although no documentary evidence of it remains.

In a series of notes written during October of 1970 in London, Javier Navarro mulled over what he called *Experiments in Situation*, a hybrid piece that he was finally able to present to an audience at the Architectural Association on November 24 of that same year. In the format of a lecture performance, Javier Navarro, along with his collaborator for the piece, the artist Henry Gough-Cooper, presented his ideas to a group of professors and students from the Architectural Association, whose ranks included two of the most influential figures in English architectural culture at the time: Charles Jencks and Paul Oliver, who hosted Navarro at the AA.[1] (Figure 1)

The title of that lecture performance was "Towards a Theatre of Situation", and the event compiled many of the spatial ideas Navarro had brought with him to London from Madrid. It centered on the relationship that is generated during a staged performance between the audience, the spatial layout, and finally the immaterial, communication-related and emotional aspects which are always brought into play by that type of mechanism (Figure 2). Javier Navarro's interest, latent for a long time during his studies of architecture and in the university theater, was focused on the possibilities that this type of architectural arrangement could offer in terms of rethinking the theater building and, by the bye, architecture as a whole. Drawing on the lecture, which is only partially documented, we can reconstruct what the Mobile Theater project would have been beyond its mere documentation as an architectural artifact, since the ambitious project was more than a series of drawings for the construction of a unique building. In his handwritten notes in preparation for the lecture, Javier Navarro defines his understanding of "situation" as follows:

The main character in the play is the very situation above the characters, and it's the situation, which develops or holds itself as the time passes, what gives for to the behaviour of the people in the play. Of course, this situation has to be a general one, which affects the whole people who intervene. The space has an important role in this theatre. It is what I would call a common breathing space and, at the same time, a self-motivated one.[2]

A series of diagrammatic drawings accompany his ideas. They place emphasis on an act of communication through a chain of terms (situation-action-reaction-communi-

cation), which connect two human bodies in a multi-sensory network, or that curl into a spiral. The first sketch (Figure 3) warns of the possibility of confusing intersubjective communication with narcissism, which would logically result in the exhibitionism of a virtuoso, as we see in the drawing, accompanied by the warning "communication or showing-off?" On the other hand, the spiral suggests another kind of development (Figure 4), which begins in the center and unravels progressively in a logarithmic spiral, until it runs up against the edges of the paper that form its borders. The border is only provisional, however, practical or even arbitrary, because according to Navarro, only "fatal destruction" or "the infinite" can put an end to a situation that has begun to develop fully and satisfyingly – in other words, once it has surpassed the merely functional act of communication, which leads to narcissistic bravura, and entered into a genuine communicative act, expansive and spiraling. The enthusiasm of these handwritten notes for a theater of situation is absolute, as are the questions raised about the need for order, limits and legibility. These theoretical materials touch on the uncertainty between stable and open forms, effective and expanded communication, infinite and limited spaces, in an unresolved and highly defiant dialectic to which the architectural design for the Mobile Theater intended to provide a practical response.

The event in London, which did not advance beyond a latent and very speculative stage, took place in one of the rooms at the Archi-

Figure 1: Javier Navarro (left) during the lecture "Towards a Theatre of Situation", facing Charles Jencks (standing on the right) and Paul Oliver (seated). London, November 1970. Courtesy of Javier Navarro de Zuvillaga.

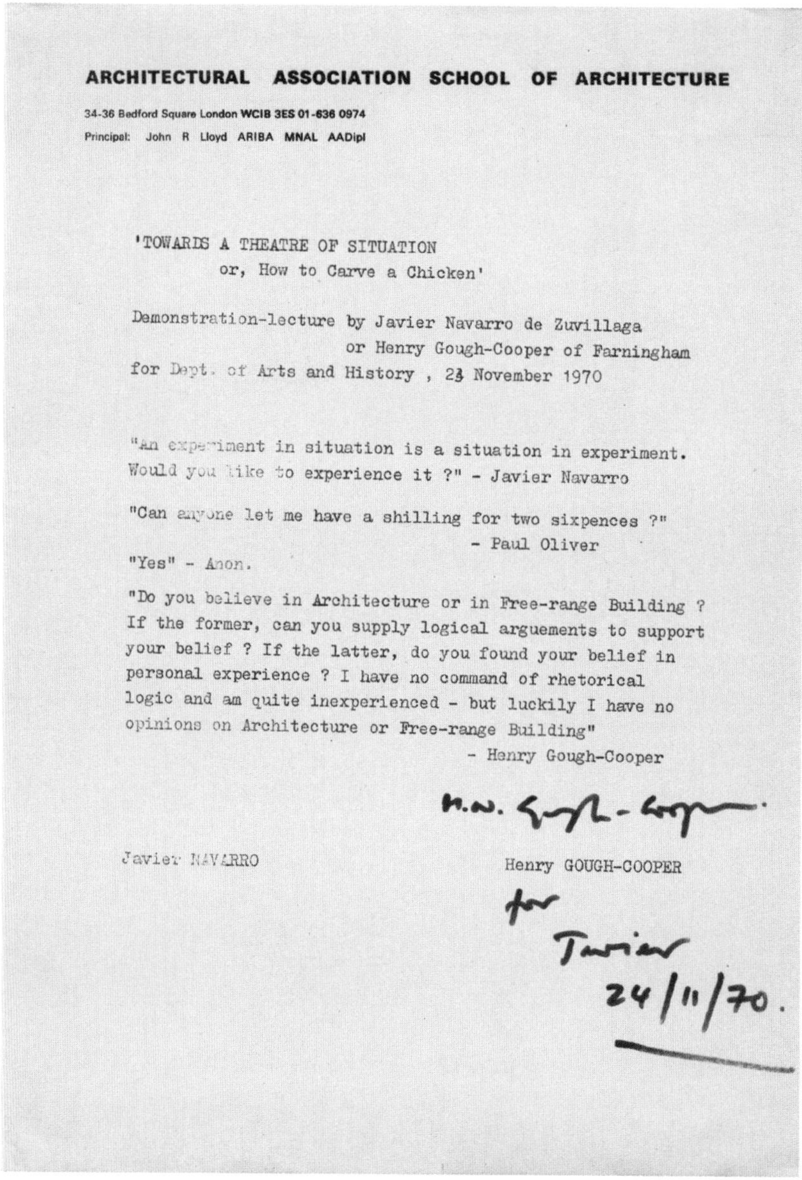

ARCHITECTURAL ASSOCIATION SCHOOL OF ARCHITECTURE

34-36 Bedford Square London WC1B 3ES 01-636 0974
Principal: John R Lloyd ARIBA MNAL AADipl

'TOWARDS A THEATRE OF SITUATION
or, How to Carve a Chicken'

Demonstration-lecture by Javier Navarro de Zuvillaga
or Henry Gough-Cooper of Farningham
for Dept. of Arts and History , 23 November 1970

"An experiment in situation is a situation in experiment. Would you like to experience it ?" - Javier Navarro

"Can anyone let me have a shilling for two sixpences ?"
- Paul Oliver

"Yes" - Anon.

"Do you believe in Architecture or in Free-range Building ? If the former, can you supply logical arguements to support your belief ? If the latter, do you found your belief in personal experience ? I have no command of rhetorical logic and am quite inexperienced - but luckily I have no opinions on Architecture or Free-range Building"
- Henry Gough-Cooper

H.W. Gough-Cooper.

Javier NAVARRO

Henry GOUGH-COOPER

for
Javier
24/11/70.

Figure 2: Leaflet from "Towards a Theater of Situation" London, November 1970. Courtesy of Javier Navarro de Zuvillaga.

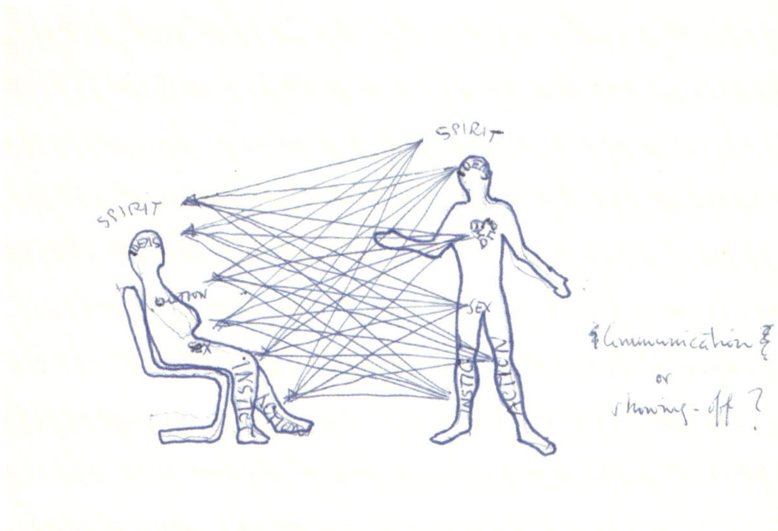

Figure 3: Preparatory drawing for "Towards a Theatre of Situation". London, October 1970. Courtesy of Javier Navarro de Zuvillaga.

Figure 4: Preparatory drawing for "Towards a Theater of Situation". London, October 1970. Courtesy of Javier Navarro de Zuvillaga.

tectural Association, which was accessed via a hallway running between haphazardly painted translucent plastic walls (Figure 5). The floor along the entryway was covered with rice and sugar cubes to encourage people to move more carefully than usual: a necessarily slow entrance, sonorous, cautious, clearly ritualized. The chalkboard in the room was covered with drawings, play programs, texts, diagrams and sketches. On one table, written material and plates of food were laid out for the guests; on another, there were two tape recorders operated by Henry Gough-Cooper, and a microphone hung from the ceiling of the room. The attendees were given pamphlets printed with typewritten texts including: "Love is communication/Make love/Communication can be love/Make Communication/If you like somebody or something/Caress it". (Figure 6)

The key to the "situation" on which the event was focused lay in providing the audience with the scheme of a situation that would be easy to understand, and the materials to construct it collectively, in order to achieve the goal laid out in the preparatory notes: "Give people a scheme of a situation, which they can make its own and, therefore, play it [...] (a situation) able to be manipulated by them." The notes and drawings show a range of experiments in situation, which refer to archetypal relationships between actor/spectator, one-on-one or in groups. We see transparent boxes with small groups of people facing grandstands, or labyrinths of mirrors and concentric hexagons for a single person, which would be triggered using equipment like tape recorders or TV monitors. (Figure 7)

The experiments fall somewhere between installations and architecture, "happenings" with the main goal of inciting communication and awareness of the surrounding space. The notes alongside one of the preparatory sketches read: "Ideas about different experiments in situation. 1 Give people schemes of their own physical situations (mirrors). A 11 A man in a labyrinth of mirrors, conscious of all the people around him are in his same situation, even physically, because all of them are his own image (conscience). Study reaction of persons (even children) in the hexagon of seven mirrors. Probably it needs some voice telling what they have been aware of. A 12 John Cage's experiment. A sound-proof room in which you can perceive two noises: your heart beating and your brain working. It's a kind of experiment of situation, in making people conscious of their noise. A 17 Stepping on sugar. Shaking upon something. Coughing cause of smoke. Feeling oppression cause of the pressure of the air".

These are the dramaturgical materials that can be designed, on an architectural scale, into the Mobile Theater – the aim of which does not lie in the particular built situation, but rather in its possibilities as an architectural artifact that can intervene in the space of the city, altering and desecrating, momentarily, its physical materiality and its social theatricality.

In a classical theater building, the stage design is the only element subject to spatial variation within a fixed architectural structure, which is often also monumental. This fact led Javier Navarro to consider the possibility of joining together a mobile ar-

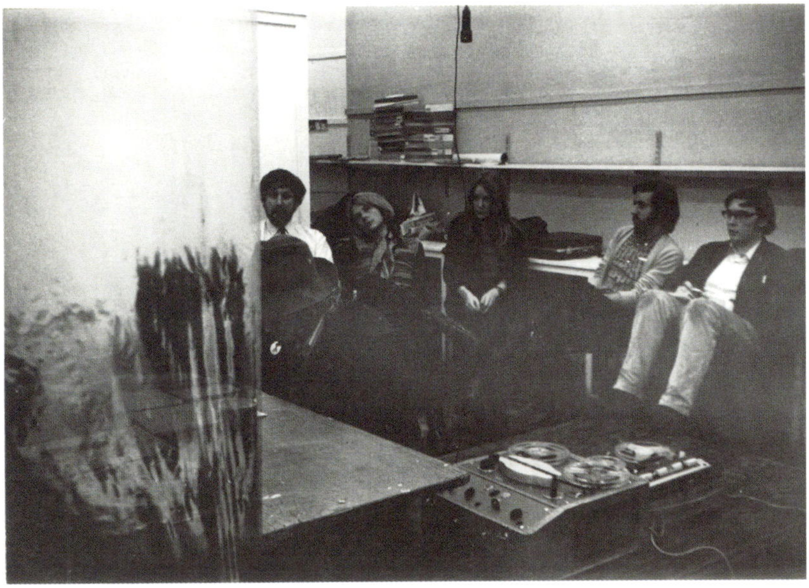

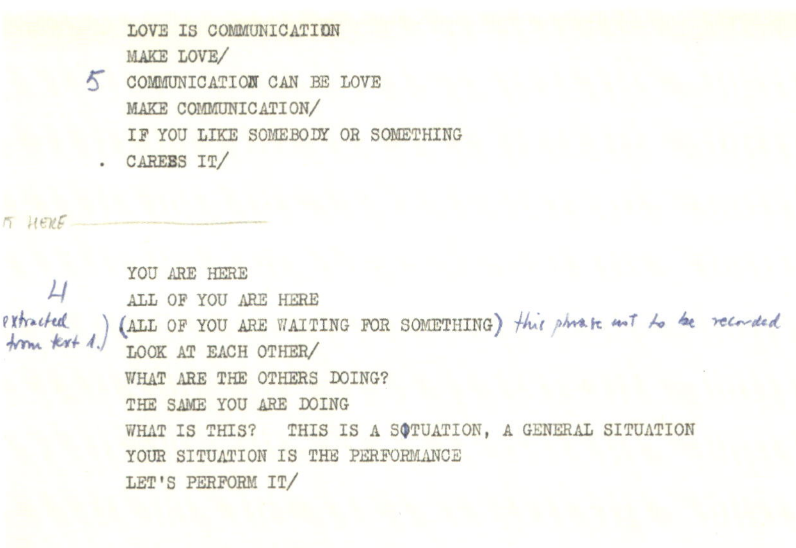

LOVE IS COMMUNICATION
MAKE LOVE/
5 COMMUNICATION CAN BE LOVE
MAKE COMMUNICATION/
IF YOU LIKE SOMEBODY OR SOMETHING
CARESS IT/

YOU ARE HERE
4 ALL OF YOU ARE HERE
extracted from text 1.) (ALL OF YOU ARE WAITING FOR SOMETHING) this phrase not to be recorded
LOOK AT EACH OTHER/
WHAT ARE THE OTHERS DOING?
THE SAME YOU ARE DOING
WHAT IS THIS? THIS IS A SITUATION, A GENERAL SITUATION
YOUR SITUATION IS THE PERFORMANCE
LET'S PERFORM IT/

Figure 5: Spectators during the lecture "Towards a Theatre of Situation". London, November 1970. Courtesy of Javier Navarro de Zuvillaga.

Figure 6: Excerpts from working materials used in "Towards a Theatre of Situation", London, November 1970. Courtesy of Javier Navarro de Zuvillaga.

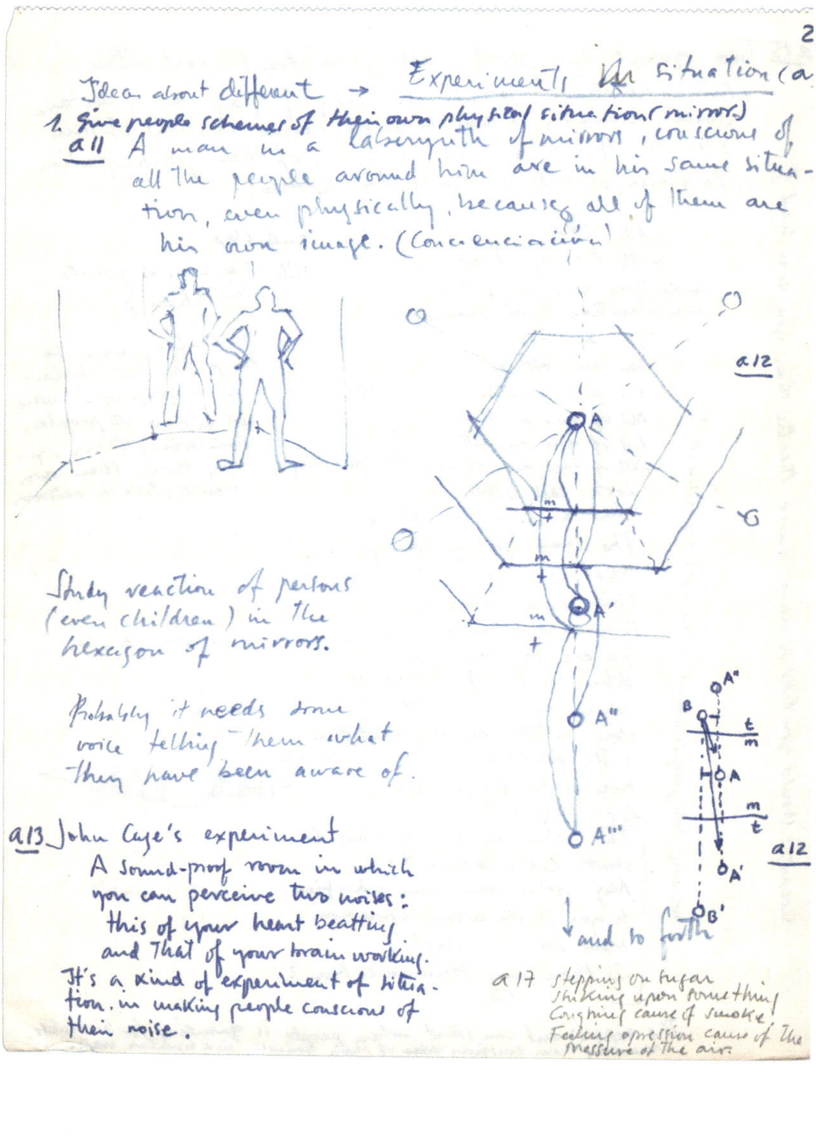

Figure 7: Excerpts from working materials used in "Towards a Theatre of Situation", London, November 1970. Courtesy of Javier Navarro de Zuvillaga.

chitecture and a mobile stage into a single element that could give rise to what he called "situations in process". With this idea, he aimed to introduce the factor of time, characteristic of the stage, into architecture, characterized by formal stability, i.e., by a form that is stable over time.

In this personal research, the popular tradition of mobile or travelling theaters was essential in the shift from a theoretical or reflective approach (the performance lecture) to direct architectural practice, or action (the design for the Mobile Theater). Following this tradition of nomadic theater, the caravan is the only element that generates an architectural constant, contrasting with the final layout that is always different on each occasion (Figure 8). The wagon is thus the fundamental and basic architecture for this type of theater, but not its final architecture, which is only defined by each configuration and each staging in a specific and, to a certain extent, unpredictable way. However, in the nomad tradition, the caravans were a subsidiary element, a mere technological support that transported the necessary materials to construct a covered space. In other cases, the caravan itself might have served as an elevated stage, around which the audience would gather.

The Mobile Theater, in contrast, pursues an exhaustive use of the caravan as an element that shapes the architectural form of the entire space. As such, mobility is a parameter that literally affects both the physical movement of the architecture itself and the transformable quality of the space for the stage and the audience – a space that will never be the same twice (Figure 9). In addition to this conceptual motivation, Javier Navarro's design touches on parameters of economy, the optimum use of resources on both a material and conceptual level, how the transportation elements are used "as storage for everything during transport, and as structural elements and exterior enclosures once at the site and, at the same time, as spaces for the theatre's services".[3]

This modular spatial structure is thus self-transportable and can be disassembled, and it follows a geometric system of organization, which "consists of forming regular polygonal enclosures, where each side=the length of the module, with the number of sides equal to 2n, where n is the number of modules used".[4] The diagram in the design consists of four trucks which, in different polygonal configurations, can generate up to 21 enclosures with different forms and sizes, using the same octagonal-shaped inflatable roof. The four trucks are supported on the ground by hydraulic footings, which replace the wheels and help to level out the floors when setting up on the site. An octagonal sheet of nylon, anchored by cables along the edges, is stretched across the ground to form the horizontal plane for the space, serving as the on-site layout, and it is surrounded on four alternate sides by the four trucks that form the exterior enclosure. The four chamfered corners are made by opening the trailer doors outward at 135 degrees, closing off the octagonal figure that outlines the edges of the space (Figure 10). The roof is a lenticular-shaped inflatable form made from a double skin of nylon with PVC, which hangs from an octagonal compression ring "anchored to eight telescopic poles that attach to the trucks at the angles of the octagon floor plan".[5]

The meticulous implementation of the system, evident in both the design drawings and the written description, is understood as an architectural performance that refers conceptually to robots and literally to the realist technology available at the time. The geometric rationality, for its part, is derived from an economic motivation, or a strictly calculated use of resources on all levels, as well as from age-old spatial concepts. Ultimately, the design puts forward a two-sided proposal: kineticism and mobility on the one hand; and stability, permanence and monumentality on the other. This conceptual duality, between dynamic technical contemporaneity and stable geometric a-historicism, perfectly characterizes this complex design, which could be considered a point of articulation between those two sensibilities through which the counterculture of the 1960s and '70s was expressed. The Mobile Theater is one of the most refined and unique examples from the limited Spanish production of experimental architecture during that period in history.

The possible fusion between avant-garde and tradition was also investigated by Javier Navarro, fueled by a personal interest in popular Spanish theater culture, but also by the atmosphere of avant-garde experimentation that permeated the AA in London in 1970. The project draws from well-known sources to which Navarro himself made reference, like the unfolding structures by Emilio Pérez Piñero for theaters or cinemas, the speculative designs by Cedric Price, or the teachings of Richard Buckminster Fuller, applied the world over, with which Navarro came into contact in London – one of Fuller's niches of influence in Europe at the time. In each instance, there was a transfer from engineering to architecture: civil engineering in the case of Piñero and Price; military engineering in the case of Fuller. They were all circumscribed, culturally and politically, by the Cold War and the techno-cultural dominance of the United States; and Spain under the Francoist regime fell within their sphere of influence. However, by the time the Mobile Theater was designed, the cultural circumstances had shifted. Pérez Piñero worked either for the government of Franco's dictatorship engaged in cultural propaganda efforts, or as an independent businessman with his portable movie theaters. Price worked as an independent, advanced speculator in conjunction with initiatives led by the British government, showing enormous perseverance yet limited success in terms of execution. Fuller, for his part, worked systematically for North American imperialist interests and for large transnational corporations. Despite the fact that Javier Navarro's project is enormously indebted technically, and even linguistically, to those illustrious precedents, the surrounding cultural climate was entirely different. It was an avant-garde climate that had integrated those innovations and focused its interests on the cultural and political effects of that kind of architectural technology. The emphasis had shifted from design to (often precarious) realization, from the artifact to the user, and from future utopias to history and archetypes. The rupture at

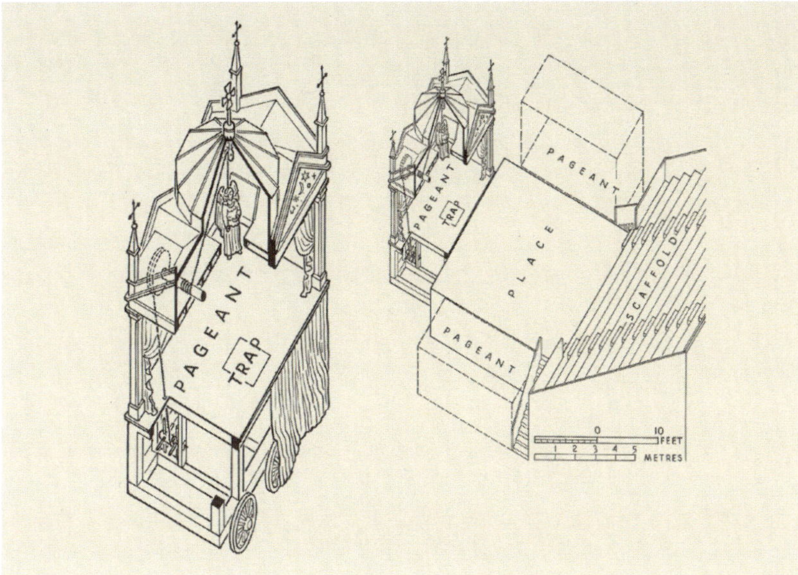

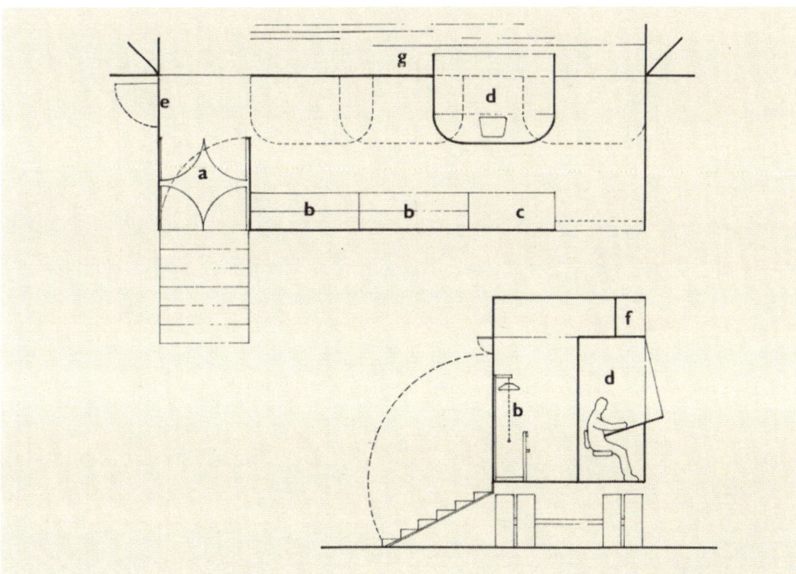

Figure 8: A reconstruction of an English pageant wagon and a ground plan of the overall playing arrangement. Source: Glynne Wickham, *Early English Stages*, Vol. I (1958).

Figure 9: Fragment of plan no. 31 for the Mobile Theater, showing the adaptation of a standard truck to serve as a shared space for a spectators' foyer and the control booth. Legend: a) entrance, b) self-service cloak room, c) vending machine, d) control booth, e) bathroom door, f) lighting truss, g) panels. London, June 1971. Courtesy of Javier Navarro de Zuvillaga.

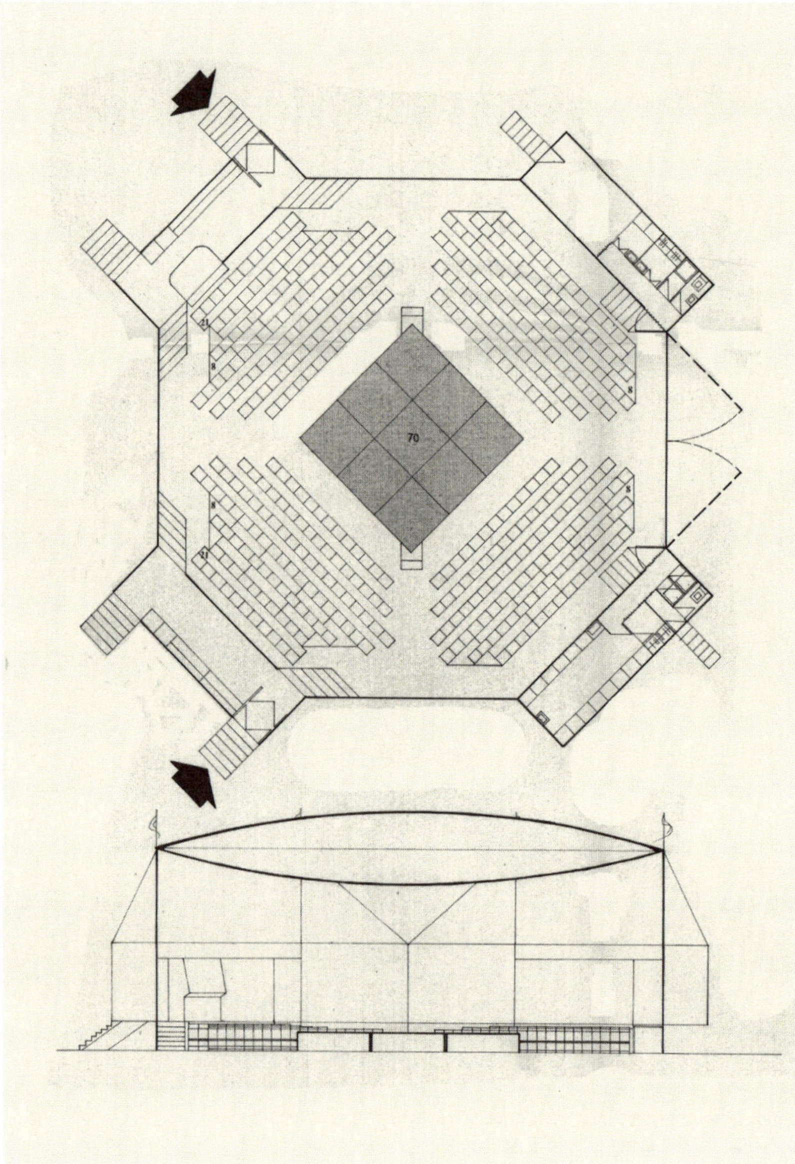

Figure 10: Plan no. 19 for the Mobile Theater project, octagonal version with a central stage and seating for 402 spectators. London, June 1971. Courtesy of Javier Navarro de Zuvillaga.

the end of the 1960s had left its mark on architectural culture.

The original design documents consist of a series of 40 A2-size plans labelled in English, which were presented for the degree project at the Architectural Association in London, plus eight A4-size hand drawings, also with notes in English, that complement some of the technical aspects of the design, specifically the components of the inflatable roof. In 1974, this documentation was rounded out with 20 A4-size hand drawings. These drawings outline the original mobile theater project with four trucks, and they introduce further variations, both in terms of the different possibilities depending on the number of trucks (from two to six), as well as the possibilities for other uses and configurations, giving rise to different spatial structures, including a repetitive structure that suggests the possibility of a minimally urban fabric – i.e., the rudiments of a city. Specifically, there are six possibilities for uses offered: theater, cinema, exhibition hall and library, with four trucks; and hospital or emergency housing, with five trucks or more. The documents provide an exhaustive exploration of the project's combinations with all its possibilities in terms of architectural form and program. The design is completed with an adaptation of the system and a railroad-based version using train cars, and with a proposal for emergency housing units presented to the Ministry of Housing and defined in six A4-size hand drawings dated October 1974. In addition, a detailed model of the building was constructed for the project's exhibition at the 13th São Paolo Art Biennial in 1975.

Notes

1. Charles Jencks (1939-2019) was only three years older than Javier Navarro. Jencks was one of Navarro's advisors at the AA and one of the people with whom he maintained personal contact. Born in the United States and trained as an architect at Harvard, where he graduated in 1965, Jencks moved to London that same year to begin his PhD under the direction of the engineer and historian Reyner Banham at University College London. He finished it in 1970 and published part of his research in 1969 and 1970, which had enormous repercussions for international architectural culture. Two of the most important themes in the work were Pop in relation to mass culture, and semiotics and its applications in architectural criticism. He taught at the Architectural Association from 1968 to 1988. Paul Oliver (1927-2017) was a historian who graduated from the University of London in 1955. During the 1960s he specialized in vernacular architecture and taught courses on the subject at the Architectural Association. In the same period, he also had a significant career as a researcher of Blues music. In 1969, he published a now classic book called *Shelter and Society*, which became very influential internationally and was published in Spain in 1978. The book compiled part of the work done by the AA's Department of Tropical Architecture, with which Oliver was a close collaborator. He was the director of the Art and History department during Navarro's time at the AA, which made Oliver his official host, together with Charles Jencks, Dix Harrison, Warren Kenton and Keith Critchlow.

2. Javier Navarro de Zuvillaga: Handwritten notes from October 1970. (Original in English).

3. Javier Navarro de Zuvillaga, *Mobile Theatre*, written report for the degree project presented to the Architectural Association School of Architecture, London, June 1971.

4. Ibid.

5. Ibid.

CHAPTER 1_ TEMPLE-MACHINE-CARAVAN

Javier Navarro's discourse is seeped with a perspective characteristic of anti-establishment counterculture, which repeatedly defended the destruction of high-brow tradition and the recovery of certain values from a less visible, but continuing tradition: popular culture – poorer and disconnected from power and the institutions of high culture. In that sense, his main leitmotif was that of spatial disintegration: "It is clear that in order to revitalize itself theatre needed to get out of theatres, although occasionally it returns to them with a new spatial approach."[1] Following in the footsteps of renovators from the modern scene like Adolphe Appia, Edward Gordon Craig, Vsévolod Meyerhold, Erwin Piscator and Antonin Artaud, the Mobile Theater suggested two complementary paths, which those renovators, each in their own way, proposed in their day: extending the space of the stage into the audience and abandoning the bourgeois architectural tradition. Javier Navarro combined these two paths into the term "disintegration", while at the same time maintaining the idea of spatial limits as an unquestionable premise. "It is clear that wherever theatre is performed, the boundaries of a theatrical space are required. But this is a space whose architecture, like theatrical space itself, must be ephemeral."[2] It is a projection, into the sphere of architecture, of the same questions about limits that were investigated in his experiments with situation.

In his research on theatrical space from 1976, Javier Navarro refers to a classification of types of theater buildings that had been established by the Italian architect Guido Canella (1931-2009) in a study on the relationships between theaters and urban morphology in Milan. This classification will provide us with the necessary principles to investigate the possibility of an urban role for the Mobile Theater. In 1966, Canella published a book called *Il Sistema Teatrale a Milano*, which analyzed the historical development of what he called a "system", referring to the relationship between the architectural type, urban form and social use of theater spaces.[3] Canella outlined a drastic differentiation between the point of view of the architect and that of the director, set designer or playwright. As far as set designers go, artists of the stage, theirs is an internal vision, associated with the performance itself, the theatrical apparatus, the technical requirements and the aesthetics characteristic of the art form. Architects take on a more relational, broader vision, incorporating the building, the city, and the social environment, which is embodied in the specific architectural relationship between stage and audience, like a miniature of the model that can be tried out to scale, but with the aim of surpassing it. Canella set up a classification into three types of theatrical spaces based on their relationship with the city, from the standpoint of an architect as opposed to a theater director: the "temple-theater", the "machine-theater" and the "mobile-theater". Navarro relied on Canella's analysis to explain the theoretical scope of his design for the Mobile Theater and its relationship with the other two types, as well as to make clear his position in the debate, as an architect.

THE TRIPLE THEATRICAL SYSTEM

There is always a diffuse social theatricality (not necessarily artistic or institutional) in the city, which theater buildings epitomize and institutionalize within their walls. This social theatricality is necessarily multiple and hard to pin down in formal terms, in the same way that the social environment may be. That is why Canella refers to a "theatrical system" to designate the urban area that surrounds a theater building, employing a direct and very effective analogy. In Canella's vocabulary, "system" refers to a physical sphere that extends beyond the architectural type of the theater and incorporates additional factors that the architect must take into account, beyond understanding and managing the available typologies of theatrical space. This category of system, in Canella's rich lexicon, is referred to by different names in some of the later analyses in his book on Milan – a more theoretical and historiographical work. For example, Canella wrote about theaters and pseudotheaters, outlining the similarities and differences between the two models of public space. The former are buildings that respond to the architectural model of a theater in the narrowest sense. The latter are urban spaces such as squares, educational spaces, associational spaces, and civic or religious representative spaces.[4] In the typical multiple stage set for representing the passion of Christ (Figure 11), hell was located on the right and paradise on the left. Lucifer's palace was accessed via a giant hellmouth, through which devils would come in and out. The space around these "mansions" was defined using the Latin term *platea*, called *plaine* or *place* in the vulgar. The mansions were lined up one after another, in a straight line or tracing a curve.

This notion is very similar to the concept of "spontaneous theater" introduced by Le Corbusier in 1948, which was influential in both architectural and theatrical culture at the time, given the author's standing and the idea's dissemination in publications with far-reaching distribution.[5] In the text, a transcription of a lecture given at the Sorbonne, Le Corbusier described with admiration scenes from his travels through Europe, North Africa and Latin America, where urban space was the setting for spontaneous social gatherings, to which he ascribed a heavy theatrical connotation, along the same lines as popular celebrations, whether secular or religious, in consolidated historic European cities. In other words, Le Corbusier looked at the streets of the traditional city, and not theater buildings, as the epitome of the spatial archetype of theatricality. In order to frame these phenomena, without generating physical or psychological coercion, in 1960 Le Corbusier designed spontaneous theaters for the Fort-Lamy Cultural Center, in Chad. The spaces were merely formalized with floors and vertical surfaces (walls, parterres, or even projection screens), which, once the performance was over, no longer represen-

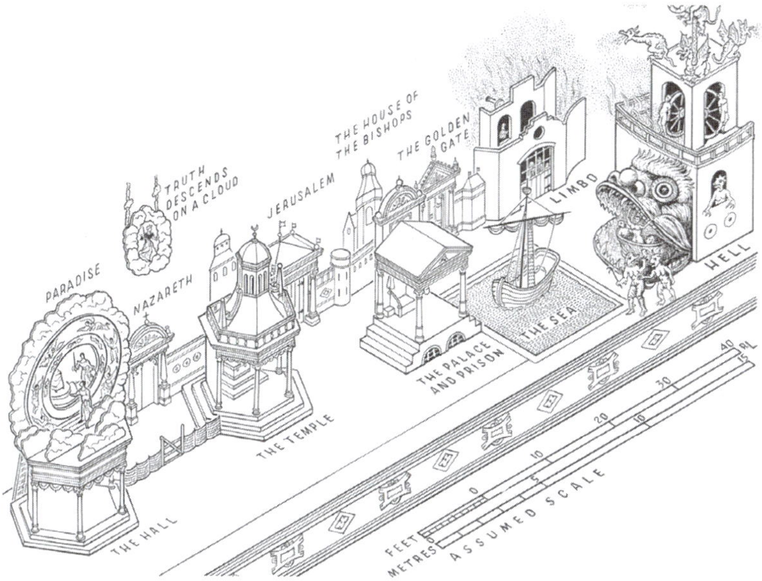

Figure 11: Mystery of the Passion of Valenciennes 1547. Source: Richard and Helen Leacroft, *Theatre and Playhouse: An Illustrated Survey of Theatre Building from Ancient Greece to the Present*, London and New York: Methuen, 1984.

Figure 12: Mystery of the Passion of Valenciennes 1547. Source: Gallica/ Bibliothèque Nationale de France.

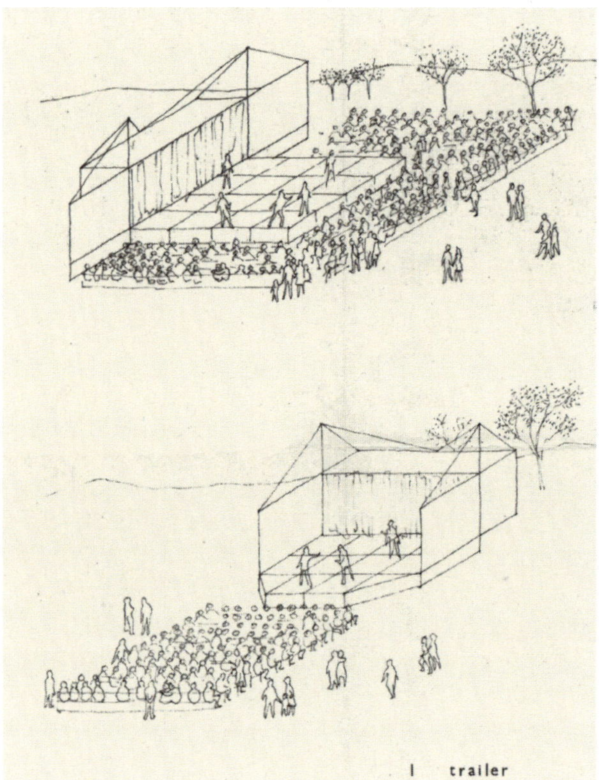

Figure 13: Le Corbusier, model for the Spontaneous Theater, Fort-Lamy Cultural Center, 1960. Fondation Le Corbusier.

Figure 14: Javier Navarro de Zuvillaga, fragment of plan no. 39 for the Mobile Theater, showing the partial configuration for one truck, uncovered, in two possible arrangements. Courtesy of Javier Navarro de Zuvillaga.

ted the limits of a stage; they simply became architectural elements that provided a vague organization of the urban space (Figure 13). The Mobile Theater, in its partial configurations without a roof and with open corners, behaved exactly like those urban spaces, pseudotheaters or performance machines, which so enthused Le Corbusier as spontaneous urban theaters and were upheld as examples in Canella's historical studies (Figure 14).

In the case of both Le Corbusier and Guido Canella, the goal was similar: to overcome the privilege historically associated with a strictly professional and technical or typological vision of the relationship between stage and audience, and its replacement with a broader social and urban vision, which conceptually disintegrates the architectural model of the theater and scatters it throughout the city, giving rise to theaters and pseudotheaters interchangeably and without hierarchies between them. To that end, both architects proposed two simultaneous methods of transcending disciplinary limitations in their respective discourses. On the one hand, overcoming the idea of the project understood as design at the service of dramatic arts on the stage – in other words, overcoming the idea of stage design as the sphere of activity that corresponds to an architect. And on the other, its systemic counterpart on an urban level: overcoming the theater model as merely the design of a container for an existing social theater, dictated by generally accepted and hegemonic social and urban behaviors. From the standpoint of the project, this implies strategies to transpose values and parameters characteristic of the stage into the architectural and urban sphere, which also have the potential to break with the dominant social order (Figures 15 and 16).

According to Canella, the theater architect should reveal, or at least promote, the multiple, spontaneous and diffuse social theatricality of the urban milieu, shaping more complex typological and programmatic systems, beyond the confines of both stage and the theater building as a whole. This guarantees a certain continuity between the more spontaneous forms of social theatricality (which tend to be ephemeral and sometimes unrepeatable) and the more institutionalized forms of the conventional theater building (which always show a marked tendency toward ritual repetition). This function of the theater architect is what Javier Navarro embraced in his project for the Mobile Theater, tied into his experiments with situation that were taking place at the same time in Madrid and London (from 1970 to 1971) and were clearly one of the sources that fed into the project.

The term temple-theater alludes to the historical period that began with the first theaters in the Renaissance and culminated in 1876 with Wagner's Bayreuth Festival Theater, the epitome of this type of theater according to Canella. Historically, it overlapped with the following type, the machine-theater, which originated with the theatrical-technological experiments of the Baroque and reached its high point with Walter Gropius' Total Theater for Erwin Piscator in 1927. The third type, the mobile-theater, has a parallel genealogy that stretches back just as far in time, with roots that connect to the same classical origins, but with an irregular historical development, a much more reduced influence, and a li-

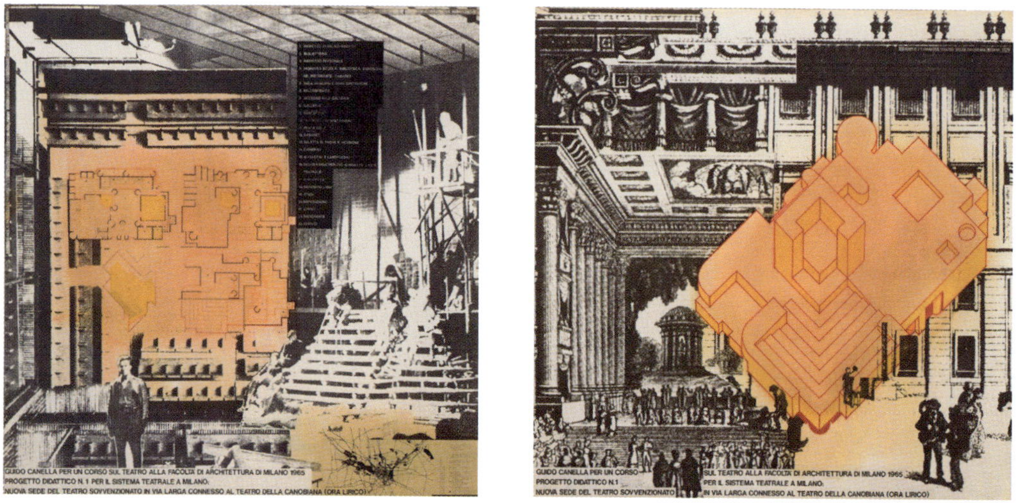

Figure 15 (Above): Guido Canella, Educational project no. 1 for the theatrical system in Milan, new public theater on Via Larga, connected with the Teatro Canobiana, 1965. Courtesy of the Collezione Francesco Moschini e Gabriel Vaduva, AAM Architettura Arte Moderna, Rome.

Figure 16 (Below): Guido Canella, Educational project no. 2 for the theatrical system in Milan, theater school, teachers' college, and department of Humanities in Sesto San Giovanni, 1965. Courtesy of the Collezione Francesco Moschini e Gabriel Vaduva, AAM Architettura Arte Moderna, Rome.

mited documentary visibility that makes it difficult to characterize, although it always maintained ties with the other two types. This rich parallel tradition of the mobile-theater was of maximum interest to Javier Navarro when it came to formalizing his own proposal for a theater building.

After Bayreuth, which marked the climax of Enlightenment-Romantic theater culture's critical stance against the European court theater of the Renaissance, the theatrical avant-garde was concentrated along three main avenues. The first was marked by an insistence on the temple-theater, experimenting with the representativity of the theater building as an urban monument and as the symbol of a particular politics, touching on its character as a secular and civic temple. The second, the machine, tried out new spatial models for the interior of the theater, experimenting with the relationships between audience and stage, drawing on developments in playwriting and dramatic formats, with particular attention to theatrical technologies, which were undergoing rapid and continuous renovations. The third, the caravan, proposed a new social role for theater, following the emergence of a new mass culture, previously unheard of, associated with large cities, which saw a certain efflorescence with the historical avant-gardes and their fascination with the metropolitan phenomenon. This taxonomy of theatrical space in relation to the urban sphere established by Canella was debated by another Italian author, cited occasionally by Javier Navarro in his text: the architect and architectural historian Mario Manieri-Elia (1929-2011). Manieri-Elia provides even more clues for a better understanding of Navarro's Mobile Theater and, more generally, any similar proposal for a travelling theater with regard, especially, to a possible urban, political and civic role.

In 1975, Navarro attended a seminar organized by the Centro Internazionale di Studi di Architettura Andrea Palladio in Vicenza, where he presented his project for the Mobile Theater in tandem with a series of lectures given by experts, which included Manieri-Elia and Manfredo Tafuri (1935-1994), the only two speakers who focused their contributions on the 20th century.[6] Although the project for the Mobile Theater was already complete, the research had not yet been written, and the design was in the process of being adapted to other possible uses (hospital, emergency housing, cultural center or even a travelling commercial space).[7] Manieri-Elia gave a talk called "Il teatro moderno", which reopened the debate begun by Canella and drew heavily on its ideological aspects, given Manieri-Elia's position as a Marxist historian.

In parallel to the triad temple-machine-caravan laid out by Canella, Manieri-Elia talked about three moments in contemporary theatrical culture – playful, productive and ritual – in order to address the possible relationship between theater and architecture within the new framework of mass consumer culture, suggested by the historical avant-garde and palpable at the time of the seminar in Vicenza. The playful moment was decried by Manieri-Elia dogmatically, considering that it disregarded architecture entirely, because architecture always pursues a social function, which is negated entirely by the gratuitous nature of the playful moment. A playful act would be anti-architectural and even anti-theatrical in the narrow sense, because "it has lost its cathartic function", which is characteristic of ritual, the main function of theater and, we might say, of its associated architecture,[8] resulting in a form of temporality that excludes the ritual dimension and, with it, the social function. Manieri-Elia clearly distinguished, and with a certain severity, between play and ritual, because ritual is inevitably connected with "a functional intention. It aims to resolve a particular pivotal situation affecting the collective,"[9] contrasted with the pure restlessness of play, the functions of which are wholly dismissive and critical. Manieri-Elia thus pinpointed the idea of ritual as the fundamental tie between theater and architecture and its political potential.

The moment or pole that he called productive, for its part, is focused on stagecraft itself, where the discourse shifts from the theoretical sphere, or the realm of ideas, to the practical sphere and its conditions within the cycle of production, management and consumption. In contrast, the playful pole implies the total dissolution of the mechanism, the "disappearance of theater" (and of architecture), an emotional explosion that does not lead to any social function of a ritual nature, in an effort that is unproductive within the symbolic economy that Manieri-Elia describes from a Marxist perspective. The productive pole, in its state of maximum theatrical intensity, leads to a complete reformulation of the social body through what Manieri-Elia calls the "theater of total conditioning". For the first case (an uncontrolled playfulness), he gives the example of Yves Klein and his empty theater, without actors or audience but with a perfectly lit ticket booth, a theater where "the actors will be paid to disappear; the audience will pay for the right to an empty seat. The theater will become an empty box that will carry out in full, in exchange for payment, its unproductive task."[10] To illustrate the second case (a total productivism), he gives the example of the project for a spherical stage by Piero Berengo Gardin (Figure 17), derived paradoxically from the space proposed by Antonin Artaud, which conditioned the spectator psychologically using a ruthless technological device, as can be determined from the descriptive text that accompanies it: "The sphere-envelope guides spectators, during their 'spectacular nutrition' (stage equals placenta) into a hypothetical 'womb-like' condition, in which the envelope 'protects' the spectator."[11]

In both cases (Klein and Berengo Gardin), the result of the supposed dissolution is a spectacle that is reinforced through two forms that are opposite but ultimately convergent in their condition as mere spectacle. In the first case, the old bourgeois temple, emptied of all meaning, whose function is the panic persistence of its own survival as a sterile institution, which precludes the emergence of new rites, only perpetuating existing ones. In the second, the renovated machine for eliciting shock, an incubator for new types of subjects who are permanently forced to adapt their own physiology and emotional systems to new technologies. For Manieri-Elia, "in these positions, one cannot help but see an exorcistic attempt to lay out new paths for the theater, and when there is an attempt to prefigure its form, the result is the exact opposite: an unexpected adjustment on the part of the audience."[12]

Between these two extremes, theater architecture had tended toward one pole or the other, without ever touching either, be-

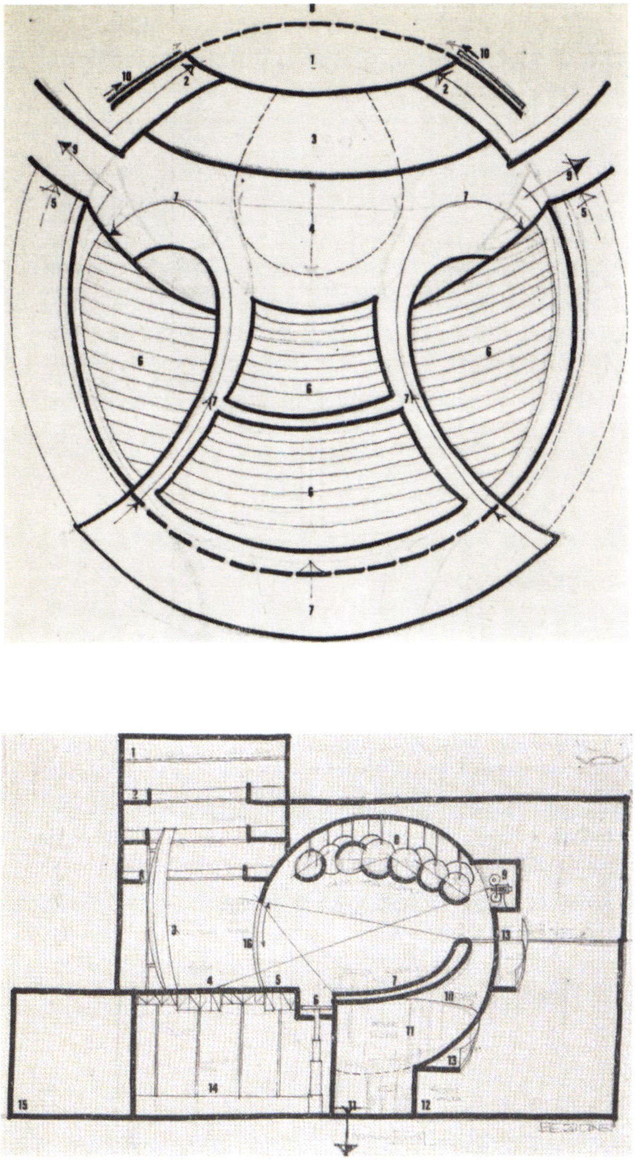

Figure 17: Piero Berengo Gardin, design for a spherical theater. Source: *I Problemmi di Ulisse*, year XXII, vol. 10, insert.

cause if it did – as we have just seen – it would disappear. The mobile-theater, Canella's caravan, is posited by Manieri-Elia as a possible model to connect theater and architecture in a mutual relationship that is different in terms of its ties with the ritual: "Contrasting with such a determining relationship between scenic device and spectacle, there emerges what we have referred to as a third type of theater: the mobile theater in its different incarnations. But, here, it is harder to talk about architecture."[13] "Here" is precisely where Javier Navarro enters the scene, with an architecture that responds to this theoretical question retroactively: his design had been finished four years before the theoretical dilemma was proposed openly, and it was based on concerns that were articulated around practical experiments. Yet, it lacked an underlying story or a narrative, which the author was only now prepared to construct: What kind of architecture, and how much, was needed for a ritual theater of situation? What precedents and valid equivalents existed at that moment?

THE METROPOLITAN CIVIC TEMPLE

Guido Canella was responding to this prickly question, regarding how much architecture is necessary for a theater that is neither a temple nor a machine, with the proposals he presented in his book about Milan in 1966, developed the previous year during his design course at the Politecnico di Milano. And his response was: a lot – unlike Javier Navarro's response, the architectural formalization of which was restrained and modest. In both cases, however, the mobility in relation to the city was essential to offer solutions that were diametrically different in terms of the architectural language used, yet extraordinarily similar on a conceptual level and in their urban and social effects.

In his study on Milan, Canella demonstrates that the social developments of the inter-war period, due to the large-scale introduction of automobiles, resulted in the transformation of both central bourgeois theaters and the peripheral ring of small stage spaces around the center of Milan. The latter were frequented by the working classes, and their programming included classical theater, popular theater, variety shows, circus and political theater. During this period, and the following post-war period, the central theaters, with some exceptions, took up a strictly commercial tendency, and the small "cinema-theaters" around the periphery became movie houses through significant architectural transformations, including the complete removal of technical equipment for the stage and the addition of underground spaces for the purpose of adding shopping areas to the buildings.[14]

Canella responded to this loss of typological variety and the resulting isolation of the building from the urban context with a series of proposals for large architectural pieces that combined the theater with the pseudo-theater, the built volume with the unbuilt, the architectural object with the urban fabric, only minimally materialized. They were groups of buildings with linear structures on a large scale, which connected train stations with parking structures for private transportation (Figures 18 and 19). Along this axis of mobility were a series of educational facilities, including elementary schools and university buildings, commercial spaces, artisanal production and theater spaces, all of them

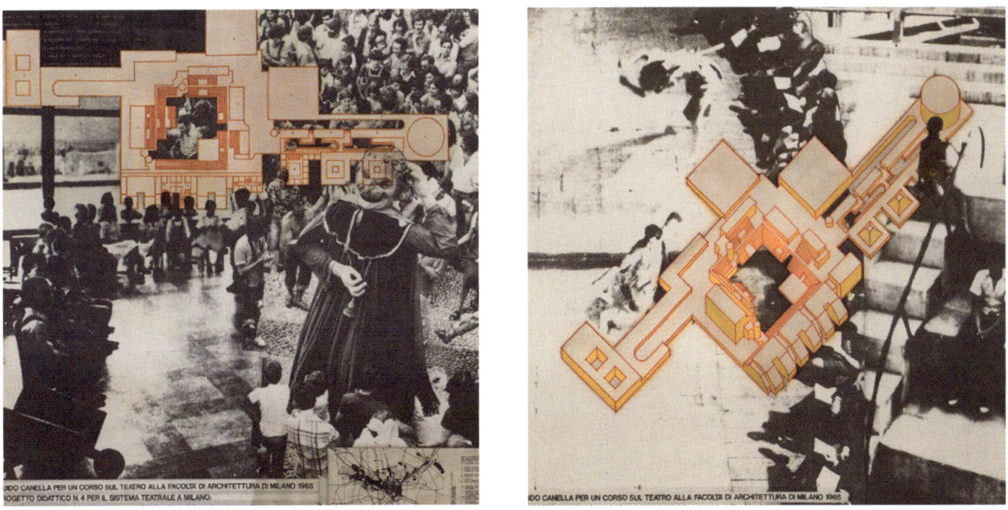

Figure 18 (Above): Guido Canella, Educational project no. 3 for the theatrical system in Milan, secondary school and furniture exhibition in Lissone, 1965. Courtesy of the Collezione Francesco Moschini e Gabriel Vaduva, AAM Architettura Arte Moderna, Rome.

Figure 19 (Below) : Guido Canella, Educational project no. 4 for the theatrical system in Milan, open-air theater and primary school in Novegro di Segrate, 1965. Courtesy of the Collezione Francesco Moschini e Gabriel Vaduva, AAM Architettura Arte Moderna, Rome.

combined with a swath of open-air seating, public squares and various types of urban pseudo-theaters.

Canella's response was, thus, not the absence of architecture or its literal dissolution, but just the opposite. Nor was it a mobile or dynamic theater, but rather an architectural organism on a metropolitan scale, which partially took up some of the aspects of the temple-theater, like its monumentality, its formal stability and its capacity for civic representativity. It was an architecture motivated by the desire to produce the city through theater as a social activity for the masses. Canella used mobility as a conceptual motor for his urban project, where the mobile element was not the theater but the audience, society itself, and class identity, thus challenging the old theatrical model because of its inability to represent novelty. On his part, Javier Navarro does not completely dissolve architecture either into a purely immaterial or merely communicative situation, as can be discerned from his insistence on the absolute need for a spatial limitation of the situation. Instead he sets it in motion, lends it dynamism and introduces the factor of time into its constitution, since the architecture can only be considered complete once it is assembled, and disassembled, following the choreographic-constructive process that imbues it with its full meaning. This setup process (Figure 20) is both architectural and theatrical; it takes place in a sequence and comprises a series of operations: 1: Laying the flooring, which defines all 21 possible layouts. 2: Positioning the trucks on alternate sides of the regular octagon defined by the flooring, and raised on top of hydraulic jacks. 3: Installing the eight telescopic poles extended from the corners of the trucks that coincide with the vertices of the regular octagon. 4: Anchoring the tops of the poles to the trucks using cables. 5: Hanging the panels that form the interior sides of the trucks from the poles using cables so that they can be easily swiveled. 6: Forming one of the 21 possible enclosures. 7: Installing the compression ring on the poles, using eight equal-length rods that generate the same regular octagon in plan. 8: Hoisting the inflatable roof structure. 9: Inflating the roof using the car-pump. 10: Installing the fabric envelope pieces in the spaces between the roof and the trucks, and between the roof and the panels. 11: Installing the seating for the audience and the stage modules, which can be done at the same time as the previous operation. 12: The finished enclosure shows its octagonal form, with the audience entering through the two trucks that form the entryway.

Canella's proposals, developed with his students in 1965, are framed, therefore, with all the nuances we have observed, by the tradition of the temple-theater. They are literally shattered revisions of the bourgeois architectural style and the ability of theater architecture to represent modern society – secular, democratic and polycentric – which, according to Canella, a single stable building could not convene in all its complexity.

THE AVANT-GARDE MACHINE

The archetype of the machine-theater, which deals not only with social mobility but also literally with its own internal spatial mobility, also saw a revisionist analogue at the exact same time, in 1965, with the design by Maurizio Sacripanti (1916-1996) submitted to the competition for the new Teatro Lirico di Cagliari.

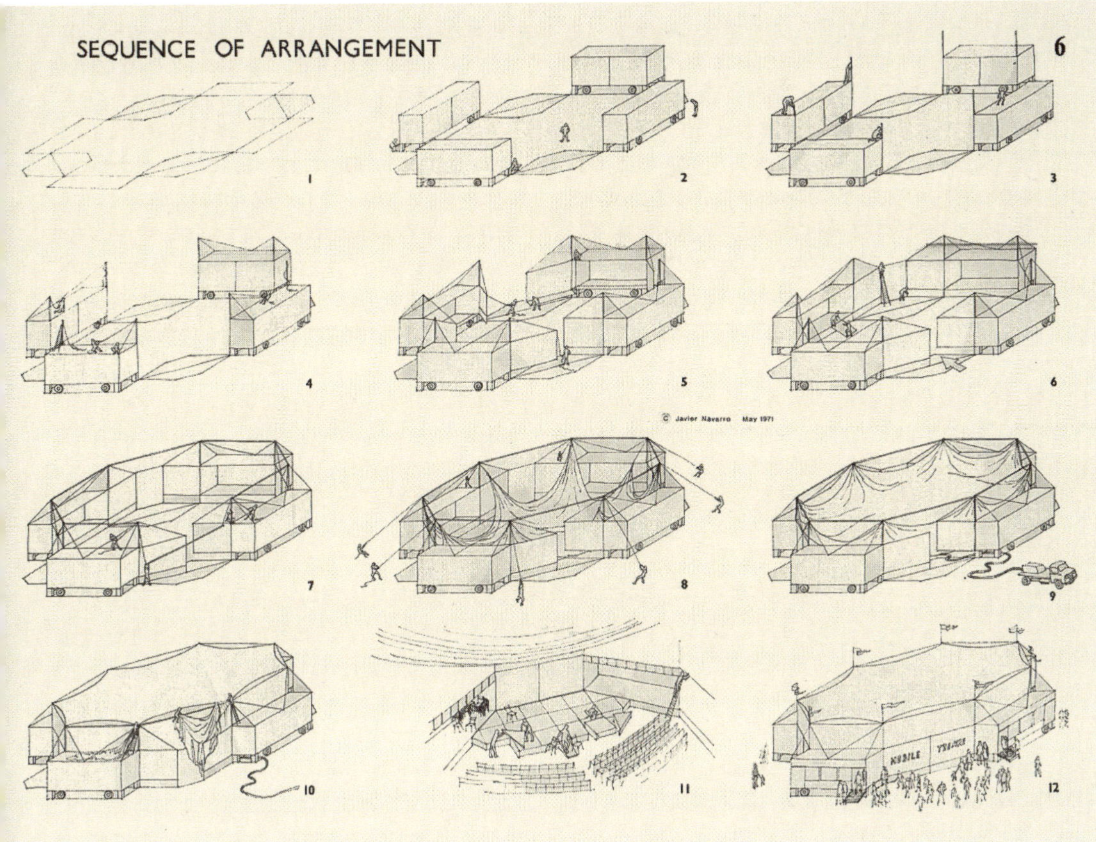

Figure 20: Javier Navarro de Zuvillaga, plan no. 6 for the Mobile Theater. Setup sequence. Courtesy of Javier Navarro de Zuvillaga.

The design, which possesses a formal and technical virtuosity seldom achieved by the Italian architecture of the period, proposed a large event space with a floor and ceiling made of telescoping square modules, using simple hydraulic mechanisms, with a perimeter corridor for circulation and services (Figure 21). It saw three successive versions, in which the interior space and the structural system underwent variations: the envelope was what changed in the second and third versions, until the complex mobile spatial system for the interior became relatively visible. The evolution of the three proposals for the enclosure takes into account the desire to generate a façade capable of transmitting the ideas of formal uncertainty in its final image. The first solution shows a very distinct vertical modulation and a top filled with linguistic signs, pure information, which speaks clearly of the desire to transmit a specific, closed meaning. The second solution maintains the vertical modulation of the façade but substitutes the informational top section with an explicit demonstration of the roof's mobile structures: the information provided coincides with the movement of the façade's internal structures. The evolution across the different variations shows that there were certain difficulties in expressing the conception of the interior space, which varied hardly at all during the evolution of the design, through a conventional façade plane, i.e., by taking the form of a temple-theater with a coherent communicative value (Figures 22, 23 and 24). This highlights the contradiction between the open spatiality of uncertainty of the interior space and the civic need to provide a stable, eloquent and pertinent façade for that changeable spatiality. In other words, the aim was to find a formal expression of the uncertainty of the space, a direct connection between atmosphere and representation.

The project brief mentions the possibility of making the intermissions during events into events in themselves. This possibility comes from programming the movements of the pieces in the floor and ceiling using punch cards, generating millimetric control over the automated movements using computer programming. Computer technology is implicated as an exact mechanism of control for mass spectacles, taking maximum advantage of space and time: nothing is beyond the scope of the spectacular and self-demonstrating component of this impressive, completely computerized mechanism (Figure 25). It is the case to such an extent, that the project defends not only a wide variety of possible uses including theater, conferences, exhibitions, markets, trade fairs or political demonstrations, but also uninterrupted operations without any limitations in terms of opening hours, seasons or social patterns of mass leisure consumption. Even the moments when scene changes are taking place, through the movements of the rectangular blocks that make up the floor and the roof, can become an event to be experienced by the audience, in a state of shock and wonderment.

The elements that make up the seating area are supported by a metallic mesh that is two meters high, with hydraulic pistons tied into the mesh. Two theater seats are installed on top, which can be oriented to face any direction in the space. As such, the possibilities for orienting the seats are nearly infinite, through the combination of varying their height and swivel. In addition, the seats can be removed, so the support can be used

Figure 21: Maurizio Sacripanti, project for the new Teatro Lirico di Cagliari. Sketch of the interior. Courtesy of the Accademia Nazionale di San Luca, Rome. Fondo Maurizio Sacripanti.

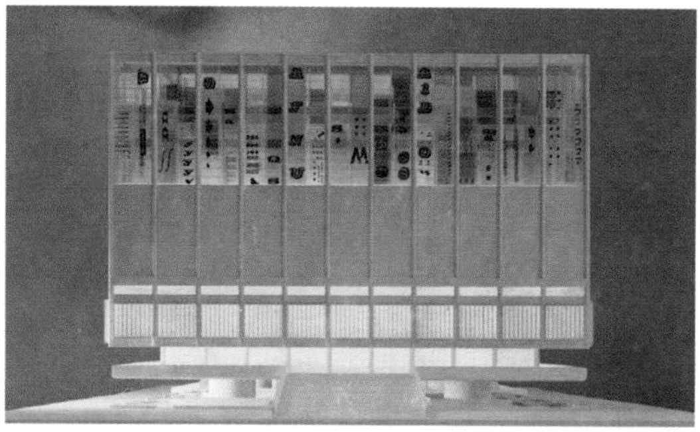

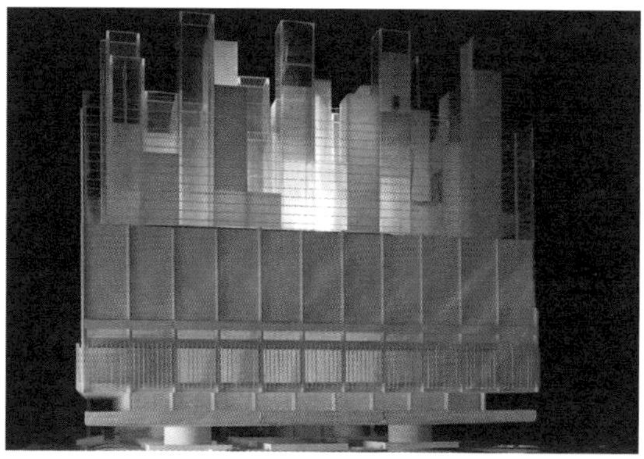

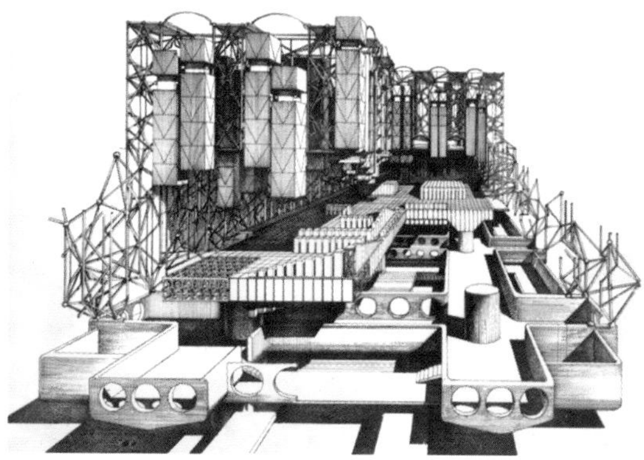

Figure 22: Maurizio Sacripanti, project for the new Teatro Lirico di Cagliari. Model of the initial design. Courtesy of the Accademia Nazionale di San Luca, Rome. Fondo Maurizio Sacripanti.

Figure 23: Maurizio Sacripanti, project for the new Teatro Lirico di Cagliari. Model of the second design. Courtesy of the Accademia Nazionale di San Luca, Rome. Fondo Maurizio Sacripanti.

Figure 24: Maurizio Sacripanti, project for the new Teatro Lirico di Cagliari. Perspective drawing of the definitive design. Courtesy of the Accademia Nazionale di San Luca, Rome. Fondo Maurizio Sacripanti.

as stage space or as a surface for another use. A similar system of adjustable rectangular blocks is proposed for the ceiling, on a larger scale, which can function as an acoustic regulator, as a support for lighting elements, or as a projection screen. Sacripanti called it a "bumper space" because of its adaptability.[15] The roof structure consists of a space frame with five-meter edges in all directions, which spans the space. The rectangular blocks fit into the gaps between the elements of this structure when they are retracted upwards, and the trusses from the space frame shape the building's enclosure in a nearly continuous envelope. Thus, the Baroque theatrical device for producing shock and surprise is recreated using computer punch card technology as a total architectural leitmotif, to which the building's overall spatial composition also refers: it is a huge cybernetic machine producing effects of light, color, sound and dynamic rhythms of all kinds (Figure 26).

Sacripanti cites the familiar history of modern theater and its crisis, which was especially intense during the 1960s.[16] This period during which historiographical research had shed enough light on modern theater to allow for a complete, empirical and systematic critique was what made it possible to propose alternatives, in parallel to the models studied by the historiographers. Sacripanti's critical narrative picks up on assertions that were frequently repeated at the time. For example, that the humanist theater of the Renaissance – for the sake of cultural representation – left behind the disperse sacred spaces of churches and their choral nature in favor of a new univocal, direct relationship between audience and stage. And along the same lines, he puts forward his project as an attempt – one more in the avant-garde line of machine-theaters – to overcome this "solidified opposition between audience and stage" (Figure 27). His design tool is an expansion of the technical principles of the stage into the seating area and, by extension (although in a completely involuntary fashion), encompassing the audience, which is similarly impacted by the building's complex automation process (Figure 28).

Sacripanti highlights the avenue of synthesis between stage and audience characteristic of the theatrical avant-garde, emphasizing the rupture that took place in the Renaissance in two ways: a specifically architectural way, with the invention of the fourth wall, implicit in the separation between the stage and the audience; and a sociopolitical way, with the emergence of professionals dedicated to the performing arts and the specialty, which, as we know, had a profound effect on the practice of architecture following the cultural break of the Renaissance. For Sacripanti, that cultural revolution did not follow the logical path of parallel development and convergence in both areas (stage and audience). According to his brief but elegant and partisan narrative, whereas the stage naturally incorporated the range of sociocultural and technical innovations and new languages, seating areas only experienced formal improvements to their physical configuration, but the role of the audience in the ritual remained fixed and even further specialized. All the evolution in theater since the Renaissance had resulted in an increase in the distance between the two spheres. Drawing on this desire for spatial synthesis, Sacripanti proposed an extension of the principles associated with the stage (changeability, temporariness and mobility) into the realm of the audience, with the cha-

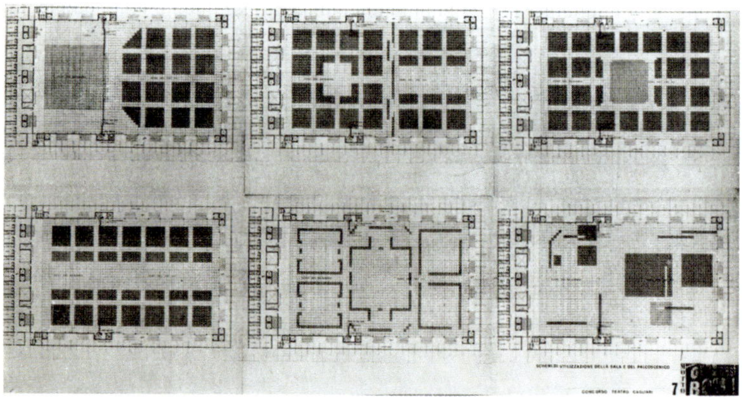

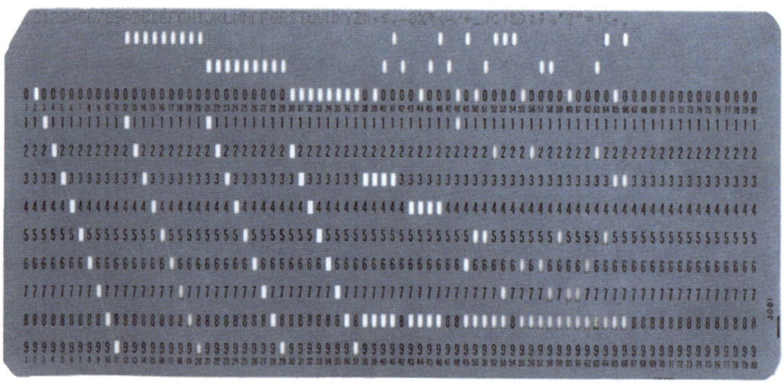

Figure 25: Maurizio Sacripanti, project for the new Teatro Lirico di Cagliari. Floor plans and schematics of the stage and seating areas. Courtesy of the Accademia Nazionale di San Luca, Rome. Fondo Maurizio Sacripanti.

Figure 26: Punch card. Courtesy of IBM.

racteristic avant-garde maneuver of making the active sphere (the stage) overflow into the passive sphere (the audience). Thus, he defined his building as a total "mise en scène", opening up the space to both classical Italian-style performances and stage configurations that could be centralized, multi-focal or even dispersed throughout the entirety of the space. He even proposed the transformability of the space for use during intermissions, eliminating breaks, for a total performance of movement and dynamism, as we have just seen. The aim was to introduce, according to Sacripanti, "a social, and thus typically modern, function" without limits in terms of the profitability of its use: everything can and should happen inside this giant theatrical and social machine over an undetermined and, in theory, infinite period of time.[17]

His project implies a radical extension of stagecraft, in that the constitutive elements that make up the building's architecture are also subject to the possibility of maneuverability. This makes the building as a whole into the object of transformation for the mise-en-scène, independently of who controls that capacity for maneuverability – something that is not indicated in the project, and which in fact becomes very problematic (Figure 29). The involvement of cybernetics in this project, thanks to collaboration from an expert consultant in computer systems, Giovanni Pellegrineschi, opened the doors to an interpretation that likens this project to Cedric Price's *Fun Palace*, not only in terms of architectural language, which is evident, but also on an ideological, social and political level.[18]

Despite the declaration of intent from the project's author, or perhaps because of the ambivalence or even the contradiction that exists between the possibility of a "social function" and the space of uncertainty of events, Manieri-Elia categorized this project as a machine-theater in its purest state: "the architecture responds to the concept of *permanence* from the temple-theater and transforms it into a manipulable mechanism [...]. The audience is seen as the purely absorbent part of this mechanism: motionless and astonished, they are at the center of an unexpected, surprising spectacle that is entirely outside of their control. With no possibility of defending themselves."[19]

Less categorical in his assessment, Manfredo Tafuri interpreted the project in a more nuanced way, as a clear attempt to generate an *opera aperta*, like Umberto Eco, an author whom Sacripanti followed very closely.[20] For Tafuri, the project employed a principle that he called "the figural organicity of the formal structure", which translated the spatialized informational structures derived from information theory and cybernetics into architectural figure. As a consequence of this operation, the building pursued "form as destruction of the traditional notion of place", resulting in the need for "a new semantic organicity of the dialectic between the availability of the structure and the specification of the physical-expressive limits programmed in the act of designing".[21]

In the early 1960s, Italy was one of the focal points for debate on the advances of linguistics and system theory, largely because of Umberto Eco. In a number of projects, Sacripanti experimented with random structures of a certain scale, in line with the idea of what he called "programmed events". At the same time, we should recall that the 1964 architecture triennial in Milan was dedica-

Figure 27: Maurizio Sacripanti, project for the new Teatro Lirico di Cagliari. Model of the interior. Courtesy of the Accademia Nazionale di San Luca, Rome. Fondo Maurizio Sacripanti.

Figure 28: Maurizio Sacripanti, project for the new Teatro Lirico di Cagliari. Model of the interior. Courtesy of the Accademia Nazionale di San Luca, Rome. Fondo Maurizio Sacripanti.

Figure 29: Maurizio Sacripanti, project for the new Teatro Lirico di Cagliari. Model of the definitive design. Courtesy of the Accademia Nazionale di San Luca, Rome. Fondo Maurizio Sacripanti.

ted to *tempo libero*, to the new ideology of mass leisure designed through government policy.[22] In that year and in following years, Italian theater culture bloomed on two very different fronts, which fueled debate: the Piccolo Teatro in Milan and other experimental theaters run by the public administration (Canella's reformist cultural milieu); and the underground scene in Rome (Sacripanti's rupturist cultural milieu). In the first case, the question centered on management, subject to the laws of competition or subject to protectionist politics that would lead leftist critics, embodied by Tafuri, to refer to "an Apollonian democratic policy of free time". For independent theater in Rome, from Carmelo Bene to Lucca Ronconi or Giuliano Vasilicò, the issue was a very different one: the continuity of the international avant-gardes represented by Antonin Artaud, Jerzy Grotowski, the Living Theater, or the Bread and Puppet Theater.

Tafuri polarized these two tendencies by associating them with two historical traditions: on the one hand, the culmination of Francesco Milizia's Enlightenment project in the case of Milan – a state theater with a moral and pedagogical character; and, on the other, the dissolution of avant-garde theater, in the case of Rome, into small venues, playhouses on the outskirts, the street or temporary circus tents, largely following the historic Cubo-Futurist, Dada, and Surrealist avant-gardes.[23] As the theatrical ritual was polarized, so was the audience, even dangerously so, becoming segmented into increasingly isolated pockets of social interaction: on the one hand, the educated bourgeois, reformist and inclusive, who tended to incorporate the working classes in terms of their habits of taste and cultural consumption; and, on the other, the new urban social class defined by a fuzzy, flexible, shifting identity, who engaged in a much more singularized kind of cultural consumption, but which progressively disconnected them from traditional class consciousness.

TAKING BACK THE STREETS

The solution to this dilemma, the third avenue, was, in the words of Manieri-Elia, the mobile-theater as a hybrid between the temple and the machine, a notable example of which is provided in his annals. It is represented by the project for the 1974 competition for the new theater in Udine submitted by Constantino (Nino) Dardi (1936-1991) and Mario Ricci. The design was never published in any professional architecture magazine,[24] but Manieri-Elia presented and discussed it at the seminar in Vicenza in 1975, and Tafuri wrote about it just a year later, in 1976, in an obscure text on the history of Italian theater architecture.[25] This fascinating project piqued Navarro's interest in Vicenza, since he saw in it an immediate analogue of his own project for the Mobile Theater. As such, he added it to his rich array of references as an example that holds enormous similarities with his own project, designed three years earlier and which addressed an identical design issue.

Navarro's concern with the dissolution of theatrical space and its consequences for architecture was shared by Manieri-Elia, who also advocated for a "theater of total disappearance" that would maintain a physical architectural support interwoven with the urban fabric and, by extension, with the social milieu. Here is where Nino Dardi and Mario Ricci's project seems to fit in perfectly. It consists of a building called the "mother theater", located on the competition site, but built using a mobile modular structure of 2.4-meter-long rods that can be disassembled, and which has the potential to occupy streets, squares and parks by transporting the modular elements using conveyors or *autotreni*. Dardi called this configuration in rods a "theatrical circulation module". (Figures 30 and 31). This operation of assembly, transport and disassembly is fully rooted in the theatrical ritual and was meant to take place for each mise-en-scène in view of the audience, who would thus participate as spectators to the ritual of the construction that would welcome them as audience directly thereafter. The scope of the ritual, of the location in which it was taking place and its relationship to architecture, was clearly enriched with the proposal for a mobile theater space.

Under the pseudonym *Lego*, the project by Nino Dardi and Mario Ricci proposed a "mother theater" made up of a cubic structure measuring 28.8 meters per side – i.e., 12 modules – and with a total height of 38.4 meters – i.e., 16 modules – three of which were located below the zero level, generating a fixed sloping seating area around a square-shaped central stage. On two sides and at the zero level, there were the entrance and exit points for the modules, the *autotreni* that could file out onto the streets, leaving the "mother theater" to set up the temporary stages. Thus, the visible mass was a perfect cube, with certain elements attached to it in the form of large-scale wedges or half-spheres with a high visual impact, as expressive additions to an ideal original Platonic space, constructed using the 2.4-meter module (Figure 32). Dardi was an architect fascinated by Platonic forms, modulation, and linear structure, which he investigated in depth in the reconciliation between abstract atavistic form and industry.[26]

However, beyond the building itself, the multiple temporary stages are what really makes this a unique project, which effects the transition from machine-theater to mobile-theater with a surprising naturalness and a minimum implication of technical resources. A large portion of the volume contained in the base of the building is disassembled and transported to open spaces in the city, forming multiple stages in the tradition of the medieval *luoghi deputati*. Some of the drawings submitted for the competition show a series of different possibilities. For example, for the Piazza Primo Maggio, the proposal shows a conventional Italian-style front-facing stage, which occupies the southwest corner of this landscaped square in Udine. For the Piazza Mateotti (Figures 33 and 34), the proposal is an elongated bridge structure made up of three connected nuclei, each of which surrounds a pre-existing element: a baldachin covering a well on one end, a free-standing column in the middle, and a fountain on the other end, to form a simultaneous or alternating three-part stage. The texts that accompany the design drawings are very explicit with regard to this function: "Action in the Piazza Mateotti. Covering over – using elements brought from the structure of the mother theater – the baldachin, the column and the fountain in the square. Linking the three protrusions with a bridge"; and also: "Section for the Piazza Mateotti. Covering over the elements generates a series of surfaces equipped with lights and projections, where actors can carry out a series of

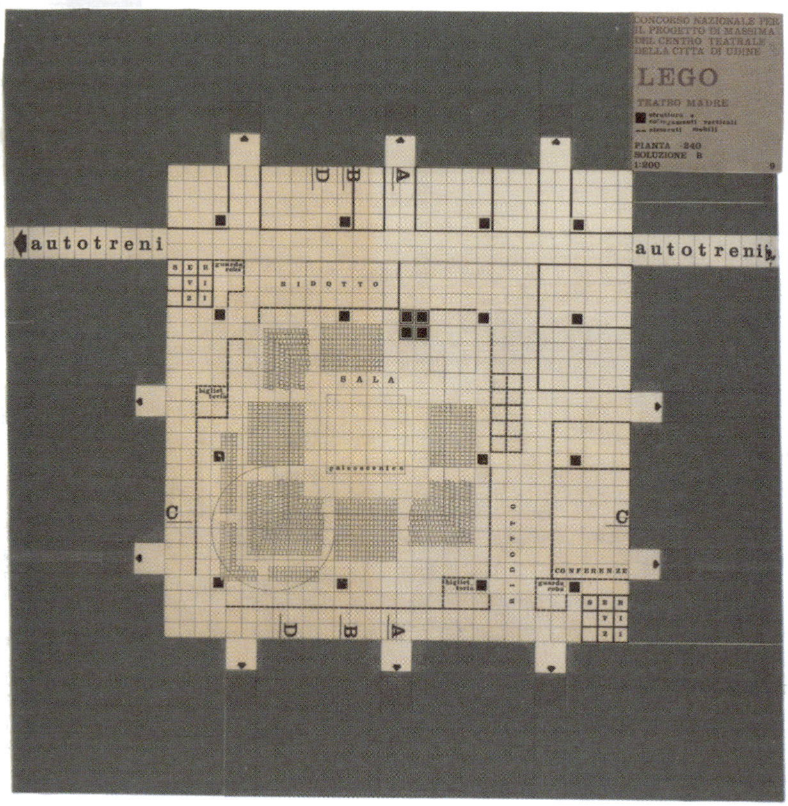

Figure 30: Nino Dardi and Mario Ricci, project for the new theater in Udine, floor plan of the "mother theater" elevation -2.40, solution B, scale 1/200. Courtesy of the Archivio Progetti, IUAV.

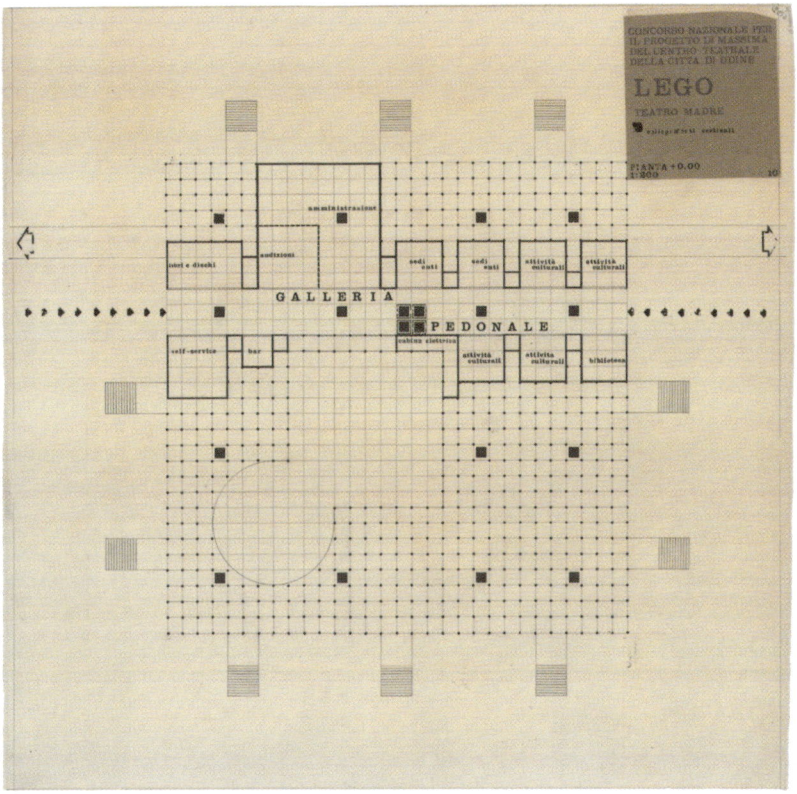

Figure 31: Nino Dardi and Mario Ricci, project for the new theater in Udine, floor plan of the "mother theater" elevation 0.00, solution B, scale 1/200. Courtesy of the Archivio Progetti, IUAV.

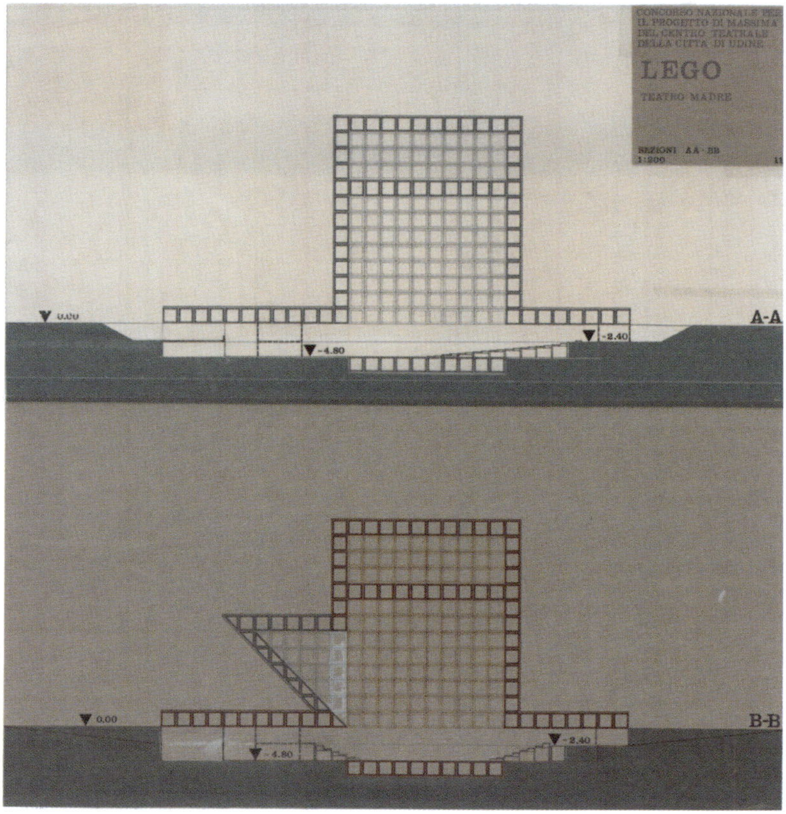

Figure 32: Nino Dardi and Mario Ricci, project for the new theater in Udine, cross-sections of the "mother theater", scale 1/200. Courtesy of the Archivio Progetti, IUAV.

multiple actions, which implicate these protrusions in the square in a spatial manner."

For the Piazza Patriarcato (similarly to the Piazza Primero Maggio), the project lays out a traditional raised stage that opens onto the square, leaving the imposing façade of the San Antonio church as the side wall for the urban stage (Figures 35 and 36). The stage in the square is the endpoint for a theatrical action that begins with the transport and linear assembly of modules along the Via Treppo, originating from the "mother theater", above and beneath which, the action takes place, accompanied by the movement of the audience, as they move to occupy their seats at the main stage. The notes explain the complete fusion of architecture and performance: "Longitudinal section along the Via Treppo. Modular elements from the mother theater that serve as the roof for a theatrical action that takes place linearly along the street"; "traditional performance presented in the Piazza Patriarcato using elements taken from the mother theater"; or "Conclusion of the action along the Via Treppo with a traditional performance in the Piazza Patriarcato".

This possibilities for occupying the city submitted for the competition demonstrated the total flexibility and variability in the assembly and types of stages and relationships between the audience and the seating areas, always motivated by the mobility of both the audience and the elements used to build the structures. The project dissolves the machine-theater (a strictly technical architecture product intended to manufacture effects) into urban space with stages that produce, as Tafuri asserted: "an uncertain and, ultimately, indeterminate relationship between urban morphology and building typology".[27]

In the triad of spatial and architectural archetypes we have just seen in detail, theatricality plays different roles, but in each of them the architecture is a threshold that must be crossed in any ritual. In the bourgeois temple-theater, architecture takes on a cathartic function, focused on reasserting a well-defined and compact social body, which architecture itself helps to construct and lionize. It is a secular body (although it is secularized based on a religious origin), which takes on coherence and community identity through processes of identification with the stage. These architectures signify a continuity with rituals that are accepted by the majority, and their main goal is to lend legitimacy and historical continuity to those rituals. The machine-theater operates in a similar way, in that it legitimizes rituals and lionizes them, but it introduces the aspect of shock into the ritual to renew it, thus producing new social rituals that bring about a substantial change in the subject. A large part of avant-garde theater operated in this fashion, achieving profound renovation from inside the theater itself, introducing changes to the roles involved in the theatrical ritual and challenging pre-existing roles. Through this shift in roles, the ritual took on new forms, but the mechanism kept more or less intact its role as an apparatus for the legitimization of a particular moral and pedagogical ideal.

However, every history has its origin, and every temple-theater was, at some seminal moment of socio-political unrest, a machine-theater aimed at renewing behavior, a fact that ties them together via an un-

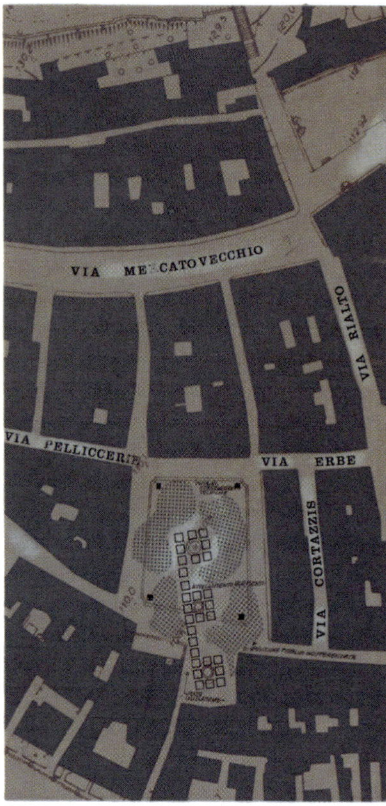

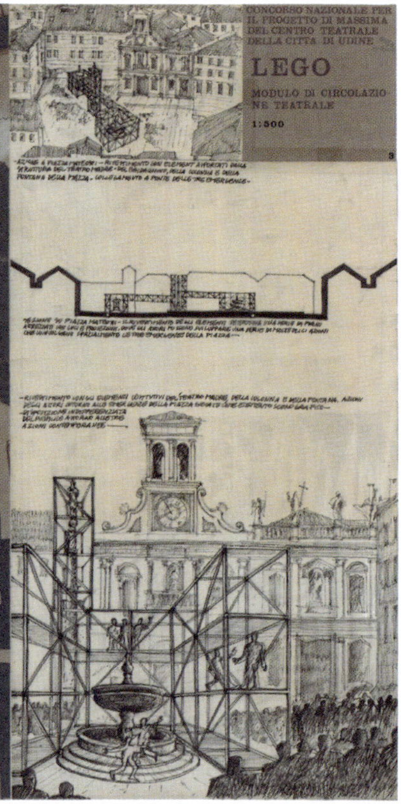

Figure 33: Nino Dardi and Mario Ricci, project for the new theater in Udine, schematic in plan for the Piazza Mateotti, scale 1/500. Courtesy of the Archivio Progetti, IUAV.

Figure 34: Nino Dardi and Mario Ricci, project for the new theater in Udine, sketch for the Piazza Mateotti. Courtesy of the Archivio Progetti, IUAV.

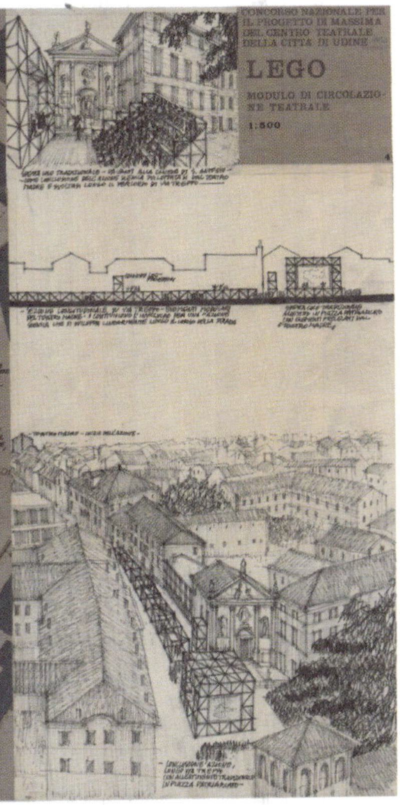

Figure 35: Nino Dardi and Mario Ricci, project for the new theater in Udine, schematic in plan for the Piazza Patriarcato, scale 1/500. Courtesy of the Archivio Progetti, IUAV.

Figure 36: Nino Dardi and Mario Ricci, project for the new theater in Udine, sketch for the Piazza Patriarcato. Courtesy of the Archivio Progetti, IUAV.

breakable link. The archetype of the mobile theater or the caravan that Javier Navarro puts into play investigates, for its part, an even more remote or earlier origin to attempt an escape from this story, whose tragic ending is always present in our minds. It is the origin where roles are still forming and reversible, that "developing situation" as a potential ritual, the space outside the theatrical mechanism, the street and everyday life, producing less stable and lasting attempts, but which are more attuned to real behaviors, which undergo any number of transformations that other architectures do not let us capture with such precision and care.

Notes

1. Javier Navarro de Zuvillaga: "The Disintegration of Theatrical Space," *Architectural Association Quarterly*, vol. 8, no. 4, 1976, pg. 24.

2. Ibid.

3. Guido Canella: *Il sistema teatrale a Milano*, Bari: Dedalo Libri, 1966. Although the whole book contains relevant texts, the first chapter "Il teatro e i compiti della architettura", compiles the fundamental ideas (pp. 7-17). Similar ideas can also be found in Guido Canella: "Il nuovo teatro cerca la città," *I Problemi di Ulisse*, year XXII, vol. 10, 1969, pp. 9-19.

4. Guido Canella: "Teatri e pseudoteatri", *Zodiac*, no. 2, 1989, pgs. 70-93.

5. Le Corbusier: "Le théâtre spontané", in André Villiers and André Barsacq (eds): *Architecture et dramaturgie.* Bibliothèque d'Esthétique, Paris: Flammarion, 1950. The text saw maximum diffusion in the architectural community through the abridged version published in various languages for the International Congress of Modern Architecture (CIAM) VIII held in Hoddesdon in 1951, three years after Le Corbusier's lecture at the Sorbonne. The English edition *The Heart of the City* was published by Lund Humphries & Co. Ltd. in London in 1955, edited by Ernesto Nathan Rogers, Josep Lluís Sert and Jacqueline Tyrwhitt.

6. Twenty-two international speakers participated in the seminar, called *L'Architettura teatrale dal Palladio ad oggi*, and all of them, except Manieri-Elia and Tafuri, focused on the history of theater from the Renaissance until the late 19th century. The disproportion in the historians' attention to different periods in history was remarkable and obvious.

7. The company Galerías Preciados studied the possibility of using the Mobile Theater as a way of exhibiting their fashion collections in spaces around the city of Madrid.

8. Mario Manieri-Elia: "Il teatro moderno", *Bollettino del Centro Internazionale di Studi di Architettura Andrea Palladio*, vol. XVII, Vicenza 1975, pg. 379.

9. Ibid.

10. Ibid., pgs. 380-381.

11. Piero Berengo Gardin: "Teatro?", *I Problemmi di Ulisse*, year XXII. Vol. 10, pgs. 25-31. In the pages of this journal, Berengo Gardin was credited as a marketing journalist. He argued for a proposal of shock mediated theatre following Gropius and Piscator, and confronted his proposal with the audiovisual mass-communication media with a spherical building, which drew from Artaud's stage designs.

12. Mario Manieri-elia, op. cit., pg. 380.

13. Ibid., pg. 386.

14. Guido Canella: *Il sistema teatrale a Milano*, op. cit., pgs. 125-136, where the author analyzes the state of the theatrical system in Milan in 1965.

15. Maurizio Sacripanti: "Il total teatro di Maurizio Sacripanti", *Domus* 437, April 1966, pgs.1-11. The design was widely published in Italy and France. In Italy, in addition to an extensive feature in *Domus*, it appeared in an article by Bruno Zevi:

"Un concorso concluso con sei voti contro cinque. Nasce in Sardegna il teatro in condominio", in the newspaper *l'Espresso*, on October 16, 1965 and as "Concorso nazionale per il teatro di Cagliari" in *L'Architettura. Cronache e Storia*, no. 123, 1966. In France, it was published as "Théâtre total" in *L'Architecture d'Aujourd'hui*, no. 128, 1966. In Spain, it appeared in the legendary issue number 28 of the journal *Nueva Forma* in May 1968, in which Juan Daniel Fullaondo shared his vision of the architecture of the period in his ambitious long-form text, "Agonía, Utopía. Renacimiento".

16. Maurizio Sacripanti: "Il total teatro di Maurizio Sacripanti", *Domus* 437, April 1966, pg. 1.

17. Ibid., pg. 1 and following.

18. Cedric Price's collaboration with Gordon Pask, an expert in cybernetics, dates from the same approximate time as Maurizio Sacripanti's collaboration with Giovanni Pellegrineschi between 1963 and 1965.

19. Mario Manieri-Elia: op. cit., pgs. 384-385.

20. Sacripanti also had close connections to Bruno Zevi, who published some of the writings by the Roman architect related to Umberto Eco's semiotics. See Maurizio Sacripanti: "Città di frontiera", *L'Architettra Cronache e Storia* 187, May 1971, pgs. 56-60; and "Maurizio Sacripanti sulla linguistica architettonica", *L'Architettra Cronache e Storia* 230, December 1974, pgs. 531-533.

21. Manfredo Tafuri: "Opera aperta e spazio polivalente", *Grammatica-Teatro*, no. 2, 1966.

22. Manfredo Tafuri: "Archittetura italiana 1944-1981", in *Storia dell'Arte Italiana VII. Il Novecento*, Turin: Einaudi, 1982, pg. 102.

23. Manfredo Tafuri: "Il luogo teatrale dall'Umanesimo ad oggi", in *Teatri e Scenografie*, Milan: Touring Club Italiano, 1976, pgs. 38-39.

24. Along with Dardi and Ricci, other collaborators on the project for Udine included Giovanni Morabito, Franz Prati and Ariella Zattera. Mario Manieri-Elia also collaborated occasionally with Dardi in his studio.

25. Mafredo Tafuri: "Il luogo teatrale dall'Umanesimo ad oggi", op. cit.

26. There is an exceptional monograph on Nino Dardi, published by Francesco Moschini, *Constantino Dardi. Semplice. Lineare, complesso*, Roma: Editricie Magma, 1976. More recently a new book has been released by Claudio Mistura (ed.), *Constantino Dardi. Forme dell'infrastruttura*, Padua: El Poligrafo, 2017.

27. Manfredo Tafuri: "Il luogo teatrale dall'Umanesimo ad oggi", op. cit., pg. 39.

CHAPTER 2_ ENVIRONMENT

Drawing on an appropriation of Guido Canella's taxonomy, Javier Navarro further divided the third type, the mobile-theater, into three different groups: "found environment", "prepared environment" and travelling theater. So-called "environmental theater" was an aesthetic current worldwide, although it was systematized theoretically in the Unites States in the 1960s, which had a widespread influence. In referring to that cultural phenomenon, Navarro aimed, first, to contribute to a better definition of the panorama of experimental theater at the time, which contained an enormous variety of practical formats. Second, he was looking for the most precise framing possible for his own project, in the context of a very broad landscape of trends. To that end, he relied on a contribution from another theater scholar, the American historian and stage designer, Brooks McNamara (1937-2009), who distinguished between what he called the "found environment" and the "transformed environment" in a text published in the *Architectural Association Quarterly*.[1] This was in the summer of 1975, when Navarro was in Vicenza, a year before his own text was published in that same journal.

McNamara's term "found environment" referred to existing spaces, whether enclosed or open-air, urban or otherwise, taken as they were, with minimum transformations, to be used as stages. He used the term "transformed environment" for spaces that were more similar to conventional theaters, specifically rooms of a certain size – also pre-existing – which were subject to successive complete, and not just partial, environmental transformations for each theater piece, and without separate areas for the performance and the audience.[2] Maintaining this classification and terminology under the wide terminological umbrella of the mobile-theater, Navarro added a third type, the travelling theater, where he logically included his own Mobile Theater in a perfectly natural way.[3] Nonetheless, his insistence on commenting on the other two types, the two "environments", in certain detail indicates a relationship between them that was only hinted at in his text. One thing was clear in Navarro's argument, however: that both the temple-theater and the machine-theater had become obsolete in the context of the renovation of theater and theater architecture. As such, the only option was to investigate the mobile-theater as a source to mine for his work.

The city as a transformed environment in theater had been an ideological wellspring for the Catholic church, which the American current picked up and turned on its head, using the same working methods and practical tools but with opposing ideological goals. The *autos-da-fé* of the Spanish Inquisition were grand stagings of power and domination. American environmental theater, however, sought out other references with aesthetic and ideological pro-

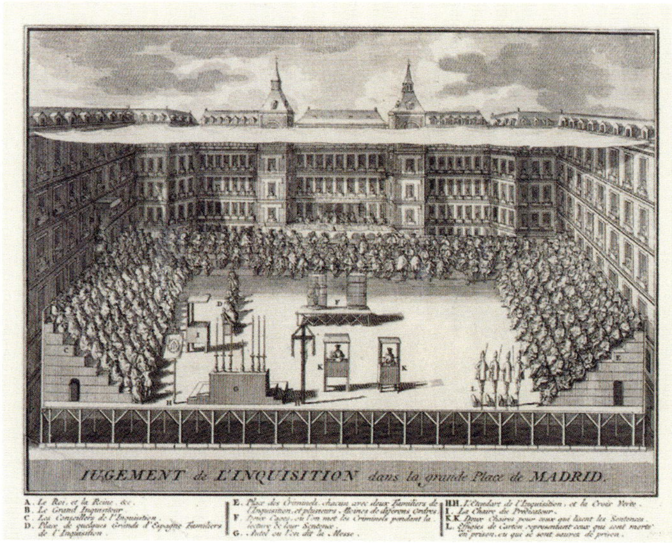

jects that coincided with its own, avoiding comparisons with those cruel celebrations (Figure 37). One of the main precedents, which is often cited as the origin of American environmental theater was *The Storming of the Winter Palace* staged as a mass spectacle and held in the square outside the Winter Palace in Petrograd on November 7, 1920 (Figure 38).

The event was created for the third anniversary of the October Revolution, and 6,000 people participated in it, including professional actors, theater students, soldiers and workers, for an audience of some 100,000 people. It was directed by Nikolai Evreinov, N. V. Petrov and Alexander Kugel. It was designed as a procession, with a series of locations arranged for actions to take place along the way, culminating in the Palace Square. There, the stage designer Yuri P. Annenkov built a series of large stages. In the center, around the Alexander Column, was a platform for the directors. Two stages were built behind, against the façade of the General Staff Building. On the left, what was called the Red City, and on the right the White City, with a bridge between them. The audience was cordoned off into two large square areas in the center of the square, on either side of the directors' platform, leaving a fifth stage in the path between the arch at the entrance to the square and the Winter Palace.

In 1981, Javier Navarro had the chance to design a complete environment for the Plaza Mayor in Madrid, which used similar mechanisms. His project made extensive use of the environmental techniques investigated years earlier by the American experimental theater scene, which he had

Figure 37: Anonymous, *Auto de fe en la Plaza Mayor de Madrid*, 1680. Museum of the History of Madrid.

studied and internalized for the conception of this Mobile Theater (Figure 39). In his 1976 article, Navarro recorded those concerns in detail, through his discussion of McNamara. First, he asserted that his Mobile Theater, and all travelling theaters in general, contain something of the machine-theater. That being said, he was referring more to the necessary technification of the apparatus in order to make it mobile than to its function as a social machine for the conditioning of subjects. This is not at all explicit in the text, but it is evident in the architectural design: he provides hardly any information on its function as a social mechanism, nor does he mention anything about the subjectivity of the audience – which is, no doubt, in addition to the phenomenon of technification, the aspect that was most stressed by the ideologues of the machine-theater. Piscator and Gropius wanted to bombard the spectator, across his entire sensorium, to transform him as a subject of perception, rather than enunciation, although they trusted that the former phenomenon would connect with the latter. Their successor, Sacripanti, was even more explicit in referring to his theater in Cagliari as a giant cybernetic machine, in which the spectator acts like one of the holes in the punch card that activates the mechanism – just another activator in the device.

Second, Navarro also asserted, citing McNamara,[4] that environmental theater did not represent a break from the nomadic street theater tradition and its power to transgress the norms of urban behaviors, as was the case of the machine-theater. Rather, it aimed to reactivate that tradition under the new conditions imposed by modernity. That is why Navarro immediately associated Canella's concept of the mobile-theater with McNamara's environmental theater. In that sense, the type of relationship between environmental theater and the city is very different from that of the machine-theater, which is essentially just a temple-theater that has been updated technically in terms of its urban role. For its part, environmental theater is dedicated to reactivating the scattered, and sometimes partisan, theatricality characteristic of the medieval travelling theater tradition. The three possibilities recognized for those purposes – the found environment, the transformed environment, and the travelling theater – are therefore

Figure 38: Yuri Annekov, *The Storming of the Winter Palace*, preparatory drawing for the staging of the mass spectacle held in the square outside the Winter Palace in Petrograd, November 7, 1920. A.A. Bakhrushin State Central Theatre Museum, Moscow.

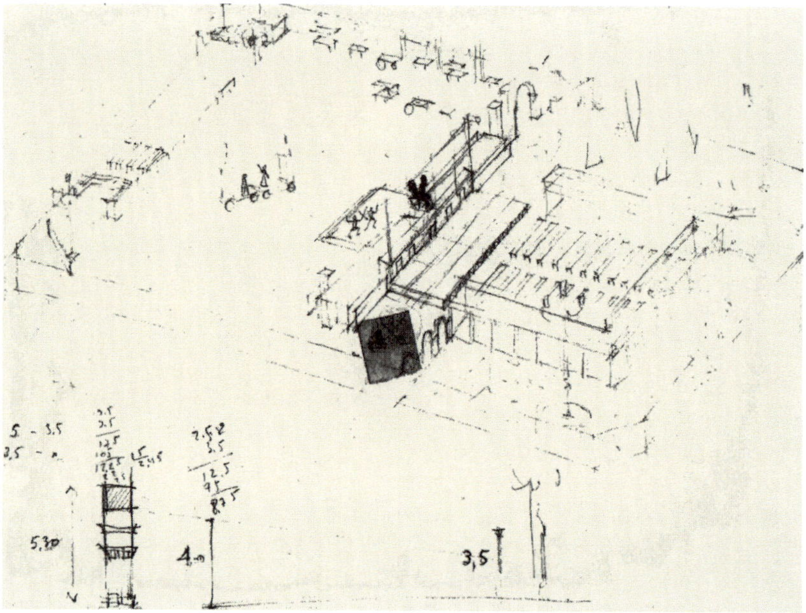

interwoven with one another, and there are many overlaps, both with regard to the performances themselves and in the underlying theory.

It could be said the one thing which most strongly characterises current theatrical practice is that instead of creating theatre in an appropriate space or place, on occasion it looks for the appropriate space to perform particular types of theatre. This phenomenon, which could easily be mistaken for indifference towards theatrical space, is, in fact, not so. It is quite the opposite: it implies greater concern for theatrical space by considering that theatrical space could well be anywhere – in an ancient or modern theater, open air or enclosed, a sports arena, a square, a park, a factory. [5]

In the theater of environment, whether found or transformed, mobility refers not so much to the stage itself as to the artistic community and the audience as part of the social fabric. The movement is either within a single theatrical space, or it leaves behind the theater building to generate a new space, which, nonetheless, has a pre-built physical base. Moreover, the main goal of this movement – whether inside or outside of the specialized space – is to overcome the dual division into stage and audience

Figure 39: Javier Navarro de Zuvillaga, *Design of the Setting for the Fiesta de los Austrias*, an homage to Calderón de la Barca for the 3rd centennial of his death. Plaza Mayor, Madrid, July 1981. Image courtesy of Javier Navarro de Zuvillaga.

characteristic of the theater building, in order to bring about a reunification through new structures that are specifically designed for that purpose. The temple-theater consciously maintained this division to ensure the continuity of orthodox theater's functions of social self-representation. The machine-theater, on the other hand, dissatisfied with this division, tested out forms of reunification or synthesis, although they were always strictly contained within the walls of the theater building. The mobile-theater, the category in which Navarro situates the two possible types of environmental theater as well as his own, tests out ways of unifying the space that are intended to leave behind the confines of the theater building in an attempt to expand that unification to encompass the city as a whole. It is only logical that the main strategy involved literally leaving behind the theater building, which occurred in parallel to visual artists moving out of studios and galleries, i.e., away from the institutional circuits of production and exhibition.

TRAGEDIES IN A GARAGE

McNamara was, along with the theater director Richard Schechner (1934) and the stage designer Jerry Rojo (1935-2018), the third core figure in American environmental theater. All three were involved in a considerable number of influential theatrical productions, whose impact was cemented through intense academic efforts

in American universities and a continued publishing practice through the magazine *TDR*, edited by Schechner, as well as a series of monographs. The initials from the title of the magazine corresponded to the Schechner's successive academic affiliations. First, in New Orleans from 1962 to 1967, it was the *Tulane Drama Review* (for Tulane University, where the first issue was published in 1957) and then, in New York from 1967 to 1969, it became *The Drama Review* (at New York University, where it is still being published today). Michael Kirby (1931-1997), another artist and official his-

Figura 40: Cover of TDR magazine *The Tulane Drama Review*, vol 10, n. 2, 1965.

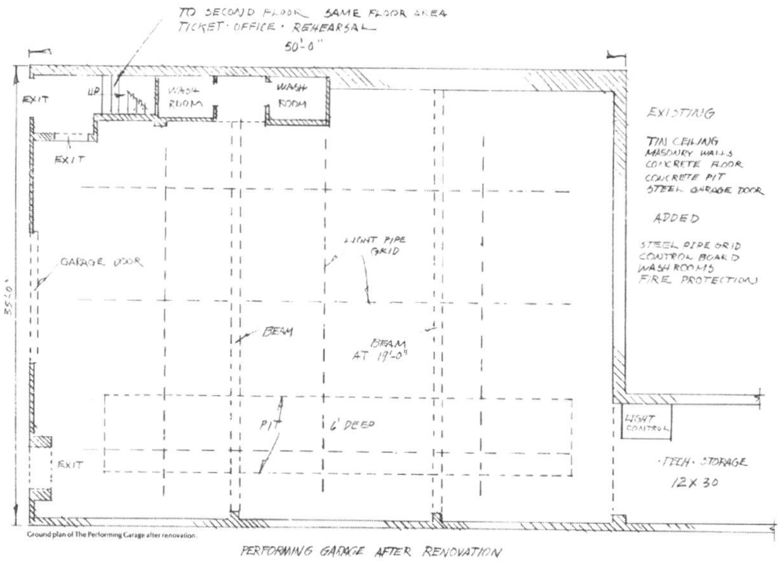

torian of happenings, was also crucial to the efforts. He was director of the magazine *TDR* from 1970 to 1986. Then Schechner took over the job again and has kept it until the present. The magazine touched on the whole of theater culture, without geographic or cultural limits of any kind. It offered broad, thematic monographs that delved into non-Western theater, role theory and game theory, popular theater, the European avant-garde, and the entire experimental theater scene at the time, on a global level.[6] Kirby edited a special issue of the *Tulane Drama Review*, which contained interviews, essays, conversations, diagrams and play reviews (Figure 40). In addition to Kirby himself, other contributors to the issue included Robert Ashley, John Cage, Ken Dewey, Letty Eisenhauer, Anna Halprin, Dick Higgins, Theodore Hoffman, George Maciunas, Jackson Mac Low, Robert Morris, Claes Oldenburg, Yvonne Rainer, Ramón Sender, Paul Sills, Kelly Yeaton and La Monte Young

Richard Schechner was the founder of The Performance Group in New York in 1967 and the main ideologue behind environmental theater.[7] The theater group had its own space, called the Performing Garage, beginning in 1968. It was located in SoHo in an old print shop, which is still in operation today: it has been the headquarters of the Wooster Group since 1980 (Figure 41). The space is 50 feet long, 35 feet wide and 19 feet high (15.24 x 10.67 x 5.79 meters). According to Schechner's description:

The building was constructed around 1960 as a metal stamping factory between two

Figure 41: Performing Garage, floor plan of the space after renovation, drawn by Jerry Rojo and reproduced by Schechner.

already existing old buildings. They threw up four steel girders, two on each side, and two cross girders and constructed the building on that frame. The ground floor has a pit that was used for the guts of the stamping machine. The space was never actually a garage, but we called it The Garage because the first time I saw it there was a garbage truck parked in it. Since we decided to call ourselves The Performing Group, it seemed appropriate to call it The Performing Garage. The floor is concrete and the walls are cinder block, and there is a 12' high, overhead door opening onto Wooster Street (the east side of the building) and two small windows where we later put two air conditioners.[8]

From 1968 to 1975, when internal tensions began to emerge in the Performance Group and a new management phase began, they staged five productions that are essential to American environmental theater, for which Jerry Rojo acted as the designer: *Dionysus in 69* (1968), based on Euripides' *The Bacchae* with text by Schechner written from improvisation sessions; *Makbeth* (1969), with text by Schechner based on the Shakespeare play; *Commune* (1970), written by the entire group; *The Tooth of Crime* (1972), by Sam Shepard; and *Mother Courage and Her Children* (1975) by Bertolt Brecht.

The first production, *Dionysus in 69*, which was later adapted for the screen by Brian de Palma, was staged using two 19-foot towers (nearly six meters), arranged in a diagonal, which divided the space into thirds, plus a three-story gallery on the north side, and three low platforms across the ground (Figures 42 and 43). According to Schechner, the group itself did most of the construction work, since they did not have the budget to hire anyone. Two scaffolding structures that they set up to paint the walls white were then used for the group's exercises in preparing the play.[9] The final form of the space was a slightly stylized version of the scaffolding. Schechner initially called in Kirby to collaborate as a sculptor, but his ideas were eventually rejected, and Rojo joined the team in his place. The two towers were built with standardized wood elements, and they became a hallmark of the Performance Group's style. The central platforms, which the group called the "sacred area", were the black leather mattresses habitually used by the company for rehearsals, as a layer of insulation against the cold concrete floor. In May 1968, just a month before the opening in June of that year, they bought black carpeting at a factory sale, which they used to cover part of the floor and the walls. The two towers were designed for the audience, although part of the action took place there. After the opening, the space was altered slightly, with two new lower towers on wheels: one at the back on the north side, and another nearer to the entrance. The space was subject to occasional variations, to the point where, given the play's success with audiences (it was presented 163 times in a little over a year),[10] a third tower was built to be included in the performance. The space generated a highly variable relationship with the audience. The central area was clearly perceived as empty and at the ready for the action to take place there, despite the complete lack of any physical barriers, and the audience took their places according to their desired level of exposure: less if they climbed to the top of the towers, and more if they stayed closer to the central platforms. With this production, Schechner brought to New York a series of

Figure 42: The Performing Group, *Dionysus in 69*, photograph of the director with the group behind, circa 1969.

Figure 43: The Performing Group, *Dionysus in 69*, photograph of Pentheus (William Shepard) addressing the Thebans from the top of one of the main towers, circa 1969. Photograph: Reanne Rubenstein.

techniques and spatial ideas he had been developing at Tulane University since 1962, and they underwent a broad evolution in subsequent pieces.[11]

ACTION, SPACE AND ENVIRONMENT

Like Schechner, Brooks McNamara had borrowed the term "found environment" from Michael Kirby, who used it in 1965 to describe how happenings in the late 1950s treated the physical space for their events.[12] Kirby's fertile terminology contained a direct appropriation of Marcel Duchamp's concept of the "found object" in order to draw a link between the European avant-garde and its American counterpart in the work of John Cage and Allan Kaprow, who are key figures in this terminological genealogy. Kirby clearly distinguished between environment as an artistic format – like a collage spread out across the three-dimensions of space – and "found environment", understood as a space onto which actions that take place over time can be projected.[13] Thus, the factor of time does not play the same role in both artistic formats. In the artistic environment, time is subjective, a product of absorbed and self-referential perception, similar to the condition of the spectator in the bourgeois theater. In the "found environment", in contrast, time is the same as everyday time, because it is determined by the found space and everything taking place in it, making it an appropriate setting for a happening.

In addition to this terminological precision, Kirby observed that, in staging their exhibitions, Dadaists used the notion of "found environment": for example, in the exhibition in Cologne in 1920, for which Jean Arp, Johannes Theodor Baargeld and Max Ernst installed their work in the back courtyard of a café, which could only be accessed through a public restroom. He also pointed out that, in 1921, André Breton encouraged his fellow Surrealists to leave behind galleries, theaters and institutional spaces and move out into the streets to arrange excursions and visits.[14] These operations theatricalized the exhibition of objects and everyday urban experiences through new social rituals, resulting in a profanation of the found space of the city and, at the same time, an attack on the institution of art.

For Richard Schechner – writing, like Kirby, in 1965 – happenings implied two main challenges, which he took up in his own project of environmental theater (Figures 44 and 45): first, the introduction into the performance space of all the semiotic richness of the street as a network of information structures; and, second, the possibility of playing with the spectators' modes of perception. According to Schechner: "Those few who have seen or participated in a Happening have undergone the beginning of a perceptual re-education."[15] This statement demonstrates his deep understanding of the protocols that the happening had brought into play as a new artistic format.

Kaprow, in 1966, also referred to these questions in one of his programmatic principles for the happening, specifically the one stating that: "G) The composition of a Happening proceeds exactly as in Assemblages and Environments, that is, it is evolved as a collage of events in certain spans of time and in certain spaces."[16] According

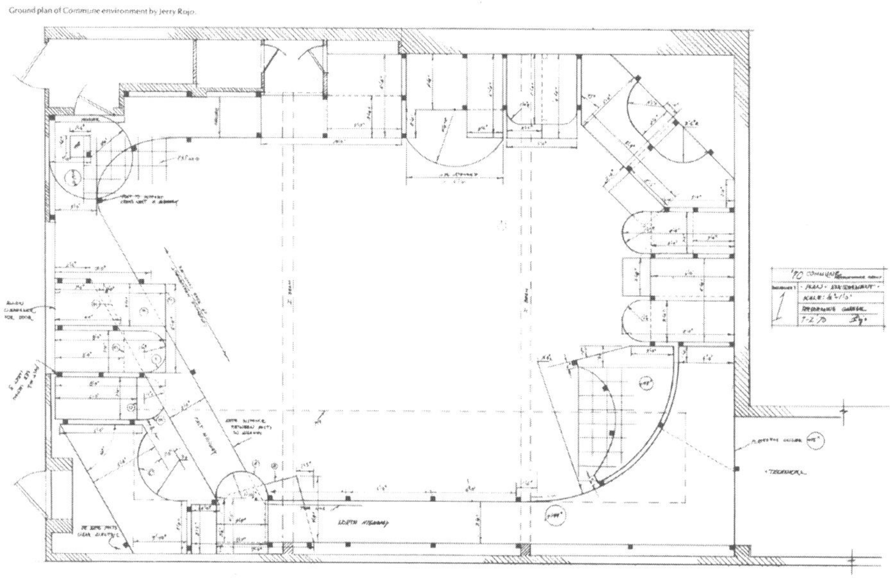

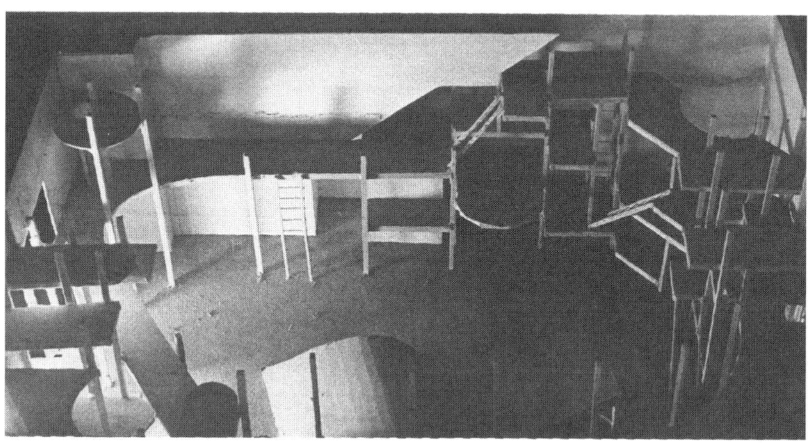

Figure 44: The Performing Group, *Commune,* 1970. Floor plan of the stage design by Jerry Rojo.

Figure 45: The Performing Group, *Commune,* 1970. Model of the stage design by Jerry Rojo.

to the definition, this mode of composition is not classical in either its organic or mechanical form, since it does not pursue unity or totality as a goal in which "the materials are taken for granted" as a means to an end. Rather, this method of composing is entirely dependent on and subsidiary to the materials themselves, which, in a stage performance, include "people and nature".[17] This mode of composition, which Kaprow inherited from John Cage, holds true for both Schechner's environmental theater and Javier Navarro's Mobile Theater, with different working scales and interests, but with very similar formal processes.

The composition through a simple juxtaposition of heterogeneous spatiotemporal materials was also very characteristic of traditional travelling theater. However, the relationship between Javier Navarro's Mobile Theater and traditional travelling theater is indirect for two reasons: because, in the travelling theater, the caravan was analogous with the stage, as separate from the audience (the street or public square was the realm of the audience); and because, instead of moving from one city to another, it would move to different locations within the same city.[18]

URBAN SCORES

One fascinating and radical precedent on an urban level is a piece that was performed on March 9,1963 in San Francisco, called *City Scale*. The project was published by Kirby and Schechner in the special issue of *TDR* cited previously, dedicated to happenings, and it was developed by Ken Dewey, Anthony Martin and Ramón Sender.[19] *City Scale* was an exceptional example of the use of the "found environment", since it constructed a score of programmed events in the city for a moving audience, with minimal transformations of space. The "found environment" was not an art gallery, a vacant lot, a gymnasium or a park, but an enormous section of the city of San Francisco, which became a huge theater during the six hours that the event lasted. The text that accompanied the publication of the project read:

City Scale was the culminating event of a season devoted to exploring performer-audience relationships. We decided to use the city environment as totally as possible, to create a trip out of which more or less controlled elements would emerge. Many of the events were purposely ambiguous so that audience members would not have the certainty of knowing whether a given incident had been planned or was happening anyway. The most meaningful events of the evening were those which impinged upon the life of the city, interacted with it, transformed it, or absorbed it into the structure of the work. The arrival of the audience in two trucks at a small park perched high on a hill overlooking the Mission coincided with a collision between two teenage gangs in the park. I had arrived early to inflate four seventeen-foot weather balloons, and noticed the kids collecting. Just as the two groups started toward each other, our trucks full of excited participants roared up. Sixty people started running across the park towards the balloons, and the teenagers scattered through the periphery. I don't know what went through their minds in the minutes that followed, as adults chased balloons and each other through the park. City Scale was a natural extension of sound experiments with which the Tape Music Center members were involved – group improvi-

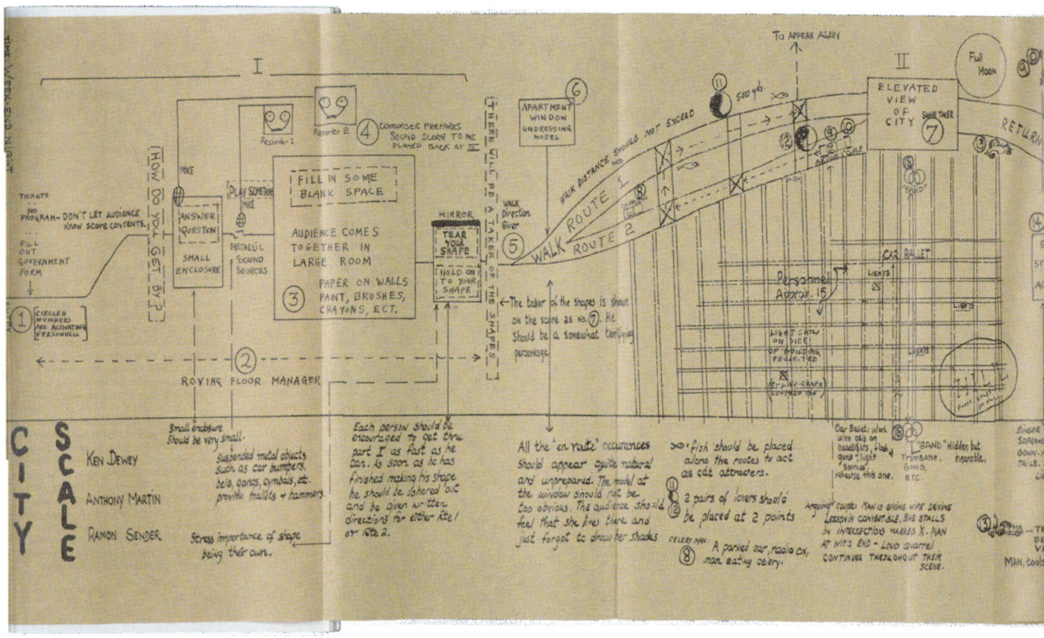

sation, or tape pieces unfolding on many simultaneous levels of control. Out of it developed our present interest in environmental works – sound and light events controlling as much of a given space as possible. (Ramón Sender).

My intention was to externalize visually the world in ourselves by providing a maze of the manmade, a sequence of events in the city (Anthony Martin).

Ramón Sender Barayón was the main driving force behind the project. The son of a Spanish-born exile, Ramon J. Sender, he received a formal musical education on the East Coast of the United States, which he completed in San Francisco, where he forged immediate ties to the local avant-garde music scene. In 1961, while he was studying composition with Robert Erickson at the San Francisco Conservatory, he took the first steps toward founding a group that was immensely important to the musical counterculture of the moment: the San Francisco Tape Music Center. After composing his first piece for magnetic tape, he set up a studio in the attic of the conservatory building dedicated specifically to that type of music, where he began creating new pieces along with Pauline Oliveros, Terry Riley and Philip Windsor.[20]

For *City Scale*, Sender was joined by two others from very different fields: Ken Dewey and Anthony Martin. Dewey had trained in sculpture, writing and the dramatic arts with two fundamental West Coast figures: Ronnie Davis, founder of the San Francisco Mime Group, a guerilla political street theater group; and the choreographer Anna Halprin, founder of the Dancers' Workshop and a pioneer of postmodern dance. For his part, Anthony Martin is a visual artist who

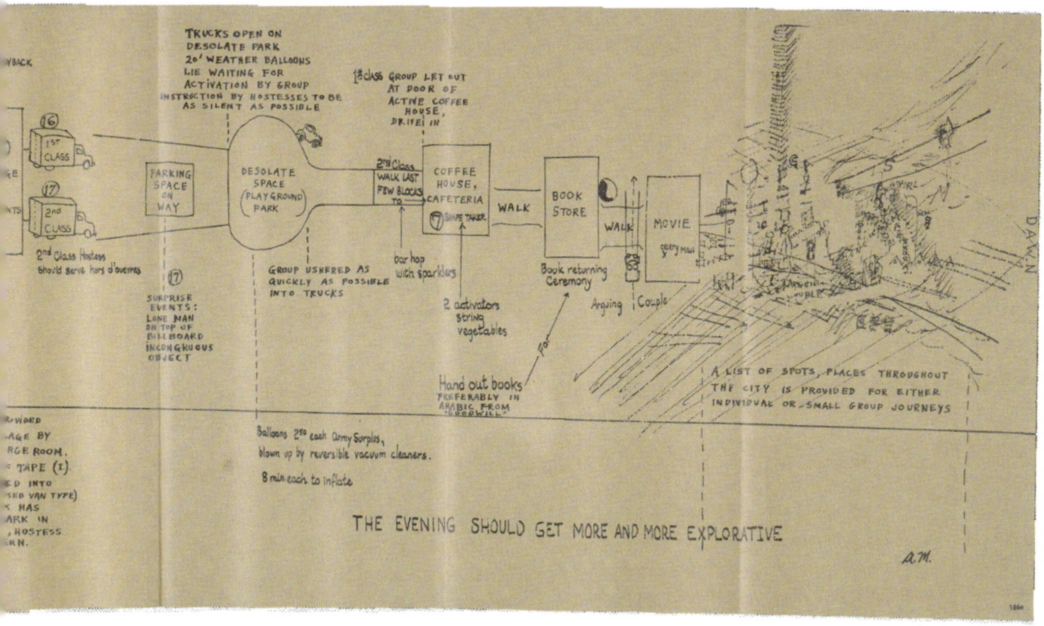

became the artistic director of the San Francisco Tape Music Center. Martin studied painting at the Chicago Art Institute in the 1950s. After graduating, he moved to San Francisco, where he collaborated with Sender. He began creating pictorial pieces using projected light, sound vibrations, reflected images, and illuminated liquid masses, which became enormously popular at the Acid Festivals in 1966.

Thus, Sender's idea of musical composition expanded into space was combined with Dewey's choreographic staging and Martin's expanded painting, as is evident in the graphic document Martin created for the project, which is extremely eloquent and vaguely recalls the restitutions of medieval multiple stages (Figure 46). There is no real scale on the map. It contains no absolute coordinates or street names: distances, times and sizes do not correspond to exact relationships of shared proportions. The only specifications are "Time: week-end night" and "full moon" to indicate the time of the event.[21] The map was hand drawn by Anthony Martin and measures 36 inches in length (nearly 92 centimeters) and it was reproduced as a fold-out insert in the special issue of the magazine *TDR* about happenings, along with a short text by Ramón Sender and a single-sentence description by Anthony Martin.

Figure 46: Ramón Sender, Anthony Martin and Ken Dewey, *City Scale*, 1963. Fold-out insert showing the map, from the magazine *TDR* vol. 10, no. 2, 1965.

It is an exercise based on a very direct and almost immediate transposition of the musical score onto urban space-time. Nonetheless, a meticulous interpretation of the map demonstrates that the apparent chaos corresponds to a three-part structure plus a coda. Anthony Martin himself described *City Scale* as follows:

People gathered in a polysensory, multimedia set up at our Jones Street space in late afternoon and spread out into the city for preorganized occurrences on the streets, hills, and tunnels. Audiences encountered surprise live and taped sound events in North Beach and a 'car ballet' on Telegraph Hill. They were driven in rented trucks to rising weather balloons on Potrero Hill. The event went on through the evening and into the night.[22]

The transfer of media was a fundamental strategy in the seminal theater of "found environment" like *City Scale*, since the practices included transpositions from one medium to another: from music to atmosphere, from score to mapped space. The Mobile Theater also worked with transfer, but on a different level. According to Navarro: "Thus, in the same way that the actor is a 'place of personalities', the theatre is the 'place of places', of all the places imaginable: it is a place-fiction."[23] By way of this analogy or transfer between actor and space, the theatrical space and its architecture can be considered a place-fiction, a space that is "acted out" by other spaces, and inundated by an infinite number of possible situations, like an actor in relation to a dramatic text. The space of the stage emerges as a container of fictions, which it is impossible to pin down in a static architecture prior to the writing of the theatrical event. Instead, it becomes a sort of variable architectural scenography, to the point of associating that variability with its physical location in space in the most general sense possible, within the city at large (Figure 47).

The space of the theater becomes mobile; it travels from one site to another. It is also kinetic; it is assembled in each location as an architectural performance or constructive choreography. And, finally, it is environmental-specific: it is configured specifically for each event for which it is used, depending on the occasion. It is a pseudo-theater, to use Canella's terminology, and it arises from a combination of found space and transformed space. Yet, it is the final element in this chain, the environmental-specific aspect that demands

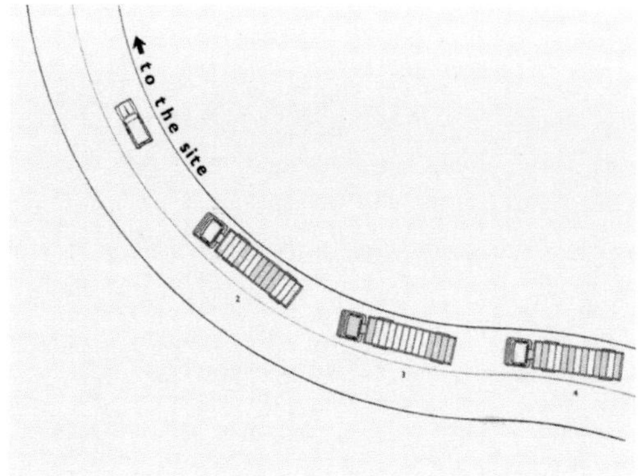

Figure 47: Javier Navarro de Zuvillaga, fragment of plan number 1 for the Mobile Theater, labeled as The Caravan, showing part of the caravan of trucks. Courtesy of Javier Navarro de Zuvillaga.

a particular physical configuration for each situation, which engenders the conceptual sequence that leads to the design and which, significantly, is much less formalized in the Mobile Theater. The design documents are intentionally dry and conventional. They hardly show the theater in operation at all, assuming that its specific configurations should not be predetermined: the design does not need to be self-demonstrative. In that sense, it does not show its origins in the situational experiments from Madrid and London, without which, nonetheless, it would never have been possible.

THE ENVIRONMENTAL CANON

The operation of transfer from dramatic text to space, or from the character as a container of fictions to space as a container of other spaces, relies on a conscientious interiorization on the part of Javier Navarro of the precepts outlined by Richard Schechner in 1967 in his famous *Six Axioms for Environmental Theater*.[24] Those axioms were:

1) The theatrical event is a set of related transactions; 2) All the space is used for performance; all the space is used for audience; 3) The theatrical event can take place either in a totally transformed space or in "found space"; 4) Focus is flexible and variable; 5) All production elements speak in their own language; and 6) The text need be neither the starting point nor the goal of a production. There may be no text at all.

The six axioms did not determine specific prescriptive norms; rather, they encouraged people to defy the normative conventions of the stage, particularly with regard to space. The second and third axioms announced by Schechner confirm the prevalence of the spatial factor in his agenda and the central idea that conventional theatrical space cannot be the setting for the type of artistic manifestations he had in mind.

In the Mobile Theater, along with the notion of fiction-place, there is a transfer from the text and/or character to the space that shares enormous similarities with Schechner's environmental theater. It stands apart, however, in that it entails a risky and ambitious shift in scale. American environmental theater dealt with bounded areas within built spaces, like the Performing Garage. Beyond the theoretical realm, however, it did not implement those ideas in the real urban sphere outside the confines of performance spaces. The artists of the "found environment" were the ones who fully developed the possibilities that Schechner investigated as future avenues for his own project. For its part, the Mobile Theater also expands the notion of environment toward a broader architectural-scenic space on an urban scale – something that other artists had been exploring continuously over the previous decade.

One of the most explicit references Navarro used to explain this possibility was the piece *Vessel* (1942) by Meredith Monk, presented in New York in October 1971, i.e., after the Mobile Theater project was designed.[25] Since 1967, Monk had worked with the idea of what she called "specific sites", with musical-theatrical pieces composed specifically for urban or natural spaces instead of theaters, galleries or museums. The piece *Vessel*, in particular, an epic opera in three acts, was performed in three different spaces scatte-

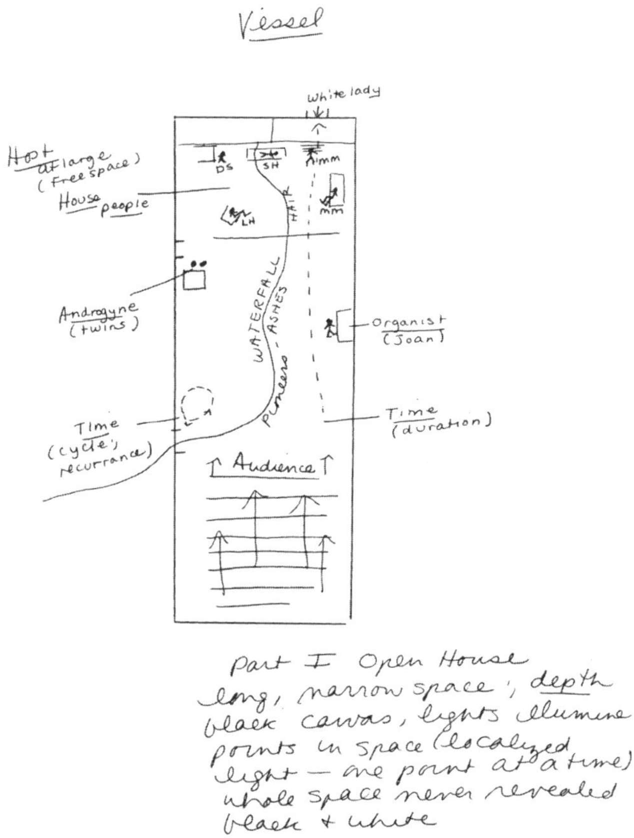

Figure 48: Meredith Monk, *Vessel*, 1971. Part 1 Overture: Open House, performed in Monk's private loft in Greenwich Village. Drawing by Meredith Monk.

Figure 49: Meredith Monk, *Vessel*, 1971. Part 1 Overture: Open House, performed in Monk's private loft in Greenwich Village. Photograph: Peter Moore.

red across the city: Monk's own loft, the Performing Garage, and finally an open-air parking lot on Wooster Street, near the theater. After attending the first act at the artist's home, the audience took a bus to the Performing Garage to see the second act, and then walked to the designated parking lot to watch the third act. This put into practice the idea of a mobile audience, which Monk had investigated in earlier pieces, and the audience's movement had its parallel in the development of the "epic movement of Monk's opera".[26]

Monk's loft, used for the first act of the piece (Overture: Open House) was located on Great Jones Street. It measured 100 ft x 25 ft (30.5 m x 7.6 m), and the ceilings were approximately 9 ft high (2.75 meters). According to Monk, the loft was suggestive of a tunnel or a long narrow space in perspective, with the wooden floorboards receding toward the vanishing point (Figures 48 and 49). The space was used with hardly any transformation at all, because of its stark "realism", in sharp contrast with the images and actions that took place there, which were very strange in both formal and aesthetic terms.

Deborah Jowitt wrote a review and a description of her experience as a spectator, which contains a wealth of details about the piece. According to Jowitt "every act is a key to every other act", so the actors reappear with different costumes and behaviors, taking the action from the private sphere of the first act to the public arena of the third. Whereas, in the first act, the atmosphere is intimate but strange, in the second it is ritual and theatrical, and in the third it is "a field of battle, a public square".[27] To get from the first setting to the second, they rented a bus, painted blue with red and yellow stripes. First, the bus drove the actors from Monk's loft to the Performing Garage, while the audience had a glass of wine. Then, the bus came back to pick them up. The bus was carpeted along its full length, with just a few seats in the rear, leaving a lot of space to sit on the floor; in other words, its spatiality resonated with that of the loft. The bus was "warm and cozy" for the purpose of contrasting with the epic inherent in the work and the fact of transporting the audience from one place to another. Monk had thought about planting actors on the streets along the way, but she realized that the fact of looking out at New York City at night through the bus windows was plenty: "having been through one theatrical experience and going to another is enough in a way".[28]

For the second act (Handmade Mountain) she used the Performing Garage just as it was, taking advantage of Jerry Rojo's structures for *Commune*, covering them with a giant piece of white muslin to make the "mountain" from the title of the second act, connecting one tower with another (Figures 50 and 51). The aim was to create a large, bright ritual space, in harmony with the intended action. At the end of the second act, the audience left the theater and walked half a block to the parking lot, a space conceived panoramically for a flat view, measuring a block wide and one-third of a block deep. The audience sat on one of the long sides, between the Canal Lumber Company on one end and the Church of Saint Alphonsus on the other, framing a shallow *tableau*. Facing the au-

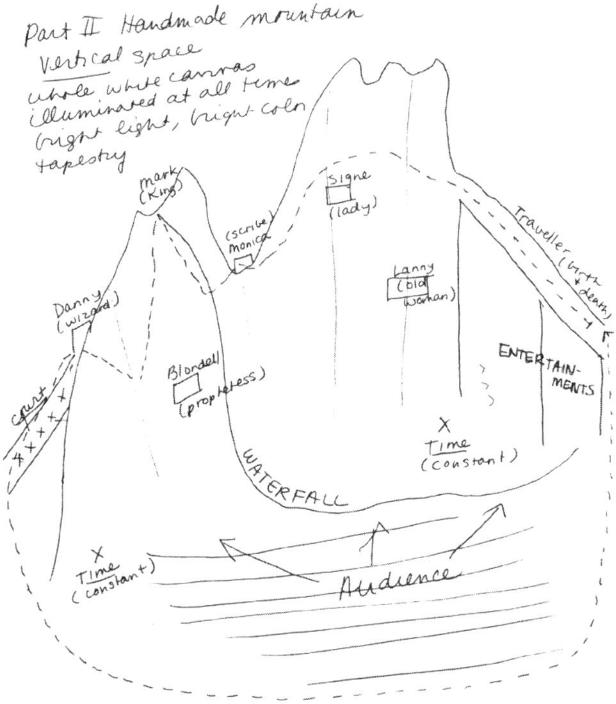

Figure 50: Meredith Monk, *Vessel*, 1971. Part 2 Handmade Mountain, presented at the Performing Garage. Drawing by Meredith Monk.

Figure 51: Meredith Monk, *Vessel*, 1971. Part 2 Handmade Mountain, presented at the Performing Garage. From left to right: Linn Varney, Meredith Monk, Coco Pekelis (front), Lanny Harrison, Daniel Ira Sverdlik, Monica Mosley, Haan. Photograph: Peter Moore.

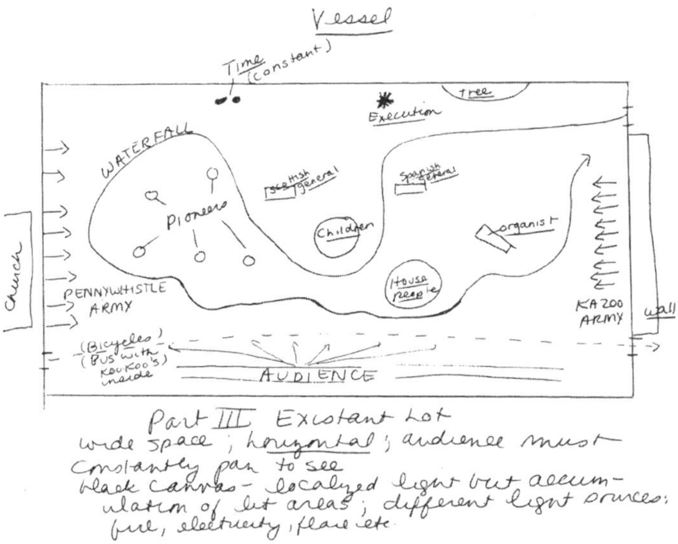

Figure 52: Meredith Monk, *Vessel*, 1971. Part 3 Existent Lot, presented in a parking lot on Wooster St. in Soho. Drawing by Meredith Monk.

Figure 53: Meredith Monk, *Vessel*, 1971. Part 3 Existent Lot, presented in a parking lot on Wooster St. in Soho. Photograph: Peter Moore.

dience was a candy factory, a decaying building with a few scattered trees in front. The ground was entirely covered in asphalt (Figures 52 and 53).

Whereas the spatial and visual structure of the loft was a long tunnel, defined by perspective – i.e., the distance between the audience and the action seemed enormous, in the Performing Garage the space was vertical and enveloping, nearby and sublime, and in the parking lot the view was flat, almost without depth, exclusively from left to right .

The element that traditionally serves to unify the variety of knowledge and practices on the stage – the text – is replaced by space in environmental theater and by the city in Monk's epic opera or Ramón Sender's experiment. As such, space takes on an absolute dominance as the focal point shared by all the agents on the stage, including the audience, in particular, as a fundamental part of the spatial composition. In some instances, the audience actually participated in the rehearsals for pieces by the Performance Group.[29] This led to a new division and distribution of the roles involved in the theatrical ritual fostered by this new treatment of space. Schechner's goal was not to further explore the audience's implication by promoting their physical, corporeal and active participation – or at least that was not the only goal. Rather, the aim was for them to achieve the ability to alternate between empathy and distance with autonomy and according to their own agency, just like what happens during experiences on a city street.[30] Emerging from a contemplative state and re-entering it freely: that was the main goal with regard to audiences that Schechner was investigating with his proposals for immersive theatrical spaces.[31]

TRANSACTIONS IN SPACE

Faced with this desire to train the spectator perceptively, which was enhanced by maneuverability, the Mobile Theater did not assert any limits regarding the events it could host, beyond the ability to form multiple possible enclosures, as noted in the texts of *Experiments in Situation* from Navarro's time in London. It is the material mechanism itself, its architecture, more than the play or the audience, which appears imbued with the axioms of environmental theater promoted by Schechner – more specifically, the first three axioms (Figure 54). In that sense, the Mobile Theater can be described as an architectural environment, which, as demonstrated by the design's successive adaptations for an enormous range of uses, can house multiple social programs beyond the realm of theater.

Schechner's first axiom determined that the theatrical event is a series of transactions that are related to one another in the following way:

The theatrical event includes audience, performers, text (in most cases), sensory stimuli, architectural enclosure (or lack of it), production equipment, technicians, and house personnel (when used). It ranges from nonmatrixed performance to highly formalized traditional theatre: from chance events and intermedia to "the production of plays". A continuum of theatrical events blends one form into the next: "Impure; life" – public events – demonstrations – intermedia (happenings) – environmental theatre – traditional theatre – "Pure; art". It is because

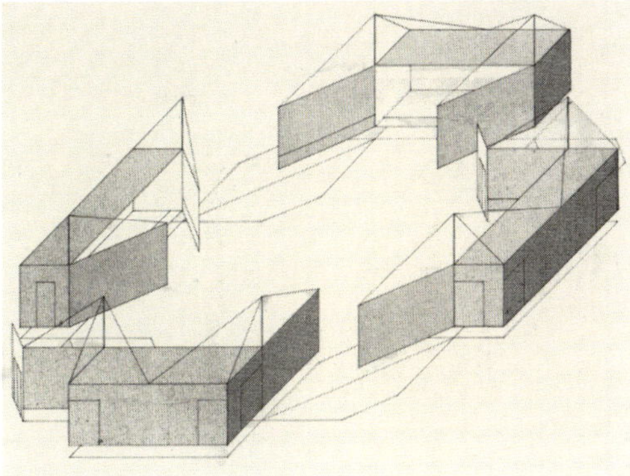

I wish to include this entire range in my definition of theatre that traditional distinctions between art and life no longer function at the root of aesthetics.[32]

Subsequently, he establishes a series of what he calls "three primary transactions", associated with the relational element inherent in the theatrical event, which can take place between actors, between different members of the audience, and finally between actors and audience members. The first transaction (relationships between actors on the stage) fits in perfectly with the Stanislavsky method, in which Diderot's fourth wall forms a radical separation between the stage and the audience in order to guarantee formal perfection and an ideal perception: self-reflective and individual. These principles can also be seen in Javier Navarro's preparatory notes for his experiments in situation from the autumn of 1970 in London. In the drawings, we find a conceptual framework of elements that can form "situations in process" involving the different variables: people, space, time, light, sound, color, air and objects. (Figure 55).

Schechner's second transaction – the relationship between members of the audience – is firmly codified in the role of the theater audience that Schechner refers to as "orthodox" in reference to bourgeois theater, but it attains its fullest capacities in events like what he calls "impure" life, such as political protests with their obvious ability to represent active social cohesion in an opposition to the powers that be.[33] This relationship between members of the audience was minimized in orthodox-bourgeois theater, where behavioral codes for the audience, in sharp contrast with those of the actors, were very limited, strict and inflexible. The aim in that mechanism was to ensure the absolute impossibility of a reversion of roles between actor and spectator, which is characteristic of political protests. Schechner cites the possibilities for working within this sphere of relationships, which he explored in his own work by incorporating the codes inherent in the rites of passage studied by anthropology, specifically the anthropologist Victor Turner.[34] As Schechner asserted:

Unlike the performers, the spectators attend theater unrehearsed; they bring to the theater adherence to decorum learned previously but nevertheless scrupulously applied now. Usually the audience is an impromptu group, meeting at the time/place of the performance but never again meeting as a defined group. Thus uncohesive and unprepared, they are difficult to collectivize and mobilize

Figure 54: Javier Navarro de Zuvillaga, fragment of plan number 9 for the Mobile Theater, showing four trucks during setup. Courtesy of Javier Navarro de Zuvillaga.

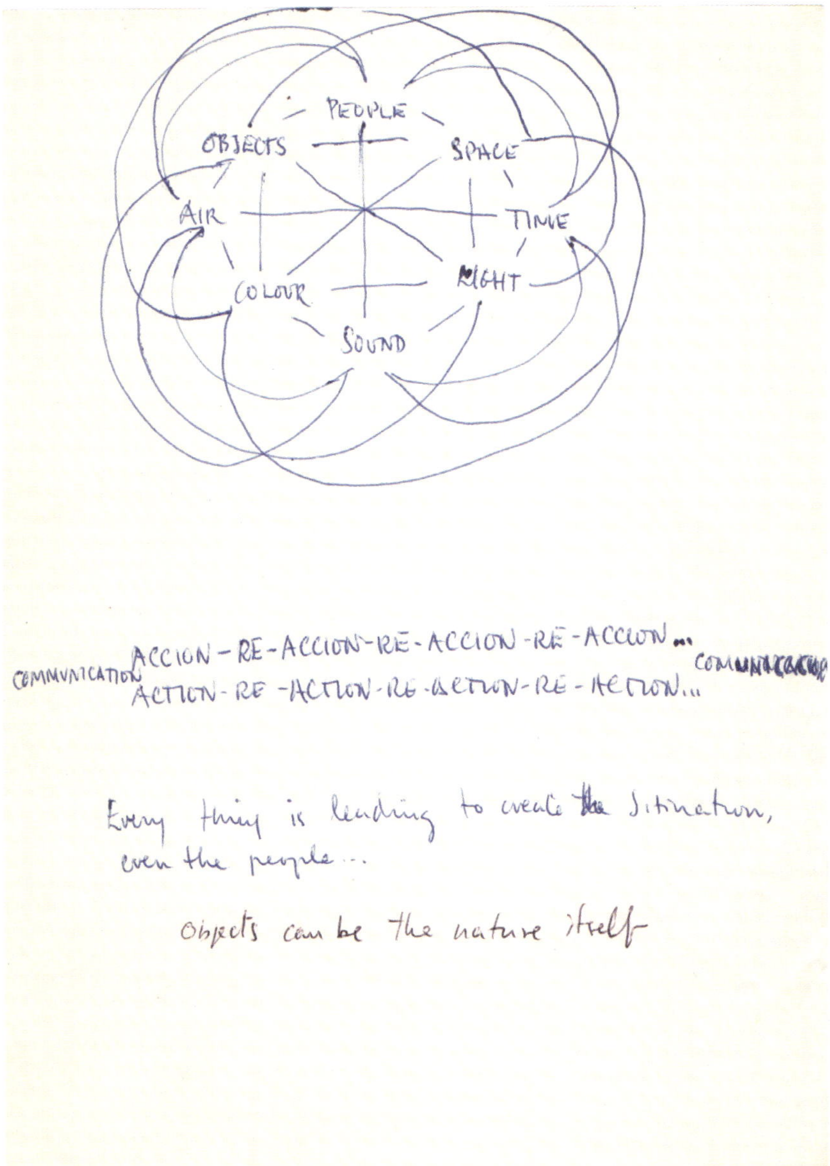

Figure 55: Javier Navarro de Zuvillaga, preparatory drawings for "Towards a Theatre of Situation", London, October 1970. Courtesy of Javier Navarro de Zuvillaga.

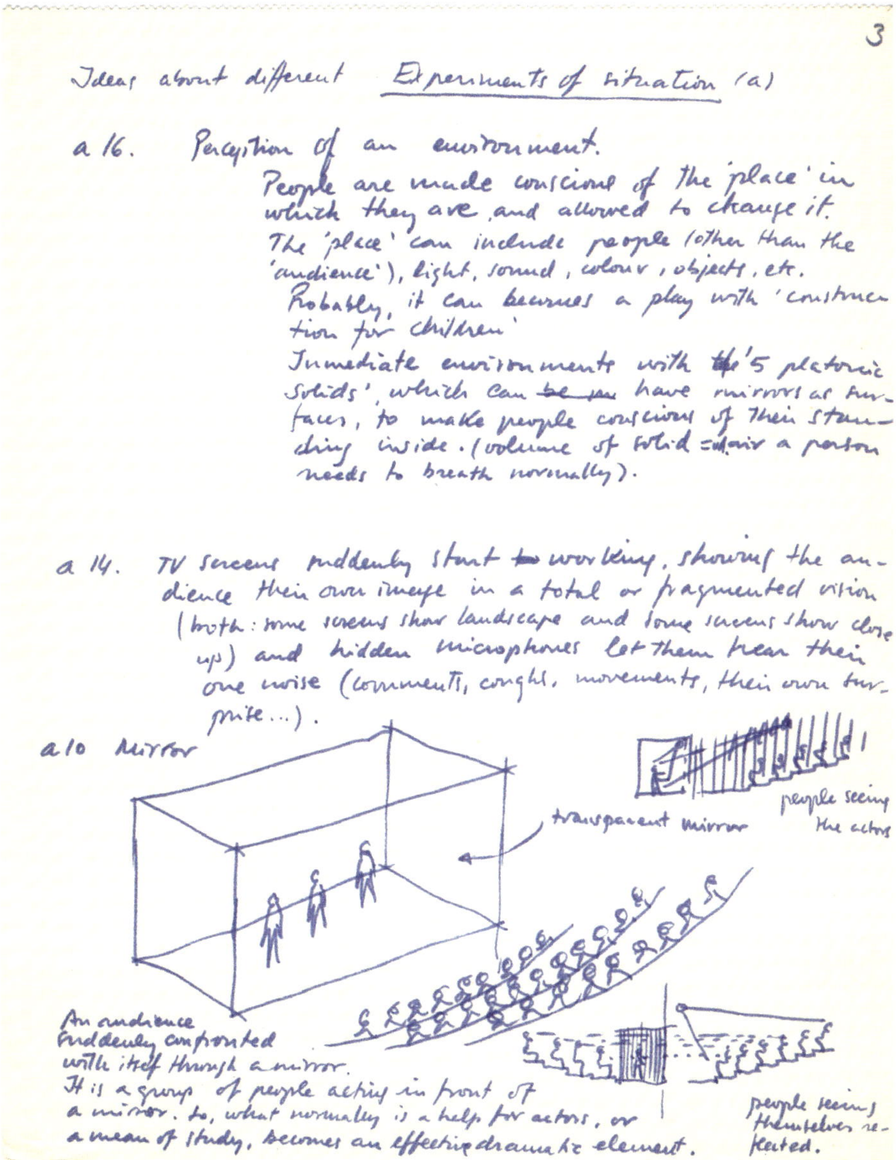

3

Ideas about different Experiments of situation (a)

a 16. Perception of an environment.
People are made conscious of the 'place' in which they are, and allowed to change it.
The 'place' can include people (other than the 'audience'), light, sound, colour, objects, etc.
Probably, it can becomes a play with 'construction for children'
Immediate environments with the '5 platonic solids', which can have mirrors as surfaces, to make people conscious of their standing inside. (volume of solid = air a person needs to breath normally).

a 14. TV screens suddenly start working, showing the audience their own image in a total or fragmented vision (both: some screens show landscape and some screens show close up) and hidden microphones let them hear their one noise (comments, coughs, movements, their own surprise...).

a 10 Mirror

An audience suddenly confronted with itself through a mirror.
It is a group of people acting in front of a mirror. So, what normally is a help for actors, or a mean of study, becomes an effective dramatic element.

Figure 56: Javier Navarro de Zuvillaga, preparatory drawings for "Towards a Theatre of Situation", London, October 1970. Courtesy of Javier Navarro de Zuvillaga.

but, once mobilized, even more difficult to control.[35]

It is clear that Schechner's environmental and immersive space incorporated the audience as a fundamental ingredient over and above any other consideration, and that this maneuver was intended to explore the clash or conflict between "learned decorum" and the codes transmitted by the performance. In this conflict, the audience had no choice but to participate in the proposed scheme, given the (constant) possibility of the reversion of roles. And given Javier Navarro's sketches and notes on his experiments in situation, that same spatial transaction centered on the audience was of maximum interest to him as well (Figure 56). In other rough sketches, we find:

A 16. Perception of an environment. People are made conscious of the "place" in which they are and allowed to change it. The "place" can include people (other than the "audience"), light, sound, colour, objects, etc. Probably, it can become a play with "construction for children". Immediate environment with the "five Platonic solids", which can have mirrors as surfaces, to make people conscious of their standing inside. (Volume of solid=vol. of air a person needs to breathe normally). A 14. TV screens suddenly start working, showing the audience their own image in a total or fragmented vision (some screens show landscapes and some screens show close ups) and hidden microphones let them hear their own noise (comments, coughs, movements, their own surprise…). A 10. Mirror/transparent mirror/people seeing the actors/an audience suddenly confronted with itself through a mirror. It is a group of people acting in front of a mirror. So, what normally is a help for actors, or a means of study, becomes an effective dramatic element/people seeing themselves reflected.

The third primary transaction is, of course, the most studied and practiced relationship in theater – the one that takes place between actor and audience, mediated by behavioral codes. Those codes are translated into decorum on the part of the spectator (in the demonstration of his impersonal identity) and into virtuosity in embodying a role on the part of the actor (in his parallel and contrasting demonstration of multiplicity and singularity). Within this rigid framework, the best possible audience would be, in orthodox bourgeois theater, one that responds harmoniously to the work in its emotional reactions – in other words, in keeping with expectations, in a way that is strictly analogous to how the actor responds with his interpretation of the text and the character. In both cases, for actor and spectator, a text acts as a mediator. For the actor, it is the text of the play, and for the spectator the social contract. For all intents and purposes, Schechner considers the two to be analogous and aims to question them down to their very root.

This series of "primary transactions" is enriched by another series of "secondary transactions", which take on a crucial importance in the case of the Mobile Theater. These secondary transactions were investigated intensely by the reformers of modern theater, and Navarro paid them special attention.[36] This second set of transactions is made up of a four-part relationship: between all the different elements of production (stage design,

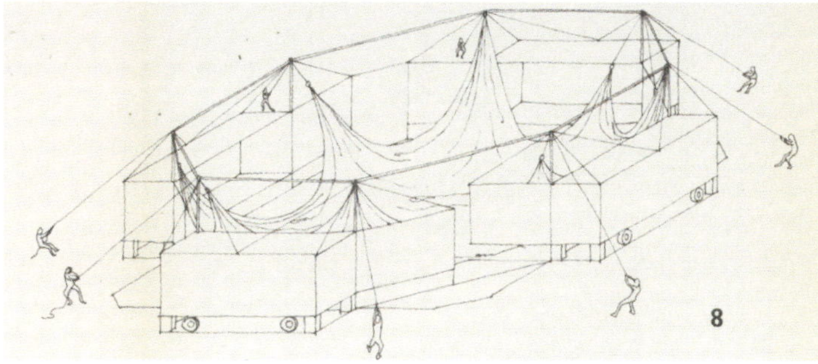

costumes, lighting, sound, makeup, etc.); between those elements and the actors; between those elements and the audience; and, finally, between the production as a whole and the space where it takes place. Moreover, those elements, which in orthodox-bourgeois theater are disconnected from the audience and are prepared without their participation – which are secondary to an extent with regard to their visibility as *work* – become primary, visible and a central point of focus. In that sense, Schechner talks about "performing technicians"[37] in the sense that they have the ability to improvise during the event to the same extent that an actor does with respect to text or score. A fundamental part of the project consists of attempting to transfer those capabilities to the audience as well. To that end, Schechner drew on his analyses of non-Western rites of passage. As a corollary: "The final exchange between performers and the audience is the exchange of space."[38] In the Mobile Theater, the assembly of the building is also a mise-en-scène, and the resource of the "performing technicians" discussed by Schechner is introduced in a very intentional way. Likewise, the possibility of this operation welcoming the audience, who can access the space during the architectural setup, paves the way for or fosters the reversion of roles aspired to by the theatrical avant-garde (Figures 57 and 58). One of the drawings of the Mobile Theater – assembly sequence number 8 – shows eight people setting up the roof while the audience looks on, acting as possible "performing technicians". For an early play, which was Navarro's first professional effort as a stage designer in 1981, he built a train car installed atop a rotating wheel, which contained all the action on stage. In the play, a conductor (Charon) takes the passengers on a train trip (Charon's ferry) against their will. All the passengers have something in common: they are patients in mental institutions and are traveling toward death and insanity.

Schechner's second axiom asserts that "all the space is used for the performance". It is

Figure 57: Javier Navarro de Zuvillaga, stage design for the play *El Cero Transparente* [The Transparent Zero] by Alfonso Vallejo, directed by William Layton at the Círculo de Bellas Artes theater in Madrid, March 11, 1980. Courtesy of Javier Navarro de Zuvillaga.

Figure 58: Javier Navarro de Zuvillaga, fragment of plan number 6 for the Mobile Theater, labeled as Sequence of Arrangement, showing assembly sequence number 8. Image courtesy of Javier Navarro de Zuvillaga.

summed up in the idea that a stable delimitation of space is eliminated or substituted by less rigid limits, drawing on two specific examples provided by anthropology: rites during which the entire space of the tribe practicing them is co-opted for the ritual; and the contemporary equivalent, the modern city street, where Schechner interprets protests as performances executed by the protesters for an audience, which is either present in person or watching on television or reading about it in the newspaper.[39] Schechner took up this idea as a concrete, specific resource for the renovation of the established theater scene. The most direct example was the Living Theater's staging of its series *Six Public Acts* in Ann Arbor in 1975 (Figure 59). In this piece, the Living Theater actors moved through the city streets from one station to the next, faithfully following the spatial framework of medieval mystery plays and their scattered urban stages.

Javier Navarro paid close attention to this kind of transfers when he was designing his Mobile Theater, and in his text he makes explicit mention of the relationship between the degree of transformation of the architectural space and the degree of representativity of the urban space, commenting on the institutional ritualization of power in its urban representations, like in secular parades or religious processions. In both cases, Navarro refers to a specific operation similar to the one laid out by Schechner, the "transgression of space" exercised by the theater over established secular or religious power, and the potential of this operation as a specific working tool characteristic of theatrical culture: the capacity for the profanation of power.

The "found environment" characteristic of the first American happenings made exclusive use of small portions of urban or natural space or the movement of the audience and the action, or even both strategies simultaneously. The goal was to delocalize the setting for art and theater in order to achieve new relationships between audience and action, spectator and actor, while fostering a reversion of roles, through a radical delocalization in physical space meant to foster that aim. This enormous centrality of real space, of the environment on any scale – not only as a backdrop but as a shared physical medium – gave rise to the possibility of interdisciplinary exchanges: music was substantiated as it took on spatial qualities; dance was objectified as it settled in place; sculpture took on temporality as it became performance. Without the spatial medium of the architectural and urban environment, none of that would have been possible.

For its part, the "transformed environment" of Richard Schechner's Performing Garage generated singular and total atmospheres for their pieces, resulting in a more controlled space dedicated to the same goals: the reversion or free circulation of roles in a single shared space, with identical conditions for all the agents involved. To an extent, it represents an analogous historical process experienced by the theater in its shift from the medieval dispersion of urban spaces and genres to the first professionalized settings of the Renaissance, but with one fundamental exception: that

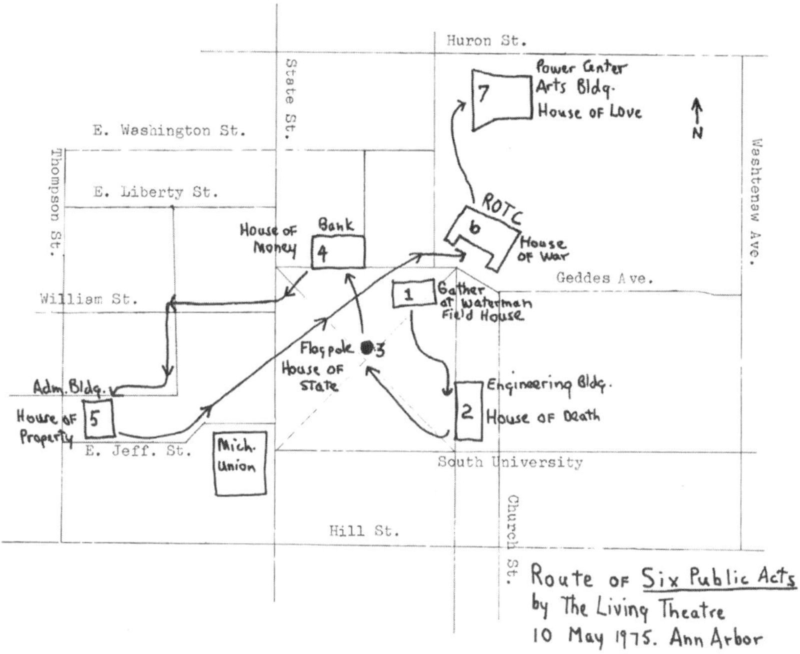

the "transformed environment" remained cautiously within the conceptual realm of the mobile-theater, without carrying over into the institutional crystallization characteristic of both the temple-theater and the machine-theater.

In that sense, Javier Navarro's Mobile Theater, like so many other traveling theaters, can be interpreted in two simultaneous and complementary ways: as a model halfway between the two types of environment, since it contains aspects of both the found environment and the transformed environment; or as a model that surpasses both the others since, paradoxically, it does not connect with cultured or avant-garde theater, but rather with the more atavistic archetypes of the wagon, the caravan or the stage. By adopting the environmental canon based on the transaction of mediums of expression in space, the Mobile Theater participated in the push toward a disintegration of the hierarchies among the different languages involved in theatrical creation. In turn, this promoted the transaction of roles and behaviors, which guaranteed a non-compartmentalized distribution of space, with little or no specialization, contrasting with the ideas of flexibility and versatility espoused by modern architecture, more based on additive compositions within larger containers.

Figure 59: The Living Theater, *Six Public Acts*, plan of the processional route described by the piece's map-score in the city of Ann Arbor, Michigan for the performance on May 10, 1975. Reproduced in Schechner.

Notes

1. Brooks McNamara: "Performance Space. The Environmental Tradition", *Architectural Association Quarterly*, vol. 7, no. 2, 1975, pgs. 3-10. The same text, with slight modifications was published under the title "The Environmental Tradition" in the book edited by Brooks McNamara, Jerry Rojo and Richard Schechner: *Theatres, Spaces, Environments: Eighteen Projects*, New York: Drama Book Specialist Publishers, 1975, pgs. 2-13.

2. Ibid.

3. Javier Navarro de Zuvillaga: "The Disintegration of Theatrical Space", *Architectural Association Quarterly*, vol. 8, no. 4, 1976, pgs. 26-27.

4. Brooks McNamara: "Performance Space. The Environmental Tradition", *Architectural Association Quarterly*, vol. 7, no. 2, 1975, pg. 4.

5. Javier Navarro de Zuvillaga, op. cit., pg. 24.

6. During Schechner's tenure, the *Tulane Drama Review* dedicated issues to the Frenchman Jean Genet (vol. 7, no. 3, 1963), to the German Bertolt Brecht and theater architecture (vol. 7, no. 4, 1963), to the Belgian Michel de Ghelderode (vol. 8, no. 1, 1963), to the Frenchman Antonin Artaud (vol. 8, no. 2, 1963), to Italian postwar theater (vol. 8, no. 3, 1964), to the Elizabethan Christopher Marlow with collaborations from Jerzy Grotowski (vol. 8., no. 4, 1964), to the Russian Konstantin Stanislavski (vol. 9, no. 1, 1964), to American theater and the Open Theater (vol. 9, no. 2, 1964), to psychoanalysis, homosexuality and the Laboratory Theater of Opole (vol. 9, no. 3, 1965), to theater from the American South (vol. 9, no. 4, 1965), to university theater, Broadway and Canadian theater (vol. 10, no. 1, 1965), to happenings and Fluxus (vol. 10, no. 2, 1965), to comedy, Pirandello and Samuel Beckett (vol. 10, no. 3, 1966), to political and guerrilla theater (vol. 10, no. 4, 1966), to expanded cinema (vol. 11, no. 1, 1966), to the British avant-garde (vol. 11, no. 2, 1966), to the Polish, Russian and Hungarian avant-garde (vol. 11, no. 3, 1967), and finally to popular, rural and non-Western theater (vol. 11, no. 4, 1967).

7. Martin Puchner: "The Performance Group: Between Theater and Theory", in James M. Harding and Cindy Rosenthal (eds.), *Restaging the Sixties: Radical Theaters and Their Legacies*, Ann Arbor, Michigan: University of Michigan Press, 2007, pgs. 313-31.

8. Richard Schechner from a conversation published in Brooks McNamara, Jerry Rojo and Richard Schechner: *Theatres, Spaces, Environments: Eighteen Projects*, New York: Drama Book Specialist Publishers, 1975, pg. 80.

9. Ibid., pg. 84.

10. Martin Puchner, op. cit., pg. 369.

11. The origin of the play can be found in Schechner's first environmental production, called *Victims of Duty*, staged at Le Petit Théâtre in New Orleans in 1967, just before he left for New York. The production is documented in detail in Brooks McNamara, Jerry Rojo and Richard Schechner: *Theatres, Spaces, Environments: Eighteen Projects*, New York: Drama Book Specialist Publishers, 1975, pgs. 154-163.

12. Michael Kirby: *Happenings: An Illustrated Anthology*, New York: E. P. Dutton & Co., 1965. Version consulted: "Happenings. An Introduction", in Mariellen R. Sanford (ed.): *Happenings and Other Acts*, London and New York: Routledge, 1995, pgs. 1-24.

13. Ibid., pg. 11.

14. Ibid., pgs. 14-15.

15. Richard Schechner: "Happenings", in Mariellen R. Sanford (ed.): *Happenings and Other Acts*, London and Nueva York: Routledge, 1995, pgs. 181-182.

16. Allan Kaprow: *Assemblage, Environments & Happenings*, New York: Harry N. Abrams Inc Publishers, 1966, pg. 202.

17. Ibid., pgs. 204-205.

18. Javier Navarro de Zuvillaga, op. cit., pg. 29.

19. Ramón Sender, Anthony Martin and Ken Dewey: "Cityscale", *The Tulane Drama Review*, vol. 10, no. 2, 1965, pg. 186a.

20. David W. Bernstein (ed.): *The San Francisco Tape Music Center: 1960s Counterculture and the Avant-Garde.* Berkeley: University of California Press, 2008, pgs. 1-35.

21. Sarah Hill: *San Francisco and the Long 60s*, New York and London: Bloomsbury, 2016. This book contains a thorough and detailed interpretation of the *City Scale* drawing.

22. Liz Glass: "Stirring the Intermix: An Interview with Tony Martin", in Andrew Blauwelt (Ed.): *Hippie Modernism: The Struggle for Utopia*, catalogue for the exhibition of the same name, Walker Art Center, Minneapolis, 2015, pg. 405.

23. Javier Navarro de Zuvillaga, op. cit., pg. 24.

24. Richard Schechner: "6 Axioms for Environmental Theatre," *The Drama Review*, vol. 12, no. 3, 1968, pgs. 41-64.

25. Brooks McNamara and Meredith Monk: "The Scenography of Meredith Monk: An Interview", *The Drama Review*, Vol. 16, no. 1, 1972, pgs. 87-103.

26. Ibid., pg. 89.

27. Deborah Jowitt, dance section from *The Village Voice*, November 4, 1971, pgs. 35-36.

28. Brooks McNamara and Meredith Monk: "The Scenography of Meredith Monk: An Interview", op. cit., pg. 96.

29. Richard Schechner: *Environmental Theatre: An Expanded New Edition Including "Six Axioms for Environmental Theater"*, New York: Applause Acting Series, 1973, 1994, pg. 69. Schechner explains that on Saturday afternoons during the preparations for *Dionysus in 69*, the rehearsals were opened to the public so that the actors could try out a scene in which they exchanged caresses with audience members.

30. Ibid., pg. 19: "In environmental theater there are endless degrees of attention, gradations of involvement. The experience of being a spectator, if you let yourself get into it, is not smooth but roller-coaster."

31. Emeline Wong Finckel: *Navigating Shared Space: Audience Agency and Passivity in Environmental and Immersive Theater*, Thesis, Faculty of Wesleyan University, Middletown, Connecticut, April 2014, pgs. 3-28.

32. Richard Schechner: "6 Axioms for Environmental Theatre", *The Drama Review*, Vol. 12, no. 3, 1968, pg. 41.

33. Ibid., pg. 42.

34. Beginning in 1967, when Schechner moved from New Orleans to New York, his interest in non-Western cultural rites expanded, and he was able to delve into the subject due to the interdepartmental infrastructure offered by New York University. Victor Turner's work had a very strong influence on Schechner, particularly his books *The Forest of Symbols* (1967), in which he studied the symbolic universe of the Ndembu people; *The Ritual Process* (1969), in which he laid out his important concepts of liminality and communitas, even comparing them with the counterculture; *Dramas, Fields, and Metaphors* (1974), in which he studied the structures and physical movements of ritual pilgrimages; and *From Ritual to Theater* (1982), in which he proposed analogies between tribal ritual processes and the theater.

35. Richard Schechner: *Environmental Theatre. An Expanded New Edition including "Six Axioms for Environmental Theater"*, New York: Applause Acting Series, 1973, 1994, pg. XXIV.

36. Richard Schechner: "6 Axioms for Environmental Theatre", *The Drama Review*, Vol. 12, no. 3, 1968 pg. 45.

37. Ibid., pgs. 46-48.

38. Ibid., pg. 48.

39. Ibid., pgs. 48-49.

CHAPTER 3_
POOR-POPULAR-POP

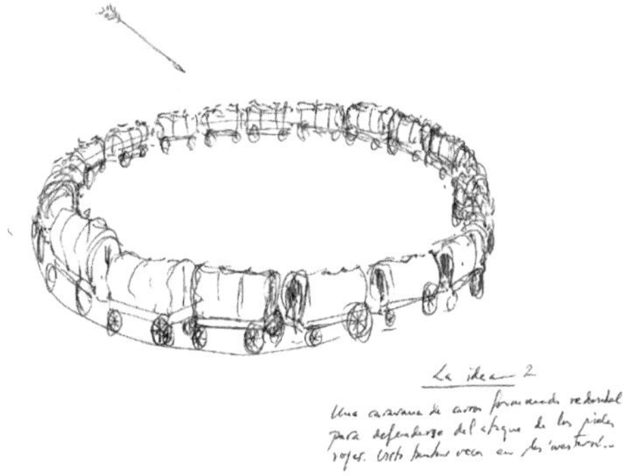

Javier Navarro set up an equivalence between the architectural rhetoric of the theater building and the textual rhetoric of bourgeois drama, and then immediately advocated for an absence of rhetoric on the stage, in what he called poor theater, borrowing terminology and ideas from Jerzy Grotowski (1933-1999).[1] It was the same operation announced by Richard Wagner in his day, when he asserted that his Bayreuth theater would be poor, perhaps made of wood, a simple enclosure or covered courtyard for performances.[2] From that time forward, the idea of the disintegration of theatrical space, understood as an institutional and perfectly formalized architectural space that needs to undergo a destructive process to be regenerated, was a constant for a fundamental part of the avant-garde.

The idea of poverty in theater refers both to a limited range of material elements and to the absence of a dependence or subordination to other artistic languages, whether text, scenery, or theater architecture, retaining the actor-spectator dialectic as the fundamental core. Contrasting with the idea of the temple-theater, which at its height implied a close collaboration among all art forms, the poor theater left behind the idea of the temple and the machine and presented itself as the theater of *environment*, with the archetype of the mobile theater (Figures 60 and 61). In the description of poor theater, poverty is contrasted with what Grotowski called rich theater, the theater of synthesis, or even total theater.[3] In its specific spatial formalization, the work of Grotowski and his Laboratory Theater belongs to the theater of environment, since its most influential and well-known work, carried out between 1960 and 1965, was in association with the architect Jerzy Gurawski (1935). Like in the American case, largely under its influence, the experiment was shaped by a very specific architectural space, the so-called *Teatr 13 Rzędów* in Opole, Poland (Theater of 13 Rows), which Grotowski took over in 1959

Figure 60: Idea 1 Wagons heading west. Drawing by Javier Navarro de Zuvillaga, n/d.

Figure 61: Idea 2 A wagon train forming a circle to protect against an Indian attack. Seen countless times in western movies. Drawing by Javier Navarro de Zuvillaga, n/d.

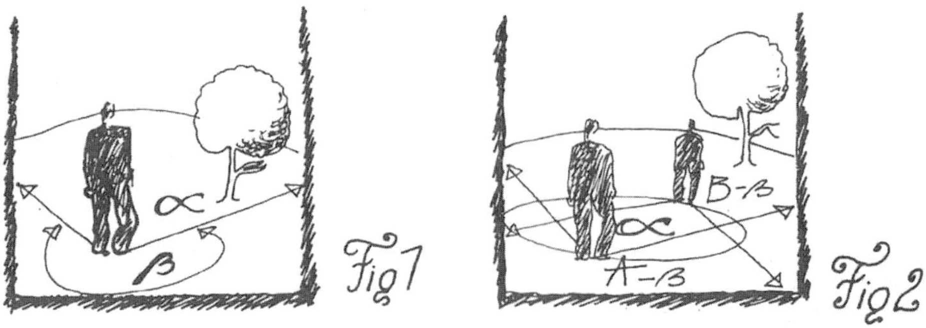

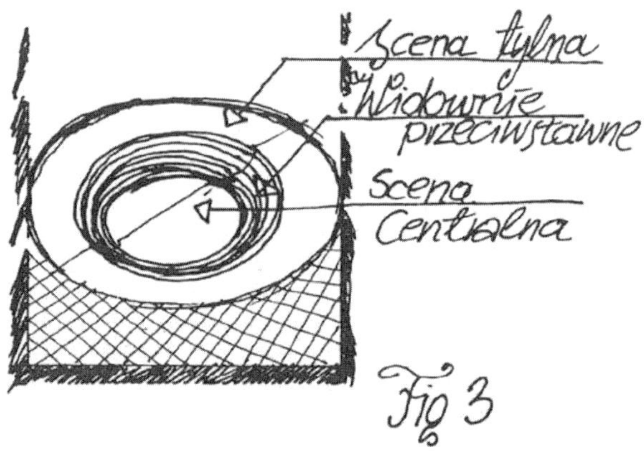

Figure 62: Diagrams 1 and 2 of the visual field according to Jerzy Gurawski, 1959.

Figure 63: Diagram 3 of the theatrical space according to Jerzy Gurawski, 1959.

at the age of 26. The space was quite small – 12 m x 7 m, and 3 m high – and there was only one entrance. As the name indicates, there were 13 rows for the audience, with a total of 116 seats maximum if the stage was set up Italian-style, which, significantly enough, never occurred.[4]

THE 13 ROWS IN OPOLE

As a student at the School of Architecture at the Technical University in Kraków in 1959, Gurawski won an award for his design for a traveling theater, inspired by the projects by Erwin Piscator and Vsévolod Meyerhold using simple moving mechanisms. For his graduation project the following year, he designed a very different theatrical mechanism drawing on other references: specifically, paratheatrical activities from popular culture, medieval mystery plays, Spanish bullfighting, the stands at traveling fairs, and circus tents.[5] What most caught Gurawski's attention were typological persistence and material poverty, tied in with the popular nature of those traditions. Because of its association with low culture and material poverty, popular tradition showed a degree of innovation that was infinitesimal compared to bourgeois theater, where permanence was constantly challenged by novelties of all kinds, namely in technical aspects.

Based on a study of the essential space of theater, Gurawski identified what he called "intuitional space", which is what surrounds a spectator beyond his or her field of vision. In an initial diagram that portrays a single spectator, he used the Greek letter α to indicate the person's active field of vision and the letter β to indicate the non-visual field, which he called intuitional space. In a second diagram depicting two spectators, where the second spectator, B, is a potential actor for the first, A, the entirety of B's space – both the visible, α, and the intuited, β – is visible space for A (Figure 62). In that sense: "The reactions of A in response to the intuitional space of B are a reflection of the impressions and the experience of events that are invisible to B." Based on this analysis, a third diagram emerges (Figure 63), in which there is an ideal theatrical space with seating areas that face one another (*widownie przeciwstawne*), a central stage (*scena centralna*), and a rear stage (*scena tylna*) that surrounds the audience.[6]

This simple diagram was what caught Grotowski's attention and sparked the beginning of a close collaboration with Gurawski. Their first joint production was *Shakuntala*, an ancient 5th-century Hindu erotic drama, which Grotowski adapted. There were two seating areas facing one another with a fixed phallic motif in the middle. The action was subject to continuous interferences from the center and from one side of the seating areas to the other, both in front and behind, simultaneously activating both visible and intuitional spaces for everyone – the actors and the audience alike. Following this spatial experiment, the Laboratory Theater produced a number of pieces with Gurawski. The collaboration ended in 1965 with *The Constant Prince*, in the new theater in Kraków, where the company moved after the Opole closed that same year.[7]

Spaces derived from the medieval popular tradition were used for all these plays, with specific allusions to the *mansions* from religious mystery plays and the characteristic absence of spatial illusion, along with a raw realism in the material conditions that fits in perfectly with the idea of poverty. In *Towards*

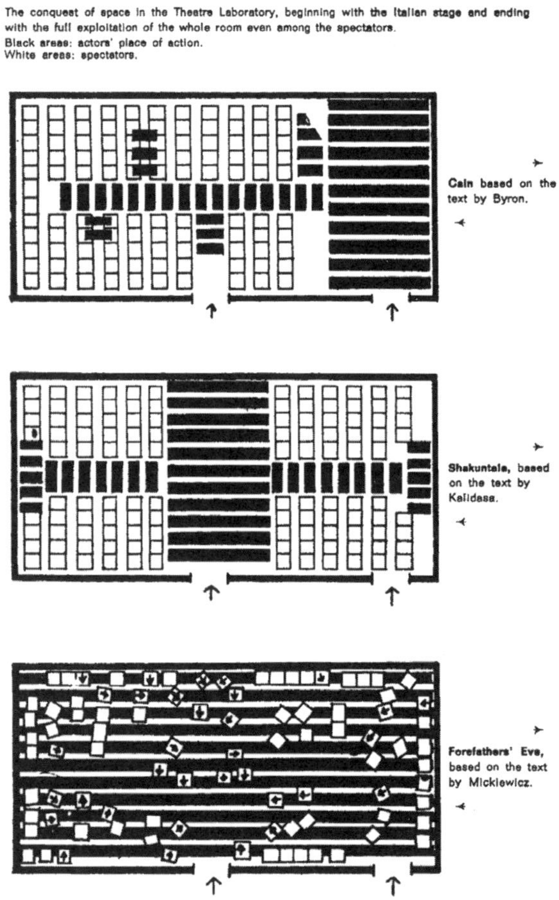

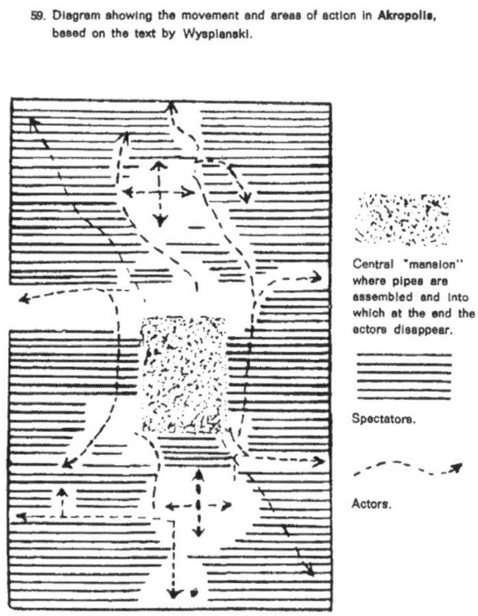

Figure 64: Diagram of the space for *Kain, Shakuntala* and *Dziady*. The caption indicates that the drawing illustrates "the conquest of space in the Theatre Laboratory". Source: *Towards a Poor Theatre*, 1968.

Figure 65: Diagram of the space for *Akropolis*. The caption mentions a central "mansion" and shows a striped area for spectators around it. Source: *Towards a Poor Theatre*, 1968.

a *Poor Theatre*, published in 1968, Grotowski included a famous diagram that presents three of the spatial layouts used by the Laboratory Theater: *Kain* (1959), *Shakuntala* (1960) and *Dziady* (1961).[8] The diagrams (Figure 64) show the space abstracted into simple forms (squares and stripes), using white for the audience and black for the actors, which is strikingly similar to a graphic abstraction of urban space in different modes of operation, inviting a rather direct comparison.

The diagrammatic drawings in Grotowski's book are a great interpretative source for drawing parallels between those theatrical spaces and urban space. The diagram of *Akropolis* (1962), with a central stage and double seating area alludes directly to the medieval French word "mansion" to refer to the central stage, surrounded by a series of stripes that correspond to the mass of spectators, crossed, in turn, by the actors' lines of movement, like dynamic vectors (Figure 65). For *Dziady* (1961) the space was built across multiple levels, with the audience spread out, so that it was never possible to perceive, all at once, all the actions taking place, scattered throughout the space. The perceptual mechanism was somewhere between a street, a square and a medieval marketplace.

For *Kordian* (1962), Gurawski placed beds all around the theater, many of which were steel-framed bunk beds, so that they would be shared by both actors and audience members (Figure 66). For a mobile spectator, the space – which recreated a mental institution – functioned similarly to the layout of the "mansions" in a medieval mystery play, where the action moved from one place to

Figure 66: Diagram of the space for *Kordian*, by Jerzi Gurawski. In white, the spectators; in black, the actors. Source: *Towards a Poor Theatre,* 1968.

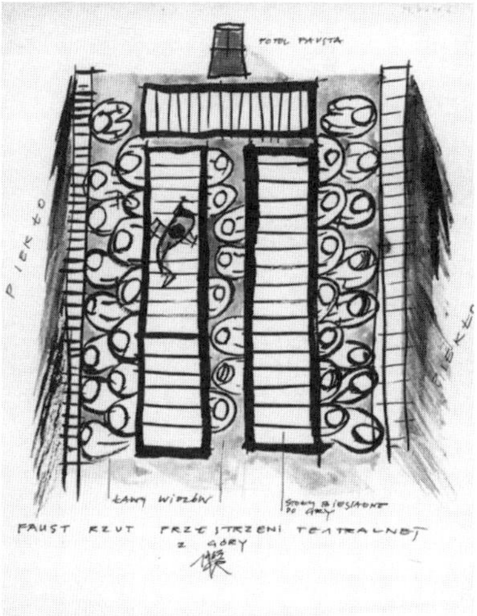

Figure 67: Diagram of the space for *Dr. Faustus*. The notes identify "Faust's chair" (above), "hell" (right and left), "benches for the audience" (lower left) and "dining tables for acting on" (lower right), by Jerzi Gurawski.

Figure 68: Space for *Dr. Faustus*. Photograph by Opiola-Moskwiak. Source: *Towards a Poor Theatre,* 1968.

another, occasionally incorporating nearby spectators who were forced to adapt their behavior upon feeling themselves observed or being treated like patients in the institution. From another possible point of view, it resembled a compact city block made up of transparent houses, which spectators could walk around or go inside, or a large house made up of interconnecting rooms in a row, linked together in both directions of the space.

For *Dr. Faustus* (1963), Gurawski built a long table with two planks crossing the entire space, capped by a perpendicular piece on one end, giving the diagram the shape of a horizontal structure in the form of a double T, made up of two long strips and one narrow one (Figures 67 and 68). The audience sat along the table, and the action took place on top of it, as Faust played out his life. The banquet, the last supper or the cabaret are the spatial structures of reference in this case. As in the other plays, the space aimed to construct a ritual situation that was familiar to everyone, belonging either to the sphere of daily life, or to the religious or secular popular repertoire.

The final collaboration between Gurawski and the Laboratory Theater closed out with the play that internationalized the company and made it famous: *The Constant Prince* (1965), an adaptation of Calderón de la Barca's work about the life of Infante Fernando of Portugal. In it, the space of the action was entirely cut off from the audience by a physical barrier, above which the spectators could observe the central scene, almost on their tiptoes. The construction was painted black and, according to Gurawski, it was directly suggested by the spatial structure of a bull

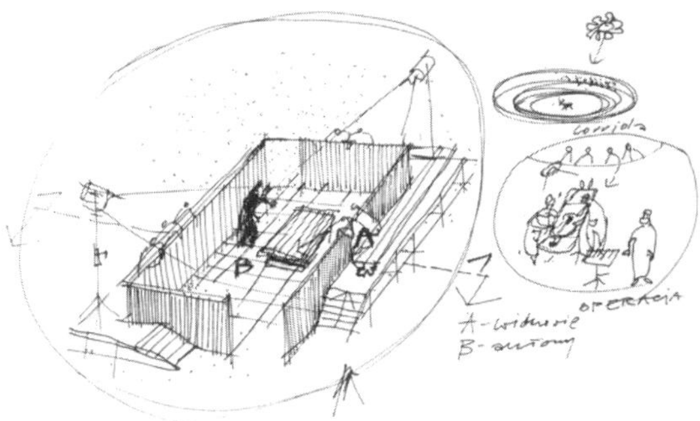

ring or an operating theater (Figures 69 and 70). The main character, Infante Fernando, was situated on the plinth/altar/tomb in the center, and around him, following the movement of a flock of birds, the members of the court gathered, keeping him prisoner, under torture.[9] The play represented a series of rituals characteristic of the Catholic Passion: mocking, acceptance of the cross, torture by flagellation, crowning with thorns, the *Ecce Homo* or the lamentation, followed by the resurrection or ascension. Perhaps even more significantly, the setup also resembled the public space of the scaffold, one of the most enduring theaters of cruelty in the history of the West, due to the tireless brutality of the Catholic church in dealing with its dissidents.

If the scaffold is the culmination, it is also the origin. Javier Navarro astutely related the medieval mystery play seen in the depiction of the martyrdom of Saint Apollonia with Grotowski's poor theater, by considering the martyrdom of the saint to be an original precedent of the mobile theater of environment.[10] In the miniature painted by Jean Fouquet for the *Livre d'heures d'Etienne Chevalier* (1465), there is a semicircular structure in the background made up of two-story *mansions* with the characteristic endpoints: heaven on the left with a staircase leading upwards, and hell on the right with the hellmouth. The martyr is in the center, suffering from a torture that involves pulling out her teeth before she dies.[11] The emperor Philip the Arab stands next to the saint, alongside two of her torturers and a figure who carries a book in his left hand and a staff in his right hand, acting as the *metteur en scène* for the spectators (Figure 71). The saint's similarities with Infante

Figure 69: Diagram of the space for *The Constant Prince*, by Jerzi Gurawski.

Figure 70: Space for *The Constant Prince*. Photograph by Bernard. Source: *Towards a Poor Theatre*, 1968.

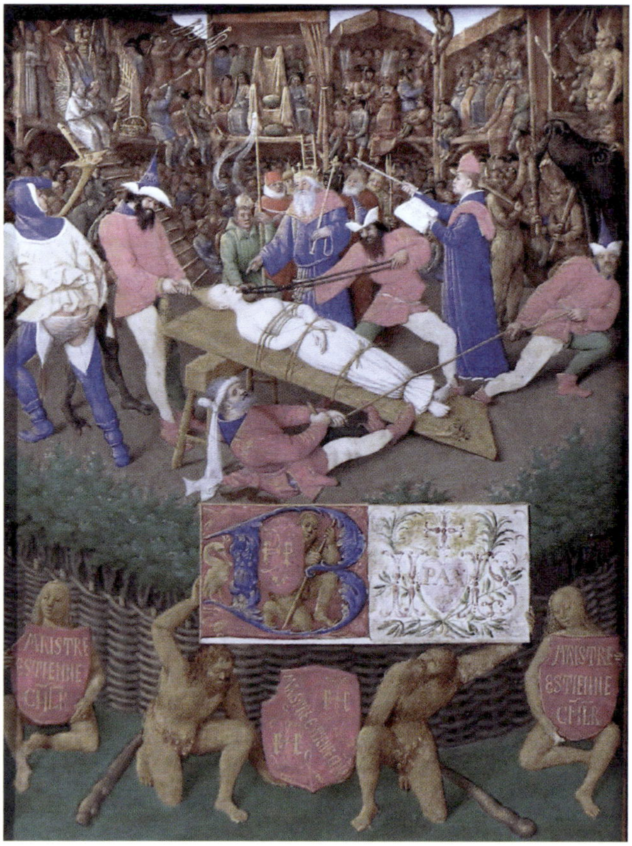

Figure 71: *Martyrdom of St. Apollonia* by Jean Fouquet, from *Livre d'heures d'Etienne Chevalier*, 1465. Musée Condé in the Château de Chantilly.

Fernando, and the torturers' with the courtesans, forming two concentric circles for the audience's attention, is glaringly obvious in a comparison of the two spatial models, in addition to generating a meta-architectural spatial mechanism that is specifically theatrical, displaying one architecture within another.

Streets, wagons, platforms, tents, and finally a scaffold were the architectural elements from the tradition of popular theater which Grotowski boiled down to their essence in each of his architectural experiments with Gurawski. Together, they constructed a highly recognizable scenographic language. The cycle finished naturally with the scaffold for *The Constant Prince* in 1965, which marked an endpoint for the Laboratory Theater's architectural experiments with the spaces of popular representation.

THE CANOPIED CONTAINER

The archetypes of spaces for popular entertainment were a major source of inspiration for avant-garde theater in the 1960s and 70s. In his 1976 text, Navarro included continuous references to those archetypes, which appear occasionally in his narrative, leaving traces that are essential to understanding the cultural atmosphere in which he developed his Mobile Theater (Figure 72). They are unconnected traces which he did not take the time to systematize. However, a more precise and ordered analysis of those archetypes was offered, ágain, by the American Brooks McNamara in 1974. He was responsible for an issue of *The Drama Review* dedicated to popular entertainment. In the introduction, McNamara defines three basic types of popular entertainment: variety theater, popular theater and entertainment

Figure 72: *Prodige de la Chimie*, engraving by Maurisset from 1839, satirizing the sale of Lion Ointment. A man with a lion's head stands on a stage, while a long line of curious people wait their turn for some of the product. In the background is a balloon that reads: *n. 537. Envoi de Pommade aux Habitants de la Lune.* Smithsonian National Air and Space Museum, Washington DC.

environments. In the article he wrote for the issue, he fine-tunes this classification, considering seven types of possible architectural spaces for those popular theatrical forms:

Traditional popular scenography may be divided into seven broad categories based on the ways in which space and design are employed by the showman: 1) booths and other arrangements of space by itinerant street performers; 2) improvised theatres; 3) the scenography of variety entertainments; 4) the scenography of popular theatre; 5) performance spaces devoted to spectacle or special effects; 6) processional forms; and 7) entertainment environments such as the traveling carnival and the amusement park, where the spectator himself organizes the event. Although nothing may be said to be universally true about these approaches to scenography, it is clear that they often involve a naive and casual view of design, a strong emphasis on trick-work, fantasy and spectacle, and a lack of interest in such conventional scenic values as verisimilitude, consistency, and so-called good taste. Popular design seems to be strongly traditional and nonacademic, far more concerned with craft than art and far more involved with objects than with ideas. At its best, it produces vital and imaginative solutions to basic problems of performance space and design.[12]

Navarro's Mobile Theater responds directly to types six and seven, in its own configuration. It is clearly a processional architectural form, intended to generate, upon reaching its destination, a non-predetermined entertainment environment. But it is also entirely open to the other possibilities, since one of the trucks can be an open-air theater booth, a complete space can be improvised using its elements, the trucks carry elemental and impoverished scenographic elements, and they are prepared to present special effects that are not directly theatrical. Moreover, Navarro used references that were specific to popular culture and theater in Spain, including Easter processions or Palm Sunday celebrations, to insert his own artefact into that tradition, where the permanence of the archetype takes precedence over typological novelty, the possibility of the emergence of fantasy over pre-designed verisimilitude, and, ultimately, objects over ideas. The fundamental references that Navarro used are also associated with itinerant theater in booths, processional forms, improvised theater and the entertainment environment, as indicated by McNamara.

The first of Navarro's references is the *envelat*, a self-supporting tent structure typical of 19th- and 20th-century Catalan culture, set up for outdoor celebrations in cities and towns across Catalonia. It is no coincidence that Navarro refers to these *envelats* in his article from 1976. The illustration he included in the article came from the influential magazine *Arquitecturas Bis*, specifically from issue number 5, published in 1975, at a time when Navarro was likely writing his text (Figure 73).[13] Part of the political agenda of the magazine, published in Spanish in Barcelona and distributed throughout Spain, was to highlight the specificity of Catalan culture, both high modern culture and, to a larger extent, popular and traditional culture, in a clear move to set up an equivalence between high and low culture, and in an attempt to recognize cultural fringe areas.[14] The article reproduced a text by the architect Lluís Domènech i Montaner, known for his influence on *modernisme*, published in *Historia General del Arte* in 1886, at the

height of the popularity of the *envelat* in Catalan culture.

Aptly enough, Domènech i Montaner included his text on the *envelats* in a curious section, the section dedicated to primitive architecture.[15] The section provided an analysis of the tents built by nomads in central Asia, the Jewish tabernacle, and Tuareg structures – i.e., geographical-cultural archetypes of ancestral architectural technologies associated with very specific cultural identities (Figures 74 and 75). This tactic lent the *envelat* a mythic, ahistorical, status and an unknown origin, integrated into the grand tradition of human construction. Following a description of the use of the *envelat* as a monumental structure, improvised in just a few hours and without interior supports, with the capacity to house up to two or three thousand people for a celebration, Domènech i Montaner provided a lengthy and detailed description of the artefact in its aesthetic principles, its dimensions, the rationality of its components and the swiftness of its assembly and disassembly. He finished the text with allusions to the unknown origin of the *envelat* and references to the Roman velarium, Eastern tents, or the Mediterranean structures that combined tents with the rigging of ships. Domènech i Montaner's reading situated the *envelat* midway between a vernacular functionalism and a monumentality awash with symbolism.

Three years before *Arquitecturas Bis*, the magazine *Serra d'Or*, published in Catalan by the Abbey of Montserrat and with a more local area of influence, included an article on the same subject by the critic Alexandre Cirici Pellicer in the issue for December 1972.[16] In this text, the *envelat* is described

Figure 73: Illustration of an *envelat* according to Lluís Domènech i Montaner, reproduced in *Historia General del Arte*, vol. 1, 1886. University of Barcelona, Humanities Library.

with even more technical precision, listing each of its elements and investigating its etymology, and including a magnificent section drawn by Cirici himself (Figure 76), showing surprising similarities with the technological structures being produced in international architecture during the same period (Figure 77). Cirici, however, unlike Domènech i Montaner, was very explicit about the cultural archaeology of the *envelat* and its historical origin, which he located with precision in 1840, and which was followed by a rapid development that achieved complete stability in 1870. Specifically, he attributed the invention of the *envelat* to the traditional knowledge of fishermen from the Maresme, a coastal region near Barcelona, drawing on small-scale canvas structures made using boat sails, booms and halyards or cord. Through this operation of intuitive technological transfer, the sailors set up canopies to provide shelter from the rain and sun on the beach during meals or celebrations.

As such, Cirici demonstrated that the *envelat* originated with DIY and sailors, a slight transgression of nautical technique in response to a social need, which does not fit in quite as easily with the greater tectonic tradition of the primitive vernacular (Figure 78). In other words, the *envelat* was more similar to the *adhocism* professed by Charles Jencks,[17] one of Javier Navarro's advisors in London, than the quasi-ontological theories of Viollet-le-Duc, which Domènech i Montaner seemed to suggest in his assessment of the popular structures (Figure 79). Cirici's reading of the *envelat* was much more historically accurate than Domènech i Montaner's, given that their respective critical objectives were very different. While Domènech i Mon-

Figure 74: Illustration number 140 from *Historia General del Arte*, vol. 1, 1886, which shows the primitive hut as rendered by Viollet-le-Duc. University of Barcelona, Humanities Library.

Figure 75: Illustration number 153 from *Historia General del Arte*, vol. 1, 1886, which shows a traditional tent in the deserts of Central Asia as rendered by Viollet-le-Duc. University of Barcelona, Humanities Library.

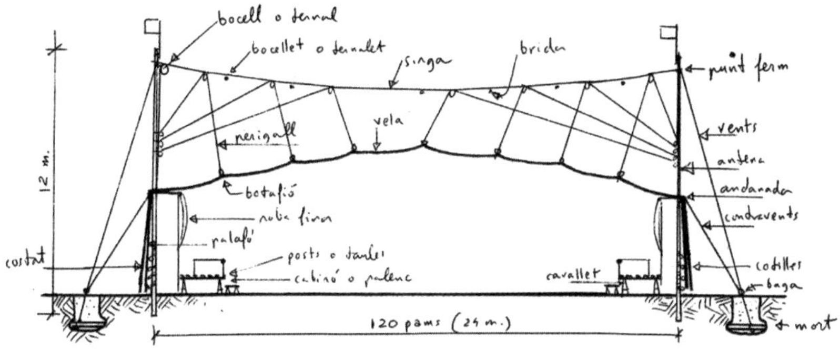

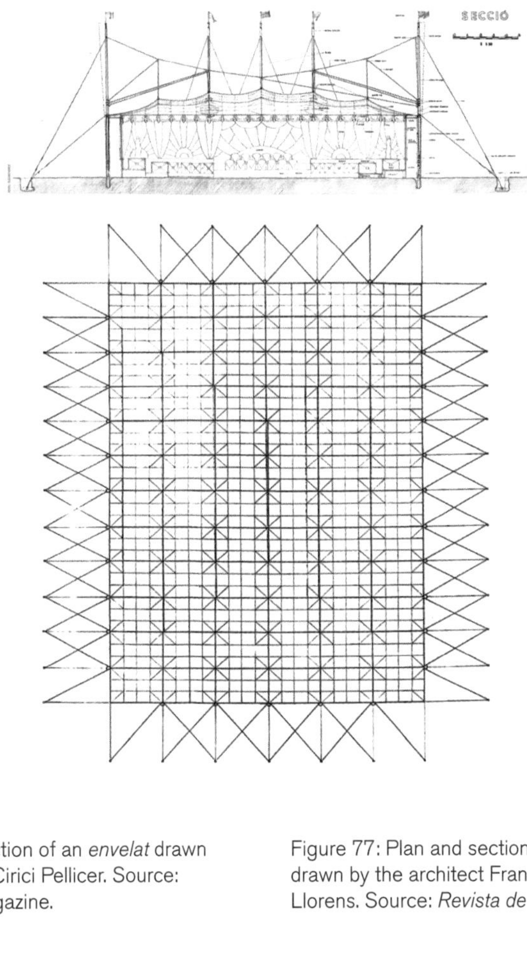

Figure 76: Section of an *envelat* drawn by Alexandre Cirici Pellicer. Source: *Serra d'Or* magazine.

Figure 77: Plan and section of an *envelat* drawn by the architect Francesc Albardané i Llorens. Source: *Revista de Girona*.

taner, with his interpretation, sought continuity with a more universal atavistic tradition, aiming to insert the *envelat* into a saga that was already assimilated into architectural high culture, Cirici engaged in a strictly historiographic reading, rather than an interpretation. Nonetheless, he also offered a contemporary understanding of the *envelat* that was very characteristic of his time: no historical interpretation can be neutral. Cirici blended the vectors of poor, popular and pop, providing a narrative of the *envelat* as an *adhocist* product, something very similar to what took place with Javier Navarro's Mobile Theater. It is not often that events corroborate history and its theories, which stubbornly seem to maintain a certain independence from events themselves, even to the point of violently imposing themselves on the facts in order to construct authoritative narratives. On this occasion, however, Cirici was the lucky beneficiary of how events played out.

Navarro's Mobile Theater as a highly technified *envelat* was another version of an alternative (even more poor, popular and pop) typological update of the type of lightweight structure with which Cirici was closely familiar. The structure in question was a temporary installation built by the artist Lluís Jové (1948-1991) in the Plaça Vella in Terrassa on December 3, 1972.[18] In the limited number of remaining photographs documenting the event, we see a structure that is built – just like the canopy of an *envelat* – without any interior supports and entirely suspended from a system of cables (Figures 80 and 81). The material used were plastic bags, opened up and tied together to create a translucent covering intended to stretch across the urban square in Terrassa and house a public event. Cirici wrote a series

Figure 78: Fishing boats on the Catalan coast. Photograph by Esteve Puig. Photographic Archive of Barcelona.

Figure 79: Dancing under the *envelat* set up by Esquerra Republicana de Catalunya (ERC) for the town festival in Santa Coloma de Gramanet, September 1, 1935. Photograph by Pérez de Rozas. Photographic Archive of Barcelona.

of notes that year about five artists who were working in that precarious, conceptual and clearly *adhocist* sphere: Josep Ponsatí, Francesc Torres, Josep Benito, Antoni Muntadas and Lluís Jové.[19] In his notes, Cirici commented that they were joined together by a set of values counter to institutional culture: a disdain for the fixed object with an intended permanence or as the manifestation of an essence, for the isolated event that aims to exist as a whole in and of itself, and for the individual event as the emanation of a personality or an inspiration. These are all values that contrast with the ones revealed by the archetypes referred to by Domènech i Montaner in his historical reading of the *envelat*, and which we can project literally onto the Mobile Theater.

The fact that the precarious and flexible spaces like *envelats* do not constitute, in and of themselves, a closed or stable cultural form or a specific individual or collective identity is because they require two elements to give them their cultural meaning and identity. Those two elements are: the semiotic contents, or the events that take place inside them; and the protagonists of those events, the social agents who activate the semiotic contents – what we call the audience. Moreover, something intriguing happens with the *envelat*, which it shares with the Mobile Theater: although *envelats* are self-supporting, self-sufficient, independent structures, they never appear outside the urban fabric in isolated areas, unlike the Jewish tabernacle or the Tuareg tent, for example. Instead, they always establish a relationship of temporary completion or culmination with respect to the existing urban milieu.

This is similar to the role of any mobile theater, which complements the urban form and its cultural life momentarily, as opposed to carrying out an operation of cultural foun-

Figure 80: Lluís Jové, intervention using plastic bags in the Plaça Vella in Terrassa, December 3, 1972. Courtesy of Antoni Verdaguer.

Figure 81: Lluís Jové, intervention using plastic bags in the Plaça Vella in Terrassa, December 3, 1972. Courtesy of Antoni Verdaguer.

dation from scratch. When they are taken down at the end of the celebrations, it will always seem, for a time, like something is missing (Figure 82).

THESPIS' WAGON WITH A COMBUSTION ENGINE

Within the same argument, Navarro also referred to a very specific theatrical initiative in Spanish history: the travelling university theater company called La Barraca [The Wagon]. The project, spearheaded by the government of the Spanish Republic in 1931, was meant to address a very specific shortfall and a devastating statistical assessment: in that year, between 34% and 44% of the country's 25 million inhabitants were reported to be illiterate.[20] The Republic implemented an enlightened reformist cultural policy centered on three complementary popular theater initiatives: the La Barraca university theater, developed and directed by Federico García Lorca and the writer and filmmaker Eduardo Ugalde; the Teatro del Pueblo [People's Theater] as part of the Misiones Pedagógicas [Pedagogical Missions], led by the playwright Alejandro Casona; and the Valencia University theater, El Búho [The Owl], directed by the writer and playwright Max Aub.[21]

The first two initiatives shared the characteristic of itinerancy, and they were all derived from the progressive liberal tradition of Krausism and its reception in Spain. In particular, they were promoted by the Institución Libre de Enseñanza [Free Educational Institution], founded in 1876 by Laurenciano Figueroa together with Francisco Giner de los Ríos, Gumersindo Azcárate, Teodoro Sainz Rueda and Nicolás Salmerón,

Figure 82: *Envelat* in the Plaça d'Espanya in Barcelona before its urban development, 1908. Photograph by Frederic Barrell. Photographic Archive of Barcelona.

among others, which remained active until the outbreak of the Civil War in 1936.[22] The Misiones Pedagógicas were begun on May 29, 1931, and each initiative, work type or format was called a "mission". Each mission travelled around the country, remaining at its destination anywhere from one day to two weeks, and the "missionaries" transported films, books or music in their portable installations. These initial missions were complemented by two others that required more specific mobile architectures, created by adapting trucks: the Museo Circulante [Travelling Museum] and the Teatro del Pueblo.

The Museo Circulante was a convoy that carried two collections of 14 copies of paintings from the collection of the Museo del Prado.[23] The initiative transported the copies of paintings by El Greco, Murillo, Ribera, Goya and Velázquez to rural areas, in trucks or even on the backs of mules when necessary, and the paintings were exhibited in institutional spaces such as town halls, schools, civic centers or workers' associations. A similar mechanism was put into place for the Teatro del Pueblo, which relied on trucks to transport the physical elements necessary to perform a theatrical repertoire of pieces by classical authors. There was a wooden stage measuring 4 m wide by 6 m deep, with a proscenium and a burlap background curtain toward the middle, with sections that opened on either side, mounted on top of a wooden frame.[24]

The university theater La Barraca was designed as a travelling theater company made up of university students who would set up a portable stage in town squares in keeping with the popular tradition of travelling theater associated with the figures called

Figure 83: La Barraca. Company members in front of the truck. Centro Federico García Lorca. Federico García Lorca Archives.

cómicos de la legua [itinerant actors of the Renaissance and the Golden Age of Spanish Theater].[25] In their song, the members of La Barraca called themselves "Thespis' new wagon with a combustion engine" (Figure 83). La Barraca was founded in November 1931, when Lorca proposed the idea of a travelling theater group to the Unión Federal de Estudiantes Hispanos (UFEH), which held an ordinary congress from November 8th to the 16th of that year. On November 25, the Minister of Justice, Fernando de los Ríos, talked to a group of journalists at the Congress of Deputies about an offer that the Federación Universitaria Escolar (FUE) had made to the Minister of Public Instruction, Marcelino Domingo, for the creation of a university theater group intended to disseminate the classics. The students presented a two-part project: on the one hand a permanent free theater, with an orchestra, for residents of the capital; and, on the other, a travelling "university stage" to visit towns and villages and perform a classical repertoire, in addition to projecting films and replaying radio broadcasts. The minister agreed to fund only the second project, which was much more profitable politically and cheaper. Lorca provided more information in an interview published in December of 1931:

La Barraca will have two stages [...] We will set up a permanent booth in Madrid, in a public park if possible, which will operate all through the winter, without interfering with the students' studies. Then, there will be a travelling stage, what you've called [referring to the interviewer] *our 'wagon'. It will travel on a truck around Madrid, and to towns across La Mancha, on Sundays and during vacation periods. During the summer months, anyone who wants to can come on a longer tour across Spain.*[26]

Once the project was given official political backing, the UFEH studied it further and took over responsibility. The winter theater was designed so it could be disassembled, to put on free performances for workers and students, and paid performances for members of the *Friends of La Barraca*. The funds raised from the latter sessions, along with the grant money from the government, helped to finance the summer tours. However, the students' difficulty in combining university studies with an intense commitment to the project, along with the possibility of attacks from professional theater companies alleging unfair competition, ultimately limited the project to just a travelling theater. When Fernando de los Ríos was appointed the new Minister of Public Instruction on December 15, 1931, the project was ensured support from the state administration. Fernando de los Ríos was a friend of the Lorca family and had offered institutional support in the past. In a parliamentary session on March 23, 1932, which included a debate on the national budget, a grant of 100,000 pesetas was approved for La Barraca.

On June 6, rehearsals began in the auditorium of the student residence hall and in premises at the Universidad Central de Madrid on San Bernardo street. On July 10, the first public performance took place outdoors in the town of Burgo de Osma. The company performed three interludes by Miguel de Cervantes with costumes and sets by Santiago Ontañón, Ramón Gaya and Alfonso Ponce de León. The reception on the part of the audience was very positive. Thereafter, performances were held across

a large portion of the peninsula up until the war broke out in 1936.

La Barraca was partially inspired by Russian agitprop trains, with which both Lorca and Eduardo Ugarte were familiar. Lorca even hailed revolutionary Russian cinema as superior to pre-revolutionary literature, alleging that the films being screened on Russian political propaganda trains were a much more efficient vehicle for communication with a largely illiterate audience, who could appreciate actions more easily than words. Moreover, Russian cinematic language held, according to Lorca, certain similarities with rural sensitivities:

Soviet Russian film, even more than pre-revolutionary literature by Dostoyevsky, Gogol, Tolstoy and Pushkin, is better understood by the Spanish people because of the harshness of its expression, its rural passion and its rhythm. As such, I believe that it is a factor to consider in the development of the culture of our people. [...] Soviet cinema teaches us a lesson that we, as Spanish intellectuals, should take to heart.[27]

The assimilation on Lorca's part was mainly technical, since he was clearly more interested in the agitprop formats than in their content. Instead of using La Barraca as a motor for agitation and direct political propaganda, Lorca turned to classical theatrical culture for his project. La Barraca's repertoire was made up of plays from the Spanish Golden Age, but the aesthetics of the stagings were avant-garde, derived from Cubist and Surrealist visual forms, as was the company's brand image (Figure 84). The 30 company members were organized in what we might call a phalanstery.[28] They were like a com-

Figure 84: La Barraca in 1933. Seated from left to right: unidentified, Federico García Lorca, Eduardo Ugarte, José Obradors, Jacinto Higueras and Diego Tarancón. Centro Federico García Lorca. Federico García Lorca Archives.

munity of erudite and emancipated cultural workers who, through their aesthetic updating of classical culture, transferred that identity onto illiterate country dwellers. The setup and breakdown of the sets took place publicly, putting on a collaborative performance for small rural communities that extended beyond the theatrical representation. The uniforms worn by the company members, a standard worker's jumpsuit with an abstract emblem designed by the avant-garde artist Benjamín Palencia, dramatized and dignified the physical labor in the eyes of the country dwellers, disconnected from their own dignity as workers and from the idea of art as work. Above and beyond the plays themselves, there was the choreographic performance of each premiere, which became an artwork in itself: that is the fundamental trait shared by both La Barraca and the Mobile Theater.

La Barraca began each of its activities as a caravan made up of two trucks, which transported the stage, the scenery and the trunks containing costumes and props, plus a bus, which they called Thespis' wagon, for the actors.[29] The group visited 64 villages and small towns, giving performances on a flat stage, measuring 6 m deep by 8 m wide, without an incline. The audience stood around the stage, normally set up in the town square, although there were times, like during the visits to Tetouan and Tangier, where, due to the lack of an available square, the performance took place on the sand at the beach.[30] The description of the setup (Figures 85 and 86) gives us a precise idea of the architectural characteristics of the stage and its enormous similarities with the smaller versions, for one truck, of Javier Navarro's Mobile Theater:

The stage was supported by a braced framework that provided stability [...] while the view of the structure was hidden by a length of black curtain that stretched from one side to the other, and through the middle. At the back of the stage, on either side, there were two sets of short stairs, with four steps; they were hidden by black curtains hung from a 3-meter-high T-shaped tube structure, installed vertically. Those curtains, acting as wings, which entered a little more than a meter onto the space of the stage, allowed actors to make their entrances, since they also hid the stairs leading off the stage and extended past the edge of the backdrop on the outer edges. If there was a need for narration from off stage, or someone to sing without being seen, an actor could also stand behind those side curtains out of view of the audience. Finally, at the back, closing off the area of the stage, a wide black curtain, rising 4 meters above the stage, was held by a steel cable stretched between two vertical iron tubes, which, in turn, to avoid slack in the back curtain, were held in place by cables or ties, also made of prestressed steel. The sets were then installed on top of the stage, which lacked a proscenium in the strict sense.[31]

In introducing the classical device of theatrical self-representation in areas of the country with no cultural institutions, La Barraca was not merely aiming to impart a specific political or ideological agenda, or to equalize large portions of the rural population with the urban bourgeoisie. The goal was much broader and never one directional, radiating outward from a cultured institutional space toward the non-institutional popular realm. In other words, it was not merely inclusivist, despite its paternalistic tone. On the contrary, it was a highly experimental project that operated in both directions between the

two realms. In generating a coalescence of the poor and popular sphere with classical theatrical culture and an avant-garde visual aesthetic, La Barraca created a momentary short-circuit between cultural vectors that traditionally operated in isolated social realms, and even in separate spaces for separate audiences, nearly always in a relationship of antagonism or competition: i.e., in open conflict. In that sense, there is a shared value that can be seen in La Barraca and the Mobile Theater and in other counterculture initiatives that took their inspiration from the historical avant-gardes and their appreciation of popular culture, whether traditional or contemporary. In both cases, and beyond the respective contributions to the theatrical medium itself, their precarious portable architectures suggest a cultural production that is far removed from the idea of a bourgeois spectacle and which sets aside social segmentation based on class, taste or historical periodization. These architectural theatrical devices seem to be demanding a new, less socially and politically segmented audience.

THE KINETIC DECORATED SHED

The period when the Mobile Theater was designed coincided fully with a new convergence between avant-garde and mass culture, which, despite certain differences, shows some parallels with the historical avant-gardes' attention to this mode of formal renovation (Figure 87). The avant-garde interest in this type of media and languages is similar over time, but there are two fundamental elements that vary: the media and languages, on the one hand; and the concept of the audience, i.e., their target. As we saw before with the case of the *envelat*, it is the critical interpretation that ultimately determines the cultural function of these material devices as they enter into history. Whereas, for Domènech i Montaner, writing about the *envelat* in 1886, and for the editors of *Arquitecturas Bis* in 1975, this unschooled structure harked back to the great Western tectonic tradition, for others like Cirici in 1972, it served to legitimize the *popular* qualities of the formal

Figure 85: La Barraca. Setup in Almazán, July 1932. Centro Federico García Lorca. Federico García Lorca Archives.

Figure 86: La Barraca. Setup in Almazán, July 1932. Centro Federico García Lorca. Federico García Lorca Archives.

and social experiments engaged in by the neo-avant-garde to which he belonged as an agitator or propagandist. In both cases, the material device serves two very different ideological goals, whose only common characteristic is that of acting as motors for cultural legitimation, albeit for separate phenomena. In other words, the popular sphere is as semantically variable as the degree of appropriation of its forms that is enacted by criticism or by history, in keeping with one objective or another. The final episode discussed by Navarro in his narrative of the popular precedents for his own architectural experiment is useful in continuing to discuss the semantic fluctuations of popular phenomena exerted by the neo-avant-garde, with which the Mobile Theater can be fully identified.

The final episode takes the form of Manolita Chen's Chinese Theater. It was a popular and commercial travelling theater, active from 1950 to 1986, which was responsible for the association of the adjective *Chinese* with all Spanish portable theaters, of which it was, by far, the most successful example. Manolita Chen (Manuela Fernández Pérez, 1927-2017) began her career in the Price Circus in Madrid in the early 1940s, and she married the Chinese businessman and circus artist Chen Tse-Ping in 1944. That was the origin of the name that made the couple famous (Figures 88 and 89). A significant part of the community of humorists, dancers, acrobats, and any number of marginal showbusiness types, passed through the troupe, joining the core of performers who offered a variety show that culminated with the super vedette's final number.[32] Con-

Figure 87: Advertisement for *The Invisible Circus* created by Dave Hodges for the 72-hour-long community happening held at the Glide Memorial Church in San Francisco, organized by The Diggers collective in 1967.

Courtesy of The Diggers Archives.

trasted with the permanent variety shows in big cities, this model explored non-urban social sectors and was characterized more by travelling and permanent touring than by stable theatrical seasons. That obligated the construction of a theatrical stage derived from the classical circus model, but with its own aesthetic, drawing on more opulent music hall precedents. In this case, the popular quality is measured using two entirely objective yardsticks: success in ticket sales, as a product; and content, i.e., variety theater or cabaret. Neither of those variables retains any similarity to the idea of *popular* meaning rooted in tradition, in ritual or classical form, but rather modern mass entertainment, with its immediacy and its fast electric messages intended for rapid consumption. In other words, it situates us firmly within the sphere of pop culture:

The tent was spacious and comfortable, designed to stand up to gusts of wind and storms, quite common during hot Spanish summers. The hall would fill up with audiences composed primarily of country dwellers and industrial workers. And the performance had nothing to do with China. It was simply a variety-style musical entertainment, only slightly more polished than other tent shows that were travelling the country around the same time.[33]

The theater was a standard rectangular steel construction with lightweight trusses, entirely covered by waterproof canvas on the roof and on three of the façades. Attached to the front façade was a decorative apparatus in the form of a marquee, displaying blown-up photographs on canvases (Figure 90). The troupe travelled in a bus, whereas

Figure 88: Manolita Chen's Chinese Theater, n/d. Courtesy of Juan José Montijano.

Figure 89: Advertisement for Manolita Chen's Chinese Theater, n/d. Courtesy of Juan José Montijano.

the owners and the stars took private vehicles, staying at inns or in rented rooms at each destination. The caravan was rounded out by the trailers where the dancers, secondary artists, and technical crew members lived during the tours. One decked-out trailer, entirely decorated using the same advertisements that covered the theater's main façade was parked next to the building and was used as a ticket booth. The mobile architectural complex would travel the highways like a real-life kinetic decorated shed, taking one step further some of the ideas laid out around the same time by Robert Venturi, Denise Scott Brown and Charles Izenour in their manifesto *Learning from Las Vegas* (Figures 91 and 92).

The tent that housed the theater was outfitted with an extravagant advertisement system of signs, bright colors and semiotic overdoses with persistently repetitive messages: "Variety revue. 50 artists and 20 lovely ladies! Manolita Chen (super vedette)", "indoor heating", "air conditioning" or "waterproof tents".[34] The messages give us an idea of the extent to which the theater's visual language was tautologically derived from advertisement, selling comfort, fun and fantasy – all of which were most probably lacking in the audience's daily lives. Moreover, advertisements were systematically distributed with newspapers on a daily basis during the theater's stay in cities, constituting an aggressive sweeping message from which it was impossible to escape.[35] As with other travelling theaters, the tent was never put up in central urban areas, but rather in sites on the outskirts, like municipal fairgrounds or other similar places in smaller cities, or even in openly marginal areas, like vacant lots that had been left barren around the peripheries of cities by the urban policies of speculative developmentalism.

The particular mix of extreme realism and extreme fantasy, enlisted alternatively by the location in a vacant lot or fairground and the spectacularity of the lit façade and the interior, is precisely what led to an appropriation of the setup by the avant-garde, interested in exploring formal codes that were both easy to understand and potentially subversive (Figure 93). The write-ups from the time coincide in highlighting this two-fold, realistic and histrionic condition so characteristic of critical, grotesque art forms – permeated, in this case, with an electrified pop aesthetic that connected directly with television, the press and other mass media. The writers Manuel Vázquez Montalbán and Francisco Umbral described it with exceptional precision, while also introducing a critical barb in highlighting

Figure 90: Manolita Chen's Chinese Theater, n/d. Courtesy of Juan José Montijano.

the similarities between this type of spectacle and the avant-garde, introducing a serious ambiguity:

This theater is truly "happening", provocation, estrangement, theater of cruelty and ceremony. Valle (Inclán) took those things as inspiration for his esperpento. But Valle died and esperpento is still here, virginal, atrocious, in red ocher and Spanish black. Toward the midway point of the performance, since there's no intermission and the end is still nowhere in sight, it's worth buying some peanuts from the hawker with the tray, mainly to have something to chew on. You'll leave this poor-man's cabaret with a hot head from all the rugged flesh and with cold feet from standing in the dirt, in the pebbles of the suburbs, on the winter ground [...] Bread and circus. Peanuts and variety shows. And as you step outside, there is the cold and dirty face of a working-class neighborhood, the pallid border between the countryside and the suburbs, nightfall on the outskirts, pulsing with trains and dogs. The girls in the troupe, workers of the stage, change their outfits amid rags and early morning dew.[36]

On October 21, 1971, the newspaper *Le Monde* published a table comparing the characteristics of the *advanced* theater culture of the 1950s with that of the 1970s. Only one month later, it was published in Spain in the theater magazine *Primer Acto* and then again, three months later, in *Serra d'Or*, which gives us a precise idea of the rapidity and liveliness of the debate.[37] The comparative table reflects the rupture brought about by the events of May '68 in France, which can be extended to Western culture as a whole, both in theater and in architecture. The table is divided into five categories: *where*, which discusses space and architecture; *for whom*, which refers to the audience; *through whom*, which alludes to cultural policies and management; *why*, referring directly to ideology; and *how*, which outlines parameters and specific tools used by the respective languages being compared (Figure 94).

The terms associated with each of the decades in the first category, which deals with the spaces themselves, are very significant in the light of everything we have seen until

Figure 91: Bus belonging to Manolita Chen's Chinese Theater, n/d. Still from the documentary by RTVE Radio Televisión Española produced in 2012.

Figure 92: Trailer belonging to Manolita Chen's Chinese Theater, n/d. Still from the documentary by RTVE Radio Televisión Española produced in 2012.

now. Whereas in the 1950s, theatrical and architectural culture were summed up in "new venues/without traditional stages/actors facing the audience", in the 1970s, the dominant characteristics were "the street, the workplace/no fixed structures/actors surrounded by the audience". With the same shift, rather than a craftsman, specialist and legitimate heir, the artist became a volunteer or amateur in the service of the audience, an activist or an agitator. A universal cultural democracy was replaced by a revolution in a constant struggle and disarray. In short, there was a move from ritual to celebration, from rigor to exuberance, from applause to slogans, and from reflection to action.[38] This fascinating comparative table employs 33 parameters which, as a whole and in pairs, describe the shift between different, yet interrelated, cultural forms. This debate introduced by *Le Monde* helps us to understand the cultural atmosphere that Javier Navarro was navigating as he promoted his Mobile Theater, and it can be very illuminating to delve further into the debate, which has been analyzed in detail by Oscar Cornago:

The new generations rejected the idea of an audience that was largely uniform socially and ideologically, as well as the didactic and paternalistic tone of a theater called "popular" which had failed to attract working-class audiences who did, on the other hand, frequent the cinema or musical variety shows. [...] New theater was looking for direct contact with the audience outside the scope of traditionally consecrated theater spaces, which had been proven ineffective. Streets, squares, garages and the most improbable spaces, emerged as ideal places for a theatrical communication that was freed from the context with which bourgeois theater had identified. The complete opposition to any culturalist attitude led to the development of different kinds of scenic languages with a markedly celebratory tone, inspired by

Figure 93: Manolita Chen's Chinese Theater, n/d. Image courtesy of Juan José Montijano.

Grelot

el jersei de la gent jove

teatre

el teatre dels anys setanta

ANYS 50 | ANYS 70

codes that were truly majoritary at the time, such as film, television, magazines, comics, or advertising, and backed up by references transplanted directly from the most immediate cultural systems: iconography, music or slogans, which appealed to the collective imagination of a society and provided an effective emotional communication. [...] Popular theater recovered a sense of spectacularity, playfulness and celebration that realist theater had never achieved.[39]

The avant-garde assimilation of popular theater culture in Spain was similar to what Brooks McNamara highlighted about the American and even international theater scene: poor and pop at the same time, austere and spectacular, grotesque and imaginative. While La Barraca only had a simple stage, at the same time they built sophisticated sets following a Cubist aesthetic, operating with limited material resources to generate large amounts of content and information, with an enormous semiotic efficiency. The goal was an effective and direct communication with the audience. Four decades later, in order to amplify and even intensify the effectiveness of that communication, there was, along with the reinterpretation of traditional popular culture, a complete assimilation of new formats like comic, television, variety theater, or circus, comparable to what had happened with the historical avant-gardes. As we can see from Javier Navarro's text, full of contemporary references to that type of register, around the time he designed his Mobile Theater there was already a broad range of avant-garde languages that were immersed in a total reinterpretation of poor, popular and pop culture indiscriminately, blending together all the formats of those codes.[40]

Figure 94: Transcription of the article *El teatre dels anys seixanta* from *Le Monde*, published in the magazine *Serra d'Or.*

Notes

1. Javier Navarro de Zuvillaga: "The Disintegration of Theatrical Space," *Architectural Association Quarterly*, vol. 8, no. 4, 1976, pg. 24.

2. Richard Wagner: *Art Life Theories of Richard Wagner*, New York: H. Holt, 1889, pg. 271.

3. Jerzy Grotowski: *Towards a Poor Theatre*, New York: Simon and Schuster, 1969, pg. 19.

4. Richard Gaffield-Knight: *Grotowski. Igniting the Flame*, Owen Daly, 1992.

5. Jerzy Gurawski: "An Architect at the Teatr Laboratorium", in Paula Allain and Grzegorz Ziólowski (Eds.): *Voices from Within: Grotowski's Polish Collaborators*, London: Polish Theatre Perspectives and The Grotowski Institute, pg. 88.

6. Ibid., pgs. 87-88.

7. For a complete study of the collaboration between Grotowski and Gurawski, see Christopher Baugh: "Play with Space: The Scenography of Jerzy Gurawski", in *Theatre and Performance Design*, vol. 1, 2005, issue 5, pgs. 281-297.

8. Jerzy Grotowski, op. cit., pg. 160.

9. The original text of the program appears in Ludwik Flaszen: "The Constant Prince", in Jerzy Grotowski, op. cit., pgs. 97-117. For a detailed description of the mise-en-scène, see http://www.grotowski.net/en/encyclopedia/constant-prince-ksiaze-niezlomny.

10. Javier Navarro de Zuvillaga, op. cit. pg. 27.

11. For a keen analysis of the importance of Jean Fouquet's image in the history of theater, see Philip Butterworth: "Jean Fouquet's *The Martyrdom of St Apollonia* and *The Rape of the Sabine Women* as Iconographical Evidence of Medieval Theatre Practice", in *Leeds Studies in English,* no. 29, 1998, pgs. 55-67, which provides a lengthy bibliography.

12. Brooks McNamara: "Popular Scenography", in *The Drama* Review, vol. 18, no. 1, March 1974, pgs. 16-24.

13. Javier Navarro de Zuvillaga, op. cit. pg. 29.

14. Lluís Domènech i Montaner: "L'Envelat", *Arquitecturas Bis*, no. 5, January 1975, pgs. 13-15. The magazine *Arquitectura Bis* is the subject of an investigation that reveals many of its ideological underpinnings. See, Joaquim Moreno: *Arquitecturas Bis 1974-1985: From Publication to Public Action*, PhD dissertation, Princeton University, 2011.

15. Lluís Domènech i Montaner, *Historia general del arte. Escrita e ilustrada en vista de los monumentos y de las mejores obras publicadas hasta el día.* Volume I, Barcelona, Montaner y Simón, 1886, pgs. 119 and 147-156.

16. Alexandre Cirici: "Els Envelats", in *Serra d'Or*, year XIV, no. 159, 1972, pgs. 92-97.

17. Charles Jencks and Nathan Silver: *Adhocism. The Case for Improvisation*, London: Secker and Warburg, 1972. Jencks was preparing the edition of his book at the time he was acting as an occasional advisor for Javier Navarro in London. In the book, Jencks and Silver advocate for a design based on reusing existing elements in the market with the idea of subverting the uses normally assigned to industrially manufactured objects.

18. Regarding Lluís Jové, see the information published online for the exhibition organized by Terrassa Arts Visuals (Ajuntament de Terrassa, Servei de Cultura) in 2016, curated by Toni Verdaguer and Miquel Mallafré: http://lluisjove-acontracorrent.com/

19. Alexandre Cirici: "Esdeveniment, environament, participació", in *Serra d'Or*, year XIV, no. 158, 1972, pgs. 43-46.

20. Information published in Azucena López Cobo: "Por caminos de piedra, charcos y olvido. Repertorios de la cultura universal: las Misiones Pedagógicas de la II República española", in *Pandora. Revue d'études hispaniques*, no. 7, 2007, pg. 83. This information is repeated systematically (with slight quantitative differences) in all the existing studies, for example in Marián Madrigal Neira: *La memoria no es nostalgia: José Caballero*, PhD dissertation, Universidad Complutense de Madrid, 2001, pgs. 96-107.

21. Acción Cultural Española (Ed.): *La Barraca. Teatro y universidad: Ayer y hoy de una utopía*, catalog from the exhibition of the same name organized by Acción Cultural Española AC/E, in 2011, pg. ii.

22. José Luis Plaza Chillón: *El teatro y las artes plásticas. Escenografía y estética teatral de vanguardia: Federico García Lorca, La Barraca y otros montajes (1920-1937).* PhD dissertation, Universidad de Granada, 1996, pgs. 198-201.

23. Martí Perán: "Del museo circulante al arte ambulante. Notas para una genealogía de la portabilidad", in *Roulotte*: 9, a special issue pub-

lished in conjunction with the exhibition *Esto no es un museo. Artefactos móviles al acecho*, organized by Acción Cultural Española AC/E in 2011, pgs. 80-95. For the program and actions undertaken by Misiones Pedagógicas, see *Las Misiones Pedagógicas.1931-1936*, Madrid: Publicaciones de la Residencia de Estudiantes, 2006; *Val del Omar y las Misiones Pedagógicas*, Madrid and Murcia: Publicaciones de la Residencia de Estudiantes/Sala Verónicas, 2003

24. José Luis Plaza Chillón, op. cit, pg. 203.

25. The origins of La Barraca are described in detail in Antonio Campoamor González: "La Barraca y su primera salida por los caminos de España", *Cuadernos Hispanoamericanos*, no. 435-436, September-October 1986, pgs. 779-790.

26. "Estudiantes de la FUE se echarán a los caminos con La Barraca. Un carromato como el de Lope de Rueda. Teatro clásico gratuito por las plazas de los pueblos", article in the newspaper *El Sol*, Madrid, December 2, 1931. Cited in Antonio Campoamor González, op. cit., pg. 781.

27. José Luis Plaza Chillón, op. cit, pg. 316.

28. Eszter Katona: "Teatros ambulantes en la Segunda República española", in *Colindancias*, no. 5, 2014, pgs. 39-61.

29. "Naturally, they needed to buy a truck to transport the scenery and the stage, along with the trunks for costumes and props; the General Directorate of Public Safety provided a bus for the actors, along with the drivers they needed. [...] Later on, right about the time I joined the theater, they bought another truck specifically to transport the scenery, trunks and props." Luis Sáenz de la Calzada: *La Barraca. Teatro Universitario*, Residencia de Estudiantes, 1998, pgs. 58-59. Originally published in *Revista de Occidente*, 1976.

30. Sáenz de la Calzada, op. cit., pg. 200.

31. Ibid., pg. 176.

32. The researcher Juan José Montijano has published a number of books on Manolita Chen and other travelling theaters, the most notable of which include: *De la carreta a la carpa. Apuntes sobre los teatros ambulantes de variedades en España*, Vigo: Editorial Academia del Hispanismo, 2011; *La vedette que desafió a Franco*, Sevilla: Ediciones Ende, 2014; and *Manolita Chen y su Teatro chino* (in two volumes), Almería: Editorial Círculo Rojo, 2015. In addition, Spanish television produced a documentary called *Teatro chino de Manolita Chen, el cabaret de los pobres*, which was first broadcast on November 9, 2011 and is available online at: http://www.rtve.es/alacarta/videos/el-documental/documental-teatro-chino-manolita-chen-cabaret-pobres/3438856/

33. José María Rodriguez Mendez: *Comentarios impertinentes sobre el teatro español*, Barcelona, Península 1972, pg. 35, cited in Juan José Montijano: *Historia del teatro olvidado: La revista (1864-2009)*, PhD dissertation, Universidad de Granada, 2009, pg. 839.

34. Magazine *El Ritmo Semanal*, Valencia, February 17, 1960, cited in Montijano, op. cit., pg. 830.

35. A look at the archive of the newspaper *ABC de Sevilla* offers any number of examples of the systematic advertisement inserts that appeared during the weeks of the Feria de abril.

36. Manuel Vázquez Montalbán and Francisco Umbral: *100 años de canción y music hall*, Madrid: Difusora Internacional S.A., 1974, pgs. 455-457, cited in Juan José Montijano, op. cit, pg. 845.

37. This important debate has been analyzed by Oscar Cornago: *La vanguardia teatral en España 1965-1975. Del ritual al juego.* Madrid: Visor, 1999, pg. 161. In this fundamental study of the Spanish theatrical avant-garde, Cornago offers a reading of the post-realist avant-garde's shift from a ritual theater toward a theater of play, as indicated by the book's subtitle.

38. Catalan version by Xavier Fábregas, consulted in *Serra d'Or*, Year XIV, no. 149, February 1972.

39. Oscar Cornago, op. cit., pgs. 165-166.

40. In his text from 1976, Javier Navarro refers to the Living Theatre, the Bread and Puppet Theatre, the San Francisco Mime Group, the Grand Magic Circus, the Teatro Campesino in Fresno, the Open Theatre and Mabou Mimes, among others. All these groups engaged in collective creation, paratheater and a fundamental renewal of the languages of popular theater, while participating in the cultural avant-garde of the moment.

CHAPTER 4_
THE ELECTRIC DECADE

When Javier Navarro arrived at the Architectural Association School of Architecture in 1970, it was a hotbed of multiple currents that did not always mesh. Moreover, the school's administration and its pedagogical tradition consciously favored a broad ideological and methodological diversity. The Architectural Association is a private institution founded in 1847 by a group of students who were reacting against the educational system in the United Kingdom at the time.

Two young architecture students, Robert Kerr, 23, and Charles Gray, 18, proposed the creation of an association of "draftsmen" who would organize their own professional training as architects, challenging the official system of professional apprenticeships and qualification. In 1862, the Royal Institute of British Architects (RIBA) established the Voluntary Examination and began issuing professional qualifications to students of the Architectural Association who passed the test.[1] The foundational spirit of the Architectural Association was imbued with the dandyism of the British upper class and its club model. Despite many ups and downs and successive crises, this educational institution is still relevant today, engaged in ongoing clashes in its facultative relationship with the RIBA and with professional architectural corporativism. The Architectural Association has always been an elite institution with a critical slant, ambivalent and paradoxical by definition, kept afloat economically by high tuition costs and maintaining its prestige through the intense dedication of its teachers and students, with a focus on critical competition. The history of this institution is the history of a continuing battle between the professional establishment of British architecture, the political power of the central government and its educational models, the intellectual independence of professors and lines of investigation, and the constant updating of funding models tied to private capital and the progressive cultural elites.

The liberal spirit of dissent was in the Architectural Association's DNA from the outset. In 1938, the students launched a magazine called *Focus*, which denounced the previous generation's grab for power as "domination". This climate of critical opposition characterized the institution enduringly. Between 1943 and 1950, from the pages of the student magazine *PLAN*, the editors challenged the English representatives of the CIAM (International Congresses of Modern Architecture), demanding their own representation to exert direct influence on the configuration of modern architecture. As a generation, the Brutalist architects were critical of the previous generation's systems of design and organization, which they classified as dogma. In its similarities with manifesto culture, the rebellious attitude characteristic of young students of the Architectural Association was rooted in the historical avant-garde of the earliest mo-

Un decreto-ley, aprobado en Consejo de Ministros, lo establece durante tres meses

ESTADO DE EXCEPCION

nuevo diario

EN TODA ESPAÑA

Quedan en suspenso los artículos 12, 14, 15, 16 y 18 del Fuero de los Españoles

El Gobierno, por unanimidad, propuso la aprobación del decreto-ley al Jefe del Estado

El Gobierno, en su reunión de ayer por la mañana, propuso por unanimidad a su Excelencia el Jefe del Estado, y así se acordó, la aprobación del siguiente decreto-ley:

APOYATURAS LEGALES

ARTICULOS EN SUSPENSO

FUERO DE LOS ESPAÑOLES

COMENTARIO DE FRAGA IRIBARNE

Figure 95: News of the declaration of the State of Exception in the newspaper *Nuevo Diario* from January 25, 1969.

dern architecture, with its multiple moments of crisis and unrest.[2]

Javier Navarro arrived during one of those frequent moments of critical transition at the institution,[3] in search of a certain cultural climate that was not to be found in 1970s Spain. He was equipped with solid, professionalist, polytechnical training, marked by a strong ideological dissidence, although its full development was hampered in Spain at the time by political repression and a lack of organization among dissidents. On January 24, 1969 the government of the dictator Francisco Franco proclaimed a state of exception in Spain for a period of three months (Figure 95). The text issued by the cabinet read: "Minor actions, yet systematically directed at disrupting the peace in Spain and breaching its public safety, have been taking place in recent months, with clear ties to an international strategy that has already been seen in a number of countries."[4] The minister Manuel Fraga Ibibarne made comments to the press that depicted perfectly the prevailing atmosphere of paranoid conspiracy:

If I may, I'd like to issue a short comment on the decree, which I think adds a clear nuance to the issue, by virtue of its conciseness. I'd like to emphasize the phrase "minor actions", since our country's social and political health is excellent, thank God. Yet, I repeat that these actions are clearly intended to sink the country into a wave of confusion and worldwide subversion, which is perfectly clear to see in the news every day. This strategy preys on the innocent generosity of young people in order to entangle them in an orgy of nihilism, anarchism and disobedience, which, furthermore, has been denounced in recent days by statesmen everywhere and all the major international platforms. In that context, a few evil and ambitious actors have tried to capitalize on the situation for their own benefit.[5]

Following the declaration of the State of Exception, the Madrid School of Architecture resumed normal activities on January 29, 1969 after months of demonstrations, strikes, sit-ins and assemblies. The teaching staff was rattled by the events, affected by acts of retaliation, unexpected academic promotions, and an overall intellectual uncertainty that lasted for a very long time.

That was the atmosphere Navarro left behind when he travelled to London in the late summer of 1970. In London, similar to other European cities, the counterculture was divided between radical anarchism and a new organized left that was preparing an institutional assault on the establishment. The critic Jeffrey Kipnis offered an eloquent description of the atmosphere at the school during that period:

London's Architectural Association 1970-72: a school awash in sex, drugs, and rock and roll, David Bowie hanging at the bar; flush to a person with experimental hysteria quickened by the visionary projects of Archigram, architecture's answer to the Beatles; galvanized, sort of, by the European action politics of May 68; intoxicated by the spontaneous American love-urbanism of Woodstock and its shadow, the erotic violence of Altamont; edified by the froth of the rumors of French intellectual thought: drawn to design, to mod and Carnaby Street, and to antidesign, to the swagger of the infinite cities of Yona Friedman and Italy's Superstudio and Archizoom. Anything goes, everything goes. For studio, write a book if you want. Dance or piss your pants if you want. Even draw and make models if you want, as long as they are 'with it'.[6]

In fact, Peter Cook, the undisputed leader of the Architectural Association at the time, had studied there and graduated in 1960, and, in addition to his intense teaching activity, was director of the Institute of Contemporary Arts (ICA) from 1970 to 1972. In the late 1950s, that institution had overturned the curatorial approach of Herbert Read, a follower of modern formalism, in favor of pop inclusivity and its ambivalent aesthetics of mass consumption, embodied by the Independent Group, an interdisciplinary group which partially espoused the Corbusian rhetoric expressed in the avant-garde journal *L'Esprit Nouveau*.[7] The ICA was the institution responsible not only for introducing the pop aesthetic following the destitution of Herbert Read, but for perpetuating it until it was exhausted. Peter Cook was a student of the Architectural Association with teachers like Peter Smithson, John Voeckler, James Stirling and Edoardo Paolozzi, many of whom participated in exhibitions at the ICA in the 1950s, such as *This is Tomorrow*, organized by Theo Crosby in 1956. The ideological sequence linking the young Jeanneret of *L'Esprit Nouveau*, the multi-format pop of the Independent Group and, finally, Peter Cook's work at the head of Archigram was nearly uninterrupted for the young English architects.[8]

THE ELECTRIC DRAMA OF DISSOLUTION

Archigram was the name invented by the young architects Peter Cook (1936), David Greene (1937) and Michael Webb (1937) for their group and the magazine they launched in 1961. The following year, for the magazine's second issue, they were joined by Ron Herron (1930-1994), Dennis Crompton (1935) and Warren Chalk (1927-1987), working professionals employed by the architecture department at the London County Council. The move was a clever maneuver to bring together two seemingly opposing fronts: academic speculation and the institutional professional practice of a segment of English Brutalism. From the outset, the magazine's influence and its propagandistic potential were decisive for certain architecture students, although they were also subject to criticism from the most politicized architects, both at the time and still today.

Although Javier Navarro did not have direct contact with Cook, or any of the members of Archigram, a certain hegemony that drew on the group's proposals imbued many of the discourses and practices at the Architectural Association at the time. Navarro's article from 1976 cites two of Archigram's fundamental references for his Mobile Theater in its enigmatic closing:

In the human environment, which is conditioned each day by man himself, the need emerges for it to possess certain flexibility which makes it capable of some degree of modification. This flexibility can be obtained in two ways; either by including it in the design of new environments – adaptability and mobility of the theatrical space – or by designing environments which can be superimposed on those already existing – environmental theatre – from the Suitaloon of M. Webb (1968) to P. Cook's Instant City (1969). As the latter suggests perhaps "the future of architecture lies in the explosion of architecture".[9]

In 1963, following intense efforts focused on graphic, pedagogical and editorial production, Archigram achieved an increase in its visibility with the exhibition *Living City* at the ICA in London, through a commission from Theo Crosby (Figures 96 and 97). Inside the ICA building, they erected a structure dedicated to the exaltation of the metropolitan experience. The material construction of this accessible artifact was a triangular faceted tent in the shape of a distorted dome, which contained a rotating lamp to generate effects similar to László Moholy-Nagy's lighting mechanisms in one of its seven areas, called "gloops" – using the word for a sticky substance to

Figure 96: Photograph of the exhibition *Living City* at the Institute of Contemporary Arts, London, 1963. Archigram Archive.

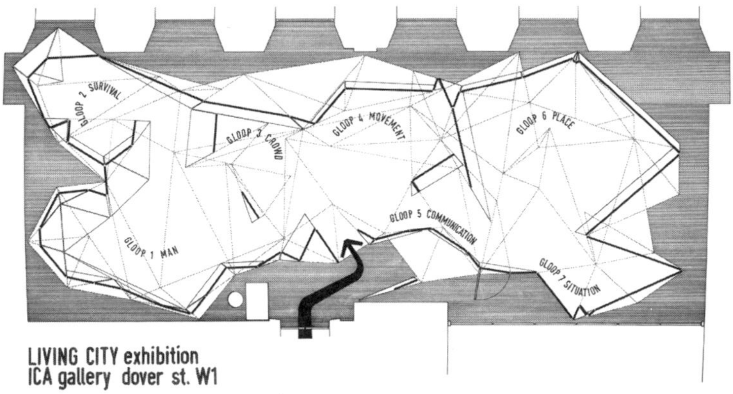

Figure 97: Floor plan of the exhibition *Living City* at the Institute of Contemporary Arts, London, 1963. Archigram Archive.

refer also to a simpleton or a fool. The installation invites a hypothetical comparison with the Mobile Theater in some aspects, specifically with regard to the dissolution of architecture into technologically assisted sensory phenomena.

Each of the seven sections of the *Living City* contained large-format graphic information and was organized around a particular theme: *man*, *survival*, *crowd*, *movement*, *communications*, *place* and *situation*. According to the historian and Archigram scholar Simon Sadler, the exhibition represented British culture's impressionistic absorption of French existentialism along with some of the Situationist mottos, decontextualized and relieved of their political overtones.[10] *Man* showed the relationships between people and objects in a "psycho-social game", similar to a game board or hopscotch court drawn on the floor; *Survival* exhibited a robot, in a tribute to the ICA and its futurist pop past from the 1950s, and it talked about the effects of augmenting the human body with mechanical and informational prostheses; *Crowd* presented a resilient individuality in the face of the teeming masses, in which a kaleidoscope of subjects, drawing on their shared perceptions, produced an aimless collective multitude, driven exclusively by boundless sensory impulses. *Movement* and *Communication* referred to the Americans Jane Jacobs and William Whyte and their respective criticisms of the modern zoned city;[11] *Place* mirrored the discourse of Team 10, an organization formed by revisionist architects critical of the Modern Movement's urban planning principles, who advocated for the recovery of urban environments on a human scale; and, finally, *Situation* alluded directly to the

French Situationist vocabulary, divested of its original political associations.

The installation was a perfect demonstration of the principles of disciplinary dissolution that the members of Archigram were debating at the time. That debate permeated student architectural culture in the 1960s in London, which aimed to confront head on the established architectural culture, inheritor of the British absorption of the Modern Movement by professional teams tied to local administrations and deployed in the form of Brutalism. In the exhibition catalog, Peter Cook wrote something that summed up the impressionist, technological and electric symphony that permeated the sensitivities of those English architects: "When it's raining in Oxford Street the architecture is no more important than the rain, in fact the weather has probably more to do with the pulsation of the Living City at that given moment."[12] In 1960, Reyner Banham published his PhD dissertation under the title *Theory and Design in the First Machine Age.* In this fundamental 20th-century volume, Banham definitively introduced Buckminster Fuller as the new canon, in a re-reading of the Modern Movement that equated the technological and compositional languages in architectural discipline. Fuller's influence as an absolute predecessor of these architectures was enormous, and it is present in the Mobile Theater to the same extent as other references.

In 1967, a comprehensive anthology of Archigram's work was published in Spain in the magazine *Hogar y Arquitectura*, directed then by Carlos Flores, which earned him a handful of reprimands from the political, academic and professional authorities (Figure 98).[13] When Javier Navarro arrived in London, he was familiar – like any architect or young student at the time with a critical perspective of the discipline – with the discourse and the images published by the English group, not only through English magazines like *Architectural Design* but also thanks to that Spanish publication.

The Spanish reception of Archigram through *Hogar y Arquitectura* is particularly interesting, because the introductory comments by Carlos Flores and the detailed analysis by the then fourth-year architecture student Francisco González Quintana were both detailed and circumspect. The magazine provided the best and broadest diffusion of Archigram's work in Spain, and it was the first to introduce them in a Spanish-language medium. It was not until following year, 1968, that the monographic issue of the Argentinian magazine *Cuadernos Summa – Nueva Visión* appeared, with an extensive distribution in Spanish-speaking countries. The Argentinian publication systematically released Spanish versions of international magazines, including *Architectural Design, Architectural Association Quarterly* or *The RIBA Journal*, to list only English-language originals. The monographic of *Hogar y Arquitectura* comprised an editorial by Carlos Flores, an article by Reyner Banham, another by the architecture student Francisco González Quintana, and a quite comprehensive collection of Archigram's work and designs.

In his editorial, Carlos Flores defended Archigram's work against critics who had labelled it a science-fiction utopia. For Flores, Archigram's projects were more attuned to real problems of the built environment than the work of critics who used what Flores called "the usual *reasonable* methods", which made his position patently clear.[14]

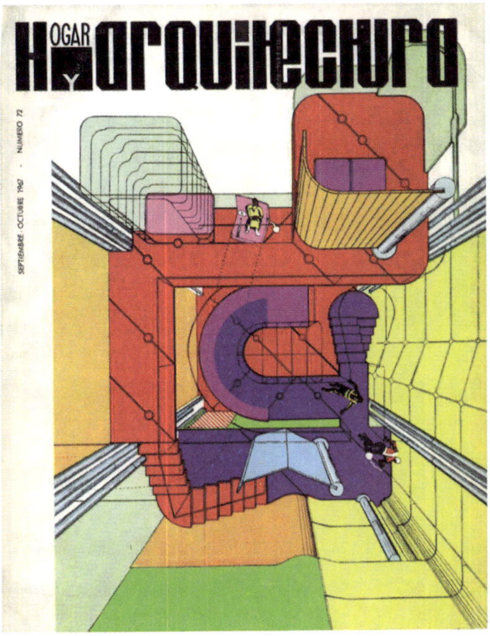

Figure 98: Cover of the magazine *Hogar y arquitectura* from October 1967. Courtesy of the ETSAM library.

Figure 99: Interior cover image from the Archigram issue of the magazine *Hogar y Arquitectura* from October 1967. Courtesy of the ETSAM library.

Banham's text draws attention to the evolution of Archigram's production, from the initial rhetorical and monumental urban projects to the later proposals, which Banham calls "environments".[15] As such, the Spanish magazine introduced its readers to Archigram's work in the context of its development, as an evolving body of work as opposed to a mere catalog of disconnected, striking images. It even offered an analysis by stages and developments, written by Banham himself, and an evolution of the group's work that culminated with designs in which tectonics were entirely dissolved or eliminated (Figure 99). Banham ended his text by asserting that: "Anyone who packs a tent, a camp stove, a flashlight and a transistor radio on the back of his motor-scooter and heads out camping is enjoying a primitive version of the new Archigram vision." For his part, Francisco González Quintana headed up his long essay with a quote by Bruno Taut, taken from one of the Crystal Chain letters.

Let us consciously be 'imaginary architects'! We believe that only a total revolution can guide us in our task. Our fellow citizens, even our colleagues quite rightly suspect in us the forces of revolution. Break up and undermine all former principles! [...] The individual personality will disappear with commitment to a higher task – if architecture reappears then the master builder will be anonymous.[16]

His shrewdness in recognizing the procedural similarities between Archigram and part of the historical avant-garde is undeniable, as is his insight in analyzing Archigram's cultural milieu. Taut's letter talks about breaking up and dissolving; the Spanish translation uses the exact same vocabulary as Javier Navarro used in his text nine years later. González Quintana was right in asserting that the keys to Archigram's international success were three strategic pillars and one tactical one. The first of the strategic pillars was a historic opportunity, in their ability to detect the exhaustion of the Brutalist discourse; the second was their widespread acceptance at the most influential architecture schools in the UK; and the third was the magazine they edited, with its enormous propagandistic potential. These three pillars, which belonged to the "academic and professional sphere", were joined by a fourth, no less important, one of a tactical order: Archigram's penetration in the "popular arena", by appearing systematically in mass media and public events, including the exhibition *A House for the Year 1990* organized by the *Daily Telegraph* and Harrods department store in London in 1967, accompanied by a special supplement in the press, or the supplement *2000*, for the mass market women's magazine *Woman's Mirror*, along with the ICA exhibition and the deluxe *Living City* catalog from 1963. Addressing all these forays in the media, González Quintana concludes that:

Archigram, with its success and the attraction it sparked among non-specialists through the constant dissemination of its designs and ideas, has demonstrated that one of the most legitimate reasons for its existence lies the fact that it can move beyond (at least potentially) that privileged environment and bring the architectural phenomenon to the general public, who actually inhabit it – which everyone always seems to forget – in a much more positive way than all the sophisticated and sterile attempts made up to date by the so-called continuers of the Modern Movement.[17]

In 1967 there were few anthologies of Archigram's work and its cultural role that were as clear and in depth; only Reyner Banham and his disciple Charles Jencks could be considered exceptions. The fact that it was a fourth-year architecture student – from an entirely marginal culture, as Spanish culture was in 1967 – who so acutely perceived Archigram's qualities and methods upon coming into contact with them, cannot be seen as a mere eccentricity, coincidence or historic fluke. Rather, it reveals a certain generational cultural awareness, to which Javier Navarro belonged – although it was by no means dominant in Spanish academic circles –as a student in the same promotion as González Quintana in Madrid. In a letter to the editor Carlos Flores, sent from London, the young student reported on these cultural incursions – halfway between astonishment and seduction – with a surprising level of immersion:

Now I'll bring you up to date on what things are like in the capital of the sixties. I'm up to my ears in "fiction architecture" and it's hard to get my head around so many new ideas. [...]

Prepare to be AMAZED: Cook and Crompton (and, this year, Herron too) are professors of 5th year design studio (the final year), and they're presenting FUTURIST ARCHITECTURE; in other words, Archigram's designs couldn't ask for a more fertile field to grow and develop – as is also the case in Virginia,[18] *where I imagine the Americans will give them a warm welcome.*

As you know, they use the tutoring system here, and each student is assigned a tutor who specializes in the subject that is the focus of that student's research. Well, the architecture students in 5th year at the AA don't all have architects as their tutors. Some of them are specialists in electronics, plastic materials, computers, etc. [...] They're constantly organizing conferences, symposia, etc. and not just at the AA. There is ongoing contact with other schools, both in England and abroad.

[...] I talked about London in my last letter. It's a shame I don't have more free time – and not precisely to spend looking at buildings, since you know lately I'm more interested in people, how they live and what they think. There is a fascinating slice of life here.

London, August 1967.

CYBERNETIC CIRCUSES

However, despite Navarro's references to the Cushicle and the Suitaloon, other Archigram projects offer better and more extensive information on some of the ideas used in his Mobile Theater, especially with regard to architectural mobility, the centrality of the industrial artifact, and, finally, the role that theater and drama could play as a tool for emancipation because of their pedagogical potential. This last element was not developed explicitly in the Mobile Theater, but it was implicit in Navarro's ideological project. The Autoenvironment designed by Michael Webb in 1964-1965 provided a fundamental speculation on the possibilities of the industry of mobile consumer artifacts in contemporary housing (Figure 100):

*If you take the car, it can be a status-symbol, male virility-object and what-have-you means of getting about that's fun to own and drive, but it can also be a mobile room

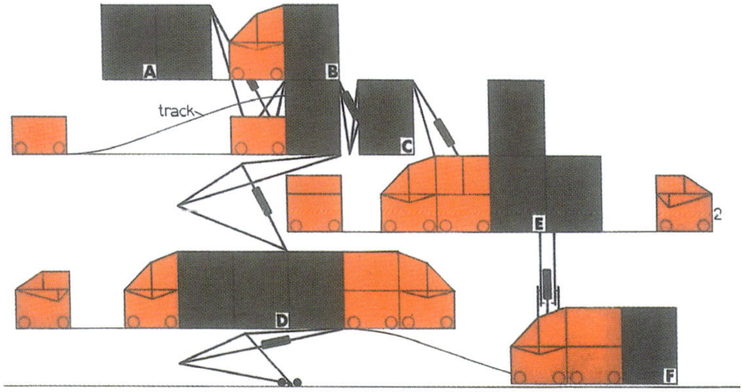

which can plug itself into a drive-in bank and become extra floor area of that bank. [...] In a drive-in home the volume at any moment is directly proportional to the number of people in it; when the family is away at the seaside the house consists only of folded up storage units; during a party as many as 30 mobile containers might gather around a unit to form a big space. So the structure has been designed to get bigger or smaller, depending on the size of the container population present.[19]

Based on his commentary on the industrialized motor homes available on the market, Michael Webb proposed a very stylized architectural adaptation, which, contrasting with the family-related social dimension of the traditional motor home, introduced the possibility of individual mobile environments, a sort of portable house for the contemporary subject – alone and without any stable social or family ties. Webb refined these ideas until arriving at the Suitaloon project in 1968, to which Navarro refers in his text, which, in turn, draws on the Cushicle, an individual inflatable room: "complete nomadic unit – and it is fully serviced", which was deployed from a core called the "armature" or "spinal system", derived formally from the automobile.[20] The more elaborate version, the Suitaloon, was a house-suit "for one rider only"[21] in which the service core and propulsion unit was eliminated, leaving only a thin, self-propelling envelope that was no longer connected to an energy supply, but rather to other users also outfitted with their own respective suits. As is evident, this line of research pursued by Archigram led directly and deliberately to individual and entirely self-sufficient structures in an exaltation of radical individuality characteristic of one of the group members' discursive avenues:

Figure 100: *Autoenvironment* by Michael Webb, Drive-In Housing showing the second phase of erection. 1966.
Archigram Archive

the analogy between architectural gadget and consumer object established by the equation "design by choice",[22] which presaged what we see today in the form of commercial customization as a vehicle for the social identification of the contemporary individual.

This line of research shows obvious similarities with the Mobile Theater in its allusions to mobility as an agent of emancipation along with a certain architectural dematerialization. However, the Mobile Theater did not *customize* the automobile industry in order to propose a radically individual habitat; rather, it harnessed the automobile in the service of a collective space design that employed only some of the parameters popularized by Archigram. In that sense, the project was more possibilistic than prospective.

The Archigram project called Ideas Circus, invented by Peter Cook in 1968, shows more conceptual similarities with the Mobile Theater than Michael Webb's individualizing structures (Figures 101 and 102). Ideas Circus was proposed as a mobile educational architectural structure that was intended to be transported across England, distributing specialized information through seminars and pedagogical activities in its installations. It was an adaptation of agit-prop for the new post-Fordist information age, which the members of Archigram formalized perfectly in some of their designs. According to the description: "*Ideas Circus* is an educational facility which is able to carry specialised information between fixed centres. [...] Responses are fed back to origin and also carried forward onto a complete circuit."[23]

The novelty of the project was relative, however, since another architect who had ties to Archigram but maintained his own individual practice, Cedric Price (1934-2004), designed a theater prototype together with the theater director Joan Littlewood (1914-2002), between 1963 and 1965, which was meant for a stable location: the uber-famous Fun Palace.[24] The artifact was intended for construction in a place called Mill Meads, near the Lea River to the east of the Port of London, in an area that was undergoing a marked deindustrialization process, with the resulting social conflict derived from a loss of jobs for the working classes, for whom the project was intended. It was a large structure using gantry cranes, which housed an indeterminate space made up of a "kit of parts" on an intermediate scale, which could be moved around and transformed across the different levels (Figure 103). Littlewood's interest in a proletarian and moralist theater with a strong educational component, developed over the decades of her work with her company the Theater Workshop, combined with Price's interest in programmatic and formal indetermination, on the one hand, and informational stimulus-response circuits on the other. In parallel, in 1965, Price developed another unbuilt project called Potteries Thinkbelt, which proposed the reuse of abandoned railroad structures in the industrial region of North Staffordshire, an area suffering from deindustrialization and unemployment – transforming them into a mobile structure for use as a technological university campus dedicated to training specialists. The project made extensive use of train cars as mobile classrooms and adapted containers to accommodate housing for students and teachers.

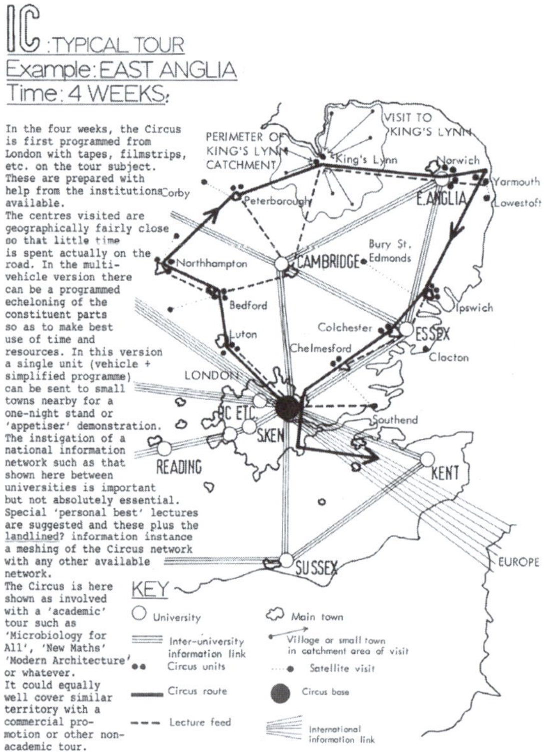

Figure 101: Ideas Circus by Peter Cook, 1968. Archigram Archive.

Figure 102: Ideas Circus by Peter Cook, 1968. Archigram Archive.

It is clear that part of the English architectural culture of the time – in which Javier Navarro was immersed during his stay in London – was intently focused on the possibilities of architectural mobility, and that the catalog of possible technical languages had reached a certain level of development in 1970. The fundamental new ingredient introduced by Archigram with respect to Price's two brilliant precedents had to do with the superposition of both concepts (mobility and education) in a single project, which lays out the models for a decentralized educational factory, so characteristic of the current post-Fordist digital economy. Today, ongoing competitive self-development is no longer a vehicle for class emancipation like it was in those 1960s projects; now it is mere survival in order to get or keep a job, and not even necessarily a well-paying job, in the information society. When those projects were drafted, the authors could not have imagined that the technological skills that those devices would introduce to the working classes not only would not help to improve their well-being by partially eliminating class barriers, but would instead tether workers even further to an economic instability, entirely dependent on the acquisition of those skills. In other words, it would exacerbate their inferior, uncertain class condition.[25] Ideas Circus set out to be a cultural antidote:

To institute a standard package of five or six vehicles that contain all the equipment necessary to set up a seminar, conference, exhibition, teaching or display. The package can be attached to an existing building. [...] The Circus can also be completely autonomous: set up in a field, if necessary. The idea would be to circulate between major provincial centres, tapping local universities, bleeding off from them personalities, documentation and such things as film of laboratory experiments: then carrying on to the next town.[26]

The description of the mechanism for the Ideas Circus is very similar to Javier Navarro's Mobile Theater in terms of the architectural formulation. (Figure 104). What differentiates them is the complete absence of interventionism on Navarro's part with respect to the epistemological content to be housed within the architectural structures. There is an even greater rhetorical, formal and apparent similarity between the Mobile Theater and Peter Cook's Instant City.

Instant City is a research project based on the conflict between local, culturally isolated, centres and the well serviced facilities of the metropolitan regions. Investigating the effect and practicality of injecting the metropolitan dynamic into these centres by means of a mobile facility carrying the information – education – entertainment services of the city, extended through the establishment of this together with the national telecommunication network.[27]

Instant City had consulting support from the expert in cybernetics Gordon Pask, who also participated in the Fun Palace, bringing about a change of course with respect to Littlewood's earlier experiments with proletarian theater. These changes tended to shift the main design goal away from the physical artifact itself and toward its role as an informational device and a mechanism for the generation of user behavior. In other words, it plunged it squarely into the

design of a new form of "decorum" among its users, to borrow the term from Richard Schechner, or "adjustment" to cite Mario Manieri-Elia, or even the terminology Cedric Price used for his Potteries Thinkbelt project: "life conditioning" (Figure 105).[28] Like in Guido Canella's mobile theaters, the artifacts designed by Price and Archigram also tended toward less disperse architectures, despite appearances and their authors' mottos. And, like Maurizio Sacripanti and Giovanni Pellegrineschi's cybernetic machine, the performative mobile architecture of Archigram and Price was ultimately targeted at the users' nervous and even emotional sensorium.

The labor disputes among unemployed workers from the docks near the Fun Palace were, ultimately, not the object of interest for the authors or the core of their architectural designs. Those conflicts unfolded in the traditional spaces of the workers' struggle, like closed factories or abandoned dockyards, thus conserving the classical representation of demonstrations, strikes or street protests, which Richard Schechner was studying almost in parallel as a possible ingredient for a new environmentalist theater. Javier Navarro's hybrid Mobile Theater navigates between all these ideological stances, without subscribing openly to any of them, but rather all of them at once in different specific aspects.

Both the Fun Palace and, to a larger extent, Ideas Circus or the Instant City demonstrate a reformist and paternalistic ideology with roots in the Enlightenment when analyzed from a distance, which shows through in an obsessive and masterful excess of design not only in the architectu-

Figure 103: Model of the *Fun Palace* by Cedric Price, 1963-1965. Canadian Centre of Architecture.

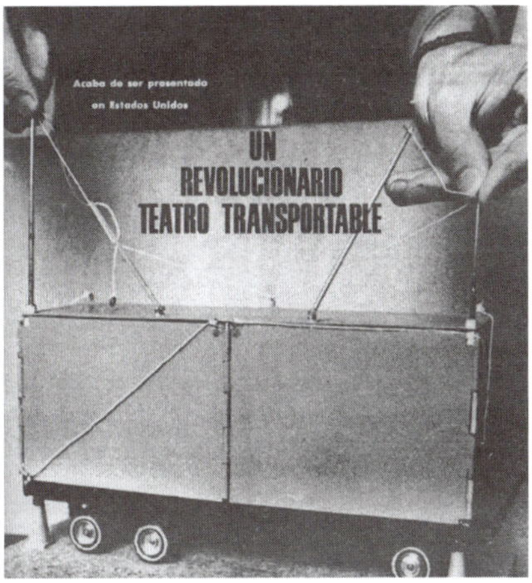

ral container, but in its semiotic contents and associated moral values. In that sense, rather than a true defiance of moralist bourgeois theater, this type of performative architecture represented a brilliant revision of the protocols of bourgeois theater and its behavioral decorum – or, in other words, of the theater-temple-machine. These traveling metropolises were meant to offer the local community:

A taste of the metropolitan dynamic – which is temporarily grafted on to the local centre – and whilst the community is still recovering from the shock, uses this catalyst as the first stage of a national hookup. A network of information-education-entertainment –"play-and-know yourself" facilities.[29]

As such, these English mobile architectures, as Manfredo Tafuri had observed with respect to their Italian equivalents, responded to a very particular social situation and atmosphere, which architects have often ignored: people were beginning to realize, at that time, that the industrial working class was entering a period of decline, which was manifesting in the dissolution of the time and space of work into a new continuous time and space of productive leisure. In that sense, the new object of design was no longer the factory, but free time. The factory and the suburban single-family home, along with their architectural dialectic, were disappearing in favor of delocalized work and commercial and leisure centers, as subsequent events have shown us. Up to that point, the leisure of the working masses had been a question dominated by the

Figure 104: Model of one of the Mobile Theater trucks by Javier Navarro de Zuvillaga. *ABC de las Américas*, New York, February 1973. Courtesy of Javier Navarro de Zuvillaga.

Figure 105: Cover of *Architectural Design* from October 1966, with Cedric Price's Potteries Thinkbelt, presented under the title "Life Conditioning". Courtesy of the ETSAM library.

state, and its architecture was modern, hygienic, lightweight and anti-monumental. These designs for electrified mobile complexes were an architectural response to the new phenomenon of the decline of the working class and its social assimilation as active consumers. It remains to be seen whether they helped to hasten it along.

THE REPOSE OF THE MASSES

In Spanish architectural culture there were similar cases of this evolution, always taking into account the exceptional nature of the Iberian context and its particular political evolution. In 1961, the young fourth-year architecture student Emilio Pérez Piñero won the International Union of Architects (UIA) competition with his well-known project for a traveling theater for 500 spectators that could be disassembled. The design was published by Peter Cook in his book *Architecture: Action and Plan*, from 1967 (Figure 106). Between 1961 and his sudden death in 1972, Pérez Piñero produced a large series of artifacts and prototypes for foldable lightweight structures, largely associated with uses that could be qualified as technocratic leisure of the state, very much aligned with Fuller's technological transfers. However, Piñero never used theoretical models of design or calculation; rather he relied on direct manufacture and craftsmanship, based entirely on spatial vision and manual skill. Most of his projects were developed based on models, rather than paper plans. With the exception of his series of designs for travelling movie theaters, developed for a family business, and his collaborations with Salvador Dalí, most of his projects were tied to General Franco's regime and its international propaganda policies initiated in the late 1950s. It is worth reaching back even a little further in time to look at proposals from Spanish architecture which, decades earlier, announced this design theme of a technocratic architecture of leisure for the masses of workers/consumers with an enormous ideological component.

In parallel to Federico García Lorca's La Barraca, which intended to offer a cultured

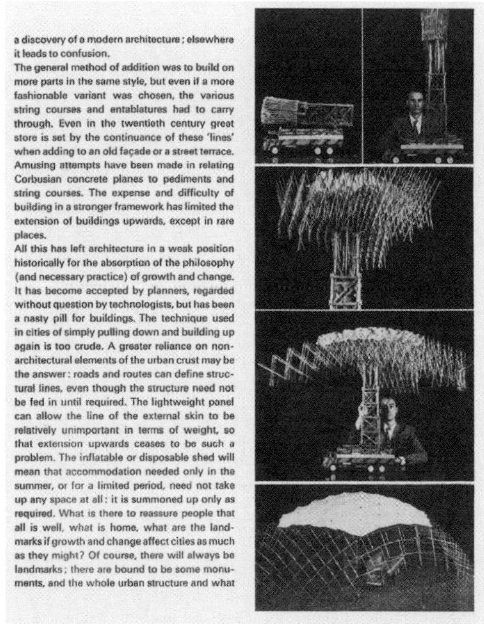
a discovery of a modern architecture; elsewhere it leads to confusion.

The general method of addition was to build on more parts in the same style, but even if a more fashionable variant was chosen, the various string courses and entablatures had to carry through. Even in the twentieth century great store is set by the continuance of these 'lines' when adding to an old façade or a street terrace. Amusing attempts have been made in relating Corbusian concrete planes to pediments and string courses. The expense and difficulty of building in a stronger framework has limited the extension of buildings upwards, except in rare places.

All this has left architecture in a weak position historically for the absorption of the philosophy (and necessary practice) of growth and change. It has become accepted by planners, regarded without question by technologists, but has been a nasty pill for buildings. The technique used in cities of simply pulling down and building up again is too crude. A greater reliance on non-architectural elements of the urban crust may be the answer: roads and routes can define structural lines, even though the structure need not be fed in until required. The lightweight panel can allow the line of the external skin to be relatively unimportant in terms of weight, so that extension upwards ceases to be such a problem. The inflatable or disposable shed will mean that accommodation needed only in the summer, or for a limited period, need not take up any space at all: it is summoned up only as required. What is there to reassure people that all is well, what is home, what are the landmarks if growth and change affect cities as much as they might? Of course, there will always be landmarks; there are bound to be some monuments, and the whole urban structure and what

Figure 106: Page 79 from the book by Peter Cook, *Architecture: Action and Plan.*

form of leisure drawing from the popular sphere, the government of the Republic promoted projects intended to organize the free time of the emerging urban middle classes, tied in with social mobility and architectural portability as its logical counterpart. Whereas the response for the rural environment with La Barraca was a temporary saturation of a culturally deserted medium, in the urban environment it was just the opposite: a de-saturation achieved through an escape into the countryside. Mobility and architectural portability thus supported ideological projects that were only apparently isolated, since they were actually complementary.

The editorial arm of GATEPAC,[30] the magazine *AC Documentos de Arquitectura Contemporánea*, published a monograph in its second year called "Es necesario organizar el reposo de las masas" [We need to organize the repose of the masses], dated 1932 (Figure 107). Among other designs, the magazine included two projects that resonate with everything we have seen heretofore: a domestic prototype for a "weekend house" and an urban prototype for a "city of repose". The weekend house is essentially a mobile, portable and disassemblable container that is entirely prefabricated. It was published along with images of groups of people travelling on trains, buses and other types of transportation. Although the weekend house is wrapped up in functionalist rhetoric, it is actually an *adhocist* architectural operation, in which a train car or a truck is adapted slightly to serve as a dwelling, operating as a mobile unit that has taken on a certain degree of stability (Figure 108). The floor plan, as schematic as Cedric Price's, barely an ergonomic diagram, is extraordinarily similar to Javier Navarro's adapted trucks. It is even capped, as can be seen in the drawing in perspective, by a playful rhetorical device – a banner – as the sole visible indication of its true function: a vacation home understood as a ludic device for rest and relaxation.

For the City of Repose, a proposal for a seaside area near Barcelona, an entire rationalist Instant City was designed, which, to an extent, like the summer home architecture in southern England that inspired Archigram's playful imagery, was a precursor of Peter Cook's idea.[31] It comprised a swimming area, a zone for summer homes, another for temporary residences, and an area devoted to "rest cures", thus articulating the architecture based on strict parameters of short-term temporary occupation: hours, days or weeks (Figure 109). The entirety of these architectures respond to a mere multiplication of functional and ergonomic ideograms, which, like the vacation home itself, were literally derived from mobile transportation devices, or the portable and temporary elements characteristic of seaside constructions. They operated, as such, to use Price's vocabulary, as a true mechanism for life conditioning, to the extent that, for the seaside cabin service, the architects stipulated "180 people per hour" for each of the cabins (Figure 110). The City of Repose and the weekend house, are, like the Instant City, nearly literal extensions of the metropolitan transportation system, which are minimally adapted in strictly architectural terms.

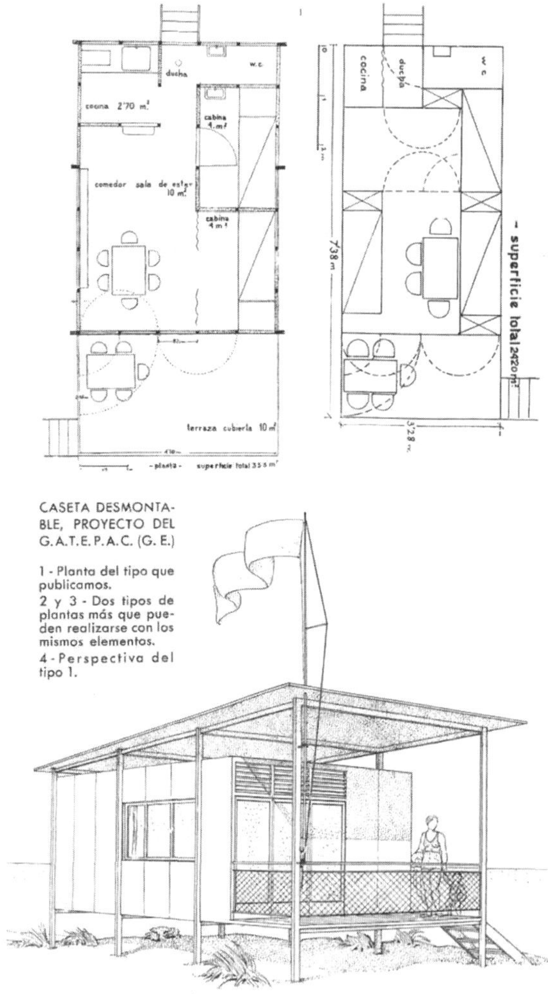

Figure 107: Cover of the magazine *AC Documentos de Arquitectura Contemporánea* from 1932. National Library of Spain.

Figure 108: Disassemblable weekend house by GATEPAC (Eastern Group) from 1932. National Library of Spain.

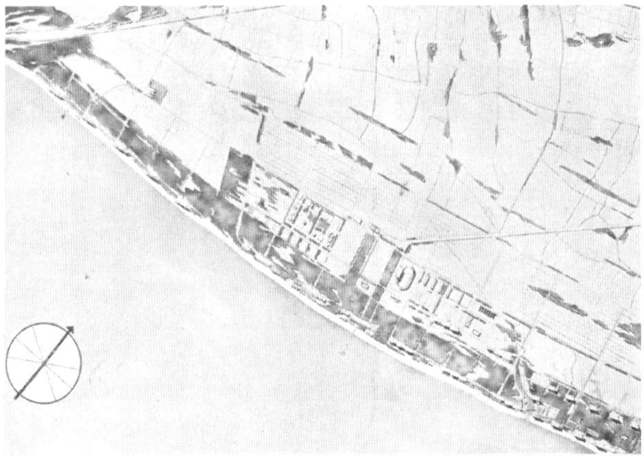

CIUDAD DE REPOSO DE BARCELONA.— Servicio de cabinas para baños. Planta de conjunto de un grupo de elementos.

Cabida por elemento: 180 personas por hora.

Cabida del grupo de cinco elementos: 900 personas por hora.

1. Cabinas para vestirse.
2. Armarios guardarropa.
3. WC, caballeros.
4. WC, señoras.
5. Duchas caballeros.
6. Duchas señoras.

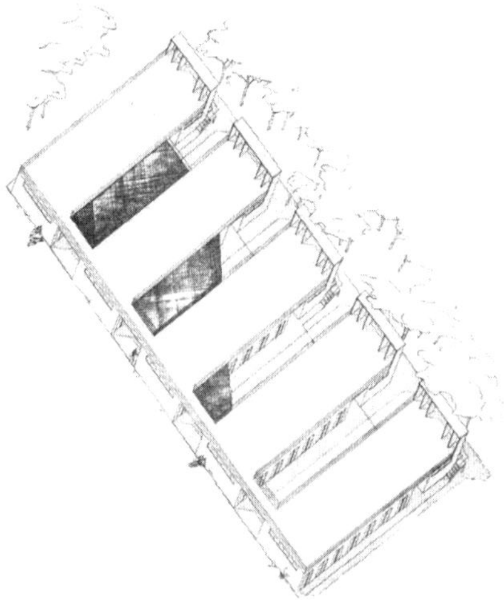

Perspectiva axonométrica de un grupo de elementos.

CIUDAD DE REPOSO DE BARCELONA. — Servicio de cabinas para baños. Detalle, planta y sección de un elemento.

Funcionamiento. La cabina responde únicamente a su fin utilitario: vestirse y desnudarse. Una vez cumplida dicha función, vuelve a quedar libre. La cabina (1 en la planta superior) tiene una pequeña abertura por donde el ocupante, una vez desnudado, entrega la ropa al encargado mediante un comprobante para que sea guardada en los armarios (2) durante el baño, quedando así la cabina en disposición de ser ocupada seguidamente (véanse fotos inferiores).

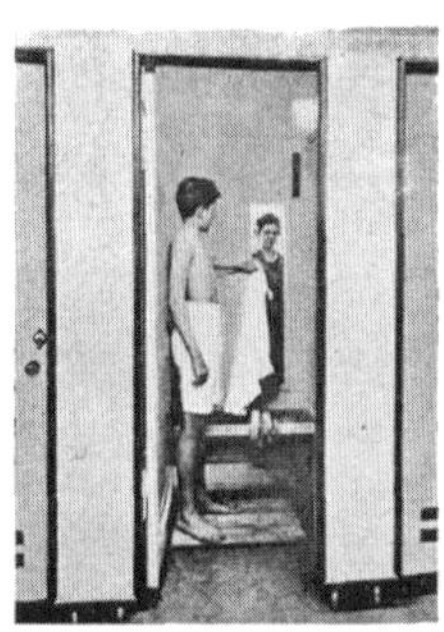

Figure 109: Floor plan for the *Ciudad de reposo* [City of Repose] by GATEPAC (Eastern Group) from 1932. National Library of Spain.

Figure 110: Cabins for beachgoers, from the *Ciudad del reposo* by GATEPAC (Eastern Group) from 1932. National Library of Spain.

Peter Cook began his 1967 book, *Architecture: Action and Plan* by asserting that "architecture can be gauged by three criteria: performance, identity, and economy of means".[32] These criteria are entirely shared by the GATEPAC initiatives involving the weekend house, which they described as follows: "It needs to be a dwelling reduced to the very minimum, with a simplified floor plan; it should transmit the feeling of contact with the sun, the earth and the air: a construction free from the social prejudices of the academic forms used up to now."[33] The city of repose should offer widespread access to those conditions, incorporating extensive mobility into the design: "Trains, streetcars, buses, subways, etc. every means of transportation that exists, are used by citizens at large who are driven by that inevitable need: to get out – to escape – from the city, to immerse themselves in a restorative and relaxing atmosphere. Repose. Physical and spiritual euphoria, a human desire shared by all social classes."[34] On the surface, there is a stark contrast between the Instant City or Ideas Circus and the City of Repose, although, underneath it all, the architectural means involved are extraordinarily similar, which generates a significant ambiguity. To an extent, Archigram was culminating the process of *organizing mass leisure* and taking it to the extreme. Using the same design resources as GATEPAC, rooted in mobility, the group definitively extended the metropolis and its associated way of life from the weekday to the weekend and from the city to the countryside.

TECHNODEVICES FOR SOCIAL EMERGENCIES

Javier Navarro's mobile device was designed as a theater, but also as a multi-use structure that could be adapted to any number of potential functions. One of those adaptations was studied in detail on a commission from the Ministry of Housing, and it became an industrialized prototype for emergency housing in 1974 (Figure 111). This adaptation affected the trucks themselves: they were reduced from eight to six meters in length and their interior configuration was adapted. Above all, however, it affected how they were connected, which initially responded to a clear design intent of generating spaces for social groups, as opposed to a series of individuals. The *urban* version of the Mobile Theater is not a city for leisure, education, or evasion, it is a temporary camp for social groups that have been displaced by catastrophes.

Javier Navarro's project for emergency dwellings incorporated a "Basic Unit" made up of four trucks measuring 6 x 2.5 meters, which formed a row of three dwellings, with courtyards covered by inflatable roofs and a shared service core located on one end of the row, housed in one of the four trucks (Figure 112). Thus, it was a miniature Mobile Theater, in which all the technical inventions were employed to generate a possible urban unit. The foundation was set up using hydraulic jacks, the partitions were formed using the truck's swiveling panel doors, the supports for the inflatable roof were extendible poles, and the plumbing, lighting and electric installations were all built in. The design proposed three groupings of these basic units, but never individual capsules:

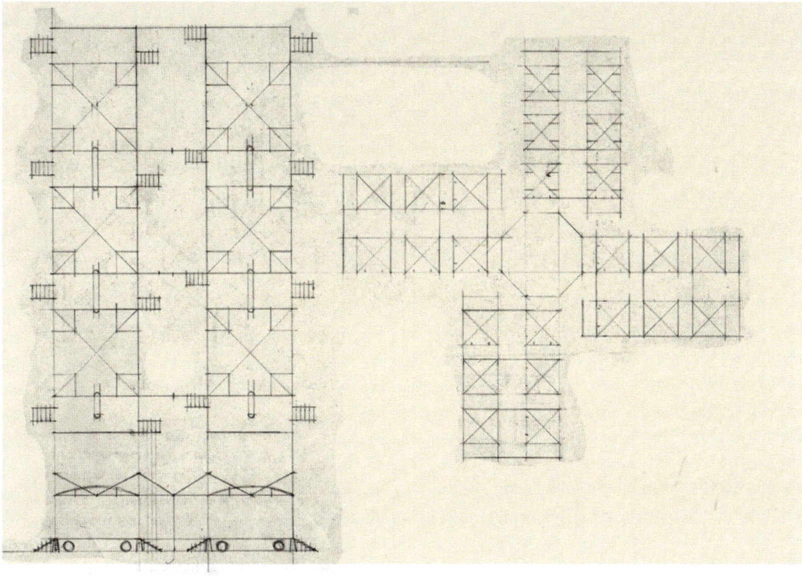

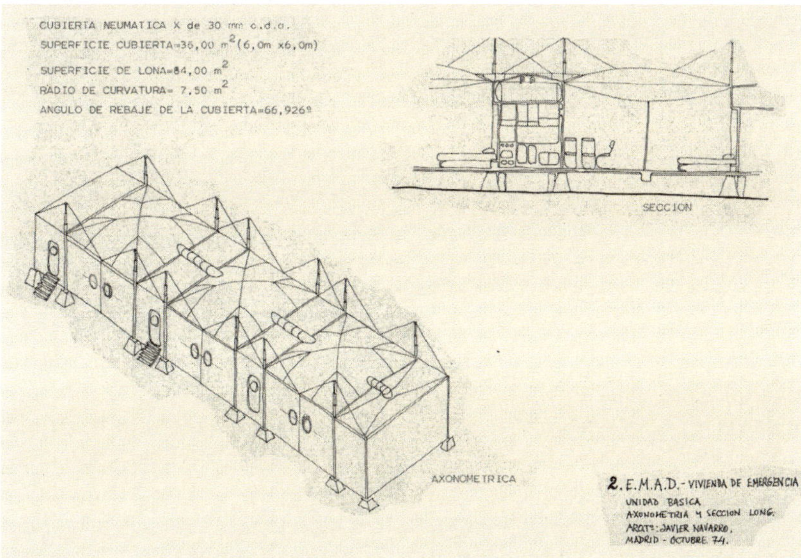

Figure 111: Sketches for the *Estructura Móvil Autotransportable y Desmontable para Viviendas de Emergencia* [Self-Transporting and Disassemblable Mobile Structure for Emergency Dwellings], October 1974. Courtesy of Javier Navarro de Zuvillaga.

Figure 112: Axonometric projection and detailed section of the *Estructura Móvil Autotransportable y Desmontable para Viviendas de Emergencia*, October 1974. Courtesy of Javier Navarro de Zuvillaga.

Grouping 1: Consists of two parallel and enantiomorphic (similar, but non-congruent) Basic Units, which, using swiveling panels that coincide with the back of each truck, enclose independent courtyards for each pair of dwellings, which can be accessed via the stairway door planned for each Basic Unit. In this case, only one of the Basic Unit trucks will be equipped with the building services to supply both units; the other truck can be given over to other uses, such as storage, first aid, etc.

Grouping 2: Four Basic Units arranged around a regular octagon formed by the four service trucks. This octagon, which may be open-air or covered, would be a common space shared by the four Basic Units; it can serve the same purpose as the courtyards in Grouping 1.

Grouping 3: Four instances of Grouping 1, arranged around a regular octagon formed by the four open trucks (not equipped with building services). These four trucks can be used for common services: laundry, first aid, day care, kitchens, etc.; the octagon (whether open-air or covered) can be used as a play space, for shared dining, etc. The uses will depend on the organization and administration of the housing system.[35]

Moreover, the design provided a "code of use", describing how the use of shared and individual services might be regulated, as well as instructions regarding the physical

mechanisms, along with "storage for salvaged household items". This insistence on shared operations, highlighted by the regulations, sets up a certain distance from Archigram's capsular designs, although it borrows from many of their technical and figurative motifs. What these emergency dwellings bring into play is the possibility of an ultimate association of the modern subject, uprooted from social class and work (the user of the capsule) with people who have lost or left behind their homes. The "emergency" of the title also, and even above all, refers to a social situation in which the domestic sphere has fallen, literally, into a profound crisis.

Figure 113: Cover of the magazine *Arquitectura* from January 1972, showing the *Unidades Sociales de Emergencia* [Emergency Social Units] by Antonio Fernández Alba and Juan Daniel Fullaondo. Source: *Arquitectura* magazine.

Javier Navarro's emergency housing drew on some of Archigram's experiments, but it was much more influenced by a more specific project developed in 1971 by the architects Antonio Fernández Alba (1927) and Juan Daniel Fullaondo (1936-1994), along with the visual artist Rafael Canogar and the student (at the time) Eduardo Sánchez. The project was the result of a commission from Carlos de Miguel, editor of the magazine *Arquitectura* for the Architects' Association of Madrid (COAM) (Figure 113). In April of that year, Carlos de Miguel was returning from a trip to Venezuela and Canada, where his experiences in "the ramshackle outskirts of Caracas and the flowery optimism of hippy communities near Montreal" led him to present the architects with the commission for the *Unidades Sociales de Emergencia.* The project was developed from April to November 1971 as a series of "growing systems of functions" to house users who had been victims of natural disasters. These growing systems could be expanded based on minimum units built in phases.

Antonio Fernández Alba asserted that the project "is presented, for the moment, as a protracted solution that falls within the theoretical, and sometimes reductionist, debates on today's socio-cultural superstructures".[36] In that sense, he framed it within the debate on industrialized capsular architectures. The whole is made up of two unit types grouped together: a scattered type, with a single story in rows and branches; and a compact type which, thanks to a rigid base grid, can be stacked vertically (Figure 114). The common module comprises three parts, which the authors called "levels of organization", phases or processes. The handcrafted process or phase is the first. It consists of a room for sleeping with four air mattresses per unit, within a structure that offers three possible building types: a rigidized canvas tent, an accordion structure and a rigid self-built grid structure. This initial phase is set up directly following the disaster and can be organized in any number of configurations. A linear configuration in rows is the option studied in detail. The handcrafted process is accompanied by "packages of provisions [...] emergency food allowances, and locations based on number tickets corresponding to each unit".[37] Shared areas built with pneumatic architectures for use as school rooms, kitchens, eating areas, self-service installations, medical services and spaces for a variety of other activities are located at the ends of the linear structures (Figure 115).

Following this initial phase of the process, the second phase begins, comprising dwellings that expand on the handcrafted phase, increasing the surface area of each unit and rounding out the initial domestic program. This second phase is called industrial, and it consists fundamentally of circular elements with three different volumetric developments, depending on the building system and the materials, identical to those in the previous phase: the result is an enlargement of the sleeping area in the shape of a dome, cylinder or cone (Figures 116 and 117). The third and final phase is the technological phase, a rigid prefabricated module with a bathroom and kitchen that is connected to the previous phase, and which can be finished with a small service yard in the back. In the case of the compact unit, the same layout is repeated, but with

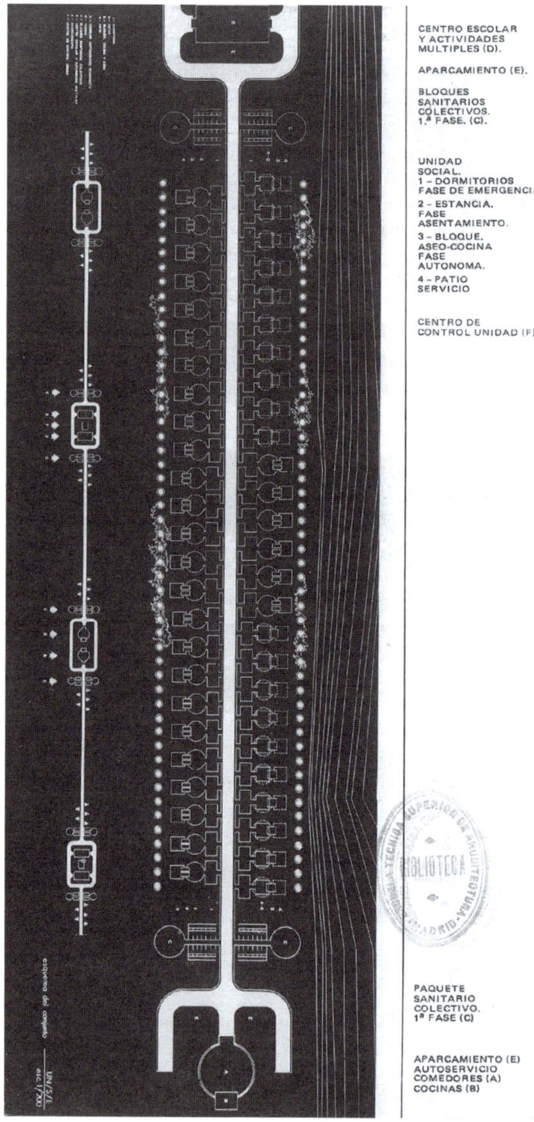

Figure 114: Axonometric drawing of the *Unidades Sociales de Emergencia*, by Antonio Fernández Alba and Juan Daniel Fullaondo, 1971. Archive of the Centre Georges Pompidou.

Figure 115: Floor plan of a possible grouping of the *Unidades Sociales de Emergencia*, Antonio Fernández Alba and Juan Daniel Fullaondo, 1971. Source: *Arquitectura* magazine.

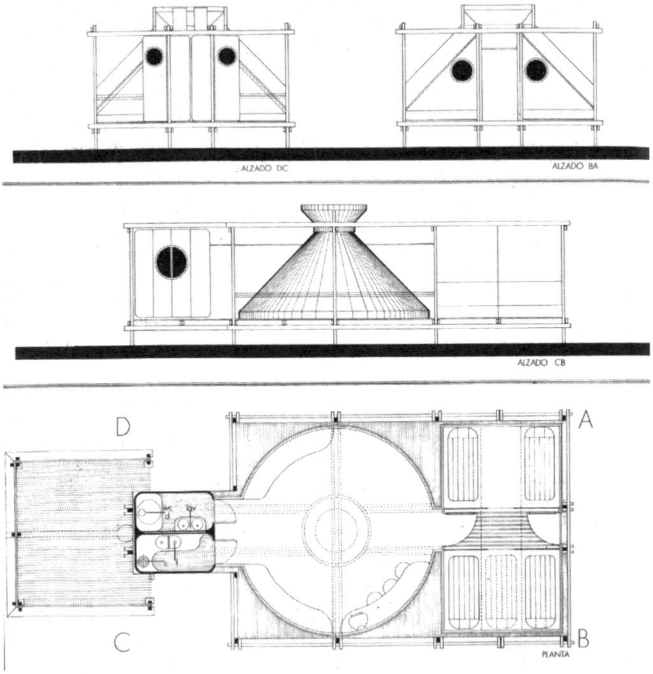

Figure 116: Plans for the Compact Unit of the *Unidades Sociales de Emergencia*, by Antonio Fernández Alba and Juan Daniel Fullaondo, 1971.
Source: *Arquitectura* magazine.

Figure 117: Photomontage of the *Unidades Sociales de Emergencia*, by Antonio Fernández Alba and Juan Daniel Fullaondo, 1971. Archive of the Centre Georges Pompidou.

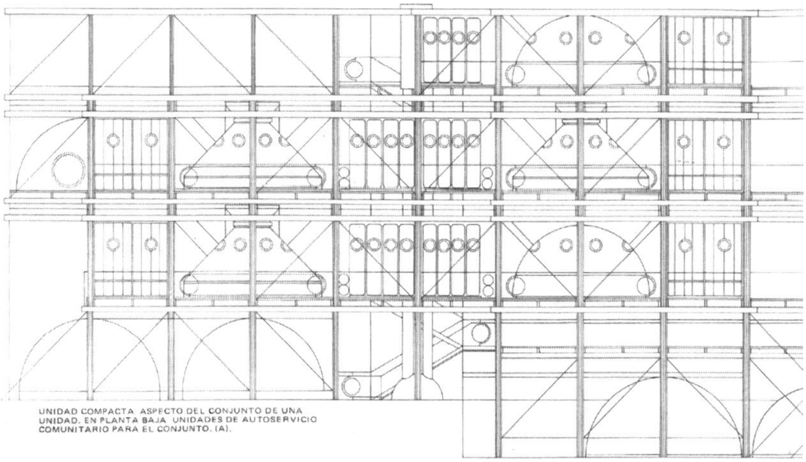

Figure 118: General section of a Compact Unit of the *Unidades Sociales de Emergencia*, by Antonio Fernández Alba and Juan Daniel Fullaondo, 1971. Source: *Arquitectura* magazine.

Figure 119: Model for the Compact Unit of the *Unidades Sociales de Emergencia*, by Antonio Fernández Alba and Juan Daniel Fullaondo, 1971. Source: *Nueva Forma* magazine.

a solid structural framework that allows for building vertically and increasing density. The diagrams show groupings of up to four stories high, with the conic volumes coinciding with the industrial phase, and with other self-service spaces and shared uses on the lower floors (Figures 118 and 119).

The project documents that were published show a series of contact sheets with different compositions of units,[38] both scattered and compact, offering a variety of different groupings that play with the dome profiles of the industrial phase and with the triangular profiles of the handcrafted phase, along with the grids of the compact units. This emphasis on the compositional aspects gives the process a certain monumentality or gravity, not because of its size, which is contained, but because of its volumetric forcefulness, fostered by the rhythmic play of repetitions. Compared with the Archigram designs, from which it clearly originates, it offers a different solution – more open than the singular, closed-off compositions of those English technical artefacts. In both cases, the composition is what confers architectural dignity to the planned complexes, although operating in a different way, even contrasting in terms of scale and, more importantly, the underlying formal structure.

This project arose largely as a critical response to the Archigram designs published a few years earlier in *Hogar y Arquitectura*, which stirred up a significant polemic among many of the Spanish architects in the professional establishment of the period. As Juan Daniel Fullaondo, co-author of this emergency housing project, little known today but broadly disseminated in its time, reminded us, Carlos Flores's monographic on Archigram was published along with the counterexample of a housing block in La Coruña by the architect José Antonio Corrales (1921-2010). This housing complex, built nearly entirely of concrete with a large-scale brink plinth, displayed all the characteristics of English Brutalism: sturdy exposed structures, *natural* materials, open

Figure 120: Interior cover image of the housing project designed by José Antonio Corrales for La Coruña, from the magazine *Hogar y Arquitectura*, October 1967. Courtesy of the ETSAM library.

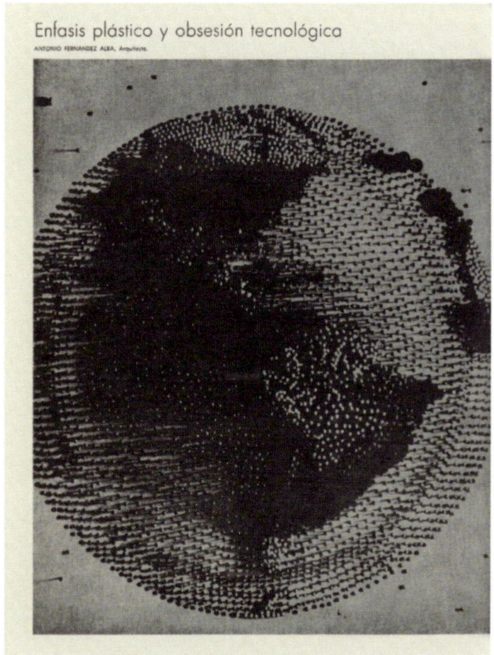
Enfasis plástico y obsesión tecnológica

ANTONIO FERNANDEZ ALBA, Arquitecto.

distribution galleries and highly articulated façades based on a grammar of openings that is canonically modern (Figure 120). Contrasted with the literal and figurative black and white of that building, the Archigram monographic with its display of fluorescent colors, incessant semiotic devices and pop imagery, offered an extraordinary contrast that was openly polemical, since it pointed out – in a very plausible interpretation – a shift in tendency. Fullaondo's chronicle in conversation with María Teresa Muñoz in 1994 leaves no room for doubt:

I remember, once, Carlos Flores [...] published a beautiful residential complex by José Antonio (Corrales) next to an extensive feature on Archigram, at its most euphoric moment. The combination was pretty explosive, evidently. And Carlos de Miguel, the editor-in-chief of Arquitectura [...] flew into a rage. He called together a few of us to prepare a sort of counterattack. How could we have confronted Corrales's fantastic design with Archigram's crazy ideas?, etc. I suggested he should keep calm and reflect a little. That we could all reflect on it together. We had a second meeting and I tried to talk to him, perhaps without much

Figure 121: Interior cover of the article *Énfasis plástico y obsesión tecnológica,* by Antonio Fernández Alba, 1968. Source: *Arquitectura* magazine.

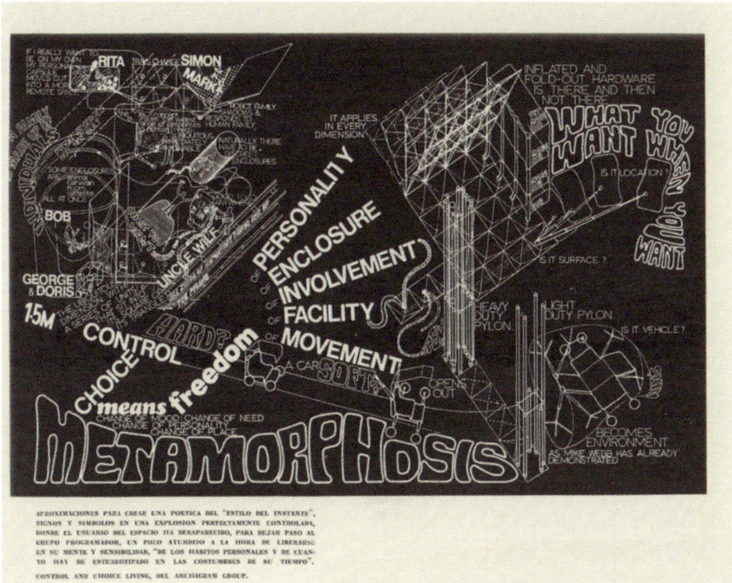

APROXIMACIONES PARA CREAR UNA POETICA DEL "ESTILO DEL INSTANTE", SIGNOS Y SIMBOLOS EN UNA EXPLOSION PERFECTAMENTE CONTROLADA, DONDE EL USUARIO DEL ESPACIO HA DESAPARECIDO, PARA DEJAR PASO AL GRUPO PROGRAMADOR, UN POCO ATURDIDO A LA HORA DE LIBERARSE EN SU MENTE Y SENSIBILIDAD, "DE LOS HABITOS PERSONALES Y DE CUANTO HAY DE ESTEREOTIPADO EN LAS COSTUMBRES DE SU TIEMPO".

CONTROL AND CHOICE LIVING, DEL ARCHIGRAM GROUP.

success, about Reyner Banham, Brutalism, Team 10, Utopie. [...] By chance, I had been able to meet Peter Cook in Paris and he didn't seem crazy to me at all. He knew what he was doing, and he was doing it with a lot of circumspection.[39]

Fullaondo was director of the magazine *Nueva Forma* at the time, one of the main publications responsible for disseminating the international architectural avant-garde in Spain between 1966 and 1975. Its role in international debates was very active and, more specifically, its assessment of Archigram was one of the most nuanced, as can be seen in his legendary essay *Agonía, utopía, renacimiento* from May 1968, a real in-depth study of the confusing international panorama of the moment, packed with lucid, though very partial, analyses that, at least, made it possible to establish a certain classificatory order and the glimmer of a horizon.[40]

For his part, the position adopted by Antonio Fernández Alba, the other architect of the *Unidades Sociales de Emergencia*, was unequivocal in its open confrontation with Archigram. An article he published in February 1968 in Carlos de Miguel's ma-

Figure 122: Caption for an illustration of Control and Choice by Archigram from the article *Énfasis plástico y obsesión tecnológica*, by Antonio Fernández Alba, 1968. Source: *Arquitectura* magazine.

gazine, called "Énfasis plástico y obsesión tecnológica" [Plastic emphasis and techonolgical obesession], laid the foundations for the confrontation (Figure 121). It is enough to look at the combative caption on an illustration of Control and Choice – which was exactly the same project Carlos Flores used to head up his monographic published a few years earlier – to understand the state of the issue at that precise moment (Figure 122):

Approaches to create a poetics of the "style of the moment", signs and symbols in a constant perfectly controlled explosion, where the user of the space disappears to make way for the group of programmers, a little bewildered when it comes to freeing themselves, in their minds and their sensitivities, "from personal habits and the stereotypes embedded in the customs of their times".[41]

And, nonetheless, the *Unidades Sociales de Emergencia* were the equitable response to this thorny debate, through a committed and mature collaboration between two architects and their respective and conflicting points of view on the question. Javier Navarro's adaptation of the Mobile Theater for emergency housing clearly takes this design as a model, but also above all, as a design mindset. The key to the resolution of that conflict can be found in an interpretation by the critic Santiago Amón (a regular collaborator with Fullaondo at the magazine *Nueva Forma*), in his introduction to the first publication of the *Unidades Sociales de Emergencia*. Amón points out something evident, that this project was conceived in a realistic vein to be built, exactly like Javier Navarro's Mobile Theater and its adaptation for emergency housing. Faced with the raw reality of non-construction, Amón coins the term "mandatory utopia" to set it apart from other possible approaches. Specifically, he refers to the antithesis laid out by Karl Manheim between ideology and utopia as positive and negative vectors in relation to the idea of progress. Whereas ideology aims to maintain the status quo, or at the most reform it, its antithesis in utopia acts as the "driving force" for deeper structural changes that can take place occasionally in the face of a breakdown of ideology. When that occurs, the utopian latency takes on an ideological significance; thus, new utopian forces appear in an ongoing dialectical engagement. As such, what is essential in the back and forth between ideologies and utopias is for the latter to become reality. Otherwise, they become *mandatory utopias*, which can only be activated by untimely recoveries – like this one. The analysis by Santiago Amón is perfectly applicable today to the Mobile Theater and its design derivatives, because the history of the project is the history of the impossibility of its construction. The cause did not lie in technical, material or economic factors (which were fully realistic), but in a series of ideological mismatches with the political environment, caused by an impermeability to the utopian vector, as Archigram demonstrated, commanded by the social environment. Amón's words at the end of his final assessment of the *Unidades Sociales de Emergencia*, citing the American poet Robert Lax, explicitly state that all those projects, beyond their varying critical frictions, when considered as a whole:

Prove that men and women, freed and cut off from their usual dwellings, people, animals and things, uprooted from habit "could come together/in a single place/occupy a field by night/set up their tents/in the early morning/perform their wonders/in the afternoon/wheel in the light/of their lamps at night".[42]

Both the *Unidades Sociales de Emergencia* and Javier Navarro's *Estructura Móvil* allude radically to new forms of human groupings. Javier Navarro published the project by Fullaondo and Fernández Alba in March 1972 with a long introductory commentary, which relates the communal socialist ideology with the counter-cultural lifestyle and the archetypes of temporary habitation, calling once again for their fusion as a possible solution to the sociological crisis of the time:

Socialists and communists, on the one hand, and beatniks and hippies, on the other, introduced this way of life, which is not new and is even supported by ideologies very similar to the ones that upheld a communal way of life throughout history, although their beliefs are very different. [...]

Fernández Alba himself says in his introduction to the subject that the hypothesis is based on "temporary environments as an alternative" which, evidently responding to the need for provisional planning in the case of an emergency, also ties in with the essence of the response that architecture should start providing for the shift we are seeing in our social structure, and to which we have referred in this introduction.

In fact, this project was developed taking into account Fernández Alba's experiences living on a commune for a short time and his ideas for the design of a Detox Center which the group had requested.[43]

The Mobile Theater, especially in its urban adaptation for people who have lost their homes, shares with the *Unidades Sociales de Emergencia* an ideological position halfway between progressive utopia and technical reality, in a staunch commitment to the material conditions of its economic and social context, which it aims to overcome by promoting existing latencies rather than generating them *ex nihilo*. In the electric decade, there was room for a certain range of proposals interested in the direct modification of users' lives through design strategies with close ties to nomadism, education and temporariness. The most utopian among them opted for the radical life conditioning of a new type of generic subject; whereas others, like Navarro's structure for emergency housing, aimed to provide more specific solutions for much more particular users, situated on the margins of material prosperity. Both architectural experiments failed in the face of the forces of inertia in the environment and its resistance to change, but they were on track in their total adherence to a commitment to the present.

Notes

1. A good overview of the history of the AA can be found here: https://www.aaschool.ac.uk/AASCHOOL/LIBRARY/aahistory.php

2. Simon Sadler: "An Avant-Garde Academy", in Andrew Ballantyne (ed.): *Architectures: Modernism and After*, London: Blackwell Publishing 2008, pgs. 33-56.

3. At the same time, the London school was in the midst of a transition affecting its studio model. For more information on the "unit"-based teaching system and its function in 1970, see, for example, Igor Marjanović: "Lines and Words on Display: Alvin Boyarsky as a Collector, Curator and Publisher", in *Architectural Research Quarterly*, vol. 14, issue 2, June 2010, pgs. 165-174.

4. The declaration of the State of Exception appeared in the Official Bulletin of the State (BOE) on January 25, 1969; the text from the quote headed up the decree-law.

5. *Nuevo Diario*, January 25, 1969. The newspaper was published by the group Prensa y Ediciones S.A. (PESA), with close ties to the technocratic branch of Opus Dei, within Franco's government.

6. Jeffrey Kipnis: *Perfect Acts of Architecture*, New York: MoMA 2001, pg. 14.

7. The events were described by David Robbins in his now classic book *The Independent Group: Postwar Britain and the Aesthetics of Plenty*, Cambridge: The MIT Press, 1990, with retrospective texts by nearly all the participants.

8. Simon Sadler: *Archigram: Architecture without Architecture*, Cambridge: The MIT Press, 2005, especially chapter 2: "The Living City. Pop Urbanism Circa 1963", pg. 33.

9. Javier Navarro de Zuvillaga: "The Disintegration of Theatrical Space," *Architectural Association Quarterly*, vol. 8, no. 4, 1976, pg. 31. The emphasis is present in the original.

10. Simon Sadler: *Archigram. Architecture without Architecture*, op. cit., pgs. 52-90.

11. These criticisms were published in the ultra-famous book by Jane Jacobs: *The Death and Life of Great American Cities*, New York: Random House 1961 and in the analyses of urban spaces known as the *Street Life Project*, by William Hollingsworth Whyte, which, although it began officially in 1969 with his activity as a consultant for the New York City Planning Commission, was widely known much earlier.

12. Peter Cook, introduction to the catalog text for the exhibition *Living City*, published in the magazine *Living Arts* no. 2, London, 1963, p. 71, edited by Peter Cook and Theo Crosby. Cited in Simon Sadler: *Archigram. Architecture without Architecture*, op. cit., pg. 55.

13. *Hogar y Arquitectura*, no. 72, October 1967. The bimonthly magazine began as the communications and propaganda organ of the Obra Sindical del Hogar [Trade Union Housing Society], an organization with close ties to the Francoist regime. The architect Francisco de Asís Cabrero was editor in chief from 1955 to 1963, when he was replaced by the architect Carlos Flores who remained in the post until 1974. After a year of inactivity, the magazine continued to be published until 1978.

14. *Hogar y Arquitectura*, no. 72, October 1967, pg. 20.

15. Reyner Banham: "La Visión de Archigram", in *Hogar y Arquitectura*, op. cit, pgs. 19-20. Banham's short text in English was published in *Hogar y Arquitectura* along with the Spanish version.

16. Bruno Taut to Gläserne Kette, Berlin, November 24, 1919, in *The Crystal Chain Letters: Architectural Fantasies by Bruno Taut and His Circle*, ed. Iain Boyd Whyte, Cambridge, MA: MIT Press, 1985, p. 19.

17. Ibid., pg. 23. The emphasis is present in the original.

18. González Quintana provided reports for the magazine focused on the teaching activities of Michael Webb, David Green and Warren Chalk in the United States, specifically at the University of Virginia School of Architecture.

19. An early version of the project, which underwent subsequent developments over a long period of time, appeared in number 5 of the *Archigram* magazine in 1964, on page 15, under the title "'Anything' space for Metropolife".

20. The Cushicle was published in *Archigram* no. 8, 1968, as insert no. 13 of the magazine in model form. Nearly all the projects in the issue refer to the architectural customization of vehicles.

21. Suitaloon always appears associated with the Cushicle in publications, and both were redrawn on multiple occasions to be published, displayed or exhibited. As with the rest of the group's work, the main source for consultation remains the catalog: Peter Cook: *Archigram*,

self-published in 1970 and reprinted by London: Studio Vista, 1972; New York: Praeger, 1972; Basel/Boston: Birkhauser, 1991; and New York: Princeton Architectural Press, 1999.

22. Reyner Banham: *Design by Choice*, Penny Sparke (ed.), London: Academy Editions, 1981. The name of this anthology corresponds to a text by Banham first published in *The Architectural Review* no. 130, July 1961, pgs. 43-48.

23. Like other projects we have cited here, Ideas Circus appeared in *Archigram* no. 8 in inserts number 17/1 and 17/2.

24. For more on Joan Littlewood, see Robert Leach: *Theatre Workshop: Joan Littlewood and the Making of Modern British Theatre*, Exeter: Exeter University Press, 2006; and Joan Littlewood: *Joan's Book: The Autobiography of Joan Littlewood*, London: Methuen, 2003.

25. For a political critique of these projects, see Anthony Iles: *Legislating for Enthusiasm: From Fun Palace to Creative Prison*, available online at http://www.arcade-project.com/sacrifice/Legislating%20for%20Enthusiasm.pdf. For the relationship between Cedric Price and Joan Littlewood in the Fun Palace, the best source is Stanley Mathews, *From Agit-Prop to Free Space*, London: Black Dog, 2007.

26. *Archigram* no. 8, 1968.

27. Ibid.

28. "Life Conditioning" was the eloquent title of the text by Price that introduced his project in specialized journals.

29. *Archigram* no. 8, 1968.

30. GATEPAC is the acronym for Grupo de Artistas y Técnicos Españoles para el Progreso de la Arquitectura Contemporánea [Group of Spanish Architects and Experts for the Advancement of Contemporary Architecture], tied to the government of the Spanish Republic as a national branch of the CIAM. It was founded in 1930 and published 25 issues of *AC Documentos de Actividad Contemporánea*, between 1931 and 1937.

31. Peter Cook and Dennis Crompton came from seaside towns with a heavy iconographic load: Cook was from Southern-on-Sea, in the southwest, and Crompton was from Blackpool, in the northeast. In both those cities, the urban landscape is intensely affected by the leisure facilities of seaside theme parks.

32. Peter Cook: *Architecture: Action and Plan*, London: Studio Vista and New York: Reinhold Publishing Corporation, 1967, pg. 5.

33. *AC Documentos de Actividad Contemporánea*, year 2, no. 7, Madrid-Barcelona-San Sebastián, pg. 18.

34. Ibid., pg. 25.

35. Javier Navarro de Zuvillaga, manuscript of the brief for the project *Estructura Móvil Autotransportable y Desmontable para Viviendas de Emergencia*, October 1974.

36. Antonio Fernández Alba: "Unidades Sociales de Emergencia", in *Arquitectura*, no. 157, January 1972, pg. 6.

37. Ibid., pg. 10.

38. The project was published in various European journals: *Arquitectura*, no. 157, January 1972, pgs. 6-22; *L'Architettura Cronache e Storia*, no. 8-206, December 1972, pgs. 536-541; *Nueva Forma,* no. 78-79, 1972, pgs. 78-79; and *L'Architecture d'Ajourd'hui*, no. 159, December-January 1971-1972, pgs. 21-23.

39. Juan Daniel Fullaondo and María Teresa Muñoz: *Historia de la arquitectura contemporánea española. Tomo III: y Orfeo desciende*, Madrid: Molly Editorial, 1997, pg. 263.

40. There are two monographic studies on Juan Daniel Fullaondo's critical activities that provide the keys to understanding the architect's role in the debate at the time. The first was written by María Teresa Muñoz, who was his collaborator from 1987 to 1994: *Juan Daniel Fullaondo. Escritos Críticos*, Bilbao: Colegio Oficial de Arquitectos Vasco Navarro, 2007; the second is the PhD dissertation written by Lucía Pérez Moreno, directed by María Teresa Muñoz and published as: *Fullaondo y la revista Nueva Forma. Aportaciones a la construcción de una cultura arquitectónica en España (1966-1975)*, Alzuza: Fundación Museo Jorge Oteiza, 2015.

41. Antonio Fernández Alba: "Énfasis plástico y obsesión tecnológica", in *Arquitectura*, no. 111, February 1968, pg. 16.

42. Santiago Amón: "Utopías obligadas", in *Arquitectura*, no. 157, January 1972. pg. 5.

43. Javier Navarro de Zuvillaga: "Emergencia. Nueva sociedad, nueva arquitectura" in *Panorámica de la Construcción*, no. 2, May-April 1972, pg. 36.

CHAPTER 5_ THE PNEUMATIC COMMUNITY

In a retrospective text about the pedagogy of the Architectural Association called "The Electric Decade: An Atmosphere at the AA School 1963-1973", written by Peter Cook and published in 1975, he calls the decade odd and eccentric. The Mobile Theater design fell within that decade, and it shows significant parallels with other projects developed by students at the school. The resemblances go beyond mere formal qualities or questions of composition and technological possibilities, shared by teachers and students in a generational continuity of interests and languages, both exemplary and critical. Cook tells of his beginnings as a professor at his *alma mater* in 1964, with just four years of experience as a graduate and a certain popularity among the close-knit circles of the London avant-garde. He describes the school's gradual process of "electrification", in its broadening disciplinary openness to social and cultural interests, which Archigram disseminated through its magazine and public appearances. This disciplinary openness, aptly characterized by Cook's statement on the relative importance of rain in Oxford Street in relation to its architecture, reached its limits at the end of this decade:

Around 1969 there were small pockets of invention, rethink, and honest-to-goodness unravelling going on... among a pervading grey. [...] And for me, the grey was magically pushed away again with the onrush of the fifth year of 1970-1971. Quite simply – they were great! Because they did things. And they could draw. And they could invent. And they had style. Sometimes the style was in their manner... the year of the mods... matured mods maybe... but with a leftover of panache. Even those with an overriding social conscience bore no resemblance to the traditional AA do-gooder... they got out there and did something about it. Graham Hobbs and Kay Jordan... they set a shop (literally a shop) in the downtrodden community and got things organised. People didn't talk about domes and inflatables... they lived inside them. And art came back.[1]

Kay Jordan, who passed away in 2011, was one of the architects from that electric class, to which Javier Navarro also belonged in his unique position as a visitor at that institution of education and intellectual production, and his time at the Architectural Association coincided fully with the *annus mirabilis* Cook talked about: 1970-1971. Jordan worked briefly in conventional architecture offices after graduating until she developed her professional specialization in community architecture: first through the Solon cooperative and, later, in 1984, when she founded the Spitalfields Small Business Association (SSBA). Operating out of East London, the association developed residential designs and workshop spaces for the Bangladeshi community in the district of Spitalfields. Jordan also created the Crown and Leek workshops, which offered training in architectural

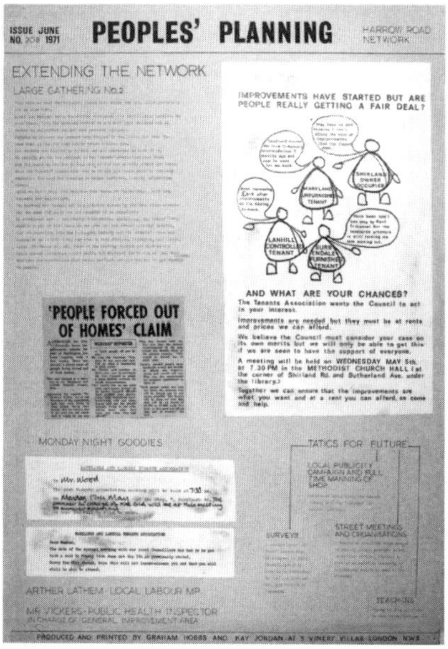

Figure 123: Graham Hobbs and Kay Jordan: Peoples' Planning, 1971.
Courtesy of the Architectural Association historical archive.

construction for residents, along with spaces for small businesses. Moreover, she played a fundamental role until her death, leading the campaign against the Crossrail, the rapid underground train slotted for completion in 2020, which will change the urban landscape in many areas of the city.[2]

Her graduation project, together with Graham Hobbs, consisted of a small-scale urban planning mechanism called Peoples' Planning, a neighborhood legal and technical consulting office that was operational for a period of time (Figure 123). Other students from the group developed projects that were much more in line with the architectural language of Archigram, although, significantly, Cook highlighted Jordan's project – so far-removed from his personal ideology – with special attention in his chronicle. Stuart Lever, another prominent student from the course, presented a design called Tree Project, which electrified a typical suburban English garden with audio and video devices, expanding the users' sensory perceptions. Mark Fisher and Simon Conolly also graduated that year, forming a team that presented a design for a multimedia tent for the Isle of Wight Pop Festival. Fisher became well known in the following decades as the designer of tents and stages for large concerts, for artists ranging from Pink Floyd to Lady Gaga. Ken Allison, who was a collaborator with Archigram from 1970 until it was disbanded in 1975, developed a graduation project called Park Hotel. It consisted of a series of bedroom-vans which, parked together in sets, formed a central collective space for an indeterminate use, under an inflatable roof.

All these designs, developed during the 1970-1971 academic year, show formal and conceptual similarities with the Mobile Theater, although their respective authors did not know one another, nor did they have the same advisors at the Architectural Association. Judging by some of the students' designs, the discourse and tools in circulation during that year seem to have been broadly shared. This new generation combined some of Archigram's initial obsessions with a series of interests of their own, which tended toward a greater professional dissolution in the social and political medium, with which Javier Navarro would fit in perfectly.

The distinctive trait of this new generation, so admired by their teacher Cook, was that their projects broke free from the radically individual agency of a society atomized into subjectivities fed by consumption and characterized by individual hyper-technological habitats; they renounced the ultraliberal ideology of the Archigram generation, which had been the cause of much criticism leveled at its members. Instead, the youngest among them adopted a sensibility that was much more attuned to collective configurations and, especially, the needs associated with shared representation – a key characteristic of the group that Cook celebrates in his retrospective narrative. The disintegration of architecture presaged by Archigram took a turn in the following generation that was surprising, but logical to a certain point: the initial rhetorical technification practiced by their teachers dematerialized into progressively more ethereal and immaterial structures until it became – in the paradigmatic case of Jordan and Hobbs' design – a pure social structure for collective service and self-representation.

THEATERS OF AIR

In this cultural process, inflatable architecture – which reached its height during that decade – played a fundamental role, and the Mobile Theater was not exempt from that influence. On the one hand, the theater formalized the service structures for what we could call, to use Schechner's terminology, "performing technicians" (which would include the actors) using industrialized elements that were only minimally customized: trucks. On the other, it used a lenticular inflatable roof to demarcate the collective space of self-representation. Based on these mechanisms, the Mobile Theater offered a response to the two main trends dominant in academic circles at the time. Similar to many of the student designs from that memorable final year at the Architectural Association, the Mobile Theater did not make use of the prospective-futuristic rhetoric typical of Archigram, nor did it propose individual inflatable habitats, bubbles or portable houses to emancipate the individual from the social sphere. On the contrary, it focused its attention on unprogrammed collective spaces. The Fun Palace's exhaustive detail with regard to social program disappeared along with the monumental technological rhetoric. Thus, a new way of working emerged, which, although it was a successor to the concerns espoused by Price and Littlewood, placed more emphasis on possibilist aspects and realizations, which were necessarily precarious.

Initially, the roof of the Mobile Theater was designed as a square floating structure shaped like a hyperbolic paraboloid, suspended from two of its corners by large helium balloons and secured on the other two corners to fixed anchor points on the trucks (Figure 124). This germinal structure was immediately refined in one respect to improve its function: the cables along the paraboloid structure were also made inflatable. In this solution, four large helium balloons were attached to the four corners, while other smaller balloons along each side of the square maintained the tension along the edges, counteracting the forces originating from the perimeter enclosures (Figure 125). Navarro arrived at this solution based on purely technical speculations, as is evident from his working notes, which seek obsessively to neutralize the stress on the structural elements by compensating tension and compression: hence, the appearance of helium balloons, inflatable elements and weights on the trucks. At the same time,

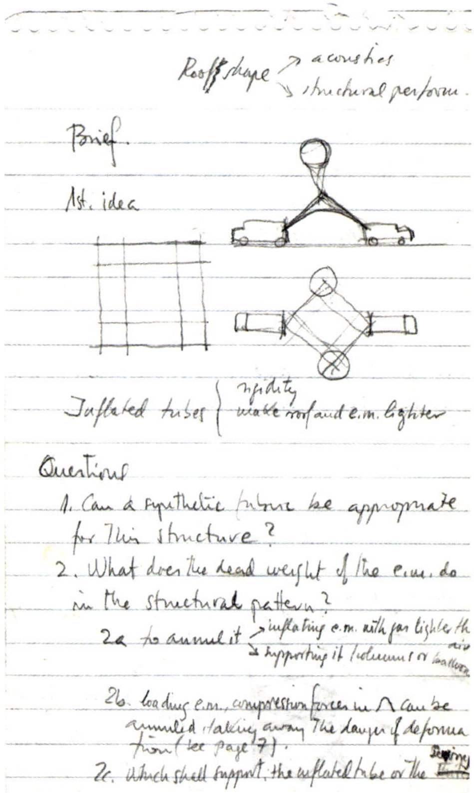

he pursued a particular and nearly tautological aesthetic for the expression of statics: the result would have been a landscape of different sized balloons, with a spectacular rhetoric of inflatability.

His speculation involving the architecture of air went even further in earlier designs that were less developed. Navarro toyed with a revision of Cedric Price's "Inflafloor" or variable inflatable floor, along with an elevated bridge for actors and audience suspended from helium balloons, and even a stage where everything would be hung from balloons, extending the principle of floating architecture not only to the roof but to the walls, curtains, lighting, and even floating seats for the audience (Figure 126). In this draft version, the square space measured 12 meters per side, based on Price's design, slightly adapted to bear the weight of 100 spectators. The dissolution of support elements into thin air is taken to the limit of its possibilities, making audience and actors the only elements with weight in this delirious collective pneumatic stage.

Curiously, inflatable architecture, which tends to be immediately associated with anti-establishment counterculture, was born – like cybernetics – out of Cold War military research.[3] The US government, hoping to conceal its radar detection systems, invested large sums at Cornell University in the late 1940s to fund the research of Walter Bird (1912-2006), an aeronautical engineer trained at MIT in Boston. Hundreds of inflatable domes were built in the 1950s in pursuit of the military objective of secrecy and concealment – the polar opposite of the goal of more experimental architectures of air. Bird built his first radar dome, a 15-meter-diameter dome which he called a Radome, in 1947-1948 in Ithaca, on the Cornell campus. The commercial applications for the prototype followed close behind. In 1955-1956, Bird cut ties with military and government agencies and universities and started the company Birdair Structures, Inc. in Buffalo, New York to sell inflatable structures for agricultural storage, greenhouses

Figure 124: Javier Navarro de Zuvillaga, Mobile Theater, sketch 1971. Courtesy of Javier Navarro de Zuvillaga.

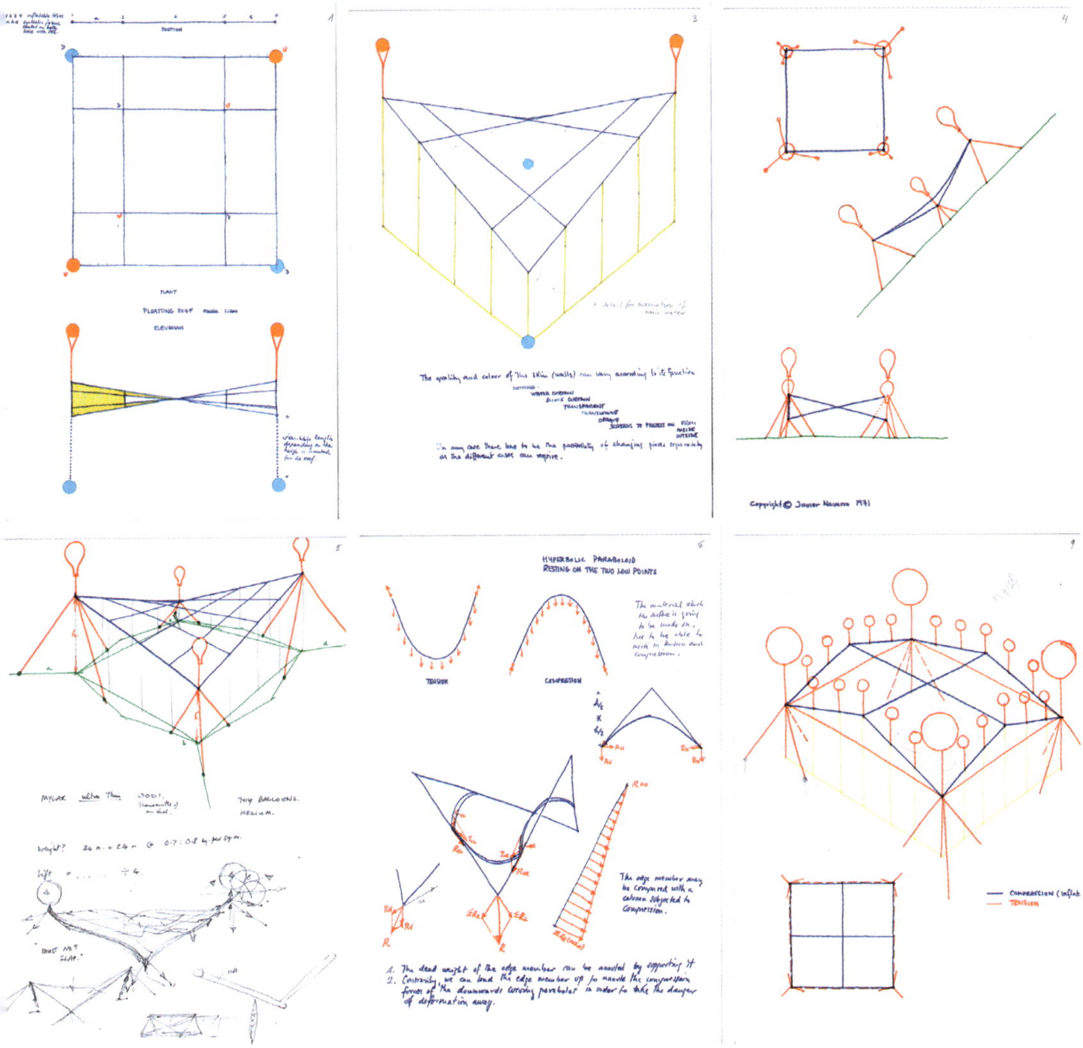

Figure 125: Javier Navarro de Zuvillaga, Mobile Theater, sequence of six sketches for the roof, 1971. Courtesy of Javier Navarro de Zuvillaga.

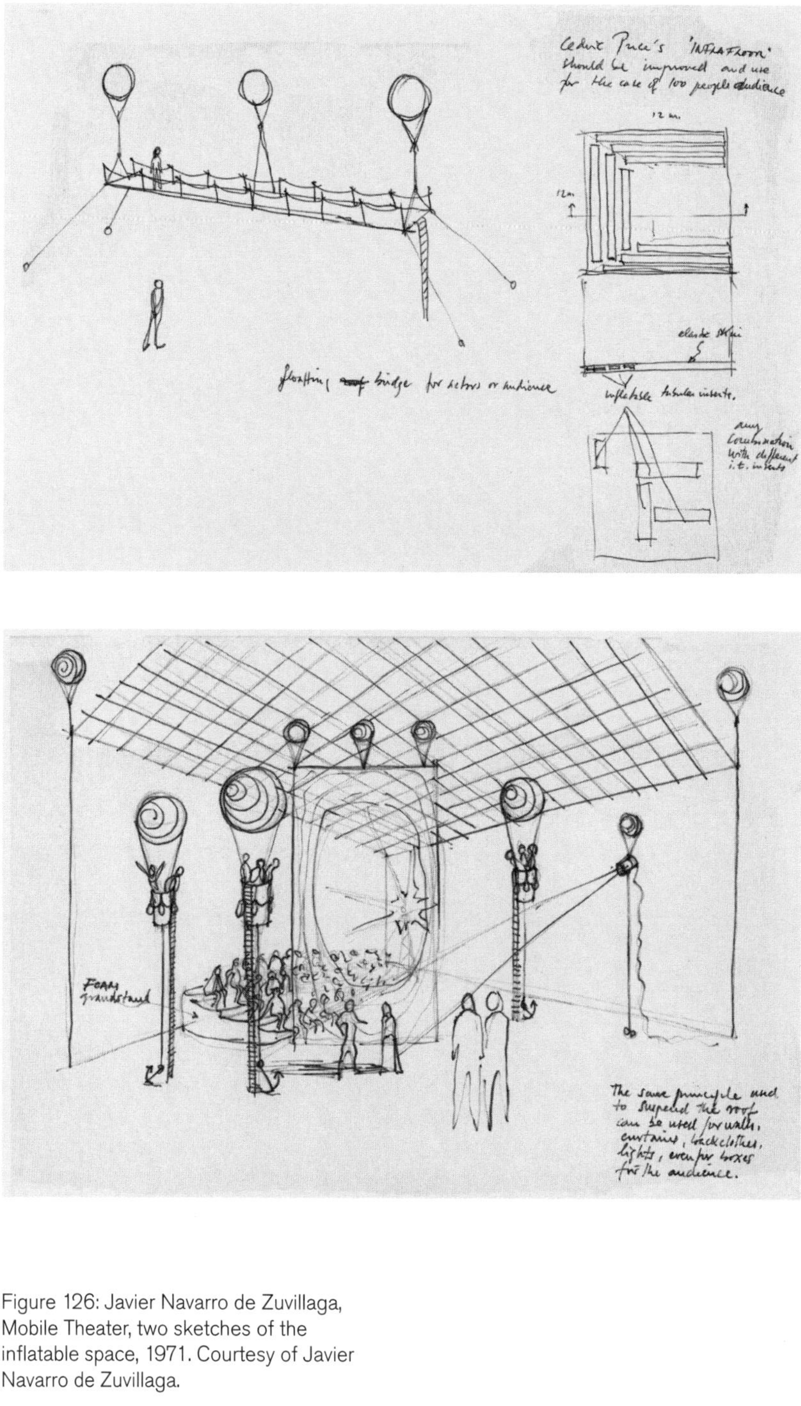

Figure 126: Javier Navarro de Zuvillaga, Mobile Theater, two sketches of the inflatable space, 1971. Courtesy of Javier Navarro de Zuvillaga.

Figure 127: Cover of *Life* magazine, November 11, 1957.

and suburban enclosures. In November 1957, one of his structures, used as a pool cover, appeared on the cover of *Life* magazine (Figure 127). The cultural transfer took a little longer, as is often the case, but not too long, and it came at the hands of the younger generations in an unexpected, but logical, turn.[4]

PEACEFUL ATOMS

The development of pneumatic architecture beginning with Walter Bird's first experiments is very telling. On the one hand, it developed in parallel with the military industry that lay at its roots along very pragmatic and functionalist lines, incorporating civil adaptations; and, on the other hand, it branched into spectacular exhibition constructions for trade fairs and events, with the distinct function of demonstrating political or corporative power – with the two clearly overlapping ideologically in the government-corporate collaborations providing financing for the constructions, which were not exactly inexpensive. A third aspect was the hybridization with art and, from there, with experimental architecture and its anti-establishment associations. The most remarkable aspect of this narrative is that the third path of development, the critical path, followed an entirely different trajectory, as though unaware of the other two, and with a temporal delay that hampered its critical efficacy despite its enormous success: time is irreversible, and inflatable architecture could not erase its origins.

A number of significant American endeavors between 1958 and 1964 demonstrated that inflatable architecture had definitively entered the civil sphere in association with established institutional powers. Pan American Airways built a spherical inflatable building, designed by Irvin Air Chute Co., for the Brussels 58 world's fair (Figure 128). A magazine article from the time described it in certain detail, explaining that, inside the sphere, there was a "theatre of stars in which Pan Am films will be shown against an astral background of moving clouds and star-filled sky. An elliptical satellite ring walkway, outside the sphere, permits a 'walk around the world' for a close-up view of Pan Am's global air routes."[5] In the following year, 1959, the architect

VISITORS TO THE BRUSSELS FAIR will, no doubt, marvel at this tinted, ocean-blue, 52-foot globe. The ingenious exhibit by Pan American Airways was manufactured by Irvin Air Chute Co. of U. S. Rubber's vinyl-coated, 18 oz. nylon fabric. Air inflated, the globe houses a "Theatre of Stars" in which Pan Am films will be shown against an astral background of

moving clouds and star-filled sky. An elliptical satellite ring walkway, outside the sphere, permits a "walk around the world" for a close-up view of Pan Am's global air routes.

Figure 128: Fragment from *Flying Magazine*, June 1958 with a write-up on the Pan Am pavilion for Brussels 58.

Carl Koch and the engineer Paul Weidlinger built the Boston Arts Center theater, with a lenticular roof suspended from posts, exactly like the Mobile Theater but larger: 44 meters in diameter, with a width in the center of 6 meters, and slightly inclined to create better acoustics.

In 1960, an inflatable structure of an enormous aesthetic and technical virtuosity was built for the United States Atomic Energy Commission's traveling exhibition. The architect responsible was someone who had intense first-hand experience of the front lines of war: Victor Lundy. Once again, the company that built it was Birdair.[6] The building was formed by two domes, connected by a band, built from a nylon double membrane covered in vinyl, leaving an air chamber between the two layers.[7] A group of four to 12 workers set it up in different locations across the United States, Asia and Latin America, taking three or four days each time (Figures 129, 130 and 131). Inside was a theater for 300 people, a technical laboratory, and reading areas. Another plastic bubble was installed under one of the domes; inside it, an atomic reactor was on display. *Architecture Forum* called the structure "a great balloon for peaceful atoms".[8]

Born in 1923, Lundy enlisted at the age of 19 while he was studying architecture in New York as part of the Army Special Training Program, a government initiative to incorporate high-level technical experts into the army. In 1944, he was deployed with the infantry as a soldier as part of the D-Day operation and sent to France. From the time he enlisted until the end of his time as a soldier, Lundy made detailed pencil drawings of his daily life in pocket notebooks. Eight of those notebooks survived, mainly containing portraits of fellow soldiers, scenes of downtime and landscapes.[9] Few battle scenes were depicted in his drawings, which were more focused on the immediate atmosphere of daily life on the front. However, three of these drawings shed some light on the ideas that imbued the architecture that Lundy would build decades later (Figure 132). One of them shows a tent with the title "home". Another shows a helmet liner in

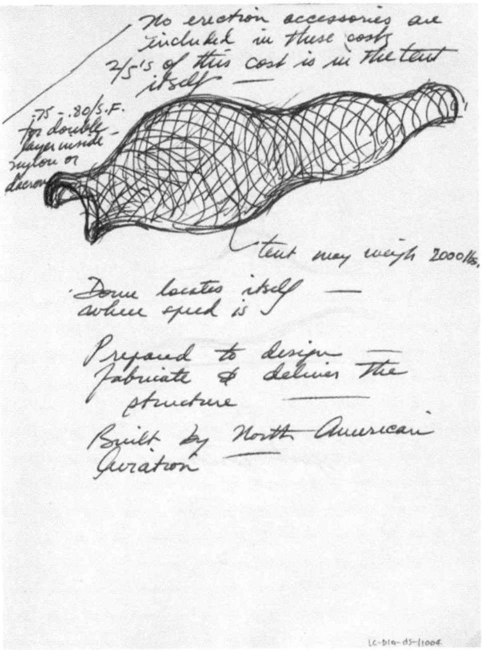

Figure 129: Victor Lundy, traveling pavilion for the United States Atomic Energy Commission USAEC from 1960, preparatory sketch. Library of Congress.

Figure 130: Victor Lundy, traveling pavilion for the United States Atomic Energy Commission USAEC from 1960, photographic sequence of the inflation process in Rio de Janeiro. Library of Congress.

Figure 131: Victor Lundy, portable exhibition pavilion for the United States Atomic Energy Commission (USAEC) from 1960. Source: *Architectural Forum* magazine.

Figure 132: Victor Lundy, drawings from his war notebooks from 1944. Library of Congress.

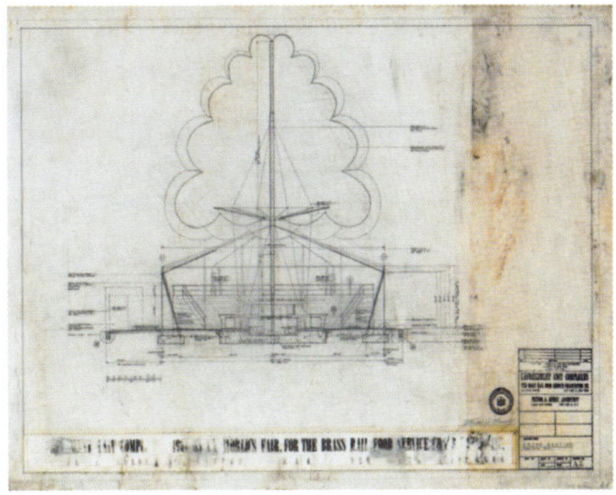

the foreground, a domed shape with stems and leaves sticking up around it, which generates an extraordinarily ambiguous iconicity through its lack of a reference scale. A third drawing shows a sea-plane hangar destroyed by the Germans in Cherbourg, an architectural structure of ribs and large-spanned curved vaults.

Shortly after the construction of the building for the USAEC, in 1963-1964 and again with Birdair, Lundy built a magnificent purely civil structure in New York for the World's Fair: the refreshment stand for the Brass Rail Food Service Organization Inc.[10] A series of these structures were dotted across the fair like clusters of bubbles, groups of balloons, or bouquets of flowers. Those were the images most commonly cited by the press, which never cited the possibility of the image of a nuclear explosion as a direct analogy (Figures 133 and 134). Ten such elements were built, with a very limited budget of just $6,000 each. One of the few influential voices that detected the importance of those modest artefacts was Ada Louise Huxtable, then a critic for the *New York Times*, who described the fair as a "happening" in her report, but in an openly pejorative sense, like the formalization of "unpremeditated chaos achieved through a series of unplanned acts with unrelated consequences".[11] Contrasting with this chaos of forms in fierce competition with one another, Victor Lundy's ten structures offered a spatial organization that regularized the perception of the whole: his peaceful atoms provided an order amid the formal chaos. This minor architecture, which garnered enormous popular success and limited critical fame, was the definitive nexus between institutional military pneumatics and the use of similar air-supported structures in art and experimental architecture. Their paradoxical aestheticization of nuclear mass destruction,

Figure 133: Victory Lundy, Model of the refreshment stand for the Brass Rail Food Service Organization Inc., 1963-1964. Library of Congress.

Figure 134: Victory Lundy, Refreshment stand for the Brass Rail Food Service Organization Inc., 1963-1964. Library of Congress.

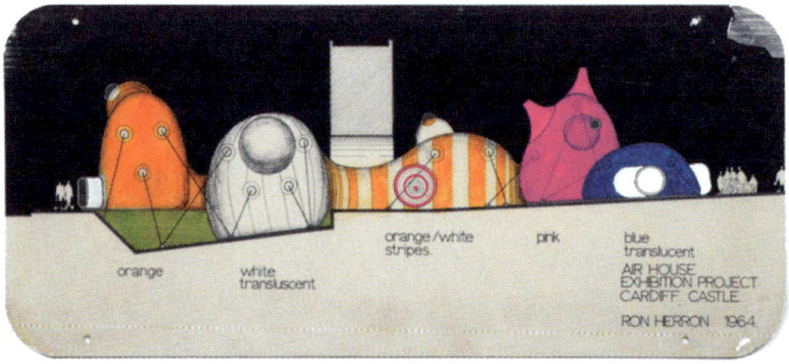

transfigured through the art of sculpture with compressed air into a collective amnesiac celebration, highlights the enormous ambivalence with which inflatable architecture was surrounded in the context of counterculture.

Ron Herron was the first Archigrammer to produce an inflatable architectural design, in 1965 for the Commonwealth Art Festival (unbuilt). Herron was most likely the first English architect to take a serious interest in this type of architecture, and his subsequent career as an architect of inflatable projects is notable. That seminal design was called Air House Strip. It consisted of a tubular profile which crossed into the walled precinct of Cardiff Castle through one of the entrance openings. Connected to this tube were five enclosures defined in the project only by the visual characteristics of their material finishes: orange, white translucent, orange/white stripes, pink, and blue translucent, in that order moving from the exterior toward the interior of the Castle (Figures 135 and 136). This new inflatable architecture functioned as a ritual threshold for crossing over. It was like a transitional atmosphere that transferred a whole series of new cultural and moral values to users as they crossed the threshold to access the historic enclosure of the Castle, which hosted the events for the festival, a celebration of the United Kingdom's imperialist multiculturalism.[12] The architecture was more motivated by environmental, perceptive and psychological questions than purely technological concerns.

That same year, in 1965, two prescriptive documents were published on the subject in the United Kingdom. The first was number 6 of *Archigram*, which showed Cedric Price's Airhouses design, along with the inevitable references to Birdair Structures, Inc. In addition to Price's research on inflatable dwellings, the magazine also published a detailed note with information on the commercialization of two different inflatable housing systems in the United States and the United Kingdom, and, lastly, Herron's design for Cardiff. The magazine never distinguished between civil

Figure 135: Ron Herron, elevation of Air House Strip, for the Commonwealth Festival in Cardiff, 1965. Ron Herron Archive.

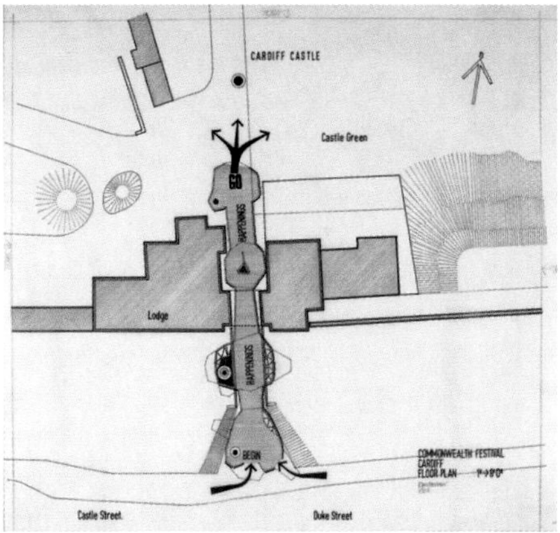

Figure 136: Ron Herron, floor plan of Air House Strip, for the Commonwealth Festival in Cardiff, 1965. Ron Herron Archive.

and military applications, in keeping with the dissolution between architecture and consumer goods, cybernetics and sociology, or high and low culture. The second crucial publication for inflatable architecture that year was the famous article "A Home Is Not a House", which appeared in the magazine *Art in America*, signed by the engineer and architectural historian Reyner Banham and the French-Moroccan graphic artist Françoise Dallegret. The article proposed an individual inflatable habitat derived from the recreational vehicle, which served as inspiration – or, more aptly a pedigreed theoretical support – for the Cushicle and the Suitaloon.

However, it was the special issue of *Architectural Design* from June 1968, dedicated to inflatable structures and titled *Pneu World*, which definitively disseminated the subculture throughout the United Kingdom and, thanks to good international distribution, a large part of the world (Figure 137). It was edited by two of Cook's disciples, Simon Conolly and Mike Davis, along with other young people in their circle, including Johnny Devas, David Harrison and Dave Martin. It provided a point of entry to appear in the magazine for an entire international movement of architects, to the point that, in subsequent years, that architectural subculture maintained a lasting presence in *Architectural Design*.

Javier Navarro's design for the roof of his Mobile Theater was based directly on Carl Koch's Boston Arts Center theater, but the system of balloons and trucks came from one of the designs published in that issue of *Architectural Design*. The project was the Itinerant Exhibition Hall for Objects of Everyday Life by Antoine Stinco, who – along with Jean Aubert and Jean-Paul Jungman – founded the group A.J.S. Aérolande in 1966 while they were still students at the École des Beaux-Arts in Paris. The following year, in the end-of-year workshop led by professors Paul Herbé and Édouard Albert, the three students requested professor David Georges Emmerich, who worked with tensegrity structures, to advise them on their graduation project. In 1967, they presented a project under collective authorship divided into three sections, which were highly defined in technical terms: Aubert designed a large container called A Travelling Theater for 5,000 Spectators, which consisted of a framework of inflatable tubes based on the geodesic projection of an icosahedron. Jungman presented a collective housing project called Dyodon, developed using inflatables based on a rhombicuboctahedron. Finally,

Figure 137: Cover of the magazine *Architectural Design*, June 1968. Courtesy of the library of the Official Architects' Association of Madrid.

Stinco presented his Exhibition Hall, comprised of two inflatable domes with interior overpressure, which supported a tensile roof. The roof structure he designed used eight anchor points on the ground, avoiding the need for a foundation. Four of those points were trucks, which contained the construction materials, and the other four were large balloons filled with water (Figures 138 and 139).[13]

With this French project, student-designed pneumatic architecture reached a high degree of technical credibility and an exceptional level of development, closely linked, paradoxically, to the radical political discourse of its authors. Aubert, Stinco and Jungman were part of the collective Utopie, founded in 1967 and active until 1978, although they left it behind for their professional practice in 1971. The group, with ties to Henri Lefebvre, was fueled by intellectual input from the sociologists Jean Baudrillard and René Lourau, and the urbanists Hubert Tonka and Catherine Colt.[14] Its publishing outlet *Utopie: Revue de Sociologie de l'Urbain*, picked up the ideology of May '68 in France and radicalized it intensely. In the editors' view, the technological emphasis among the architectural avant-garde of the moment was a continuation of the 1920s modern rhetoric, implying a mutation, of sorts, of the original functionalism, resulting in the highly bureaucratized behavioralism of the 1950s and 60s.[15] The event that ushered in the new French pneumatic culture – the exhibition *Structures Gonflables* in 1968, curated by Stinco, Aubert and Jungmann – fell into disrepute after Jean Baudrillard expressed his disconformity with the experiments and following the three architects' departure from the group the following year.[16]

Javier Navarro's attitude with respect to inflatable architecture was more ingenuous and less reflexive, more pragmatic and tied to British optimism – by virtue of direct contact, than to intellectualized French criticism. In his theoretical notes on the possibility of a fabric roof attached to helium balloons, in which he analyzed how to offset the opposite static forces in order to cancel them out to guarantee the stability of the system, he slipped in the following comment, which harks back to the Fun Palace by Cedric Price and Joan Littlewood: "The quality and colour of the skin (walls) can vary according to its function: nothing, water curtain, smoke curtain, transparent, translucent, opaque, screens to project on inside/outside." The fact that

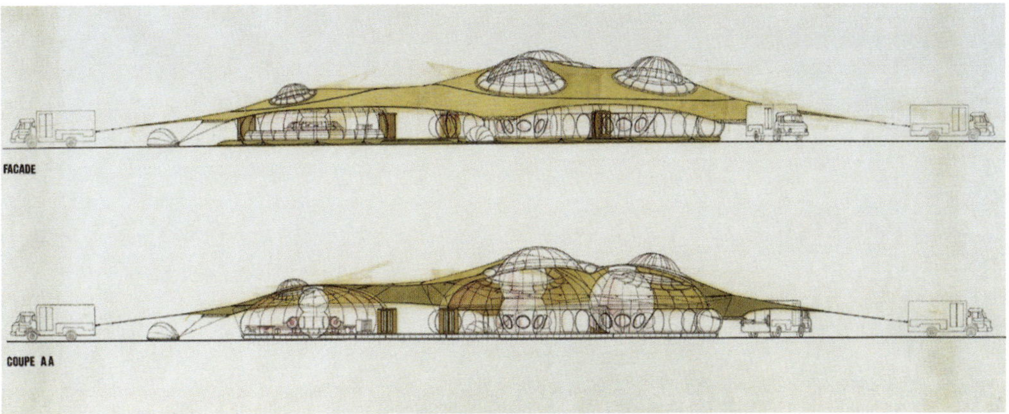

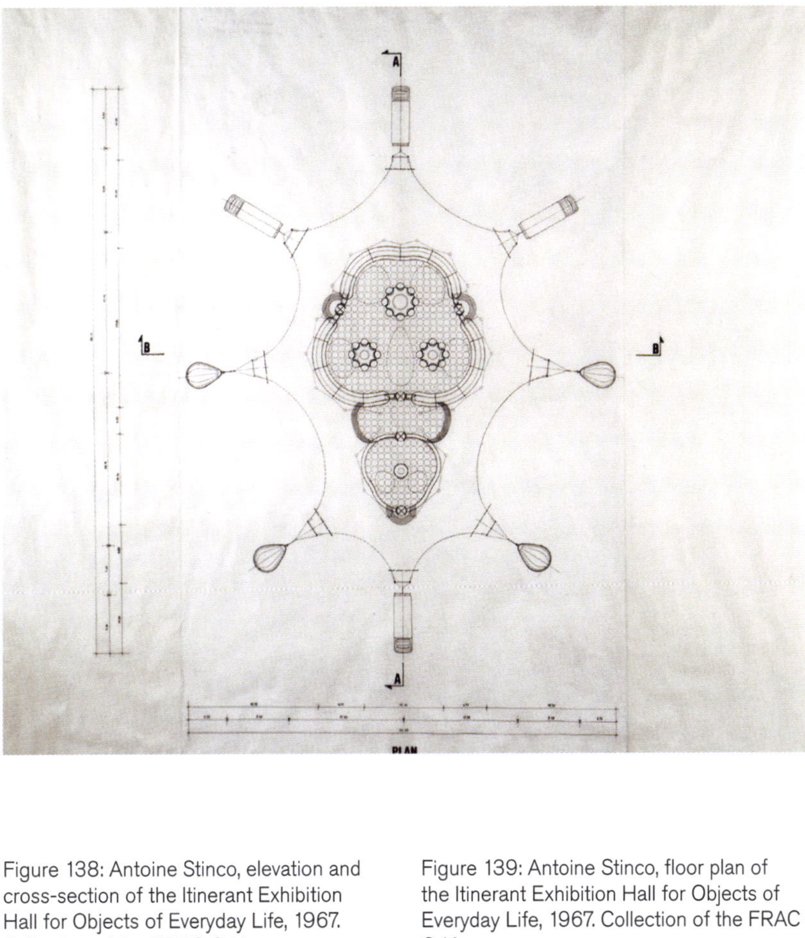

Figure 138: Antoine Stinco, elevation and cross-section of the Itinerant Exhibition Hall for Objects of Everyday Life, 1967. Collection of the FRAC Orléans.

Figure 139: Antoine Stinco, floor plan of the Itinerant Exhibition Hall for Objects of Everyday Life, 1967. Collection of the FRAC Orléans.

an architectural dematerialization is what resolves the underlying conflict of opposing forces is nearly a political metaphor: faced with this quandary, the response is static neutralization, the reduction of a force through its opposite – about which architecture, as it is traditionally understood, seems to have little to say.

THE DISSOLUTION OF THE GREAT MACHINE

The Fun Palace, as an artifact and particularly as an idea or manifesto, is an essential reference in this narrative, not only for what it should have become if it had been built, but for what it gave rise to in its wake. Joan Littlewood's idea for a "university of the streets", as she called the Fun Palace, combined popular and large-scale forms of historic mass entertainment, exemplified by the Vauxhall Pleasure Gardens, with the cutting edge technology of cybernetics. Although the Vauxhall Gardens in Southbank date back to the 17th century, for the Festival of Britain in 1951 they were transformed into a kind of monument to leisure to serve as propaganda touting the country's prospective economic power following the tough postwar period. It was one of the most emblematic settings for the event intended to promote the British Welfare State, which updated the age-old world's fair format to put the United Kingdom on the map of progressive modernity in the wake of the war. The Fun Palace was a direct response to Vauxhall Gardens and what it represented, since it was connected directly to some of Littlewood's interests, which closely followed the sociological speculations put forward by Richard Hoggart and Raymond Williams.[17] Both those men analyzed how the increasing technification of mass consumption and mass media – largely originating in the United States – was producing a particular type of subjectivity in the Welfare State, a perceptively passive subject, bringing together both poles and establishing direct connections between them. Littlewood published a series of texts espousing those readings, asserting in one such text that:

Figure 140: Ken Turner, exercises from the course in Environmental Design from Barnett College, circa 1966. Courtesy of Ken Turner.

Those who at present work in factories, mines and offices will quite soon be able to live as only a few people now can: choosing their own congenial work, doing as much or as little of it as they like, and filling their leisure with whatever delights them.[18]

The Fun Palace project was meant to activate spectator-consumer behavior, eliminating the gap between production and consumption, the hierarchies between high and low culture, between active participation and casual observation.[19] One of its most important features was that, because of its configuration as a kit of parts, it not only permitted but encouraged swift shifts in spectators' attention, turned towards the kits themselves. Spectators' behavior was expected to be distracted. Foreseeably, they would be engaged in a single activity for a short time before moving on to another, since the entire menu of possibilities was unabashedly visible and on display: "Many who start by wandering half attentively, or even skeptically, through the complex will be drawn into these and other elementary exercises in social observation."[20]

Littlewood met Cedric Price in 1961 and put together a committee of experts made up of herself, Buckminster Fuller, Yehudi Menuhin, Lord Ritchie Calder and the Earl of Harewood, all familiar names in circles of power. The history of the Fun Palace is well known: in 1964, it came close to being built when it was made part of an ambitious initiative for territorial regeneration: the Civic Trust's Lea Valley Development Plan. However, due to political disagreements in 1966, it was excluded from the urban plan, once again unmoored and without a fixed site. The Lea Valley Regional Plan ultimately dismissed the construction of the Fun Palace, which just two years earlier had seemed an almost certain reality. From that moment forward, Littlewood engaged in ongoing promotional activities in all kinds of media: she developed advertisements, a film and a very commercial theatrical production to raise money for the project, once again foreseeing the current behaviors and protocols of a self-promoting cultural producer.[21]

This situation of uncertainty surrounding the Fun Palace was compounded by an urban planning operation that affected the theater where Littlewood was in residence at the time: the Theatre Royal. When, in the mid-1960s, the municipal authorities on the Newham Council proposed the demolition of the area surrounding the Theatre Royal, in Stratford, she saw an opportunity for the future of the Fun Palace project, which had remained up in the air. In addition to demolishing the Victorian houses and small businesses surrounding the theater, the new urban planning for Stratford included demolishing the theater as well, and the entire area was to be replaced by a shopping center, offices, parking structures and apartment blocks. Gerry Raffles, the theater manager, succeeded in putting a stop to the speculation by having the theater building declared cultural heritage in 1972. Spurred on by the struggles affecting both her major projects – the Fun Palace and the Theatre Royal – between 1967 and 1975 Littlewood produced a large number of events in the neighborhood surrounding the theater, reinforcing her strategy of a "university of the streets" and erecting temporary structures designed especially for children.[22] Through these activities, Littlewood redirected the ideas from the Fun Palace, given its failed realization, toward dematerialization and dispersion, through smaller scale temporary interventions, which lacked the technical monumentality of the ini-

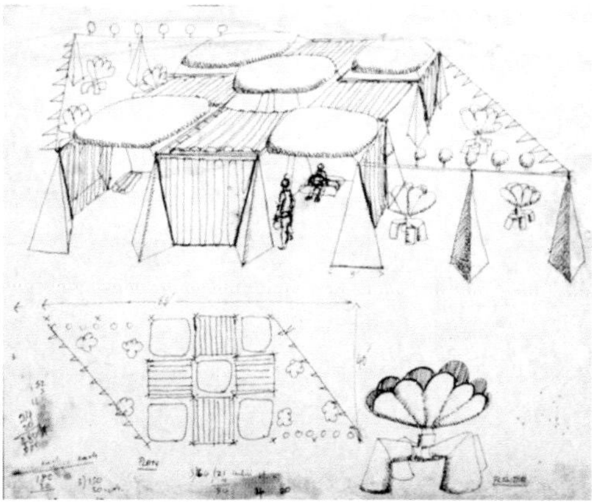

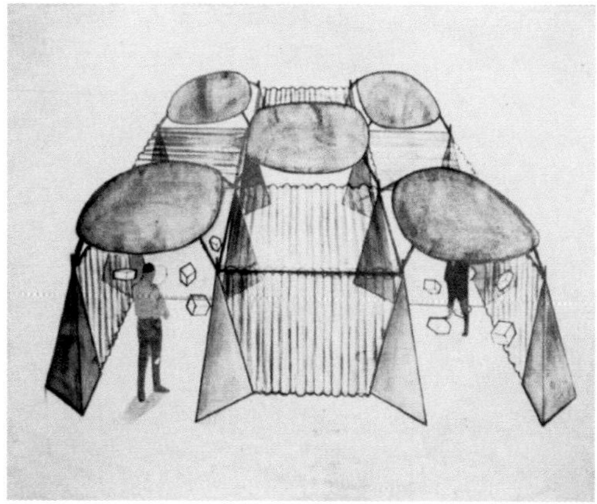

tial project. This was also in full concurrence with the generation shift detected by Cook – a change which, in its own way, was also visible in the work and discourse produced by Archigram during the same period.

Littlewood focused on two strategies: first, the practice of social activism, paralyzing initiatives rooted in speculation and introducing leisure artifacts into the affected areas, as demonstrated by her response to the urban planning operations impacting her theater; second, the generation of events with institutional support, like her Bubble City projects or what she called Pavilions in the Parks. In 1968, she was responsible for curating the Summer Fair in London, for which she proposed inflatable structures to be set up for three months in Chelsea, having contacted Allan Kaprow to act as a consultant.[23] For the City of London Festival that same year, Littlewood proposed a project for a travelling fair, called Bubble City, in which inflatables played a major role. Collaborators included Peter Cook, who designed an action called "Blow Up a Column", providing proof of his direct (if marginal) implication in the events he described in his retrospective account from 1975.

That being said, Cook was not the most significant collaborator on Bubble City; that role fell to the pair of artists and teachers Ken and Mary Turner and their community theater group called Action Space. Javier Navarro's article from 1976 included an image of Action Space from *Time Out* magazine from that same year, depicting a public protest action that took place in Trafalgar Square. In the photograph, a standing man wearing a gas mask looks inquisitively at the camera, next to a seated woman dres-

Figure 141: Ken Turner, preparatory sketches for Plastic Garden 1968. Courtesy of Ken Turner.

sed as a housemaid in grotesque makeup. Action Space was a pioneering group in the use of inflatable structures for activist events from 1968 on. Ken Turner was a teacher at Barnett College (from 1966 to 1969) and at the Central School of Design (from 1967 to 1990). He taught a course in Environmental Design in which he worked with his students on the construction of environments using objects, loosely inspired by the foundational courses at the Bauhaus, but with a notable expansion in space, reaching an architectural scale (Figure 140). Littlewood was familiar with his large-scale experiments with participatory environments built using wood, metal and plastics in the context of an introductory course for artists in training, and she suggested he get involved with her own projects for physical environments in the city of London. Specifically, for the Bubble City project in summer 1968, Ken Turner proposed an inhabitable installation called Plastic Garden (also known as Paradise Garden), located near the Tower of London, in All Hallows-by-the-Tower. According to his own account, he worked with the models in his study in Hampstead, made using perforated wood elements in the form of a pylon, combined with inflatable elements supported somewhat precariously on top (Figure 141). At the same time, Mary Turner was working with children in a playgroup, following the ideas of the influential psychoanalyst John Bowlby, well known for his investigations on attachment theory. Once Turner's small installation was built for Littlewood's festival, it occupied 600 square feet (about 56 square meters), with its pyramid-shaped wooden pylons and an inflatable roof, kept at a steady pressure by a household vacuum cleaner (Figure 142).

Figure 142: Ken Turner, model for Plastic Garden 1968. Courtesy of Ken Turner.

In addition to the Action Space installation, Littlewood's project that summer displayed a humanoid inflatable structure by Bruce Lacey called Journey through the Human Body, as well as the Inflatable Fun Structure, by Simon Conolly, Mike Davies, Johnny Devas and Dave Martin, and an impressive pneumatic construction by Jeffrey Shaw, Theo Botschujiver and Sean Wellesley-Miller, called Airground, in the form of a transparent pyramidal dome, under which an accessible yellow inflatable floor was used as a surface for play (Figure 143).[24]

Between 1970 and 1971, the members of Action Space built large pneumatic structures in different areas of London, including Camden, Bethnal Green and Islington, with support from the Arts Council program called Blow 71 (Figure 144). The Arts Council was, to a large extent, the same committee that had been responsible for the failure of the Fun Palace as a public undertaking, which shows the important shift that the policies determining arts subsidies were undergoing in parallel with these dissolutions. In other words: cultural management was not exempt from the phenomenon of dissolution, the loss of agency, of scale and ambition, compensated by decentralized built developments.[25] The Turners were very aware of the inflatables designed by other artists and architects whom they had met, including Jeffrey Shaw, Graham Stevens, and the joint work of Maurice Agis and Peter Jones. The dense international network of artists, architects and so-

Figure 143: Jeffrey Shaw, Theo Botschujiver and Sean Wellesley-Miller, Airground, for the Summer Festival in London, 1968. Courtesy of Jeffrey Shaw.

cial activists involved with pneumatic artifacts was especially robust in London at the end of the "electric decade" cited by Peter Cook. The opportunities for a young person living in the city in 1970 or 1971 to come into contact with that type of subculture were ample: they included secondary galleries, more consolidated art centers, and even, above all, public space during spontaneous or institutionally sponsored events. Aside from the circle of architects associated with those constructions, led by Price and Cook (perfectly formulated through their editorial pursuits and their collaborations with artists), there was another parallel circle, showing many areas of overlap (as demonstrated by the map of temporary constructions).

Even the BBC participated in the cultural current with two radio programs from the *Third Programme* series, called "Five Generations. Part 1: The Changing Environment", and "Five Generations. Part 2: The Response to Environment", broadcast in December 1967 and January 1968, with the participation of Ken Turner and Maurice Agis, among others. Moreover, the British public broadcaster covered similar demonstrations in a television program called *Tomorrow's World*, which dealt with cutting-edge technological developments, especially those related to electronics and cybernetics. The program began emitting in 1965, and in 1970 one of its studios hosted the installation of a piece by Jeffrey Shaw, Theo Botschujiver and Sean Wellesley-Miller called Airground Mattress. It was exactly what the name suggests: a huge air mattress described by its authors as an "event structure", similar to the one built for Littlewood in 1968, in white and without a roof (Figure 145). In contrast with these structures, which were entirely indeterminate with regard to their public use, Action Space always introduced programmed content related to theatricality. That was the basis for their fertile collaboration with Joan

Figure 144: Action Space, inflatable structure in London for the summer festivals, 1971. Courtesy of Tony Murchland.

Figure 145: Jeffrey Shaw, Theo Botschujiver and Sean Wellesley-Miller, Photograph from the BBC shoot with the installation Airground Mattress, 1970. Courtesy of Jeffrey Shaw.

Littlewood and their unique position in this complicated history – a much more central role than the marginality of their productions might suggest:

The Action Space that we developed was a programme to initiate the practice of performance, music and dance in order to bring a sense of drama into large scale structured environmental events. These disciplines were integrated into the physicality of the structures as stories and narratives, woven as if into the membrane of surfaces and the structural function of air as it pulsated, alive and breathing and circulating throughout the heaving sculptural body. Thus in themselves, the drama intensified the atmosphere and mood of the instant built/blown environment of the air structures. We as artists and operators took on roles or characters to play out dramas that nowadays (Ken Turner wrote this in 2011) *are named as Durational Performance Art.*[26]

The obsession with inflatables was mentioned in the *Guardian* on June 8, 1970. The article highlighted the nearly simultaneous large exhibitions held in 1968 in Philadelphia and Paris focusing on the interconnections between art and architecture in inflatable structures. More specifically, it referred to the activities of the Eventstructure Research Group, formed by the young Australian architect Jeffrey Shaw, then 26 years old and a habitual figure in the London gallery scene, together with Theo Botschujiver, based in Amsterdam; both were collaborators with Littlewood for her urban festivals. This new performance art in inflatable environments, adeptly supported by the Arts Council, was thus officially considered a genre and disseminated in the media, including public radio and te-

Figure 146: José Miguel de Prada Poole. Smart Structure from the *Expoplástica* exhibition in Madrid, 1968. Courtesy of Prada Poole.

levision and a national newspaper with a huge circulation.

THE COUNTERCULTURE CAMPAIGN

In Spain, only the architect José Miguel de Prada Poole (1938) participated in this subculture ahead of the Mobile Theater project, for which he also served as a technical advisor for the inflatable roof when Navarro returned to Madrid to publicize his project and try to build it. In 1975, Javier Navarro was invited to participate in the São Paolo Biennial, taking his Mobile Theater project to be included in the exhibition. The Theater Institute financed the construction of a model, made by the craftsman José Vila, which suffered technical difficulties when it came to creating a scale version of the lenticular inflatable roof Navarro had designed five years earlier, fueling so many technical speculations. Prada Poole provided advice on the form, dimensions and details of this technological intuition, which, like the entire Mobile Theater project, encountered enormous difficulties in realization due to the cultural mismatch between the proposal and the agents to whom it was directed.

Prada Poole had begun his research into inflatable and responsive structures, which he called "smart structures", at the Madrid School of Architecture (ETSAM), where he built two prototypes before presenting his "variable response structure" for the *Expoplástica* exhibition in Madrid in 1968. This structure, built in dome form using hexagonal inflatable tesserae (pneumatic pillows) connected by zippers, was meant to be plugged into a computer and subject to tests that would modify its behavior and form (Figure 146). The whole was meant to be an enormous flow computer, which never came into being because only the stable prototype was ever built. In the following year, 1969 he built a large structure called *Elipsoide* in the gardens of the Madrid School of Architecture, where it remained for seven years. It temporarily housed a smaller structure beneath it, which the author called *Jonás*, or *Gusano Móvil* [Mobile Warm]. In 1971, Prada Poole realized his first large-scale inflatable, the Instant City in Ibiza, built in October on a commission from the International Council of Societies of Industrial Design (ICSID). The design was published in *Architectural Design* in the December issue from the same year, just two months after Javier Navarro's time in London.[27]

The Instant City in Ibiza was a commission from the organizing committee for the ICSID Congress, specifically for the architects Fernando Bendito and Carlos Ferrater, to house the attendees with limited resources, mainly students and young designers and artists. Although it is known as an inflatable structure, the design included four different zones, of which the CN or *Ciudad Neumática* [Pneumatic City] was the third, also called the "coherent zone". Next to it were the three other zones – disconnected, organized and meeting – all separate from the CN and similar to a free campsite. From a head made up of four inflatable bubbles (health center, common area, storage and waste management, and CAS (*Centro de asistencia de diseño* [Center for Design Aid]), a tubular structure stretched out, which users could enter, choosing between three unit types – for two, four or six people, with a dome or vault, and the corresponding "proportional section of the general duct or canal to distribute pneumatic energy",[28] as the circulation areas were

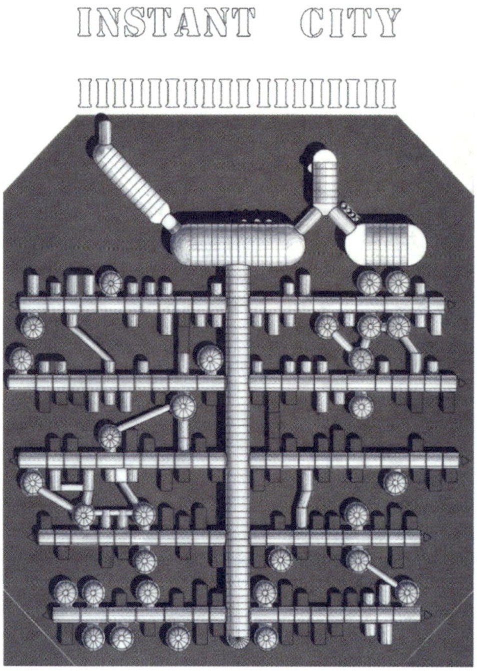

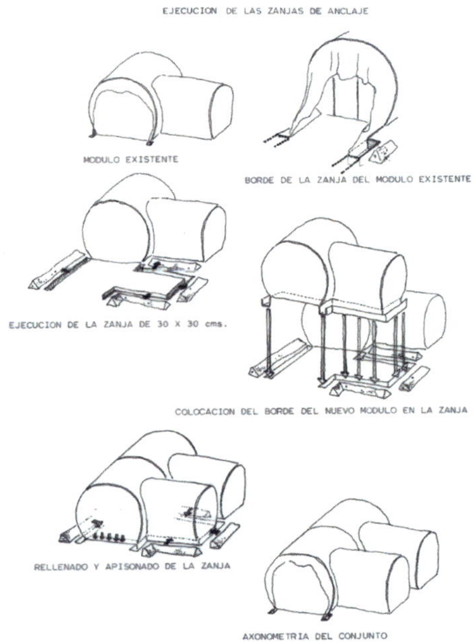

Figure 147: José Miguel de Prada Poole. Overall organization of the Instant City in Ibiza, 1971. Courtesy of Prada Poole.

Figure 148: José Miguel de Prada Poole. Assembly notebook for Instant City in Ibiza, 1971. Courtesy of Prada Poole.
Figure 149: José Miguel de Prada Poole. Instant City in Ibiza, 1971. Courtesy of Prada Poole.

called, in keeping with the design's rhetoric (Figure 147).

Initially, the organizers imagined building a tent to house events and for the storage of light building materials, to which attendees would have access for use in building their own accommodation – mainly using strips of wood and canvas. According to Prada Poole's calculations, however, given the available budget the proposal was unfeasible, since each participant would be allotted "part of one strip of wood, a couple sandwiches, with nothing between the bread, and enough canvas to make a coin purse".[29]

Prada Poole developed a counter-proposal that used a single material for the entire complex in a unified framework, reducing costs and guaranteeing a certain overall coherence; it was accepted immediately. By reducing the material range to just PVC and the formal range to cylinders and domes, the project was given a very controlled grammar. This technical vocabulary was recorded in two documents: a guide or user's manual – a "passive user's guide to grammar" – designed in ten days, providing explanations along with simple diagrams of how to set up and attach the additions to the central tube (Figure 148); and an "active user's guide", which consisted of the oral instructions to be issued by the volunteers at the CAS [Center for Design Aid] to participants upon their arrival. Prada Poole associated this aid work with "the purest tradition of learning among primitive cultures, oral transmission regarding practical execution in the territory".[30]

Thus, although it was initially conceived by the organizers as a simple temporary shelter, Prada Poole reoriented it toward greater complexity by introducing the necessary elements to generate a veritable social drama in the form of an experiment. This revealed a series of conflicts between the two broad groups at the congress, and even among the youngest participants installed in the *Instant City*. Prada Poole referred to this in an interview:

In the sociological history of this city, from its foundation to its death – in the space of less than a month – there were a series of incredibly curious transformations: trade appeared, speculation appeared, private property appeared[;] [...] it was truly a real city [...]. There were even political meetings, a government was formed that wasn't a government, since the decision was made – in the initial meetings – that the city should be governed without a government: i.e., regulated by each and every one of its inhabitants.[31]

The other authors of the project, in a text signed by Fernando Bendito, Carlos Ferrater and Prada himself, laid out all the main themes of the unresolved conflict that their pneumatic experiment enacted with an enormous precision: 1) the premeditated coalescence of work and information; 2) the contradiction between a highly precise technological system and a precarious and handcrafted execution; 3) the identification of leisure as a technological product; 4) the propagandistic power of the event, which rapidly became an advertising platform; and 5), the paradoxical contrast between the pristine, futuristic appearance of the exterior and the grubby, dirty interior of the space.[32] The laboratory condition, as a climatic bubble for the maximum control of a situation in permanent risk of bubbling over, is what best characterizes this important cultural event (Figure 149). It is precisely that condition of a controlled bu-

FIGURE 11.—A 60-bed surgical hospital displayed the use of MUST (Medical Unit, Self-contained, Transportable) equipment in a demonstration at Camp Bullis, Tex., in September 1968. (Army Medical Pictorial Service photograph by William W. Warrell.)

bble, clearly separate from a disconnected and even hostile exterior, that establishes a possible conceptual continuity between the Instant City and one of the corollaries of military pneumatic architecture that closes the circle initiated by Walter Bird: the so-called MUSTs (Medical Unit, Self-contained, Transportable) developed by the US government for the Vietnam war in chronological parallel with the Western craze for inflatable architecture (Figure 150).

Given the unique nature of the military counter-insurgency in the Vietnam war, the military hospital systems had to be reimagined for combat zones. Since there was no clear battle front but rather a slew of base camps scattered across the territory, these tactical installations for care, treatment and rescue were designed using pneumatic technologies.[33] The concept combined a quick setup with energy self-sufficiency as well as the capacity for rapid disassembly and relocation. The first MUST was deployed for a combat situation in South Vietnam in 1966 following tests on American soil, and the structures remained in use until the end of the war in 1975 and beyond (Figure 151). They were outfitted with complete systems for water supply, waste management, toilet facilities, water purification, an incinerator, operating rooms, treatment rooms and patient wards, X-ray machines, defibrillators, and a range of other healthcare services.[34] Connected with base camps, the MUSTs formed true instant cities with an activity that was divi-

Figure 150: Medical Unit, Self-contained, Transportable with 60 beds, demonstration in Texas, 1968. Source: Army Pictorial Service, photograph by William W. Warrel.

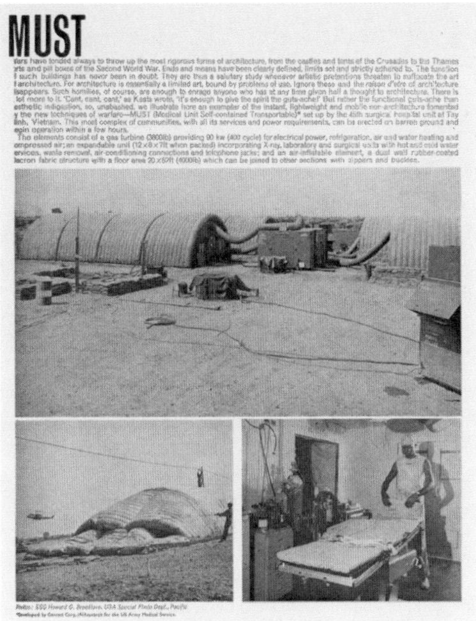

Figure 151: Medical Unit, Self-contained, Transportable. Source: *Architectural Design* magazine, April 1969.

ded between two contradictory aims – destroying and saving human lives – in the two spaces they defined, separated only by the thin inflatable walls and roofs into one area for destruction (the exterior) and another for salvation (the interior). In their architectural configuration, the MUSTs were identical to the Instant City in Ibiza. They were formed by one functional element, onto which were attached a series of longitudinal naves, measuring 15 meters long by 6 meters wide and extendible via ring segments. The assessment of these objects provided by Roger N. Dent in his PhD dissertation from 1968 is decisive and provides a very complex closure to the narrative:

> *Design of military equipment tends toward miniaturisation, functionalism and portability, and these are indeed characteristics of pneumatic construction. Military design strictly adheres to clearly defined limits and within this design the function is never in doubt. Such design work provides a valuable stimulation for architects, who so often become 'bogged down' by their aesthetic partialities and ignore the fact that architecture is an art bounded by functional parameters.*[35]

If we accept this hypothesis, we are in a position to conclude something that we contended from the outset: that civil inflatable structures, even the most anti-establishment of them, were in complete and involuntary continuity with their military predecessors. They were not exempt from the contradictions that implied; moreover, their historical and cultural value resides in having succeeded in constructing veritable social dramas out of the contradictions stemming from their origins, according to which, far from instilling peace, every Western citizen was also, as Victor Lundy understood, a soldier. The confluence of technology, architecture, theater and art in a global pneumatic community was an unprecedented event full of internal contradictions that remain entirely open to this day.

Notes

1. Peter Cook: "The Electric Decade: An Atmosphere at the AA School 1963 73", in James Gowan (ed.): *A Continuing Experiment: Learning and Teaching at the Architectural Association*, London: Architectural Press, pgs. 137-146.

2. Tribute to Kay Jordan after her death, in *The Guardian*, February 20, 2011.

3. Patrick Sisson: *More than Hot Air: The Lasting Impact of Inflatable Architecture*, available online at http://www.curbed.com/2016/1/21/10844774/inflatable-architecture-geodesic-dome-design-legacy.

4. This idea appears in Chapter 12 "A Range of Methods" of Reyner Banham's *The Architecture of the Well-Tempered Environment*, London: Architectural Press 1969.

5. *Flying Magazine*, vol. 62, June 1958, pg. 10.

6. Roger N. Dent: *Principles of Pneumatic Architecture*, London: The Architectural Press, 1971, pgs. 42-43. The book, published in 1971, drew on Dent's PhD dissertation, called *Pneumatic Structures in Architecture with Special Reference to Artic and Lunar Applications*, defended in 1968 at the University of Liverpool. It is the first in-depth investigation of the subject, and the graphic and technical documentation it contains is exceptional.

7. Frei Otto: "Exposition de l'énergie atomique", *L'Architecture d'Aujourd'hui*, no. 102 June-July 1962; pgs. 86-88.

8. David Allison: "A Great Balloon for Peaceful Atoms", *Architectural Forum*, vol. 113. no. 5, November 1960, pgs. 142-146.

9. Victor Lundy's legacy is preserved, in part, in the Library of Congress, which provides open access to his war drawings. The drawings can be consulted at https://www.loc.gov/rr/print/coll/628_lundy.html.

10. "Foire exposition de New York 1964", *L'Architecture d'Aujourd'hui*, no. 117, November-January 1964-1965, pgs. 18-22.

11. Ada Louise Huxtable: "Architecture: Chaos of Good, Bad and Joyful", April 22, 1964 *New York Times*.

12. The Commonwealth Arts Festival of 1965 was a governmental initiative with close ties to immigration policies in the UK at the time. It was held in London, Liverpool, Glasgow and Cardiff, i.e., strategically scattered across the territory. The motto was "At Home with the Empire". It was produced coinciding with the so-called White Paper of July 1965, which toughened the conditions of the Commonwealth Immigration Act of 1962, regulating the entry of immigrants into the United Kingdom originating from its colonies. For more detailed information, see Gail Low: "At Home? Discoursing on the Commonwealth at the 1965 Commonwealth Arts Festival", *The Journal of Commonwealth Literature*, vol. 48(1), 2013, pgs. 97-111.

13. These three projects were published broadly, for example in the December 1967 issue of *L'Architecture d'Ajourd d'hui*, in the Paris exhibition from March 1968 *Structures Gonflables*, and in issue no. 8 of *Archigram* magazine from 1968. The catalogue for the collection of the FRAC in Orléans, *Architectures Expérimentales*, edited by Marie-Ange Brayer, offers an extensive reproduction of Stinco's design on pages 86 to 89.

14. For an in-depth study of the group, its publications and activities, see Craig Buckley and Jean-Louis Violeau: *Utopie: Texts and Projects, 1967-1978*, Los Angeles: Semiotext(e), 2011.

15. These ideas appeared in an important article signed by Hubert Tonka, Jean-Paul Jungann and Jean Aubert, called "Architecture as a Theoretical Problem", published for the first time in *Architectural Design* in June 1968. Following the polemic unleashed by the article and the events of May, the text was expanded, revised and published in other media.

16. Marc Dessauce: *The Inflatable Moment: Pneumatics and Protest in '68*, New York: Princeton Architectural Press and Architectural League, 1999, pg. 8.

17. Nadine Holdsworth: *Joan Littlewood*, New York: Routledge, 2016, pg. 32.

18. Joan Littlewood published these ideas successively in: *New Scientist*, Vol 22, no. 391, May 14, 1964, pgs. 432-434 and *Theatre Drama Review*, edited by Richard Schechner, no. 3, summer 1968.

19. Nadine Holdsworth, op. cit, pg. 34.

20. Joan Littlewood, *New Scientist*, op. cit.

21. Nadine Holdsworth, op. cit, pg. 35.

22. Ana Bonet Miró: "Sigma Portfolio and Bubble City: Ludic Sites for a Mobile Fun Palace Programme", *Architecture and Culture*, vol. 4, no. 1, pgs. 137-161. In this article, the author analyzes the official document for Bubble City, presented publicly by

Joan Littlewood and published by the Fun Palace Trust in 1968.

23. Fatine Bahar Karlidag: *Reading the Old Left in the Ewan MacColl and Joan Littlewood's Theatre Workshop and Beyond: in Joan Littlewood's Post-Theatrical Engagements in the 1960s*. PhD dissertation, University of Washington 2017, pgs. 38-39.

24. All the information regarding Action Space can be found in two anthologies dedicated to the group's activities. Ken Turner: *Crashing Culture 1954 to 2016*, CreateSpace, 2016 and Mary Turner: *Action Space Extended*, CreateSpace, 2012.

25. Juliet Rufford: "'What Have We Got to Do with Fun?': Littlewood, Price, and the Policy Makers", *New Theatre Quarterly*, vol. 27, no. 4, November 2011, pgs. 313-328.

26. Ken Turner, op. cit., pg. 57.

27. The best source for Prada Poole's work and thought is Nuria Prieto González: *La arquitectura de José Miguel de Prada Poole. Teoría y obra*, PhD dissertation, 2013 Universidad de La Coruña. See also José Miguel de Prada Poole y Fabián López Ulloa: "José Miguel de Prada Poole y las estructuras neumáticas en España, 1960-1980", in Pepa Casinello, Santiago Huerta, José Miguel de Prada and Ricardo Sánchez Lampreave (eds.): *Geometría y proporción en las estructuras*, Madrid: Lampreave 2010, pgs. 365-38; Antonio Cobo: "Huellas de una arquitectura peredecera", *Circo M.T.M.*, no. 191, 2013; and Antonio Cobo: "La arquitectura inteligente de José Miguel de Prada Poole", *Pasajes de arquitectura y crítica*, no. 134, 2014, pgs. 16-18. The museums of contemporary art of Sevilla and León, CAC and MUSAC respectively, have recently staged a complete exhibition about Prada Poole, curated by Antonio Cobo, see Antonio Cobo (ed.): *José Miguel de Prada Poole. La arquitectura perecedera de las pompas de jabón* [The pesishable architecture of soap bubbles], Sevilla: Recolectores Urbanos Editorial, 2019.

28. José Miguel de Prada Poole: "Zonificación de la Ciudad Instantánea", *Arquitectura,* no. 154, January 1972, pg. 30.

29. José Miguel de Prada Poole: "Senderos", unpublished text included in Nuria Prieto González, *La arquitectura de José Miguel de Prada Poole. Teoría y obra,* op. cit. Vol. 2, pg. 79.

30. José Miguel de Prada Poole: "Una ciudad inflexible", in Nuria Prieto González, op. cit., pgs. 61-63.

31. Carmen Castro: "La Ciudad Instantánea. La Ciudad Cambiante. Entrevista a Prada Poole", *Arquitectura,* no. 154, January 1972, pg. 25.

32. Fernando Bendito, Carlos Ferrater and José Miguel de Prada Poole: "Albergue para congresistas. ICSID, 1971", *Quaderns d'Arquitectura i Urbanisme*, no. 83, 1971, pgs. 85-88.

33. Major General Spurgeon Neel: *Medical Support of the US Army in Vietnam 1965-1970*, Washington DC: Department of the Army, 1991, pg. 59.

34. Lieutenant General Hal B. Jennings, Colonel William S. Mullins jr; Rose C. Engelman (eds.): *A Decade of Progress: The United States Army Medical Department 1959-1969*, Washington DC: Department of the Army, 1971, pgs. 178-180.

35. Roger N. Dent: *Principles of Pneumatic Architecture*, op. cit., pg. 184.

CHAPTER 6_ SACRED GEOMETRIES

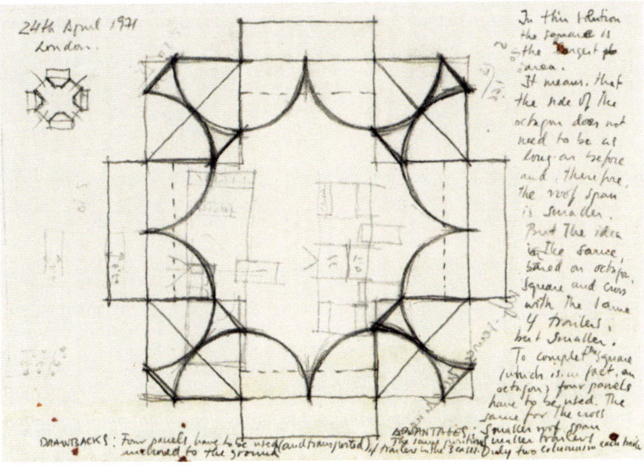

A drawing by Javier Navarro dated April 24, 1971 ended up becoming the logo for the Mobile Theater. It is a very abstract sketch of the design, which seems even somewhat hermetic as an image, since it provides very little information on what the artifact it depicts is and how it is used (Figure 152). The sketch is a geometric study of the form of the building, which illustrates the economy by which it must be governed on all levels. It is shocking that this should be the logo, the project's visual identity, as opposed to a diagram that explains its mobility or transformability. Nonetheless, the logo took up this geometric diagram, which transmits stability and a certain gravity (Figure 153). The commentary that accompanies the drawing is misleading if we interpret it literally. We must look beneath the surface to understand its scope:

In this solution the square is the largest area. It means that the side of the octagon does not need to be as long as before and, therefore, the roof span is smaller. But the idea is the same, based on octagon, square and cross with the same four trailers, but smaller. To complete the square (which is in fact an octagon), four panels have to be used. The same for the cross. ADVANTAGES: smaller roof span. Smaller trailers. The same positions of trailers in the three cases. Only two columns in each trailer. DRAWBACKS: four panels have to be used anchored to the ground (and transported).

Figure 152: Javier Navarro de Zuvillaga, sketch of the Mobile Theater, 1971. Courtesy of Javier Navarro de Zuvillaga.

Figure 153: Javier Navarro de Zuvillaga, logo for the Mobile Theater, 1974. Courtesy of Javier Navarro de Zuvillaga.

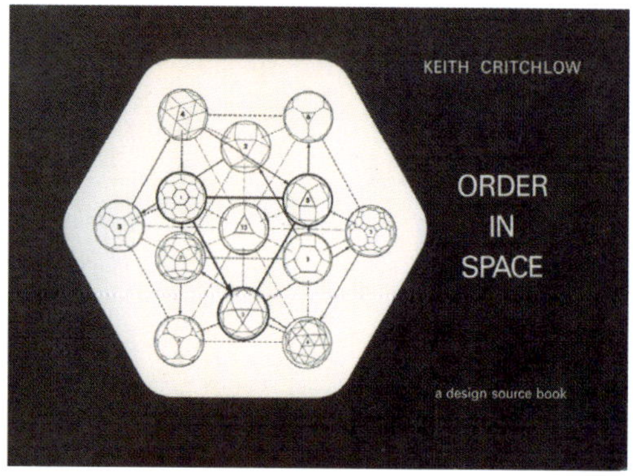

Upon his arrival in London, Navarro was already very familiar with geometry, a discipline of utmost interest to him, in which he placed an intense epistemological trust – even more so than in technology. Those were perhaps the only two certainties in which his design confided, in a cultural medium full of all kinds of uncertainty. His meeting then with Keith Critchlow (1933) at the Architectural Association was fundamental: of all the professors with whom Navarro came into contact, Critchlow was the one who gave the most attention to the Mobile Theater. He was the person with whom Navarro maintained the most ongoing relationship during his stay, attending his classes regularly. Critchlow was a professor at the AA for 12 years, an activity he combined with teaching at the Bournemouth College of Art. At both schools, he taught courses in geometry and the creation of cellular prototypes. He studied painting at the Royal College of Arts and worked with Richard Buckminster Fuller, whom he met in 1960 and of whom he was a very loyal disciple in the UK (Figure 154). In 1969, he published a book called *Order in Space: A Design Source Book*, of which Javier Navarro attempted to publish a Spanish edition, unsuccessfully (Figure 155). The book saw wide distribution in the years following its release and provided a practical approach to different models of what the author called "closepacking space".[1] It had an educational, visual format and dealt with regular polyhedrons and their configurations and possible groupings. The influence of some of the ideas contained in the book was largely important in the development of the Mobile Theater, and Critchlow's personal influence on Javier Navarro was very significant. For both men, geometry and architecture are bodies of knowledge whose purpose is rooted in the understanding and basic organization of space. As such, the two disciplines share a remote common origin, wherein their possible future development also lies. That was Critchlow's main interest and the fundamental premise to which he dedicated his work.

Figure 154: Anonymous photograph from 1960. On the left, Richard Buckminster Fuller and on the right, Keith Critchlow.

Figure 155: Cover of *Order in Space*, by Keith Critchlow, 1969.

ORDER, TECHNOCRACY AND INDUSTRY

In the primitive stages of architectural culture, which appear mythicized in Critchlow's imaginary, the built habitat was constructed using repetitive elements that were found, manipulated to a minimum, and with the limited motivation of providing shelter. Yet the selection of those elements, such as rocks or blocks of earth, although they fulfill identical functions, and the methods of combining them, provided, from the outset, an aesthetic component to even the most elemental constructions.

The organization of the ground and the wall, the horizontal plane and the vertical plane, introduced a linguistic factor by establishing rules of syntax to manage the elements in superior structures comprising more than just one of the elements on its own. The structured subdivision of the plane and of space thus introduces the concept of weaving and tesselation, whereas the ordered repetition of elements or components to cover space or fill it up introduces the concept of pattern.[2] These were the main themes of Critchlow's work at that stage of his professional life, and they are partially compiled in *Order in Space*, which continued Buckminster Fuller's studies on the mathematical structuring of nature. The book and Critchlow's teachings were particularly focused on packaging solids in three-dimensional space and stimulating ideological ties with industry, an approach which shares close similarities with the early years of the Bauhaus. *Order in Space* analyzed the geometric properties of the bodies that fill space and the typological ties between solids, grids and weavings pursuing a maximum economy of perimeters.

Critchlow had extensive experience in the development and construction of cellular polyhedral prototypes. From 1967 to 1971 he tested and built a series of them, including the Hexagon Houses, the so-called Polyhedral Constructions, the Polydomes, and the Square Spin House (Figure 156). All the structures were similar, with variations in the shape of the basic polyhedron and the materials used in the construction. The description of the *Hexagon Houses* gives a clear idea of Critchlow's design philosophy:

The Hexagon House is a light-weight, easy and quickly erected multi-purpose shelter. It has been designed to gain the maximum structural performance from Tri-Wall Pok triple-corrugated board, hence its unusual faceted appearance. Its geometrical configuration gives unlimited planning possibilities for either single or grouped units. It can be used to house people, goods or equipment, can be arranged as dwellings for families, as offices, store rooms or any activity requiring an enclosure comparative to a conventional building, but at a substantially lower cost.[3]

To sell his patents, for a time Critchlow ran a business called Polyhedral Developments Ltd. One of his prototypes, the Square Spin House was a temporary emergency shelter, built using walls made up of four panels, to which were added a roof, an entrance module and a door unit (Figure 157). The material was triple-corrugated board, normally used for storage in heavy industry because of its load-bearing capabilities. It was finished with a plastic-based resin, which was expected to give it a durability of 25 years, while making it water-resistant and UV-resistant. The joints between the panels were finished with fiberglass rope, generating a continuous, waterproof and stable envelope. Although the rhetoric is direct and refers exclusively to criteria of flexibility and economy, when

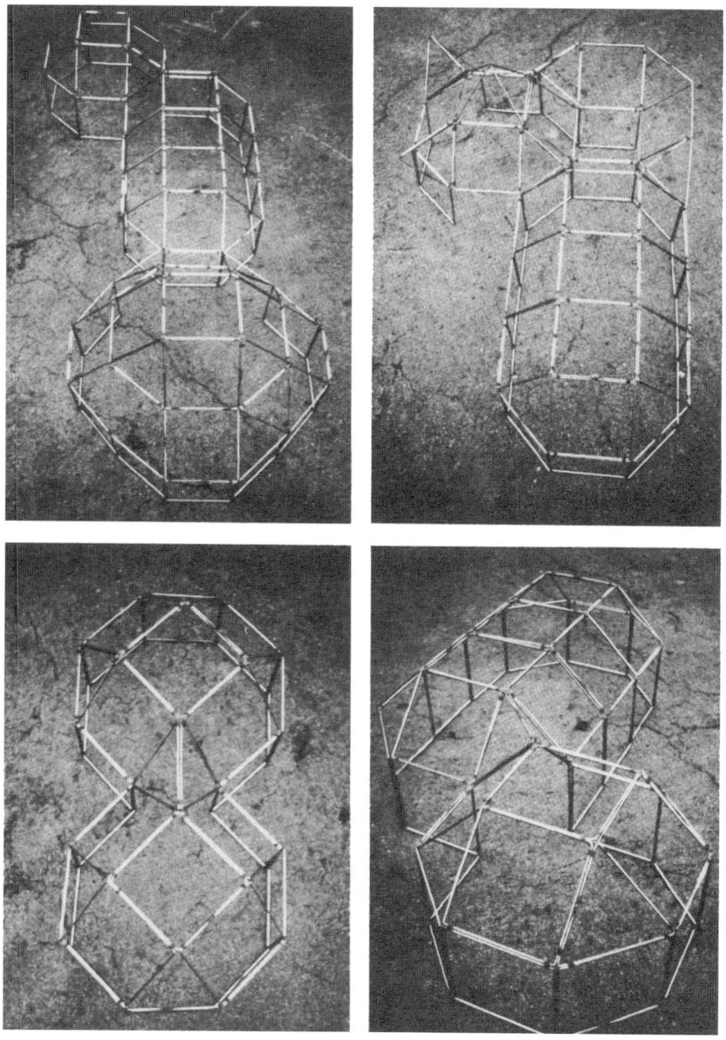

Figure 156: Keith Critchlow, Square Spin Houses, a tubular system with two compound models, 1971. Source: *Zodiac* magazine.

these structures were actually tested as built prototypes they were systematically tied in with recreational or pedagogical counterculture contexts and distanced from the construction industry, engineering or the military apparatus. They were prototypes proposed and examined as part of Critchlow's design courses, a real research niche focused on form and material that entirely supplanted the usual industrial apparatus (Figures 158 and 159). The contexts in which Critchlow's structures were tested out and used offer us more information than the artifacts themselves, which ultimately belong to the extensive catalogue of constructions derived from the teachings of Buckminster Fuller.

In March 1971 an announcement was made giving the results of a competition that had been organized by the Pavilions in the Parks Advisory Service,[4] the same organization where Joan Littlewood had worked some time earlier, just before the competition was launched. The first prize was awarded to a structure by Peter Rice, a brilliant engineer from Arup, who was also participating at the time in the competition for the Centre Pompidou with the team that went on to win the commission. An honorable mention was awarded to Critchlow's proposal, from his Polydome series, which was also built, along with winning structure, and was used by a Leeds-based street theater company, founded in 1968, called The Welfare State.[5] Four years later, the same structure was purchased by another theater company called the Bubble Theater. It was used for the company's tours from the time of its founding in 1972 until 1974 when they acquired a larger structure (Figures 160 and 161). Critchlow's structure ended up in the hands of a third company, called the Balloon Theater Company, with its headquarters on the south coast, in Christchurch.[6] The fate of this structure, derived from Fuller's investigations of direct transfers from the military industry to civil industry, is truly surprising. At one point, its evolution follows a backtracking path in a return to war: it was used as a mobile theater to dramatize wartime social conflicts and their consequences on postwar society.

The Bubble Theatre's first show, from 1972, called *The London Blitz Show*, toured the neighborhoods on the outskirts of London, with official support from the Greater London Arts Association, from May 1972 until September 1973 (Figure 162). The Blitz refers to the bombings of London carried out by the German Luftwaffe in 1940 and 1941. In the mise-en-scène for the play, Critchlow's Polydome was used to represent an air-raid shelter, and the actors, who called themselves "The Happy Shelterers", played civil defense workers who were tasked with entertaining the

Figure 157: Keith Critchlow, construction from the Polyhedral series using eight components, called the Guilford Cluster, 1969. Source: *Zodiac* magazine.

Figure 158: Keith Critchlow during the final session of his course at the Bournemouth College of Art in 1971, with a Polydome prototype. Source: *Zodiac* magazine.

Figure 159: Keith Critchlow, construction from the Polyhedral series using eight components, called the Guilford Cluster, 1969. Source: *Zodiac* magazine.

audience, confined to the shelter during a night of bombing. Using a variety show format, the performance was based on a series of numbers that took place on a central stage, entirely surrounded by a small audience of about 100 people maximum. Audience members were received and treated like hosts in the shelter, with the goal of generating an atmosphere of comradery among the group, simulating what might have been the case in wartime, with the ties of solidarity forged between citizens under threat. The performance made extensive use of nostalgia, using references, news articles, and local press items from the period, which were adapted to each particular location, to elicit a direct and emotional identification among the older members of the audience (Figures 163 and 164). The press highlighted the formal continuity between this theatrical format and the famous play by Joan Littlewood *Oh! What a Lovely War* from 1963, which achieved great commercial success in London's West End.[7] One of the many press reviews of *The Blitz Show* highlights a fundamental aspect which, in contrast to the others, presents a critical and premonitory reading. According to the journalist who wrote it, the play "relies too heavily on a cosy sentimental nostalgia and never rams home, with sufficient force, the situation's tragic irony: that the classless cooperation engendered by war scarcely survived into peacetime and has now disappeared almost entirely."[8]

The diagnostic was incredibly apt. The subsidized political theater appealed to subjective individual emotions, beyond the collective consciousness and its potential for feeling, reconstructing, through fiction, a classless society broadly intertwined by the values of comradery, which – it seemed – could only be awakened in modern industrialized society by a context of violence or, to the extreme, war. It is significant that Critchlow experienced a very particular personal evolution beginning in 1972, the date when this war-themed play was presented. At that moment, he completely abandoned his research into the geometry of industrialized packed spa-

Figure 160: Keith Critchlow, Polydome from the Polyhedral series, as it was used by the traveling theater company The Bubble Theatre, circa 1972.

Figure 161: Keith Critchlow, Polydome from the Polyhedral series, as it was used by the traveling theater company The Bubble Theatre, circa 1972.

ce, and he shifted his focus onto the historic analysis of sacred Eastern geometries, especially those of Persian origin, although he did have longstanding interest in the subject. In 1975, he began teaching courses on Islamic art at the Royal College of Arts, and in 1984 he founded VITA (Visual Islamic and Traditional Arts), which eventually fused with the most conservative of British educational institutions: The Prince's Institute of Architecture. Prince Charles himself is a patron of the Temenos Academy, co-founded by Critchlow, which originated as a journal specialized in sacred geometries and is still in operation today.

THE GREAT MYSTIC CAMPOUT

Over time, Keith Critchlow took his interest in geometry to great lengths, toward a complete and militant cultural anachronism, asserting that geometry is the "key" to the sacred: "Sacredness is as simple as breathing,"[9] he said in an interview in 1999, to explain his insistence on the use of geometry to organize living spaces. On a methodological level, the direct influence of Buckminster Fuller can be seen as an almost absolute continuity. However, the original values of Fuller's legacy were slightly distorted by Critchlow's unique contributions as they gradually took on a vaguely religious component, which could effectively be called esoteric, and from which Fuller was not entirely disconnected – although in his own way, always remaining technocratic.

Figure 162: Keith Critchlow, Polydome from the Polyhedral series, as it was used by the traveling theater company The Bubble Theatre, circa 1972.

Figure 163: Photograph of a moment from *The Blitz Show*, by the traveling theater company The Bubble Theatre, circa 1972.

Figure 164: Poster for *The Blitz Show*, by the traveling theater company, The Bubble Theatre, circa 1972.

These close ties between technology and geometry were central to the countercultural front as a whole:

Fuller and his "comprehensive design" offered many in the 1960s a way to embrace the technologies, the technocratic politics and the flexible, collaborative work styles of the Cold War military and industrial worlds, even as they built their own alternative communities.[10]

The singularity of Critchlow's teachings throughout his time at the Architectural Association lay in the strange connection between industrial technology and spirituality, which was mediated by geometry as the link that tied the two spheres of knowledge together – which industry had profoundly and definitively dissociated. Critchlow responded directly to this dissociation with his techno-conservative intellectual project:

I found the prime axiom of Euclid "a point has a position, but it has no magnitude" unacceptable as Einstein seemed to have pointed out that in relativistic cosmology the geometrical properties of space are directly related to and not independent of the distribution of matter.[11]

This link between geometry, space and matter anchors geometry to solid bodies. It makes it impossible to look at geometry as something immaterial; it ties it to a place. As such, geometry is perceived as a form of control and power that is not abstract but concrete, physically embodied and not immanent, as Fuller saw it. That is where Critchlow lay the essential fundaments for his unique critique of modernity, without turning his back on the progress of the pure sciences and, as a later consequence, the applied sciences and technology. In that sense, he asserted that "we cannot have position (in space) without substance (matter) and time (duration) — all our experience down to the bubble chamber would seem to point this way."[12] Critchlow's main goal seems to be the same as so many traditionalist intellectuals who were critical of modernity[13] and who helped to shed light on the apparent dilemma Javier Navarro highlighted with the Mobile Theater: the difficult compatibility between the dissolution of architecture (its radically inclusive dimension) and the need for spatial limitation (its radically exclusive dimension). Like Critchlow, Navarro also seemed

to acknowledge, especially with his *Experiments in Situation*, the hidden metaphysics in the separation between intellection and sensory perception, in search of an overlap between those spheres of knowledge. In his notes from October 1970, he wrote that he was trying to design an "inflatable communal space", which could also be "self-motivated". It had to be communal because it was the same for everyone and for every activity, without specialization, with the potential, even, to house different simultaneous events, and self-motivated because "it pulsates and breathes with the situation".[14]

Recalling the pop and nihilistic atmosphere at the Architectural Association, as Jeffrey Kipnis described it, the institution given over to the education of architects encompassed, in the 1970-1971 period, a variety of very different niches simultaneously. One of those niches, Critchlow's, was highly influenced by the ties between geometry, mechanical efficiency, and a vague, amateur spirituality (Figure 165). A former student of architecture commented:

I went to the second Glastonbury Festival in the summer of 1971. [...] I bumped into Keith Critchlow at the Festival, and he suggested I join him at the Architectural Association in London when I got back. [...] Somehow, I managed to raise the fees and enrolled for a diploma at the Architectural Association in London. This place, it became clear later, was also a nursery for students of Beshara. Keith Critchlow was an inspiring teacher, and became a good friend who was generous with his knowledge and enthusiasm. Keith knew of Reshad's search for a design for the dome (the "Mihrab") that was to be built within a stone barn at Swyre Farm in Gloucestershire, and was intended as the place of meditation, and a venue for talks and other events. We worked on a scheme and presented it. Our design was accepted, and I went to live there in February 1972 to oversee its building. (It

Figure 165: Geodesic construction at the Beshara farm with Halim Tollemache, Hakki Bey, David Hornsby, Rashida and an unidentified person, summer 1972.

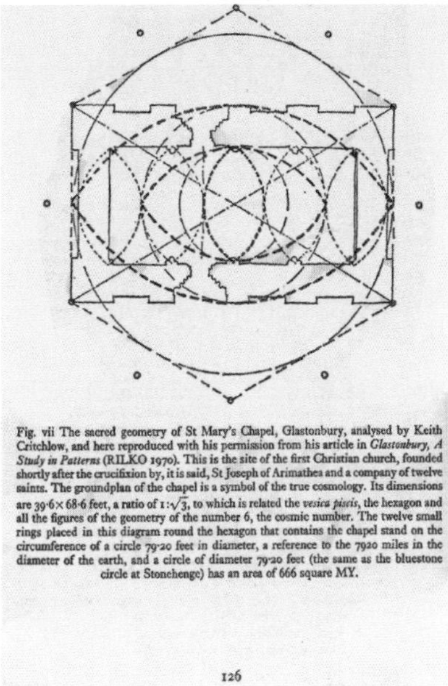

Figure 166: Diagram by Keith Critchlow for RILKO, with his study of Glastonbury Abbey, reproduced in John Michell's book *The View Over Atlantis.*

was to be my project for that year of study at the Association).[15]

In 1969, Critchlow founded a cultural association called Research Into Lost Knowledge Organization (RILKO), in conjunction with a prestigious scholar of medieval literature named Mary Williams and with John Michell (1933-2009). Michell was a dilettante from a rural aristocratic family, Eton educated, who dedicated the early years of his professional life to the family business, buying and selling large real-estate properties, and the following years to the extensive dissemination of a curious and syncretic esotericism that had an enormous repercussion in English counterculture. Critchlow, Williams and Michell shared a common fascination for the Arthurian legend of Avalon, the island from Celtic mythology that some have associated with Glastonbury, where there would theoretically have been an island before the marshland was drained to be made habitable. In that sense, Critchlow's research into polyhedral structures at the Architectural Association at the time was already colored by his esoteric interests. In September 1969, RILKO published a pamphlet called *Glastonbury: A Study in Patterns*, which contains Critchlow's analyses of the geometry of Glastonbury Abbey (Figure 166). According to Critchlow, the ruins of the abbey contain the same pattern used in the construction of Stonehenge. This continuity marked an ideological vein that Critchlow and Michell explored to its farthest possibilities.

During the 1970-1971 academic year, Critchlow collaborated closely with the organizers of the Glastonbury Festival, held in June 1971 to celebrate the summer solstice. Michell was a central figure in the event due to the broad impact of his 1969 book *The View Over Atlantis.*[16] The festival emerged as an alternative to the Isle of Wight Festival, held the previous year, which suffered from organization problems, leading to criticisms about commercialization from a large part of the attendants. The businessman Andrew Kerr, who had worked in Randolph Churchill's cabinet, developed the project for a free festival in collaboration with Arabella Churchill, granddaughter of the famous politician.

In September 1970, what is now considered the first edition of the Glastonbury Festival took place at Worthy Farm, outside the town. The official name was the Pilton Pop, Blues and Folk Festival and it was organized with support from the farm's owner, a farmer named Michael Evis. Tickets cost £1, and the event lasted just a few hours, with an estimated audience of some 1,500 people. For the next year, Kerr, Churchill and Evis organized a free music festival which they called Glastonbury Fayre. From the outset, it was set up as an event meant to be dominated by the esotericism that characterized the mythical site. The press referred explicitly to these reasons for choosing Glastonbury as the location for the event, highlighting both Michell's book and Kerr's mission, which was nothing less than to recreate, for the solstice, a "prehistoric science, whose huge energies are not recognized by modern society".[17]

Kerr commissioned the design of the main stage to Bill Harkin, a young architect who had studied in Liverpool. Harkin drew on Critchlow's geometric studies to design a pyramid, which reproduced the Great Pyramid of Giza on a scale of 1:10. It was used as a stage for the musicians, with a 75-foot base and a height of 48 feet (Figure 167). The assembly was carried out by a small group of volunteers during a few weekends in June, using a Kwikform scaffolding system – specifically a patent developed for shipbuilding called Kwikstage – which was used, here, for the first time to build a stage (despite what the name suggests). It went on to become a standard system for such purposes. The construction was entirely financed through donations from the festival organizers, in particular Andrew Kerr, Arabella Churchill and Jeff Dexter. The structure was covered with 300 expanded metal panels, which created a shiny metalized finish (Figure 168).

Figure 167: Main stage at the Glastonbury Festival for the solstice 1971, designed by Bill Harkin. Courtesy of Tony Murchland.

We already had the makings of an audience looming in front of the stage. Taking advantage of the many willing hands we soon had a greatly enlarged crew passing sheets of expanded metal up the face of the Pyramid. From afar they looked like leaf cutter ants swarming over the framework, moving sheets up and wiring them on, this is why so many of that '71 audience feel that they were part of the creation of the Pyramid Stage.[18]

Thanks to this cladding, the pyramid had five million little facets of metalized material, which meant it could be turned into a luminescent object using just two Mole Richardson 10 kW lights. The stage for the musicians was located at a certain height, so the audience had to stand back from the front row to get a good view. That meant a security barrier was not needed to separate the audience from the stage. The pyramid was outfitted with a series of platforms, in addition to the stage for the musicians: one for the camera operators, one for the lighting and sound equipment, and a third for dressing rooms (Figure 169). Around the pyramid, a network of small constructions was set up, with the participation of professors and students from a variety of educational institutions. They were joined by pseudo-vernacular structures built by the attendants themselves, all together forming an instant city of from 7,500 to 10,000 people.

Hi my name is Margy, my boyfriend at the time now my best friend Paul and I were at the 1971 festival it was amazing. There was very little in the way of accommodation, by accident we slept in a Hari Krishna tent one night, a big no no for women apparently but they were sooo lovely and gave us breakfast the next day, news from the farm came down that we could build shelters as long as we only used dead wood, Paul and I made a great "tent" which, we found out much later was awarded BEST home made tent of the festival

Figure 168: Main stage at the Glastonbury Festival for the solstice 1971, designed by Bill Harkin. Photograph by Matt Williams.

Figure 169: Audience members in front of the main stage at the Glastonbury Festival for the solstice 1971, designed by Bill Harkin. Photograph by Matt Williams.

DRAWING DOWN THE ASTRAL ENERGIES

Keith Critchlow

in an architecture mag, wish to god I had kept that picture, what beautiful memories.[19]

The magazine to which Margy refers was, in fact, *Architectural Design* (Figure 170).[20] The community of students and designers in Critchlow's circle attended the festival with him and the homeopath Julian Carlyon. They brought along the prefabricated pieces necessary to build an 8-meter plywood dome in front of the farm, from the Polydomes series, which a few weeks earlier had been the graduation project for the students in Bournemouth. It was used as a rest stop for lost hikers and was burned following the festival. Mark Fisher and Jonathan Park, with a direct connection to Archigram, built a small inflatable structure which housed some of the attendees who did not have their own tents. Zee Chamoe, from the US, built a 6-meter diameter tent using a system he had developed in the 1950s. His real name was Donald James Hamrick (1935-2011) and he had studied architecture and physics. He left behind a successful professional career to found the Harbinger commune, active from 1967 to 1969, which was associated with an alternative learning center called Harbinger University. The designers Roger Heighton and Roger Tuffs, two of the stagehands, built a structure they called the Dark Star. Set on a hill, it was made from black plastic wrap and formed in the shape of a star. The catalog of geometries and technologies used at Glastonbury was a clear extension of the most radical experimental learning environments of the time. They were perfectly intertwined in a strong network, structured largely according to Michell's syncretic work and his countercultural best-seller *The View Over Atlantis*, from which nearly all the ideas put into practice for the festival were taken. Through

Figure 170: Double-page feature by Keith Critchlow on the Glastonbury Festival, published in *Architectural Design* in August 1971, with commentary on the structures built by students and festival attendants.

the eyes of an outsider, and according to a journalist who was present at the event:

Many people here are gentle misfits, living life in its margins and looking for a mainstream credo to replace distrusted inherited values. They have assembled in a place where the broad and ancient beliefs in astrological religions has been changed and narrowed gradually into the creeds of Ebenezer chapels in the villages round about.[21]

The exact site selected for the festival was located on farmland, just a few kilometers from the archaeological ruins of Glastonbury Tor, a cone-shaped hill topped by a Gothic tower. It is the only remains of a conventual construction of great literary and mythological (more than archaeological) prestige, which was part of the heritage site, with its famous abbey, measured and analyzed by Critchlow for RILKO in 1969. According to Michell, the abbey was built, like nearly all English churches, at the intersection of two "ley lines", which might be referred to today as regulation lines or law lines. "Ley", a word with its origins in the Latin *lex*, refers to the rule or regulation established by a superior authority to regulate some aspect of social relationships, but it can also refer to the set of rules in a religion or, finally, to pastureland or land used temporarily for agriculture. It has a direct relationship with the Greek word *nomos*, as well as its triple meaning of legal rule or law, religious dogma, or a cultivated field as opposed to a natural meadow. Michell asserted that the lines formed a direct link connecting Stonehenge with Glastonbury and the ruins of the abbey, crossing through Worthy Farm, where an exact point on the line was calculated for the location of the pyramid.

LINES AND TIME TUNNELS

A document distributed by Kerr during the festival explained the ideology behind the chosen site. Kerr defined Stonehenge as an "astronomical instrument, it's a clock, it's a calendar, it's a meeting place for force lines and for people, it's a computer and a stimulator" (Figures 171 and 172). This improbable connection between communication networks and geodesic and topographic networks was perfectly aligned with Critchlow's assertions about the falsity of Euclid's prime axiom, which asserts that a point is an abstraction, a merely intellectual entity, and not a tangible place in physical terms. In *The View Over Atlantis*, Michell took to an extreme this idea of the tie between ley lines and the immaterial aerial network that would virtualize them in the air as a mirror system of orientation, at a certain distance from the Earth's surface.

Michell's book begins by laying out an idea that organizes all his arguments: similar to how people can have identical ideas at the same time in different places, without there being any communication between them, that synchronicity can also transcend the limits of time. Moreover, it follows a precise geometry: the ley lines. Thus, the remote past and the present can forge an absolute connection. That is the phenomenon to which Michell was responding, drawing on the work of a series of historical figures, including John Aubrey, William Stukeley, Katharine Maltwood and Alfred Watkins, who were his predecessors in the undertaking.

John Aubrey (1626-1697) is still well-known for his short biographies of famous figures, including his teacher Thomas Hobbes, among others, for his analyses of English folklore,

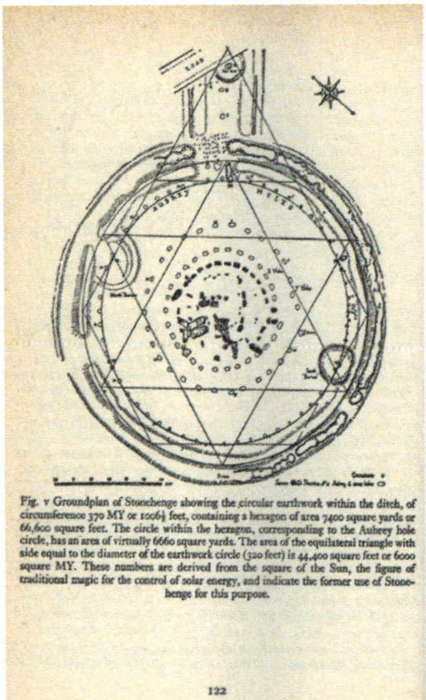

Fig. v Groundplan of Stonehenge showing the circular earthwork within the ditch, of circumference 370 MY or 1006½ feet, containing a hexagon of area 7400 square yards or 66,600 square feet. The circle within the hexagon, corresponding to the Aubrey hole circle, has an area of virtually 6660 square yards. The area of the equilateral triangle with side equal to the diameter of the earthwork circle (320 feet) is 44,400 square feet or 6000 square MY. These numbers are derived from the square of the Sun, the figure of traditional magic for the control of solar energy, and indicate the former use of Stonehenge for this purpose.

122

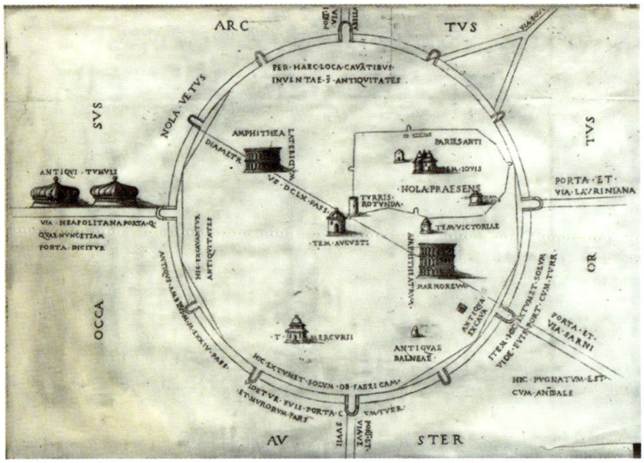

and for his studies of ancient architecture, in particular the megalithic ruins of Avebury and Stonehenge, to which he dedicated 30 years of his career, from 1663 to 1693. His erudite studies were never published and became known in manuscript form, in four volumes, under the title *Monumenta Britannica.* The first volume is called *Templa Druidum* and deals with the archaeological ruins of Avebury and Stonehenge. This was the work that sparked Michell's interest in his own cultural project. Aubrey was the first to assert that the Britons achieved an advanced cultural, technical and political level before Romanization. The fortunate coincidence of his assertions with the restauration of the British monarchy, following the republican parenthesis under Cromwell, just a decade after his ideas began to be disseminated, was key to his success among politicians and intellectuals of the ruling classes and is a clear indication of his political inclinations.[22]

William Stukeley (1687-1765) was a doctor, and later an Anglican clergyman, who also researched the same megaliths (Figure 173). His intellectual project was inseparable from his religious and cultural activism, which were entirely intertwined. He was also the biographer of a great figure, Isaac Newton, which had its own significance: Aubrey and Stukeley's fondness for biography suggests

Figure 171: Geometric diagram of Stonehenge showing a hexagon inscribed in the circular ditch that surrounds the monument, from John Michell's book *The View Over Atlantis*, 1969.

Figure 172: Mystical diagram of the city of Nola according to Ambrogio Leone, from his work *De Nola Opusculum*, Venice 1514. Leone was an Italian philosopher and humanist who reconstructed the city of his birth, Nola, in this map, a drawing Michell reproduced in *The View Over Atlantis*, although he provided no information about it. Historical Library of the UCM.

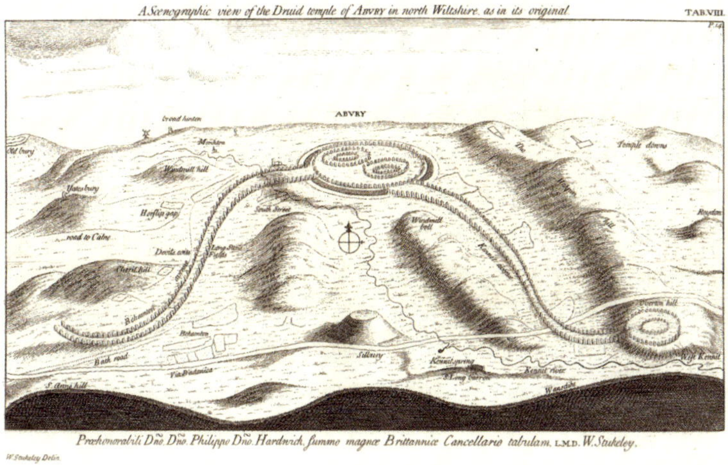

their concern for the construction of history, as well as their self-awareness in engaging in that type of activity, and for the power of writing. Stukeley's archaeological theory was based on the belief that the druids were direct descendants of the biblical patriarchs. As such, they developed a monotheistic religion, which, seen in that light, directly rivaled Catholicism, based on a clear historical connection – which had overt political implications. In his study, *History of the Temples of the Ancient Celts*, which focused on those megalithic ruins, Stukeley challenged the hypotheses of Inigo Jones and John Webb, the maximum authorities on the subject until that time, who maintained that the Romans were responsible for the constructions. Stukeley's counter-hypothesis drastically altered the panorama and introduced an aspect of cultural nationalism that fit in perfectly with British imperialism. He later revisited the subject with *Stonehenge*, from 1740, insisting on the hypothesis of the druid patriarchy as a direct mirror of Anglicanism, with the goal of neutralizing certain dissident religious fronts, which Anglican hegemony considered to be a threat (Figure 174).[23]

Michell's assimilation of the two authors is symptomatic, since he attributed to Aubrey a revelation in his "discovery" of the Avebury megaliths, which led him to his own idea of a trans-historical synchronicity.[24] This rhetorical maneuver was obviously directed, at its height, back toward Michell himself: his version of Aubrey is clearly a self-portrait. In

Figure 173: William Stukeley, *Abury, A Temple of the British Druids, with Some Others, Described*, London 1743. The image shows the region of Avebury and its megalithic ruins, and it was reproduced in Michell's book *The View over Atlantis* from 1969. Belton House, National Trust Collections.

beginning his book by connecting Aubrey's archaeological interests with a kind of religious revelation, Michell was clearly hoping for the reader to identify with the man who was illuminated by the material he was about to present – an endeavor in which he was successful, judging by the enormous success of the book.

From Stukeley, Michell borrowed his refined rhetorical technique, rooted in comparative religion (what we would call Cultural Studies today). He then took a flying leap that resulted in a tightening of the connections Stukeley had drawn between different belief systems and historical time periods, the Britons and the Jews, through his comparative studies of the Bible and Celtic mythology. Projecting Stukeley's theories into the present, Michell dug a time tunnel that connected the Britons and pre-Roman Celtic culture not only with other non-Christianized or non-Romanized groups in a monotheistic global world, but also with the modern English society of his time. Michell thus forged a direct connection between those pre-Roman or, more accurately, pre-continental, cultures and mass consumption, mass media, an incipient electronic technology, and (by flatly negating the 19th-century idea of materialist historicity) a radical political alterity. His key to *accessing* that time tunnel was, of course, geometry, a field of knowledge that had managed to remain intact and impermeable despite the succession of cultural revolutions since its mythical origin, which he situated among the Britons.

To round out his narrative, Michell turned to Katharine Maltwood (1878-1961), who published a fascinating book called *A Guide to the Glastonbury Temple of the Stars* (Figure 175).

Figure 174: William Stukeley, *Stonehenge: A Temple Restor'd to the British Druids*, London, 1740. The image shows Stonehenge and its megalithic ruins, and it was reproduced in Michell's book *The View over Atlantis* from 1969. Tatton Park, National Trust Collections.

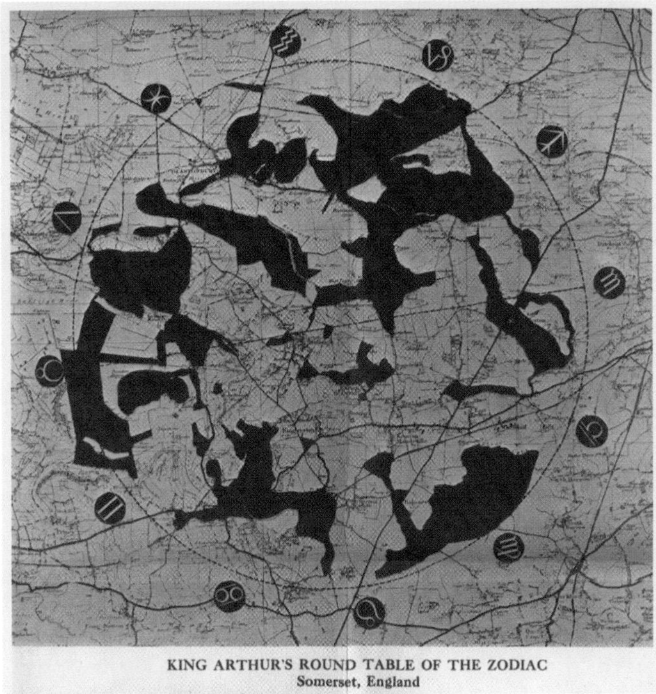

The book opens with a comment from the author which offers the key to the project: aerial photography allowed Maltwood – in a way that had been impossible previously, combined with a series of official maps called *Ordnance Survey Maps* – to identify a complete zodiac circle in the landscape of Glastonbury, lending meaning to its literary legends.[25] Not just meaning, but also scientific credibility and epistemological continuity. The modern science of cartography and aerial photography provided a validation of the myths to the extent of establishing a fluid continuity between myth and territorial form. Maltwood's book contained very elaborate maps in which fragments of the territory can be seen floating in a dark mass, enclosed in the shapes of the signs of the Zodiac, representing their perfectly recognizable animal forms (Figures 176 and 177). Michell interpreted, once again, Maltwood's work as a revelation, as a powerful thread of continuity – while failing to mention the mediation of the topographic and photographic devices to which Maltwood refers in the introduction to her text.

A final author who supports Michell's astonishing tale, over and above all the others, is Alfred Watkins (1855-1935), an amateur whom Michell systematically over-interpreted in an authentic operation of cultural appropriation. Watkins was in the brewing business in Hereford, but he was also an excellent photographer, well-versed in the

Figure 175: Illustration by Katharine Emma Maltwood called *King Arthur's Round Table of the Zodiac*, from her book *Guide to Glastonbury's Temple of the Stars: Their giant effigies described from air views, maps, and from "The High History of the Holy Grail"*, London, 1929.

Plate

VIRGO

The Cary River outlines her bonnet, face, sleeve, and breast which is marked by Wimble Toot, meaning Augur's teat.
The 'Kern Baby' is inset at the corresponding angle. The Hyperborean priestesses "In the celebrating of the mysteries, held handfuls of corn".

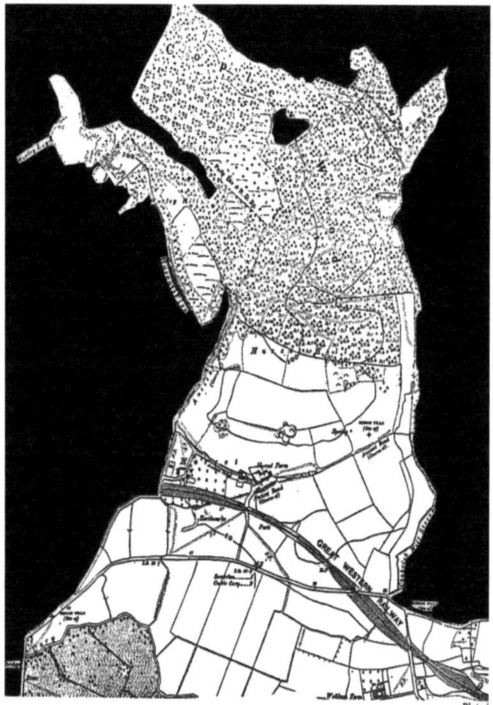

Plate :

LEO

Chabrick Mill Stream outlines the nose and mane, "Ancient Road" the neck, and "Linches" the jaw.

Figure 176: Illustration by Katharine Emma Maltwood showing a part of Somerset in the shape of Virgo, from her book *Guide to Glastonbury's Temple of the Stars: Their giant effigies described from air views, maps, and from "The High History of the Holy Grail"*, London, 1929.

Figure 177: Illustration by Katharine Emma Maltwood showing a part of Somerset in the shape of Leo, from her book *Guide to Glastonbury's Temple of the Stars: Their giant effigies described from air views, maps, and from "The High History of the Holy Grail"*, London, 1929.

mechanics and optics of photography, and a lover of landscape and geography (Figures 178 and 179). To get an idea of the scope of Michell's appropriation, it is sufficient to compare his description of how Watkins' interest was piqued by the phenomenon of ley lines, of which he is considered the main inventor, with Watkins' own words on the subject:

One hot summer afternoon in the early 1920s Alfred Watkins was riding across the Breadwardine (sic) hills about 12 miles west of Hereford. On a hilltop he stopped, meditating on the view below him. Suddenly, in a flash, he saw something which no one in England had seen for perhaps thousands of years. Watkins saw straight through the surface of the landscape to a layer deposited in some remote prehistoric age. The barrier of time melted and, spread across the country, he saw a web of lines linking the holy places and sites of antiquity. [26]

For his part, Watkins described the same moment during a lecture in September 1921, which he gave to a group of naturalists from his hometown, in a very different way, also revealing Michell's error when referring to the name of the place where the supposed revelation took place, Blackwardine:

A visit to Blackwardine led me to note on the map a straight line starting from Croft Ambury, lying on parts of Croft Lane past the Broad, over hill points, through Blackwardine, over Risbury Camp, and through the high ground at Stretton Grandison, where I surmise a Roman station. I followed up the clue of sighting

Figure 178: Photograph by Alfred Watkins, sacrificial stone in the region of Herefordshire, 1922. Alfred Watkins Collection. Herefordshire County Library Service.

Figure 179: Photograph by Alfred Watkins, Arthur's stone in Dorstone, 1922. Alfred Watkins Collection. Herefordshire County Library Service.

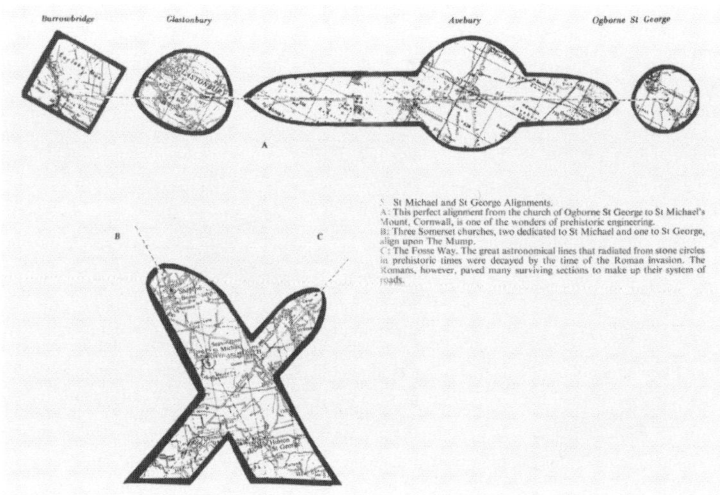

from hill top, unhampered by other theories, found it yielding astounding results in all districts, the straight lines to my amazement passing over and over again through the same class of objects, which I soon found to be (or to have been) practical sighting points.[27]

Thus, Watkins explained, to a very incredulous audience and with extreme prudence, two fundamental questions, which Michell cleverly obscured in his bold maneuver. Watkins' first explanation is that his observations were not derived from any theory. They were not intended to demonstrate anything, but rather to point out something that was the product of direct and systematic observation. The second explanation is that the origin of the *discovery* of the lines was not a revelation standing before the landscape, but rather a geometric operation on a map, which he only corroborated later by walking in the area (Figure 180). Michell switched the order of the events as Watkins described them, asserting that, following a revelation experienced in the landscape, brought about through a meditative state, Watkins later confirmed his vision on the map. With this inversion in the initial pages of his book, where Michell lays out the sophisticated scholarly mechanism that supports his thesis, beginning with Watkins, he was then able to follow his own interpretive avenues in every possible direction.[28]

Throughout his book, Michell drew connections between Watkins' system of ley lines, geomancy, Feng Shui, the Nazca Lines in Peru, and the geometric structure of the Great Pyramid of Giza, thanks to a highly developed weft of scholarship and a masterful writing style using a brilliant and very persuasive rhetoric (Figures 181 and 182). All these systems, which are, from his point of

Figure 180: John Michell, *Saint Michael and Saint George Alignments*, from his book *The View Over Atlantis*, from 1969.

view, synchronic epistemological disciplines, led him to conclude that the *Atlantis* from the title of his book was a real possibility, which, in a lucky turn of events, was put into practice by the Glastonbury Festival just two years later. The fifth chapter of Michell's book is dedicated exclusively to establishing a direct relationship between Stonehenge and Glastonbury. As its main reference, it relies on the polemic work by the astronomer Gerald Hawkins, well known for his 1965 publication *Stonehenge Decoded*, in which he interpreted the ruin as an extraordinarily sophisticated sundial, to the point of considering it the direct precedent of the computer: the very idea Andrew Kerr used in his advertisement for the festival.

TECHNOWALDEN

The Glastonbury Festival was thus a crystallization of the possible overlap between an archaic global universe, organized in a planetary network of ley lines, and a modern electronic culture, intent on reactivating that network through an operation of excavation into the past. The result takes us from an astrological garden[29] to an electric Eden.[30] In this Eden, the ley lines would recover their total visibility and functionality, which could only be brought about by a complete geographic transformation entirely based on digging up the past. The Eden in question is, of course, in typical English fashion, superior to any other model for occupying the territory, introducing into Michell's work an even more radical nationalism than the one proposed by

Figure 181: Old Sarum ley line, 18 kms long between Stonehenge and Frankenbury Camp, from the book *The Ley Hunter's Companion: Aligned Ancient Sites: A new study with field guide and maps*, by Paul Deveraux, London 1979. Deveraux, a veteran of LSD culture, was John Michell's most loyal follower.

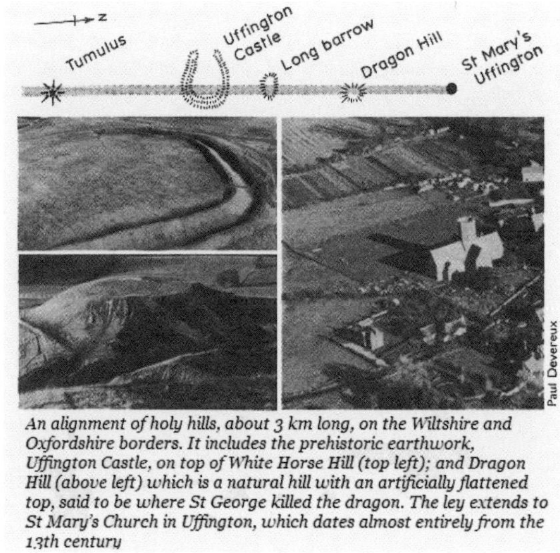

his illustrious imperialist predecessors, who, in his vision, become profoundly sublimated as national heroes.

Dr. Stukeley saw the work of old British geomancers at Avebury and extended his vision to encompass the entire country. Mrs. Maltwood looked with a geomancer's eye at the Somerset plains and understood in a flash the secret of the zodiacal giants hidden in the landscape. Alfred Watkins, envisioned on the Breadwardine hills, perceived the veins and arteries standing out clear against the Herefordshire fields. Blake, Wordsworth, Coleridge, Tennyson and many others sought the vital spots to penetrate the layers of time that cover the face of the country. The feeling they all shared was of some forgotten secret. They glimpsed at a remote age of science, poetry and religion in which the vast works they saw in the landscape were accomplished. Each of these English visionaries knew that what he saw was but a fraction of the great mystery, the key to which had been lost. Britain, they felt, was the holy land under enchantment.[31]

British literature, poetry, art and music are full of secret gardens, wonderlands, and paradises that have been lost, interrupted or recovered. Michell's electric Eden pointed to fictitious realms that could secretly seep into the present to construct alternative speculations – sometimes built, like the Glastonbury festival, and sometimes unbuilt, like the Mobile Theater. In the late 60s and early 70s, the fear of annihilation, technological progress and the vision of alternative societies ente-

Figure 182: Ley line from Tumulus to Saint Mary's Church in Uffington, from the book *The Ley Hunter's Companion: Aligned Ancient Sites: A new study with field guide and maps*, by Paul Deveraux, London 1979.

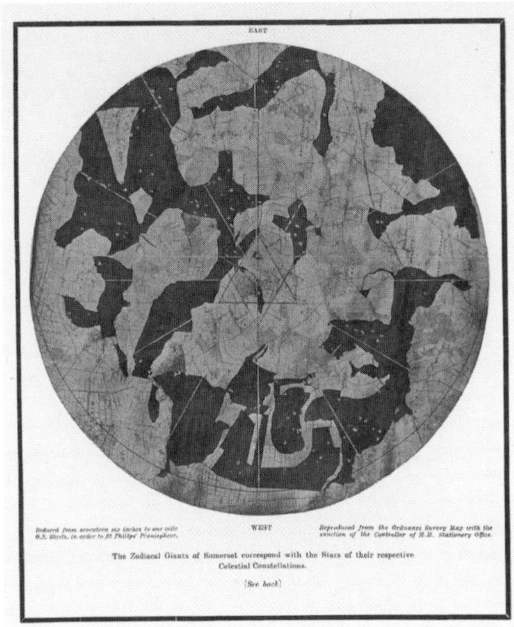

red popular and culture and art, conspiring to foster the idea of a "return to the garden".[32]

Only three years separate *Ideas Circus* from the Glastonbury Festival, with the Mobile Theater occupying, once again, an ambiguous, tangential and intermediate position between them. Maps of lines cover the territory of these new Arcadias in a network, half virtual and half real, that spreads knowledge, customs, behaviors and attitudes, equating its users in a global community. It replaces the existing networks and their artifacts with others of a nature that is mobile, sometimes precarious, extraordinarily functional, and entirely subsidiary to that network. A map of the United Kingdom showing an accurate distribution of prehistoric settlements and their networks of ley lines would be the exact opposite of a map showing the current population density,[33] something which Maltwood's drawings suggested: Zodiac islands floating in a black sea, connected to one another in an almost inaccessible network (Figure 183).

While beginning a narrative takes effort and carries all kinds of uncertainties, ending it is even more difficult. The threads off the skein take on a certain life of their own which, as you advance, it gets harder to keep them woven together in a fabric of meaning. And if, as is the case here, the threads aren't perfectly intertwined, but rather scattered all over in multiple places, the task becomes especia-

Figure 183: Illustration by Katharine Emma Maltwood called *The Zodiacal Giants of Somerset correspond with the Stars of their respective Celestial Constellations*, from her book *Guide to Glastonbury's Temple of the Stars: their giant effigies described from air views, maps, and from "The High History of the Holy Grail"*, London, 1929.

lly demanding and complex. To that end, it is useful to turn to an expert in belief to help us gain some insight; the greatest connoisseurs of disjointed structures are the poets, because, through their art, they create meaning where there was none, from isolated words.

Wystan Hugh Auden (1907-1973) was an important English poet, uprooted geographically, but also a very curious soldier. At the end of the war in 1945, he joined the so-called Morale Division of the U.S. Strategic Bombing Survey, a US public agency created to analyze the effects of Allied military campaigns on the German population. He was named as a Major in the Army to study the psychology of the population affected by the disaster of the war, visiting many of the German cities that had been devastated.[34] Throughout his poetry and essays, Auden wrote about the Happy Place time and again, having seen the effects of the civilizing military apparatus, in the search for possible models to overcome the state of absolute crisis brought about by the technology of war.

What Auden called the Happy Place, where there is no pain or suffering, was exemplified in two personality types, which are moral and political, as well as two associated urban models.[35] He called one Eden and the other New Jerusalem. The Arcadian goes in pursuit of Eden, the Utopian searches for New Jerusalem. Although a single individual is perfectly capable of conceiving the two characters, of understanding them, feeling drawn to them and valuing them equally, Auden considers them to be incompatible, because one cannot ascribe to both, despite the comprehension or inclinations one might feel. Whereas the Arcadian searches for Eden in a time that precedes all conflict or contradiction, in other words, a past before original sin (in whatever form it may take, for example, a brutal war), the Utopian New Jerusalem is always to be found in the future, at a time and place where the conflicts and contradictions have been resolved, overcome and left behind. Between these two spaces and times lies the present, the place where we inhabit conflict, contradiction and the desire for something other.

In Eden, everyone does what they want, and people are governed by the motto *Do what thou wilt is here the Law*. In New Jerusalem obligation is pleasure; it is ruled by *In His will is your peace*. They coincide in one fundamental aspect: the moral imperative does not exist in either. In Eden, there are no universal laws. In New Jerusalem, the law does not prescribe what people may or may not do, rather, it dictates the behaviors of those who belong. Although the inhabitants of both realms are happy, the inhabitants of Eden are pleasant and agreeable, whereas the inhabitants of New Jerusalem are good, with the distinguishing nuances that implies. You cannot enter Eden; you can only be born into it. You cannot be born into New Jerusalem; you can only enter it once you have acquired the goodness that grants you entrance.

While the Arcadian knows and accepts that his city is a dream, because he has been cast out of paradise and is thus unconcerned with his own original sin or his actions, the Utopian believes that New Jerusalem can and

should be built, and thus his actions should serve that goal, independently of their consequences. That is why, according to Auden, the Utopian needs images, and the Arcadian does not; similarly, Arcadian architecture has its sources in literature and poetry, whereas the architecture of Utopia looks to other architectures and, in general, their images. When Auden wrote about these questions after the war, he was thinking about the utopia of totalitarianism, but instead of delving into the Utopian temperament, if only to refute it like Theodor Adorno did, he turned his focus to the details of the Arcadian personality, establishing ten characteristics of the temperament and denying any further space for action or critique to Utopia. In that sense, his own inclinations were made very clear. This is not the place to address all the characteristic of the Arcadian. It is worth mentioning just one, however, which pertains to architecture in particular, number six of the ten characteristics he describes: space is both safe and open; there are walled gardens, but there are no jails; there are open roads in all directions, but there is no wandering in the desert (Figure 184). Auden's argument provides the conclusion to the last of the facets that helped give rise to the Mobile Theater as a faithful representative of an attitude and a very precise moment in history. The links between geometry and the sacred allowed for constructing an ideological bloc of resistance with close ties to a possible Edenic Arcadia, albeit, in this case, electrified.

Figure 184: Audience at the Glastonbury Festival during the solstice in 1971. Photograph by Matt Williams.

Notes

1. Keith Critchlow: *Order in Space: A Design Source Book*, London: Thames and Hudson 1969.

2. Keith Critchlow: "Closepacking", in *Zodiac* no. 22, 1972, pgs. 172-178.

3. Keith Critchlow: "Polyhedral Structures Conform", in *Zodiac* no. 22, 1972, pgs. 194-195.

4. *Architectural Design*, March 1971, pgs. 183-184.

5. *Architectural Design*, September 1971, pg. 530.

6. http://www.theatrecrafts.com/archive/cue/cue_07_25.pdf

7. The information comes from two news sources: *Financial Times*, May 4, 1972, article by Michael Coveney; and *Richmond and Twickenham Times*, May 26, 1972, article by Nick Smurthwaite.

8. Michael Billington: "Blitz Show", article in *The Guardian*, May 2, 1972.

9. From an interview with the newspaper *The Independent* published on November 5, 1999.

10. Fred Turner: "A Technocrat for the Counterculture", in *AV Monografias* no. 143, Madrid 2010, pg. 103.

11. Keith Critchlow: "Towards a New Philosophy of Structure", in *Zodiac* no. 22, 1972, pgs. 180-187.

12. Ibid.

13. For a reflection on Critchlow's significant influence on counterculture, see: Mark Sedgwick: *Against the Modern World. Traditionalism and the Secret Intellectual History of the Twentieth Century*, Oxford and New York: Oxford University Press, 2004. Especially the chapter "Europe after 1968", pgs. 207-221. Jay Kappraff: *Connections. The Geometric Bridge Between Art and Science*, New York: McGraw-Hill Inc., 1990, which makes constant references to Critchlow.

14. Handwritten notes contained in a labelled folder "Theater of situation. Experiments in situation. London 1970-1971", with notes written in English and Spanish.

15. Suha Taji-Farouki: *Beshara and Ibn'Arabi: A Movement of Sufi Spirituality in the Modern World*, Oxford: Anqa Publishers, 2007, pgs. 442-443.

16. John Michell: *The View over Atlantis. Secrets of the Ancient Mysteries Revealed*, New York: Ballantine Books, 1969.

17. Article published in *The Observer*, a section of *The Guardian* newspaper on June 20, 1971.

18. Bill Harkin, available online at http://www.pyramidstage-glastonburyfestival.co.uk/

19. http://www.ukrockfestivals.com/glasto-71-recollections.html

20. The journal *Architectural Design* published a short writeup in its August 1971 issue, with an extensive double-page photo feature, signed by Keith Critchlow himself.

21. John Cunninghman: "The Mystic Misfits", in *The Guardian*, June 22, 1971.

22. The bibliography on Aubrey is immense. One of the sources that focuses on his archaeological activity is Aubrey Burl: *John Aubrey & Stone Circles: Britain's First Archaeologist, From Avebury to Stonehenge*. Amberley: Stroud, 2010.

23. The bibliography on Stukeley is equally extensive. For an examination of the figure himself, see Stuart Piggott: *William Stukeley: An Eighteenth-Century Antiquary*. London: Thames & Hudson, 1985.

24. John Michell: *The View over Atlantis*, op. cit., pg. 15.

25. Edition consulted, Katharine Emma Maltwood: *Guide to Glastonbury's Temple of the Stars: Their giant effigies described from air views, maps, and from "The High History of the Holy Grail"*, London: The Women's Printing Society, Ltd., 1934, pg. viii.

26. John Michell: *The View Over Atlantis*, op. cit., pg. 21.

27. Alfred Watkins: *Early British Trackways, Moats, Mounds, Camps, and Sites*. Hereford: The Watkins Meter Co., 1922, pg. 6.

28. Michell introduced a continuous flow of information of dubious credibility, such as his suggestion that Watkins and his sister had developed a way of communicating with each other telepathically. John Michell: *The View Over Atlantis*, op. cit., pg. 23.

29. Chapter seven of Michell's book is called *The Astrological Garden*.

30. Rob Young: *Electric Eden: Unearthing Britain's Visionary Music*, New York: Faber and Faber, 2011.

31. John Michell: *The View over Atlantis*, op. cit., pg. 54.

32. Rob Young: *Electric Eden: Unearthing Britain's Visionary Music*, op. cit., pgs. 5-7.

33. John Michell: *The View Over Atlantis*, op. cit., pg. 67.

34. Cornelia D. J. Pearsall: "The Poet and the Postwar City", in *Raritan*, Fall 1997, 17- 2, pgs. 104-120.

35. Wystan Hugh Auden: "Dingley Dell & the Fleet", in *The Dyers Hand and Other Essays*, London: Faber and Faber 1948, pgs. 409-410

CONCLUSIONS

The Mobile Theater is a rich metaphor in its possible interpretations. Its specific incarnation in the design by Javier Navarro de Zuvillaga is wholly symptomatic of the period in which the design was conceived and developed. But the fact that it was never built is also a symptom of something more deep-seated than contingencies or adversity. Under no circumstances should the Mobile Theater, in its double condition as an archetype and a specific object, be considered an escapist utopia. Its precise initial technical development and its decidedly possibilist nature are clear indicators of its realism. The wide range of design offshoots that emanate from it, at their center, is also a good example of its historical relevance: it was proposed in the right place, at the right time and under optimum specific conditions. Perhaps that is why it could never be made a reality.

If the present, as Auden announced in his digression on Arcadia and Utopia, is the site of critical conflict between one and the other, built architecture can only rarely match up: it is paradoxical to cement contradiction, to solidify crisis into cultural artifacts with as much gravity as buildings, which systematically resist becoming critical objects. That was the main goal of the generation of architects and artists who appear in this book, and that is their invaluable legacy. In the face of a series of crises experienced at a dizzying speed, their response was positivity, a leap forward that combined three sensibilities: criticism, reflection and action, which have seldom been seen simultaneously in the way they were then. The Mobile Theater is a hybrid cross between those reactions to a series of crises, rather than an espousal of one of them over and above the rest.

The first of the crises observed by those architects and artists was the crisis of representation and, more specifically, social representation in the public medium – in the city, which lost its credibility as a place of cohesive representation. Faced with the predominance of spectacularity in the social sphere, there was a shift toward recovering the ritual aspect of the public sphere, with architecture as the most legitimate threshold for that ritual: not as a mere representative container that literally disappears into darkness when the audience enters it – as is the case with the enclosed bourgeois theatrical temple – or that melds with the architecture in a continuum of effects – as is the case with the modern machine theater, in complete continuity with the metropolitan exterior, which is domesticated and contained within its walls. The dynamic and performative construction of the Mobile Theater is an alternative that also implies the ritual production of work, as it is fully on display, which engenders the real possibility of a reversion of roles, because they are no longer subordinate to one another, and the establishment of a new foundation for the ritual of shared representation in the public milieu.

The second crisis was that of the specialization of space. The notion of "environment" had its critical heyday in the period under study, although its inner history dates back to the 19th century, and the transfers between biology and the social sciences remained ongoing for more than 100 years. The notions of environment, milieu, ambience or atmosphere have been characteristic of architectural and theatrical culture from Romanticism to the present, but they do not always possess a clear critical content. The use of the concept of environment in the Mobile Theater was critical in that it pointed out the fallacy of the neutrality of modern space, showing that a theater building can impede, rather than facilitate, the emergence of meaning from the space, which is equivalent to negating its true function. In parallel chronologically with visual artists' leaving the white cube, what this phenomenon revealed was a specific ideology from which people were distancing themselves politically – escaping from its influence – and aesthetically – generating their own, autonomous contexts. That is why medial transactions became essential in the composition of space, as opposed to the specialization that had characterized modern architectural space up to that point.

The third crisis was that of type as an embodiment of function, of a particular mode of use, and the proposal of the archetype in its place. Entirely associated with the crisis of specialization, the crisis of type not only affected the space itself and its form, but also its material conditions, which were suspended in order to reveal the space itself, laid bare. Stripping things down toward poverty is a characteristic attitude of moments in culture with high moral ideals, as is absolutely the case of the period investigated in this book. And it is also characteristic of the culture of the inopportune. The recovery of archetypes in opposition to the idea of type is a critical operation, just as it is, and in the same measure, an operation of sclerosis and typological novelty, which leads us to two correlative phenomena: first, the exhaustion of the existing types as a symptom of the exhaustion of the institutions represented by those types, as well as their mutual relationship of correspondence; and, second, an anachronistic and cross-cutting perspective, through the updating of archetypes, to which there is a return for the purpose of shattering the deterministic relationship between architectural type and social institution, in pursuit of a broader, more inclusive and more complex formula. In that sense, close attention had to be paid to what was new, in order to foster a coalescence between the novel and the ancestral, in languages as well as in forms, with the aim of reassembling an audience that was seen to be incredibly segmented.

The fourth crisis was that of the dialectical dislocation between dissolution and form, place and non-place, subjectivity and belonging, which took place in the context of the new sociological conditions of leisure, entertainment and learning, contrasted with the prior dominant coordinates of work and production. The challenge consisted in proposing an architecture – by and for the community and its representation – in a context of the intense crisis, affecting both community and representation, which was brewing at the time, and which has only continued to accelerate and peak in the present with technological developments and the processes of subjectivation mediated by those developments. Modern architecture was more technocratic than participative, because the sociological context contributed to that; counterculture perceived that phenomenon and criticized it harshly, positing new liberating models of subjectivation, which, in part and in return for that liberation, accelerated the absolute disconnection of the subject from the social structures rooted in traditional models: family, social class and occupation all began openly disintegrating in the new consumer and information society.

The fifth crisis was technological, the coincidence of enormous technical advances with the loss of a belief in the capabilities of technology to bring about direct improvements in the quality of life of the broadest sectors of the population. The transfer of state-of-the-art military and aerospace technologies into architecture represented a clear attempt to overcome that situation by looking for the inroads that the most advanced and ideologized industries could offer. The reversion of the oppressive and negative role of technology through the domestication of violence and technocratic power was central to those contexts, although there was a certain amount of naiveté in the transfers that took place, a burden inherited from modern technocracy. Thus, tactics took over from strategies, nomad war machines replaced the great military apparatus, and networked environments supplanted pyramidal organizations. The consequences were seen immediately and translated into atmospheres with an unusual, and even radical, level of social experimentation, which, nevertheless, have been partially surmounted through their gradual absorption.

The sixth crisis was that of value systems and belief systems, such that it contained the previous crises, or part of them, in one way or another. The society of affluence, or the society of access, which postwar modernity instated in Western countries, immediately revealed its double: that of vagrants, the poor, the homeless and other marginalized figures. Some young people at the time went through a process of identification with that counterpart, not so much literally as in their processes of subjectivation, when it came to constructing themselves as subjects in environments that were largely organized technocratically. That led to the need for a networked reorganization, for the espousal of political commitments and the formation of communities. The idea of a network was fundamental in breaking away from the possibility of exclusion; and the idea of community in escaping from pure nihilism. Arcadia offered solid value systems that could hold up against the dominant values of the time on two levels: that of pedigree, because they were belief systems that had been tested by consensus; and that of advancement, because in being updated to electric Arcadias through their intersection with cutting-edge technology, the belief systems embodied in them took on a radical novelty.

It is not difficult to see how these crises have not only failed to fade out of existence but have undergone new mutations that have even made them more acute. As they have gotten stronger, however, so can our resistance to them. That is the ultimate conclusion here, having taken a look back at the experiments in this book, because they tell us more about the times in which they were conceived than about what happened immediately after. It is still a mystery what the architecture of the present should be to deserve the label of presentness, but there is no question that the most engaged architecture today still has its sights set on that idea.

Photocollage for the presentation of the Mobile Theater, Javier Navarro de Zuvillaga 1971.

Fernando Quesada is Associate Professor of Architecture at Universidad de Alcalá, Madrid. He is also a member or Artea, an association for practice research in the performing arts. He has been a visiting scholar in the Netherlands (TU Delft 2009-2010), Mexico (UNAM-MUAC 2013), and Philadelphia (Penn Design 2019).

Mobile Theater
Architectural Counterculture on Stage

Fernando Quesada

Published by:
Actar Publishers, New York, Barcelona

Edited by:
Fernando Quesada

Graphic Design: Actar

Printing and Binding:
Arlequin

All rights reserved
Edition ©: Actar Publishers
© of the texts: Their authors
© of the images: Their authors

This work is subject to copyright. All rights reserved, over all or part of the material, specifically the rights of translation, reprint, reuse of illustrations, recitation, transmission, reproduction on microfilm or other media and storage in databases. For any type of use, permission must be obtained from the copyright owner.

Distribution:
Actar D, Inc. New York, Barcelona.

New York
440 Park Avenue South, 17th Floor
New York, NY 10016, USA
T +1 2129662207
salesnewyork@actar-d.com

Barcelona
Roca i Batlle 2
08023 Barcelona, Spain
T +34 933 282 183
eurosales@actar-d.com

ISBN: 978-1-945150-80-7
Publication date: 2021